Angel Flying

ON THE

Ground

LETTERS OF A GENTLEMAN'S PURSUIT

Angel Flying

ON THE

Ground

LETTERS OF A
GENTLEMAN'S PURSUIT

SECOND EDITION

Compiled & Edited by

Courtney Jo Barr

First Edition Published 2020
Second Edition Published 2022

ISBN: 978-1-7365738-0-8
ISBN (eBook): 978-1-7365738-7-7

Book Cover and Interior Book Design by
Casey L. Jones — CaseyBelle.com

"When was the last time you read these letters?

Tell me your memories as you read these stories, Grandma."

I would LOVE to have been blessed to have had this conversation. Why did I never?

Growing up, the family all kind of knew about the letters, yet their existence didn't really reveal themselves until 2005 when I flew from Maryland to Columbus, Ohio, for a visit. While there, my Aunt invited me to drive out to Grove City to see what items of Grandmas I might like to keep in her memory. Turns out, I was the very last relative to visit before the donation cycle was to start, and so a lot of our grandparents' items had been sifted through and grabbed up.

It was perfect, actually.

I found lovely, low-ball Santa glasses, which I use daily; tall 1970s green, hand-blown glass that as a little girl, my pinky would make suction sounds in the pock marks on the sides when I took a sip. Then there's the infamous 1970s yellow ashtray with memories of Grandpa's many cigarettes, plus other miscellaneous useful, historical kitchen items.

As I walked into the den—or second bedroom where I used to sleep during my visits—I was immediately drawn to her small, brown desk. This is the desk where she wrote letters, did her finances, and kept her life organized. Next to her desk was a small, round table. True to my curious nature, I lifted the blueish tablecloth, and there sitting peacefully on the cross stand underneath the table, sat a plain white box. A sudden energy pulsated through my body, like little Angel goose bumps. Both my Aunt and I were in awe to see three orderly rows of WWII-era love letters tied in string, peeking out from under white tissue paper. There they were, patiently waiting for me to discover them, no doubt.

Decades later, I joyfully bring our grandfather's loving words into the light to share with my family, friends, and the world.

These now eighty-one-year-old string-tied, organized letters laid dormant until January of 2020, when I decided this is the year. Serendipitously, I had no idea it was also the 75th Anniversary of the end of the WWII European Theatre.

To know I am the only one who has read these since my grandma last did is humbling. I can't help but wonder, "How many times did Grandma reread these in her lifetime?"

I have laughed at my Grandpa's words, cried at his antics, shook my head at some of the phrases, but realize too, this was all written eight decades past: a much different time.

As you read along, it is my true hope you also laugh, cry, and shake your head in appreciation of how life moved then, how societal norms were just plain different. Family goals were local, simple, and uncomplicated. I am proud that 80 years ago, my grandma, Evelyn Lucille Stark, knew how to change a tire, was a college graduate in 1939, and had the precipitous wherewithal to save these letters for all of us to enjoy. She waited three years before she told Grandpa she loved him. She stayed true to her independence and values first, like she didn't even want to marry until age 25. She married at 24, and as you'll discover when you read the letters, Grandpa's love was hard to ignore. He saw in her, as do I, a truly wonderful woman, whom in my opinion, serves as an excellent example of what it means to be a matriarch.

My grandpa is affectionately remembered for his colorful language—I'm amused his phrases could be applied to regular clean English vernacular words as well. Some of the new words I learned were: betimes, weather eye on, pizen, studes, bangtails, hutments, and boon companion. Words that again bring us back to a different era.

For purposes of the title to this work—and as a tribute to the woman Grandpa loved dearly, *Angel Flying on the Ground*, is inspired by one of the letters where Grandpa addressed her as so. There are other allegories he used that might make you smile:

"I'd marry you tomorrow standing naked in a snowstorm."

"You're the center of every castle."

"If you want the moon, I'll try and get a step ladder someplace, and climb after it for you."

Grandma is a real Angel now, flying in the air (And believe me, she's near too.). As Grandpa so eloquently stated in his writing . . . *"Life goes on as it has a habit of doing."*

Courtney Jo Barr

Disclaimer: Please keep in mind that as I typed my grandfather's handwritten letters, I strived to type them exactly as he had originally written them. However, a number of minor punctuation changes have been made, just as a way of making the letters a bit easier to read for a modern audience.

7

1939–1940

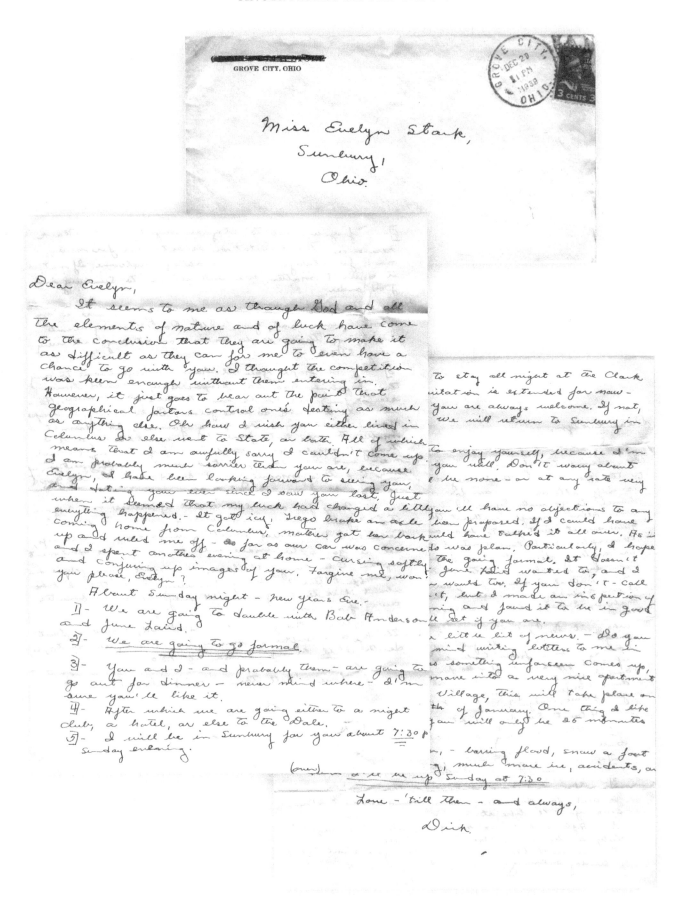

POSTMARKED GROVE CITY, OHIO—DECEMBER 20, 1939

Dear Evelyn,

It seems to me as though God and all the elements of nature and of luck have come to the conclusion that they are going to make it as difficult as they can for me to even have a chance to go with you. I thought the competition was keen enough without them entering in. However, it just goes to bear out the point that geographical factors control one's destiny as much as anything else. Oh how I wish you either lived in Columbus or else went to State, or both. All of which means that I am awfully sorry I couldn't come up. I am probably much sorrier than you are, because Evelyn, I have been looking forward to seeing you, and dating you ever since I saw you last. Just when it seemed that my luck had changed a little, everything happened. It got icy, Trego broke an axle coming home from Columbus, mother got her back up and ruled me off—so far as our car was concerned, and I spent another evening at home—cursing softly, and conjuring up images of you. Forgive me, won't you please, Evelyn?

About Sunday night—New Years Eve-

1. We are going to double with Bob Anderson and June Laird.

2. We are going to go formal.

3. You and I—and probably them—are going to go out for dinner—never mind where—I'm sure you'll like it.

4. After which we are going either to a night club, a hotel, or else to the Dale.

5. I will be in Sunbury for you about 7:30 pm, Sunday evening.

6. If you want to stay all night at the Clark residence the invitation is extended for now—and for always. You are always welcome. If not, it doesn't matter. We will return to Sunbury in good order.

7. Be prepared to enjoy yourself, because I'm almost sure that you will. Don't worry about drinking, there'll be none—or at any rate very, very, little.

8. I hope you'll have no obligations to any thing which has been proposed. If I could have seen you, we could have talked it all over. As it is—all I could do was plan. Particularly, I hope you don't mind going formal. It doesn't matter to me, but June Laird wanted to, and I thought maybe you would too. If you don't—call me—and we won't,

but I made an inspection of my tux this morning and found it to be in good shape, so I'm all set if you are.

Now for one little bit of news. Do you think you would mind writing letters to me in Columbus? Unless something unforeseen comes up, we're going to move into a very nice apartment up in Olentangy Village, this will take place on or about the 12th of January. One thing I like about it is that you will only be 25 minutes away from me.

Well Evelyn, barring flood, snow a foot thick and drifting, much more ice, accidents, or death I'll be up Sunday at 7:30.

Love—'til then—and always,

Dick

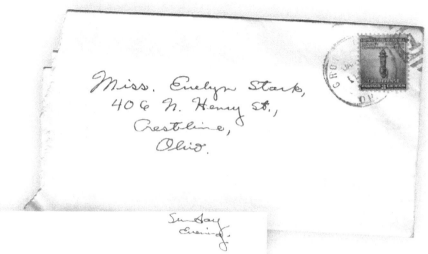

Miss. Evelyn Stark,
406 N. Henry St.,
Crestline,
Ohio.

Sunday
Evening.

Dear Evelyn,

Here we are at the end of a week and the beginning of a new one. Time certainly passes swiftly. Since I last wrote, I haven't done anything very much. I've read a couple of books, I've taught at school, I've begun to make changes - laying the plans for next year's classes. Also - oh wonder of wonders - I've been thinking. My thoughts for no very good reason seem to revolve around the problem of what's happening, or is likely to happen, to America. Maybe you won't be interested, but here are the conclusions I've reached:

1.- In 1942 and '43 we are going to have a greater period of prosperity than America has ever seen. There will be full employment, high prices, easy credit, and everything that makes up a boom period. All this will be brought about by the Defense Program, which of course must be paid for by all of us through taxation. We will be able to make those payments as long as the war lasts; when the war is over, if England and we immediately close our tremendous arms-spending program, which soon will result in depression. Or, if Germany wins, we will continue our program until we no longer have money enough to pay for it.

2.- In either case there will eventually - within the next ten years - be a depression greater than anything that has preceded it. Compared to it, the depression of the early thirties will look like rosy prosperity. Through an involved process, which I'll explain to you when I see you, the government must either become bankrupt, or else tax the people to the point of revolution. - The result of either of these eventualities will be a government different from anything we now have. Either it will be Communistic, Nazi, or some form of State Socialism. At any rate, our money, our government bonds, our negotiable securities will not be worth the paper they're printed on, and the banks, wholesale and retail business, and industry as we now know it, will be wiped out completely. The only people who can be sure of security are engineers, farmers, and professional people. The one secure investment - land. I've also figured out

make a tremendous profit from. However I'll bore you with which I see reminds me that I've probably bored you for now.

to the subject to something considerably why haven't you answered my it that you've been too busy, far sick; or are you deciding that you to me anymore? I expected to hear last week, and when no letter was I got sadder and sadder, until Saturday was unfit to live with, I was so down that Plymouth just sort of drooped all over for me. Anyway, I hope there is and I do wish you'd write to me, and I can see you real soon. (I'm not hinting to come to Sunbury or Crestline this coming I see the girl I'd like to think I of suppose you could talk to her and see like that?) - I sure hope she would, though she doesn't care so much love her like the very devil, and I ing her answer my letters, and I miss her laugh, and voice, and lips, and goes into the makeup of the most I've ever known, or ever will meet, Evelyn Stark, will you tell her ask her to write once in a while, and to him? I'm sure that if she knew all this to listen to the humble supplica- lonely, very sincere young feller, and to try a little anyway I what to

Dick.

Sunday evening

Dear Evelyn,

Here we are at the end of a week and the beginning of a new one. Time certainly passes swiftly. Since I last wrote, I haven't done anything very much. I've read a couple of books, I've taught school, I've begun to make changes—laying the foundation for next year's classes. Also—oh wonder of wonders—I've been thinking. My thoughts for no very good reason seem to revolve around the problem of what's happening or is likely to happen, to America. Maybe you won't be interested, but here are the conclusions I've reached:

1. In 1942 and '43 we are going to have a greater period of prosperity than America has ever seen. There will be full employment, high prices, easy credit, and everything that makes up a boom period. All this will be brought about by the Defense Program, which of course must be paid for by all of us through taxation. We will be able to make those payments as long as the war lasts; when the war is over, if England wins we will immediately cease our tremendous arms—spending program, which soon will result in depression. Or, if Germany wins, we will continue our program until we no longer have money enough to pay for it.

2. In either case there will eventually—within the next ten years—be a depression greater than anything that has preceded it. Compared to it, the depression of the early thirties will look like rosy prosperity. Through an involved process, which I'll explain to you when I see you, the government must either become bankrupt, or else tap the people to the point of revolution. The result of either of those eventualities will be a government different from anything we now have. Either it will be Communistic, Nazi, or some form of State Socialism. At any rate, our money, our government bonds, our negotiable securities will not be worth the paper they're printed on, and the banks, wholesale and retail business, and industry as we now know it, will be wiped out completely. The only people who can be sure of security are Engineers, farmers, and professional people. The only secure investment—land. I've also figured out a way to make a tremendous profit from all of

this, which I'll bore you with when I see you. Which reminds me that I've probably bored you enough for now.

To change the subject to something considerably more personal, why haven't you answered my last letter? Is it that you've been too busy, or have you been sick; or are you deciding that you shouldn't write to me anymore? I expected to hear from you all last week, and when no letter was forthcoming, I got sadder and sadder, until Saturday I just about was unfit to live with. I was so downhearted that even my Plymouth just sort of drooped all over, out of sympathy for me. Anyway, I hope there's nothing wrong, and I do wish you'd write to me, and I surely hope I can see you real soon. (I'm not hinting but I'd like to come to Sunbury or Crestline this coming week end, and see the girl I'd like to think I go with, do you suppose you could talk to her and see whether she'd like that?) I sure hope she would, because even though she doesn't care so much about me, I love her like the very devil, and I miss not having her answer my letters, and I miss her smile, and her laugh, and voice, and lips, and everything that goes into the makeup of the most wonderful girl I've ever known, or ever will meet. So, if you are Evelyn Stark, will you tell her all this, and ask her to write once in a while, and to see me real often? I'm sure that if she knew all this she'd be willing to listen to the humble supplications of a very lonely, very sincere young feller', and maybe respond to them a little anyways. What do you think?

Dick

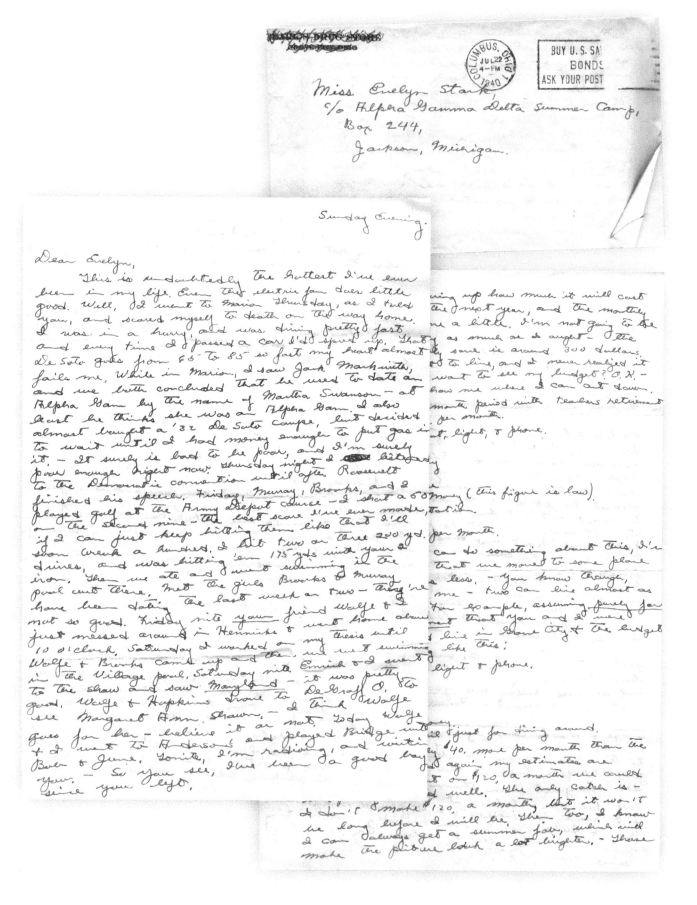

figures represent a pretty higher standard of living too, — I'm not exactly trying to sell you on the idea, but I'll bet you can't figure out a much better budget, can you? — Who started this anyway?

Honey, I'll sure be glad to have you back once more. The moon has been very lovely this week, and every time I look at it, it makes me feel so very lonely. How I should like to be sitting in your porch swing with you, looking at the moon, listening to the chirp of the crickets, or being overcome by the quietness of the country, and by the loveliness of the spell you cast over me — or perhaps the spell God casts over us. I wish I were with you tonite looking out over the shimmering reflection in Michigan looking out over the cool water, and perhaps being like of the moon on the cool water, and perhaps being like the mouse — nibbling a bit at the delicacy of your nose and ears, and perhaps sampling the sweetness of your lips — 'till eleven, and that before you then be in bed — So — Give me a drag on that before you then be in bed — So it away Clark! — Or, you'd better quit drinking that, and think & dream of stuff Clark, it's "pizen"!

By the way, a year 'ago yesterday I asked you to go hear Artie Shaw with me. I'll bet you didn't expect to still be dating me, did you? — I was hoping from the first that we could get along. — I'm still hoping, but I never was that lucky. — This letter was interrupted here while Tom White, Wolfe, and I went for a ride to cool off. Wolfe said he wished he had a date tonite — I think he must be changing. White is painting a bridge just outside of Delaware on the way to Sunbury.

Wolfe, Hopkins, White, Julian and myself are all going to be orphans next week end. Our folks are all going to be away. We're planning an all night poker session Friday night. — You'd better get home and rescue me. By the way, have you decided yet when I get to see you? Is it to be Saturday, Sunday, Monday or when? — Not to mention how if it's Saturday or Sunday. Personally, I think it would be a good idea for you to come down and cook Sunday dinner for me; but if it's this hot, I wouldn't want you to.

POSTMARKED COLUMBUS, OHIO—JULY 22, 1940

Sunday Evening

Dear Evelyn,

This is undoubtedly the hottest I've ever been in my life. Even the electric fan does little good. Well, I went to Marion Thursday, as I told you, and scared myself to death on the way home. I was in a hurry, and was driving pretty fast and every time I passed a car I'd speed up. That DeSoto goes from 65 to 85 so fast my heart almost fails me. While in Marion, I saw Jack Markwith, and we both concluded that he used to date an Alpha Gam by the name of Martha Swanson—at least he thinks she was an Alpha Gam. I also almost bought a '32 DeSoto coupe, but decided to wait until I had money enough to put gas in it. It surely is bad to be poor, and I'm surely poor enough right now. Thursday night I listened to the Democratic convention until after Roosevelt finished his speech. Friday, Murray, Brooks and I played golf at the Army Depot course—I shot a 50 on the second nine—the best score I've ever made, if I can just keep hitting them like that I'll soon break a hundred. I hit two or three 200 yd. drives, and was hitting 'em 175 yds with your 2 iron. Then we ate and went swimming in the pool out there. Met the girls Brooks & Murray have been dating the last week or two—they're not so good. Friday nite your friend Wolfe & I just messed around in Hennicks & went home about 10 o'clock. Saturday, I worked on my thesis until Wolfe & Brooks came up and then we went swimming in the Village pool. Saturday nite Emrich & I went to the show and saw Maryland—it was pretty good. Wolfe & Hopkins drove to DeGraff O. to see Margaret Ann Shawn. I think Wolfe goes for her—believe it or not. Today Wolfe & I went to Anderson's and played Bridge with Bob & June. Tonite, I'm radioing, and writing you. So you see, I've been a good boy since you left.

I've been figuring up how much it will cost me to live during the next year, and the monthly figures astounded me a little. I'm not going to be able to save nearly as much as I ought—the most I can possibly save is around 300 dollars. It surely costs a lot to live, and I never realized it before. Do you want to see my budget? O.K. Maybe you can show me where I can cut down.

Salary over 12 month period with teachers retirement taken out—$104 per month

$29.85	Rent, heat, light & phone
18.00	Food
2.00	Laundry
10.00	Clothes
3.00	Insurance
1.20	Spending money (this figure is low)
5.00	Transportation
$79.85	Total
24.15	Saving per month

I surely hope I can do something about this. I've suggested to mom that we move to some place where the rent is less. You know though one thing astounds me—two can live almost as cheaply as one. For example, assuming purely for the sake of arguement that you and I were married we would live in Grove City & the budget would be something like this:

$38	Rent, heat, light & phone
30	Food
20	Clothes
3	Insurance
2.4	Spending Money
4	For gas & oil just for driving around
$119.00	

This is only $40 more per month than the other figure, and again my estimates are darned high. But on $120, a month we could live pretty darned well. The only catch is—I don't make $120, a month, but it won't be long before I will be. Then too, I know I can always get a summer job, which will make the picture look a lot brighter. Those figures represent a pretty high standard of living too, I'm not exactly trying to sell you on the idea, but I'll bet you can't figure out a much better budget, can you? Who started this anyways?

Honey, I'll sure be glad to have you back once more. The moon has been very lovely this week, and every time I look at it, it makes me feel so very lonely. How I should like to be sitting in your porch swing with you, looking at the moon, listening to the chirp of the crickets; being overcome by the quietness of the country, and by the loneliness of the spell you cast over me—or perhaps the spell God casts over us. I wish I were with you tonite in Michigan looking out over the shimmering reflection of the moon on the cool water, and perhaps being like the mouse—nibbling a bit at the delicacy of your nose, and ears, and perhaps sampling the sweetness of your lips. Give me a drag on that before you throw it away Clark! Oh, you'd better quit drinking that stuff Clark, it's "pizen"!

By the way, a year ago yesterday I asked you to go to hear Artie Shaw with me. I'll bet you didn't expect to still be dating me, did you? I was hoping from the first that we could get along. I'm still hoping, but I never was that lucky. This letter was interrupted here while Tom White, Wolfe, and I went for a ride to cool off. Wolfe said he wished he had a date tonite—I think he must be changing. White is painting a bridge just outside of Delaware on the way to Sunbury.

Wolfe, Hopkins, White, Julian and myself are all going to be orphans next week end. Our folks are all going to be away. We're planning an all night poker session Friday night. You'd better get home and rescue me. By the way, have you decided yet when I get to see you? Is it to be Saturday, Sunday, Monday or when? Not to mention how if it's Saturday or Sunday. Personally, I think it would be a good idea for you to come down and cook Sunday dinner for me; but if it's this hot, I wouldn't want you to.

Well honey, it's about a quarter till eleven, and time for all good little boys to be in bed. So write P.D.Q please and love me and think and dream of me a little, because you have all my love, and all my thoughts and dreams.

Dick

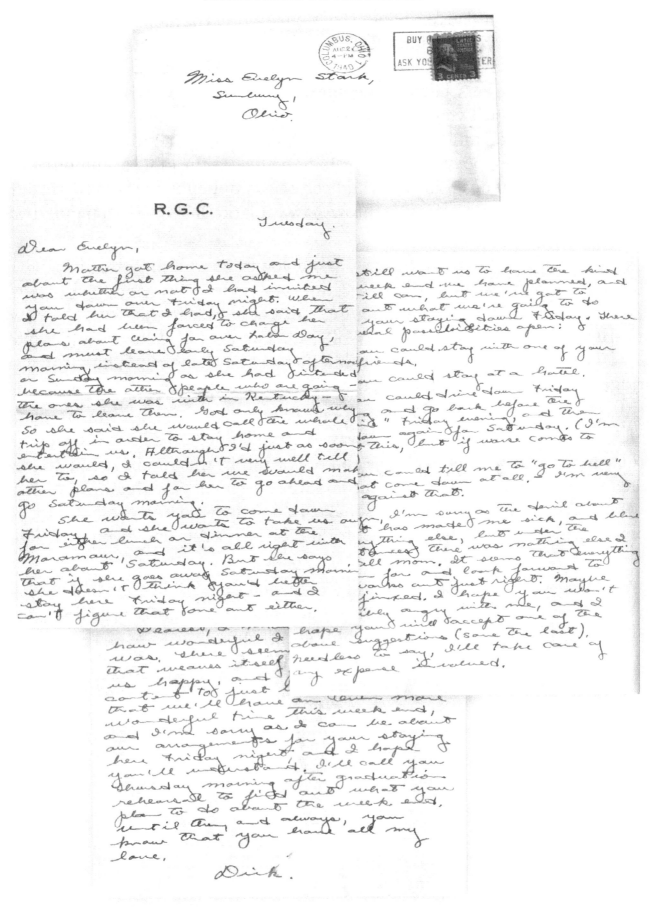

R.G.C.

Tuesday.

Dear Evelyn,

Mother got home today and just about the first thing she asked me was whether or not I had invited you down over Friday night. When I told her that I had, she said that she had been forced to change her plans about closing for over Labor day, and must leave early Saturday morning instead of late Saturday afternoon or Sunday morning as she had intended, because the other people who are going — the ones she was with in Kentucky — have to leave then. God only knows why. So she said she would call the whole trip off in order to stay home and entertain us. Although I'd just as soon she would, I couldn't very well tell her to, so I told her we would make other plans and for her to go ahead and go Saturday morning.

She wants you to come down Friday, and she wants to take us out for either lunch or dinner at the Maramaur, and it's all right with her about Saturday. But she says that if she goes away Saturday morning she doesn't think you'd better stay here Friday night — and I can't figure that one out either.

...still want us to have the kind week end we have planned, and we still can, but we've got to about what we're going to do your staying down Friday. There several possibilities open:
you could stay with one of your friends,
you could stay at a hotel,
you could drive down Friday and go back before the "Friday evening", and then down again for Saturday. (I'm ...this, but if worse comes to ...you could tell me to "go to hell" ...not come down at all. I'm very against that.

I'm sorry as the devil about ...has made me sick, and like anything else, but under the ...there was nothing else I tell mom. It seems that everything for and look forward to ...works out just right. Maybe ...jinxed. I hope you won't ...angry with me, and I ...you will accept one of the above suggestions (save the last). Needless to say, I'll take care of any expense involved.

Dearest, ... how wonderful it was. There seems that weaves itself us happy, and content too just ... that we'll have an even more wonderful time this week end, and I'm sorry as I can be about our arrangements for your staying here Friday night and I hope you'll understand. I'll call you Thursday morning after graduation rehearsal to find out what you plan to do about the week end. Until then and always, you know that you have all my love,

Dick.

POSTMARKED COLUMBUS, OHIO—AUGUST 27, 1940

Tuesday

Dear Evelyn,

Mother got home today and just about the first thing she asked me was whether or not I had invited you down over Friday night. When I told her that I had, she said that she had been forced to change her plans about leaving for over Labor Day, and must leave early Saturday morning instead of late Saturday afternoon, or Sunday morning as she had intended, because the other people who are going—the ones she was with in Kentucky—have to leave then. God only knows why! So she said she would call the whole trip off in order to stay home and entertain us. Although I'd just as soon she would, I couldn't very well tell her to, so I told her we would make other plans and for her to go ahead and go Saturday morning.

She wants you to come down Friday, and she wants to take us out for either lunch or dinner at the Maramour, and it's all right with her about Saturday. But she says that if she goes away Saturday morning she doesn't think you'd better stay here Friday night—and I can't figure that one out either.

I still want us to have the kind of week end we have planned, and we still can, but we've got to figure out what we're going to do about your staying down Friday. There are several possibilities open:

1. You could stay with one of your girl friends.

2. You could stay at a hotel.

3. You could drive down Friday morning and go back before our "deadline" Friday evening, and then come down again for Saturday. (I'm against this, but if worse comes to worse.)

4. You could tell me to "go to hell" and not come down at all. I'm very much against that.

Evelyn, I'm sorry as the devil about this, it has made me sick, and blue, and everything else, but under the circumstances there was nothing else I could tell mom. It seems that everything we plan for and look forward to never works out just right. Maybe we're jinxed. I hope you won't be terribly angry with me, and I hope you will accept one of the above suggestions (save the last). Needless to say, I'll take care of any expense involved.

I have been investigating the job situation, and it isn't very promising. Business, according to Mr. White, is very poor in Columbus right now, and Lazarus is the only firm hiring anyone. The rest are laying them off. The woman I want to contact about a Lazarus job was not home yesterday, but I'll get in touch with her before the week end. Those department store jobs only pay $15.00 a week, by the way.

Dearest, I know that you know how wonderful I thought Sunday was. There seems to be a spell that weaves itself around us, to make us happy, and peaceful, and content to just be together. I hope that we'll have an even more wonderful time this week end, and I'm sorry as I can be about our arrangements for your staying here Friday night, and I hope you'll understand. I'll call you Thursday morning after graduation rehearsal to find out what you plan to do about the week end. Until then, and always, you know that you have all my love,

Dick

Miss Evelyn Stark,
To Crestline High School,
Crestline,
Ohio.

Dere Missus Stark,
Please X cuse Mary Jane from
Fiz Ed. 2 day as she wus drunk
last nite and still has a auful
hangover.
Thank U.,
Mrs. Zilch,

Dear Evelyn,
How is the teaching going thus far? I
surely hope everything is well under control,
and I'm pulling for you all the way. This
teacher has been pretty busy the last 2 two
days, although I'm getting used to it now, and
I'm having a lot of fun!
Perhaps you're wondering why I'm writing
so soon, and probably you will wonder why
it is so short. The last question shall be
answered first: I'm writing you while waiting
for supper. I've just gotten home, and I'm
going to go to an executive meeting as soon as I eat.
The reason for my writing now instead of waiting
to hear from you, or until I have more time,
is to re-affirm my statement of Saturday that
I would like very much for us to go hear
Tommy Dorsey this Saturday night. Probably
some of the other fellows are going, and I know
we can have a swell time. Of course, most
important of all is that we'll be together.
So, if you can, and want to, please come
home. Write me so that I'll know whether or
not you're coming. If so, I'll be up about

to get there early to get a seat.
whenever you can get down, and
long letter as soon as I hear

me missed me, and wished that
I know you haven't had time
that, and that you probably
anyway. So —— write & tell me
down, and know that
have —
My Love,
Dick

POSTMARKED COLUMBUS, OHIO—SEPTEMBER 10, 1940

Dere Missus Stark,

Please Xcuse Mary Jane from Fizz Ed. 2 day as she wuz drunk last nite and still has an awful hangover

Thank U.,

Mrs. Zilch

Dear Evelyn,

How is the teaching going thus far? I surely hope everything is well under control, and I'm pulling for you all the way. This teacher has been pretty busy the last two days, although I'm getting used to it now, and I'm having a lot of fun.

Perhaps you're wondering why I'm writing so soon, and probably you will wonder why it is so short. The last question shall be answered first: I'm writing you while waiting for supper. I've just gotten home, and I'm going to go to an executive meeting as soon as I eat. The reason for my writing now instead of waiting to hear from you, or until I have more time, is to re-affirm my statement of last Saturday that I would like very much for us to go hear Tommy Dorsey this Saturday night. Probably some of the other fellows are going, and I know we can have a swell time. Of course, most important of all is that we'll be together. So, if you can, and want to, please come home. Write me so that I'll know whether or not you're coming. If so, I'll be up about 7:30—You've got to get there early to get a seat. If not, I'll see you whenever you can get down, and I'll write you a long letter as soon as I hear from you.

I hope you've missed me, and wished that I was around, but I know you haven't had time to do anything like that, and that you probably won't miss me anyway. So— write & tell me whether you can come down, and know that you will always have—

All My Love,

Dick

Miss. Evelyn Stubbs,
40 6 North Henry St.;
Crestline,
Ohio.

Dear Evelyn,

I, like Longfellow, have come to the conclusion that "life is real and life is earnest." Like Pepys I was "up betimes," taught six classes, attended a teacher's meeting, went to football practice; and to a meeting of the Wilkie Club. After which we had an executive meeting, so I've been pretty busy today. Tomorrow I teach, go with the football team to play South, then go with Pete to scout Gahanna in their opener, Friday I shall teach, and then rest, in order to be at my best for a date with my love on Saturday.

I guess I shouldn't have written you yesterday, but I wasn't sure whether you were going to get down or not, and I wanted you to awfully much. You see, I really think about you, and miss you, and love you all the time; and I know you'd like to hear Darcy, so I thought I'd better tell you again that going is a wonderful idea. As I said in yesterday's letter, if it's O.K. with you, I'll be up about 7:30 Saturday evening, and we won't get back very early — so there!

Honey, it is wonderful that you're getting along so swell with your teaching, and I know you'll like it more and more as you get into the swing of things. (What I'm afraid of is that I'll never be able to persuade you to quit teaching, and start taking care of me.) The idea of your training the cheerleaders intrigues me. I'll bet you really dream up some new wrinkles. Wait until they put you in charge of the campfire girls, the girl scouts, the athletic association for girls, ticket sales for plays, the girl reserves; and whatever else they have in the way of school activity. I'd like to be a little mouse in your study hall to watch you look stern, and listen to you give the kids hell. — I hope you don't get so used to the idea that you keep it up on me — I probably need it though.

little news around the community
... — Trego says she's a cinch
... is now second Lieutenant
..., Regular Army, Fort Hayes
..., is wonderful, Wolfe is
... to get him to get a date for
... don't. I think we'll meet
...(his love) at the Dale, and
... they will go,
... so sleepy I can barely
... with truck into bed. I know
... cause you're always in my
...p — love does that — don't it?
...soon honey, I was a little blue
... you've cheered me up again.
...nch you miss me, but I
... think of me, and love me
... I do you.

...ling, I love you, and will
... more than anything else in

POSTMARKED COLUMBUS, OHIO—SEPTEMBER 12, 1940

Dear Evelyn,

I, like Longfellow, have come to the conclusion that "life is real and life is earnest." Like Pepys I was "up betimes," taught six classes, attended a teacher's meeting, went to football practice; and to a meeting of the Wilkie Club. After which we had an executive meeting, so I've been pretty busy today. Tomorrow I teach, go with the football team to play South, then go with Peter to scout Gahanna, in their opener. Friday I shall teach and then rest, in order to be at my best for a date with my love on Saturday.

I guess I shouldn't have written you yesterday, but I wasn't sure whether you were going to get down or not, and I wanted you to awfully much. You see, I really think about you, and miss you, and love you all the time; and I know you'd like to hear Dorsey, so I thought I'd better tell you again that going is a wonderful idea. As I said in yesterday's letter, if it's O.K. with you, I'll be up about 7:30 Saturday evening, and we won't get back very early—so there!

Honey, it's wonderful that you're getting along so well with your teaching, and I know you'll like it more and more as you get into the swing of things. (What I'm afraid of is that I'll never be able to persuade you to quit teaching, and start taking care of me.) The idea of you training the cheerleaders intrigues me, I'll bet you really dream up some new wrinkles. Wait until they put you in charge of the campfire girls, the girl scouts, the athletic association for girls, ticket sales for plays, the girl reserves; and whatever else they have in the way of school activity. I'd like to be a little mouse in your study hall to watch you look stern, and listen to you give the kids hell. I hope you don't get so used to the idea that you keep it up on me—I probably need it though.

There is very little news around the community. Cherry Cap runs tomorrow, Trego says she's a cinch to win—ha! Murray is now second Lieutenant M.M. Montgomery, U.S. Regular Army, Fort Hayes Garrison, which, I think is wonderful Wolfe is no different. We tried to get him to get a date for Dorsey, but he wouldn't. I think we'll meet Brooks (and Helen—his love) at the Dale, and possibly Pete and Betty will go.

Darling, I'm getting so sleepy I can hardly see, so I guess I'd better tumble into bed. I know I'll dream of you, because you're always in my mind—awake or asleep—love does that—darn it! Thanks for writing so soon honey, I was a little blue when I got home, and you've cheered me up again. I don't know how much you miss me, but I hope you miss me, and think of me, and love me just half as much as I do you.

Goodnight you darling, I love you, and will <u>love</u> you always —more than anything else in this world,

Dick

Miss. Evelyn Stark,
406 North Henry St.,
Crestline,
Ohio.

Sunday Evening.

Dear Evelyn,

I didn't wait until Monday to write you, because I'm not sure I'll be home Monday evening. — I guess I've got to talk to the Buckeye Republican Club for a few minutes tomorrow evening, which means that I stay down town until late.

This has been a very peaceful day for me. I got up about noon — which was much too early — ate breakfast, read the newspaper from cover to cover; went down to the bowling alley with Hopkins and Wolfe. Then took a nap, ate dinner, dozed and listened to the radio. It is about nine o'clock, and I'm going to bed when I finish this letter — I'm convinced that Sunday ought always to be a day of rest. — Although I would a little rather rest with you around than alone. It's more fun that way.

Darling, last night seemed very wonderful to me (some few about an hour when I was mad at you.) I thought Dorsey was very good, I liked the dancing in the moonlight, in short, I liked it all; but I'm afraid I would not have been nearly so wonderful had I been with anyone else. Even though you don't feel quite as I do, we both — I hope — have a pretty wonderful time together, and for me at least, nothing serves as an acceptable substitute for you. — A quiet contentment settles over everything, and there is nothing lacking when we're together. I wonder sometimes whether any other couple were ever more suited for one another or more happy together than we are. — Today has been one of the days when I felt very near to you, as though you were actually with me, and oh how I wish you were! I love you so very much that the thought of you, the image of you, your smile, your voice, your lips are almost a part of me.

Yet, today every thought has not been a pleasant one. Two things keep destroying the perfection of my peace of mind. First, if you come down next week end, I shan't have the car Saturday night. — Mom is going to some kind of a party, and wants it. Of course, Sunday is another matter, and the car will be available, I could probably figure out some

... whenever, if you do come home. ... that has been bothering me is a ... busy I'm sorry, maybe my ideas ... I'll see why it's necessary ... entertainment for the visiting ... dating you lately. If it doesn't ... you fix him up with ... there is no one around there, why ... I'd guarantee any date to be ... that gets me is that you'd ... the same day. It seems too much ... dates for me. I know, and so do ... with you, you wouldn't like ... surely be more burned up than ... seen you specially asked me to ... been out with some other girl. ... under the bridge, I've got no ... I can do or can't do, and you ... about having other dates. ... when I'll want a little ... about it. I have a better time ... quiet it. I do with any girl other than ... to have other dates would be to ... competition, and since you ... it hardly seems worthwhile. ... makes off my chest I feel much ... then all about it, so don't worry ... I'd better tell you how I feel about ... I miss dates, and tell that ... out other dates. I'm not! ...

... look now, and I think I'd ... still sleepy, you keep me ... can't get you to go in, and I ... thought it was the other way ... I guess it is at that. No feeling ... the time you just won't be ... all, because once I'm near ... you. How I wish we could ... never tire of it I'm sure. ... I know what it is to be ... know what it is to me — Darling, don't ... neither do we. Twice this week, ... together if I write oftener than we write. Be a good ... it brings us nearer together of those kids if they get tough. ... girls, don't bounce any all night, ... Tell 'em I said it was all right,

All My Love, — Always,

Dick.

Dear Evelyn,

I didn't wait until Monday to write you, because I'm not sure I'll be home Monday evening. I guess I've got to talk to the Buckeye Republican Club for a few minutes tomorrow evening, which means that I stay down town until late.

This has been a very peaceful day for me. I got up about noon—which was much too early—at breakfast, read the newspaper from cover to cover; went down to the bowling alley with Hopkins and Wolfe, then took a nap, ate dinner, dozed and listened to the radio. It is about nine o'clock, and I'm going to bed when I finish this letter. I'm convinced that Sunday ought always to be a day of rest. Although I would a little rather rest with you around then alone. It's more fun that way.

Darling, last night seemed very wonderful to me (save for about an hour when I was mad at you) I thought Doug was very good, I liked the dancing in the moonlight, in short, I liked it all; but I'm afraid it would not have been nearly so wonderful had I been with anyone else. Even though you don't feel quite as I do, we both—I hope—have a pretty wonderful time together, and for me at least, nothing serves as an acceptable substitute for you. A quiet contentment settles over everything, and there is nothing lacking when we're together. I wonder sometimes whether any other couple were ever more suited for one another or more happy together than we are. Today has been one of the days when I felt very near to you, as though you were actually with me, and oh how I wish you were! I love you so very much that the thought of you, the image of you, your smile, your voice; your lips are almost a part of me.

Yet, today every thought has not been a pleasant one. Two things help destroy the perfection of my peace of mind. First if you come down next week end, I shan't have the car Saturday night. Mom is going to some kind of party, and wants it. Of course, Sunday is another matter, and the car will be available, I could probably figure out some way to get up Saturday, however, if you do come home.

The other thing that has been bothering me is a rather bad case of jealousy. I'm sorry, maybe my ideas are all wrong, but I can't see why it's necessary for you to promise the entertainment for this visiting fireman who has been dating you lately. If it doesn't mean anything, why don't you fix him up with someone else? Or, if there is no one around there, why not let me fix him up? I'd guarantee any date to be pretty smooth. The thing that gets me is that you'd have two dates in the same day. It seems too much like running them in shifts for me. I know, and so do you that if I did that with you, you wouldn't like it either, and you'd probably be more burned up than I was if I were late when you specially asked me to be early, just because I'd been out with some other girl. However, that's water under the bridge, I've got no right to tell you what you can do or can't do; and you do whatever you feel like about having other dates. There may come a time when I'll want a little variety myself, although I doubt it. I have a better time out with the boys than I do with any girl other than you. The only reason I'd have other dates would be to provide you with a little competition, and since you aren't around to see it, it hardly seems worth while.

Well, with these remarks off my chest I feel much better, and now I've forgotten all about it, so don't worry any at all. I thought I'd better tell you how I feel about it all though. Please don't misunderstand, and think that I'm demanding that you not have other dates. I'm not!

It's about ten o'clock now, and I think I'd better get to bed. I'm still sleepy, you keep me up awfully late. I just can't get you to go in, and I try so hard too. Oh, you thought it was the other way around did you? Well, I guess it is at that. No fooling honey, I'm afraid that sometime you just won't be able to get rid of me at all, because once I'm near you it's so hard to leave you. How I wish we could be together always. I'd never tire of it I'm sure. Brooks and Helen don't know what it is to be together maybe, but neither do we. Darlingest, don't be surprised if I write oftener than twice this week. It brings us nearer together when we write. Be a good girl, and bounce any of those kids if they get tough. Tell 'em I said it was all right.

All My Love—Always,

Dick

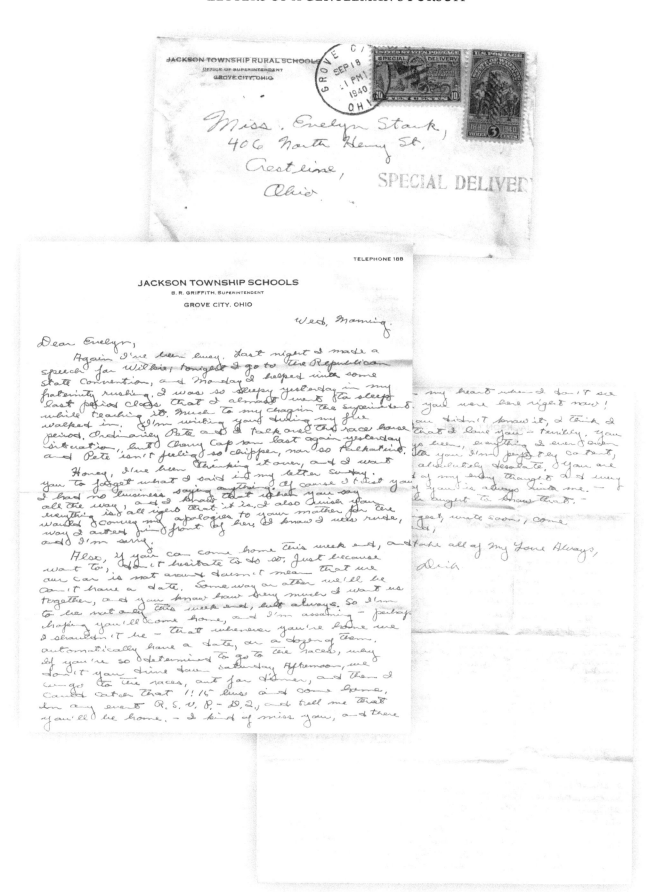

Wed. Morning

Dear Evelyn,

Again, I've been busy. Last night I made a speech for Wilkie; tonight I go to the Republican State Convention, and Monday I helped with some fraternity rushing. I was so sleepy yesterday in my last period class that I almost went to sleep while teaching it. Much to my chagrin the superintendent walked in. I'm writing you during my free period. Ordinarily Peter and I talk over the race horse situation, but Cherry Cap ran last again yesterday and Pete isn't feeling so chipper, nor so talkative.

Honey, I've been thinking it over, and I want you to forget what I said in my letter Sunday. I had no business saying anything. Of course I trust you all the way, and I know that when you say everything is all right that it is. I also wish you would convey my apologies to your mother for the way I acted in front of her. I know I was rude, and I'm sorry.

Also, if you can come home this week end, and want to, don't hesitate to do so. Just because our car is not around doesn't mean that we can't have a date. Some way or other we'll be together, and you know how very much I want us to be not only this week end, but always. So I'm hoping you'll come home, and I'm assuming— perhaps I shouldn't be—that whenever you're home we automatically have a date, or a dozen of them. If you're so determined to go to the races, why don't you drive down Saturday afternoon, we can go to the races, out for dinner, and then I could catch that 1:15 bus and come home. In any event R.S.V.P.—D.2., and tell me that you'll be home. I kind of miss you, and there is a dull ache in my heart when I don't see you. How I wish you were here right now!

Just in case you didn't know it, I think I ought to tell you that I love you—terribly. You are, and have always been, everything I ever even dreamed about. With you I'm perfectly content, without you I'm absolutely desolate. You are a part of me, and of my every thought and every deed. The memory of you is always with me. I just thought you ought to know that.

So please darlingest, write soon, come home this week end,

And take all of My Love—Always,

Dick

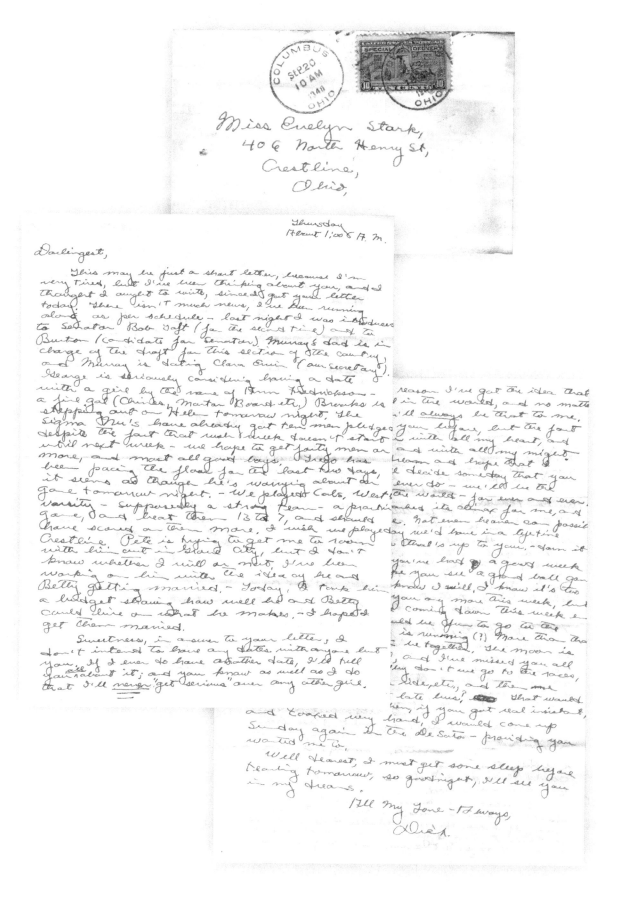

Thursday About 1:00 A.M.

Darlingest,

This may be just a short letter, because I'm very tired, but I've been thinking about you, and I thought I ought to write, since I got your letter today. There isn't much news, I've been running along as per schedule—last night I was introduced to Senator Bob Taft (for the second time) and to Burton (Candidate for Senator.) Murray's dad is in charge of the draft for this section of the country, and Murray is dating Clara Erwin (our secretary.) George is seriously considering having a date with a girl by the name of Ann Freduckson—a fine gal (Chimes, Mortar Board etc.) Brooks is stepping out on Helen tomorrow night. The Sigma Nu's have already gotten men pledged, despite the fact that rush week doesn't start until next week—we hope to get forty men or more, and most all good boys. Trego has been pacing the floor for the last two days, it seems as though he's worrying about our game tomorrow night. We played Cols. West's varsity—supposedly a strong team—a practice game, and beat them 13 to 7, and should have scored on them more. I wish we played Crestline. Pete is trying to get me to room with him <u>out</u> in Grove City, but I don't know whether I will or not. I've been working on him with the idea of he and Betty getting married. Today, I took him a budget showing how well he and Betty could live on what he makes. I hope I get them married.

Sweetness, in answer to your letter, I don't intend to have any dates with anyone but you. If I ever do have another date, I'll tell you all about it; and you know as well as I do that I'll <u>never</u> "get serious" over any other girl.

For some strange reason I've got the idea that you're the only girl in the world, and no matter what you do, you'll <u>always</u> be that to me. I think I've told you before, but the fact is that I love you with all my heart, and with all my soul, and with all my might. And the greatest dream and hope that I have is that you'll decide someday that you love me. If you ever do—we'll be the happiest couple in the world—for ever and ever. Life will have then reached its climax for me, and I shall ask no more. Not even heaven can possibly match the eternal joy we'd have in a lifetime together, but I guess that's up to you—darn it!

Honey, I hope you've had a good week teaching, and I hope you see a good ballgame tomorrow night. I know I will. I know it's too late to hear from you any more this week, but I'm hoping you're coming down this week end I still think it would be fun to go to the races—Cherry Caps is running (?) more than that, I just want us to be together. The moon is still very beautiful, and I've missed you all week, <u>no fooling!</u>

Why don't we go to the races, out to dinner, for a ride, etc., and then I come home on that late bus? That would be a fine date. Then, if you got real insistent, and coaxed very hard, I would come up Sunday again in the De Soto—providing you wanted me to.

Well dearest, I must get some sleep before teaching tomorrow, so good night, I'll see you in my dreams.

All My Love—Always,

Dick

Monday
Evening.

Dear Evelyn,

Last night, after I had gone out for dinner with mom, I went down to the fraternity house and saw all the good brothers, went to Hennicks for a coke, and then played bridge at White's. Today I was out of sorts for some reason or other, and everything seemed to go wrong. I kicked a couple of kids out of class, and then I really booted young Breckenridge. It was really like Monday. To top it off, I had to attend P.T.A. meeting, which wasn't particularly good entertainment. But, tomorrow is Tuesday, another day, and I hope a better one. After Tuesday there are only four more days until Saturday, and then I may be allowed to see my honey again.

Do you know I've been doing a large amount of thinking since yesterday, but I haven't come to any conclusions about anything except on one subject. And that's this business of not planning ahead on seeing one another. When I made the remark that we'd probably have to go to the Michigan game, but that we wouldn't plan on it definitely, I had reference to last year's O.S.U. Homecoming which we had planned for in advance. I don't want anything like that to happen again, of course, I did not have in mind, however, that we should not plan on seeing one another whenever you come down for the weekend. I'm not "demanding" that we make any such plans now. I feel that if I rate very much with you that you will make it a point to see me whenever you can. I'm quite sure that's the way it is with me. I always want to see you, if I could be with you every minute of every day I would be content. All I want to say on the subject is this: If you honestly want to have better dates on the week ends that's your privilege; if you feel that "settling down" to dating me is too burdensome and cramps your style, then by all means don't do anything like that. But, if that's the way you intend for things to be, and if you want to continue just being someone you like to see occasionally — maybe once every two or three weeks — I fully intend to have other dates, as many as I want whenever I want them. For example, had I based on indication that you were just dating me Saturday because no better opportunity presented itself, I would not have broken the date I had. My idea of the way things ought to be is for us to have dates with one another whenever and as often as possible, and to try and make it possible. Then, when we couldn't be together, other dates would be in order.

Please don't think I'm being demanding, I'm meaning to be, all I want is to gain some sort of an understanding of how we're going to handle this problem. You know as well as I do that whatever you want to do will be done, but I just wanted you to know what I think. If I'm wrong please tell me about it, and point out my error.

The only thing that bothers me so much is being not at all sure of you.

Honey, I didn't mean to lecture you in this letter. Indeed, I'm not lecturing you, though it may sound as though I am. I hate — I'm so much in love with you that even the smallest cloud on our horizon worries me, I feel so close to you that I know you'll always know how I am, and will consider anything I say. If I didn't have that feeling, I'd never tell you about anything that bothers me.

Darlingest, I don't know whether I told you yesterday or not, but I was awfully happy Saturday night. I really had a wonderful time with you. It proved something to me that had been bothering me a little and that was that we can still be happy together out in a crowd. I felt the same happiness that we have always — together. Sunday too was wonderful for me, although there was something wrong part of the time, — I don't know quite what. Examples: Your sudden desire to go someplace (which was perfectly O.K., but which surprised me a little, because earlier you had no apparent desire to move around). Your discourse on how we were not suited for one another, because of the idea that I was a little storm — when you and I both know that we are more suited for one another in every way than any two people in the world. The idea of my being any mental giant is utter damned foolishness, and you know it as well as I do. Then there was the remark that you were in no wise ready to settle down, and the indication that our getting serious was almost an impossibility.

I guess I'd better go to bed now, I'll write tomorrow again, and surely Wednesday. Plans for a weekend together remain in your hands, whatever you say goes — but here's hoping I see you. Which just proves that a week is a long time to go without you, that's for sure. I know I'll be thinking long four years are I know I'll be thinking about you dearest, I almost always do, I know that I love you, that I truly miss you, and that you're the only girl in the world I'll ever possess. All my Love — Always,

Dick.

Miss Evelyn Stark,
40 E North Henry St.,
Crestline,
Ohio.

Monday evening

Dear Evelyn,

Last night, after I had gone out for dinner with mom, I went down to the fraternity house and saw all the good brothers, went to Hennicks for a Coke, and then played bridge at White's. Today I was out of sorts for some reason or other, and everything seemed to go wrong. I kicked a couple of kids out of class, and then I really booted young Breckenridge. It was really blue Monday. To top it off, I had to attend a P.T.A. meeting, which wasn't particularly good entertainment. But, tomorrow is Tuesday, another day, and I hope a better one. After Tuesday there are only four more days until Saturday, and then I may be allowed to see my honey again.

Do you know I've been doing a large amount of thinking since yesterday, but I haven't come to any conclusions about anything except on one subject and that's this business of not planning ahead on seeing one another. When I made the remark that we'd probably have to go to the Michigan game, but that we wouldn't plan on it definitely, I had reference to last years' O.S.U. Homecoming when we had planned far in advance. I don't want anything like that to happen again, of course. I did not have in mind, however, that we should not plan on seeing one another whenever you come down for the weekend. I'm not "demanding" that we make any such plans now. I feel that if I rate very much with you that you will make it a point to see me whenever you can. I'm quite sure that's the way it is with me. I always want to see you, if I could be with you every minute of every day I would be content. All I want to say on the subject is this: If you honestly want to have other dates on the week ends that's your privilege; if you feel that "settling down" to dating me is burdensome and cramps your style, then by all means don't do anything like that. But, if that's the way you intend for things to be, and if I'm to continue just being someone you like to date occasionally—maybe once every two or three weeks then I fully intend to have other dates, as many as I want, whenever I want them. For example, had I possessed an indication that you were just dating me Saturday because no better opportunity presented itself, I would not have broken the date I had.

My idea of the way things ought to be is for us to have dates with one another whenever and wherever possible, and to try and make it possible very often. Then, when we couldn't be together, other dates would be in order.

Please don't think I'm being demanding, I'm not meaning to be, all I want is to gain some sort of an understanding of how we're going to handle the problem. You know as well as I do that whatever you want to do will be done, but I just wanted you to know what I think. If I'm wrong please tell me about it, and point out my error.

Darlingest, I don't know whether I told you yesterday or not, but I was awfully happy Saturday night. I really had a wonderful time with you. It proved something to me that had been bothering me a little and that was that we can still be happy together out in a crowd. I felt the same happiness that we have always—together. Sunday too was wonderful for me, although there was something wrong part of the time. I don't know quite what. Examples: Your sudden desire to go someplace (which was perfectly O.K., but which surprised me a little, because earlier you had no apparent desire to move around.) Your discourse on how we were not suited for one another, because of the idea that I was a brain storm—when you and I both know that we are more suited for one another in every way than any two people in the world. The idea of me being any mental giant is utter damned foolishness, and you know it as well as I do. Then there was the remark that you were in no wise ready to settle down, and the indication that our getting serious was almost an impossibility.

Finally, I felt that you'd have been happier had I not been around when those fellows (the "visiting fireman") came to see you. But in the main Sunday was another wonderful day. I think the thing that bothers me so much is that I'm not at all sure of you.

Honey, I didn't mean to lecture you at all in this letter. Indeed, I'm not lecturing you even though it may sound as though I am. Actually, I'm so much in love with you that even the smallest cloud on our horizon worries me, and I feel so close to you that I know you'll understand how I am, and will consider anything I say accordingly. If I didn't have that feeling, I'd never tell you about anything that bothers me.

I guess I'd better go to bed now, I'll probably write tomorrow again, and surely Wednesday. The plans for a weekend together remain in your hands, whatever you say goes—but here's hoping I see you. Which just proves that if a week is a long time to go without you, think how long four years are. I know I'll dream about you dearest, I almost always do, and you know that I love you, that I truly miss you, and that you're the only girl in the world who will ever possess.

All My Love—Always,

Dick

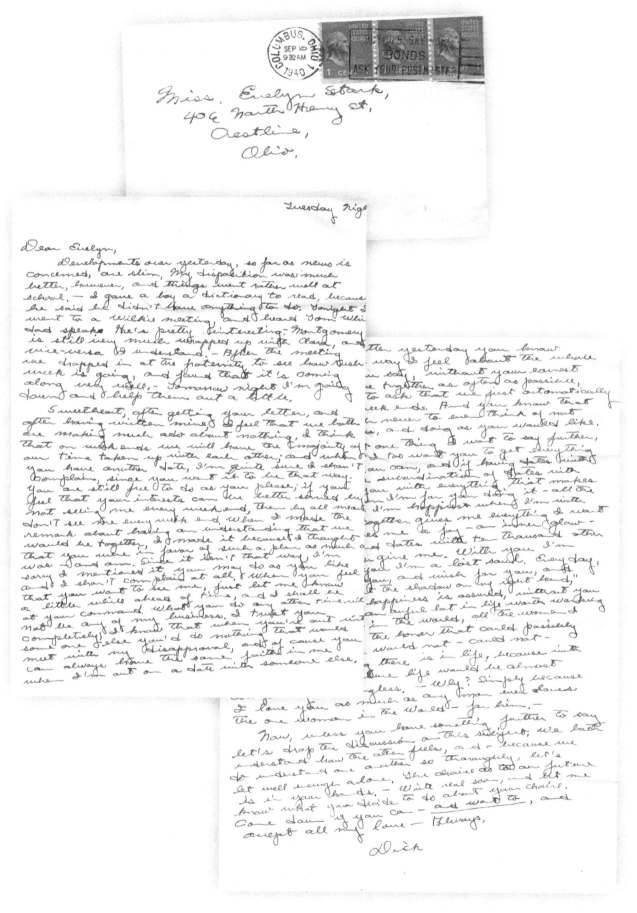

Miss. Evelyn Stark,
406 North Henry St,
Crestline,
Ohio,

Tuesday Night

Dear Evelyn,

Developments over yesterday, so far as news is concerned, are slim. My disposition was much better, however, and things went rather well at school. — I gave a boy a dictionary to read, because he said he didn't have anything to do. Tonight I went to a Wilkie meeting, and heard Tom White dad speak. He's pretty interesting. Montgomery is still very much wrapped up with Clara, and vice-versa to understand. — After the meeting we dropped in at the fraternity to see how rush week is going, and found that it's coming along very well. — Tomorrow night I'm going down and help them out a little.

Sweetheart, after getting your letter, and after having written mine, I feel that we both are making much ado about nothing. I think, that on week ends we will have the majority of our time taken up with each other; and when you have another date, I'm quite sure I shan't complain, since you want it to be that way. You are still free to do as you please; if you feel that your interests can be better served by not seeing me every week end, then by all means don't see me every week end. When I made the remark about having an understanding that we would be together, I made it because I thought that you were in favor of such a plan as much as I was, and am. Since it isn't that way, I'm sorry I mentioned it. You may do as you like and I shan't complain at all, and when you feel that you want to see me, just let me know a little while ahead of time, and I shall be at your command. What you do any other time will not be any of my business. I trust you completely; I know that when you're out with some one else you'd do nothing that would meet with my disapproval, and of course you can always have the same faith in me when I'm out on a date with someone else.

... after yesterday you know ... way I feel about the whole ... you say, without your earnest ... be together as often as possible, ... to ask that we just automatically ... week ends. And you know that ... never to even think of not ... , and doing as you would like. ... one thing I want to say further, ... too want you to get everything ... you can, and if having dates with ... a subordination of dates with ... you with everything, that makes ... I'm for you doing it — all the ... I'm happiest when I'm with ... together gives me everything I want ... me a joy — an inner glow — ... dates with ten thousand other ... give me. With you I'm ... I'm a lost soul. Every day, ... you, and wish for you, and ... the shadow on my right hand, ... happiness is assured, without you ... an awful lot in life worth working ... the world, all the women ... the honor that could possibly ... would not — could not — ... there is in life, because with ... life would be almost ... Why? Simply because ... as any man ever loves ... the one woman in the world — for him. —

Now, unless you have something further to say let's drop the discussion on this subject, we both understand how the other feels, and — because we understand one another so thoroughly, let's to understand one another well enough alone. The choice as to our future is in your hands. — Write real soon, and let me know what you decide to do about your chance. Come down if you can — and want to —, and accept all my love — Always,

Dick

41

POSTMARKED COLUMBUS, OHIO—SEPTEMBER 25, 1940

Tuesday Night

Dear Evelyn,

Developments over yesterday, so far as news is concerned, are slim, my disposition was much better, however, and things went rather well at school. I gave a boy a dictionary to read, because he said he didn't have anything to do. Tonight I went to a Wilkie meeting, and heard Tom White's dad speak. He's pretty interesting. Montgomery is still very much wrapped up with Clara, and vice-versa I understand. After the meeting we dropped in at the fraternity to see how rush week is going, and found that it's coming along very well. Tomorrow night I'm going down to help them out a little.

Sweetheart, after getting your letter, and after having written mine, I feel that we both are making much ado about nothing. I think that on week ends we will have the majority of our time taken up with each other; and when you have another date, I'm quite sure I shan't complain, since you want it to be that way. You are still free to do as you please; if you feel that your interest can be better served by not seeing me every week end, then by all means don't see me every week end. When I made the remark about having an understanding that we would be together, I made it because I thought that you were in favor of such a plan as much as I was—and am. Since it isn't that way, I'm sorry I mentioned it, you may do as you like and I shan't complain at all. When you feel that you want to see me, just let me know a little while ahead of time, and I shall be at your command. What you do any other time will not be any of my business. I trust you completely, I know that when you're out with some one else you'd do nothing that would meet with my disapproval, and of course you can always have the same faith in me when I'm out on a date with someone else.

From my letter yesterday you know pretty much the way I feel about the whole idea, but as you say, with out your earnest wish for us to be together as often as possible, I have no right to ask that we just automatically be together on week ends. And you know that I love you enough never to even think of not accepting your ideas, and doing as you would like.

There is just one thing I want to say further, and that is that I too want you to get everything out of life that you can, and if having dates with other people to the subordination of dates with me will provide you with everything that makes for happiness, then I'm for you doing it—all the way. But, I know I'm happiest when I'm with you. Just being together gives me everything I want from life. It gives me a joy—an inner glow—that ten thousand dates with ten thousand other women could never give me. With you I'm content, with out you I'm a lost soul. Every day, every hour, I miss you, and wish for you and want you. "Thou art the shadow on my right hand," with you complete happiness is assured, with out you there wouldn't be an awful lot in life worth working for. All the liquor in the world, all the women I have ever seen, all the honor that could possibly ever come to me would not—could not— give me everything there is in life, because with you out of the picture life would be almost completely meaningless. Why? Simply because I love you as much as any man ever loves the one woman in the world—for him.

Now, unless you have something further to say let's drop the discussion on this subject. We both understand how the other feels, and—because we do understand one another so thoroughly, let's let well enough alone. The choice as to our future is in your hands. Write real soon, and let me know what you decide to do about your choice. Come down if you can—and want to, and accept all my love—Always,

Dick

Beta Nu Chapter
OF
Sigma Nu Fraternity
22 SIXTEENTH AVENUE
COLUMBUS, OHIO

GILBERT A. PETERSEN
EMINENT COMMANDER

WILLIAM R. McGOUGH
LIEUTENANT COMMANDER

ROBERT K. WILLIAMS
TREASURER

WALTER A. DRYJA
RECORDER

Dearest Evelyn,

This will necessarily have to be short. I've been rushing for Sigma Nu, and I've put the pin in the pocket of a couple of boys myself, and I'm going to try hard to get some more. They've got me interested in Sigma Nu again. Outside of rushing I've been doing very little since I last wrote. Teaching has been coming along O.K. so far this week, no trouble at all with classes, and I've given a couple of tests this week.

Sweetness, again I'm missing you, and wanting to see you. — I guess it must be because I'm in love with you — do you suppose? At any rate, I hope that if you come home, you call me, or someway let me know when I can see you, If I can see you Saturday, we'll go out with Murray & Clara — he's still going for her. — If I can't see you, or if you aren't coming home, I'll write you a long letter Sunday. — But gosh I hope I can <u>see</u> you, and be with you either Saturday, or Sunday, or <u>both</u>! — That is if you don't think that would be "practically going steady." — Well, honey, I'm off to work and rushing again, so please come down & let me see you. If you call me, call me Sat. noon Saturday, or, if you want to write, send me a special when you get this, and I'll get it in time, set time & date

and I'll be there.

Dearest, please know that I will miss you, and want you, and that you always the most wonderful...

All my love now, and forever and ever

Dick.

Postmarked Columbus, Ohio—September 27, 1940

Dearest Evelyn,

This will necessarily have to be short. I've been rushing for Sigma Nu, and I've put the pin in the pocket of a couple of boys myself, and I'm going to try hard to get some more. They've got me interested in Sigma Nu again. Outside of rushing I've been doing very little since I last wrote. Teaching has been coming along O.K. so far this week. No trouble at all with classes, and I've given a couple of tests this week.

Sweetness, again I'm missing you, and wanting to see you. I guess it must be because I'm in love with you—do you suppose? At any rate, I hope that if you come home, you call me, or someway let me know when I can see you. If I can see you Saturday, we'll go out with Murray & Clara—he's still going for her. If I can't see you, or if you aren't coming home, I'll write you a long letter Sunday. But gosh I hope I can see you, and be with you either Saturday, or Sunday, or both! That is if you don't think that would be "practically going steady." Well, honey, I'm off to work and rushes again, so please come down & let me see you. If you call me, call me by noon Saturday. Or, if you want to write, send me a special when you get this, and I'll get it in time. Set time of date in your letter, and I'll be there.

And darlingest, please know that I will always love you, and want you, and that to me you'll be always the most wonderful girl in the world.

All My love now, and forever and ever,

Dick

Miss Evelyn Stark,
406 North Henry St.,
Crestline,
Ohio.

Dear Evelyn,

Since I last wrote you I have been a pretty busy boy. Friday I saw two football games. Saturday I saw Ohio State open by walloping Pitt. — I guess you didn't lose any money since Muskingum and Wesleyan played to a tie. Saturday night I helped with rushing, and then went down to the Deshler to the Post Master's Convention. Sunday I helped with rushing, went to Buckeye Lake, played poker, and helped with formal pledging, but came and got about three hours sleep before time for school this morning. — Needless to say, I'm tired.

How has school been going at Crestline? Swell, I hope! I was plenty sorry you couldn't see your way clear to come down. — No kidding. I really miss you when I don't see you for a while. I'm not at all sure when I do see you that you'll be altogether safe, because I'm ——— definitely in the mood.

Evelyn, so far this letter is just about as full as all the others I've written lately. For some reason or other, I've been afraid to let go, and say what I'd like to say the way I'd like to say it. The truth of the matter is I have a feeling that we're not pulling together as we usually do. It worries me, because I can't figure out what the trouble is. Honestly though, Sweet, there are several things that are bothering me. Some of which I told you about in an earlier letter. To enumerate:

1) — I can't imagine what was wrong the day I came to Sunbury. As I told you, I had a feeling that you wished I was someplace else. I don't think it was because of the trips past your house by the "inviting fireman", and I surely hope that wasn't it, but darn it all, what was it?

I'm not at all sure that I understand it your attitude is going to be in regard to having dates. And I definitely am against the of my having to beg for dates in order to one once every two or three weeks. — Damn it when I say I miss you I mean it! I see you as often as I possibly can, and heaven if I were with you every week end, we us it wouldn't be often enough for me. Of co jealous as the devil when you have other da it burns me up, but I still can see that if think you want to have them, that you sho but not at the expense of my not being whip in with a major percentage of dates of you, I won't say anything about it, and I'll come around anytime you'll let me, as long I'll let me, but I really think I ought to major portion of your time. — Maybe I'm w if I am please tell me so.

You don't seem to be nearly as enthused abou like me as you were. Frankly, the last letter to was just about as cold as one I'd write grandmother. It read as though you were force self to write me at all, and since then, I have begun to hear from you.

All three of the items listed above worry m ly, and they cause me to ask you what is ng. If you're tired of seeing me, or would rath see me, or have You or somebody else for one sake tell me. If all of this stuff is my gination tell me that too, I'd sure hope it is darlingest. I don't want to lose you no ter what happens, I love you. Whenever you o, I want you for ever and ever, because I believe we're made for one another. I know d be wonderfully happy together whenever we hose words. — If ever. —

Honey, that's all I'm going to say about all ews stuff. If you feel like answering my doubts, I'd appreciate it, if not — that is alright too. I hope you won't think I'm a first-budget, b I really don't know what the score is right now

and
If you don't
would just like
gladly come & get
other idea sands
grabbed would, of

Dearest, please do come down someway or anoth anything you say is law with me, and whatever you want things to be averaged — thus shall it be. However, I wish you would answer this letter right away, as soon as you decide what you're going to do, in order that I can plan with the grandmother, and if you will stay here, so that I can tell mom. I'd hate special I've always wanted to get one anyway.

Well, I've got to get to bed in order to awake bright and cheerful on the morrow, so please accept, an keep, and cherish — All My Love, Always,

Dick.

Dear Evelyn,

Since I last wrote you I have been a pretty busy boy. Friday I saw two football games. Saturday I saw Ohio State open by walloping Pitt. I guess you didn't lose any money since Muskingum and Wesleyan played to a tie. Saturday night I helped with rushing, and then went down to the Deshler to the Post Master's Convention. Sunday I helped with rushing, went to Buckeye Lake, played poker, and helped with formal pledging. Got home and got about three hours sleep before time for school this morning. Needless to say, I'm tired.

How has school been going at Crestline? Swell, I hope! I was plenty sorry you couldn't see your way clear to come down. No kidding. I really miss you when I don't see you for a while. I'm not at all sure when I do see you that you'll be altogether safe, because I'm definitely in the mood.

Evelyn, so far this letter is just about as dull as all the others I've written lately. For some reason or other, I've been afraid to let go, and say what I'd like to say the way I'd like to say it. The truth of the matter is I have a feeling that we're not pulling together as we usually do. It worries me, because I can't figure out what the trouble is. Honestly though, dearest, there are several things that are bothering me—some of which I told you about in our earlier letter. To enumerate:

1. I can't imagine what was wrong the day I came to Sunbury. As I told you, I had a feeling that you wished I was someplace else. I don't think it was because of the trips past your house by the "visiting fireman," and I surely hope that wasn't it, but darn it all, what was it?

2. I'm not at all sure that I understand what your attitude is going to be in regard to our having dates. And I definitely am against the idea of my having to beg for dates in order to get one once every two or three weeks. Damn it all, when I say I miss you I mean it! I want to see you as often as I possibly can, and heaven knows if I were with you every week end, the whole time, it wouldn't be often enough for me. Of course I'm jealous as the devil when you have other dates. It just burns me up, but I still can see that if you think you want to have them, that you should go ahead, but not at the expense of my not being able to whip in with a major percentage of dates. As I told you, I won't say anything about it, and I'll still be coming around anytime you'll let me, as long as you'll let me, but I really think I ought to get the major portion of your time. Maybe I'm wrong, and if I am please tell me so.

3. You don't seem to be nearly as enthused about writing me as you were. Frankly, the last letter you wrote was just about as cold as one I'd write to my grandmother. It read as though you were forcing yourself to write me at all, and since then I haven't even begun to hear from you.

All three of the items listed above worry me plenty, and they cause me to ask you what's wrong. If you're tired of seeing me, or would rather not see me, or have found somebody else, for heavens sake tell me. If all of this stuff is my imagination tell me that too. (I sure hope it is.)

Darlingest, I don't want to lose you no matter what happens. I love you. Whenever you say so, I want you for ever and ever, because I really believe we're made for one another. I know we'll be wonderfully happy together whenever you say those words. If Ever.

Honey, that's all I'm going to say about all this stuff, if you feel like answering my doubts, I'd appreciate it, if not—that's allright too. I hope you won't think I'm a fuss-budget, but I really don't know what the score is right now.

Sweetness, in regard to this week end coming. May I humbly ask you for a date—or twenty? Saturday night, the Sigma' Nu's are having their first dance of the year at the house. I've been invited, and if you'd like to go—we'll go. If you'd like to just have a date we'll do that, if you'd like a party it can be arranged. Probably we'll have a party & dance too. Tom, Murray, Wolfe, Anderson etc., are all planning to take in the dance, and they cordially invited you to join in. Would you like that? Just purely as a suggestion, I thought that maybe you'd like to drive down Saturday in time for the Purdue–State game, go with me—since I don't have a season ticket. Go out for dinner, and then meet the rest for the evening. That way, however, I'd either have to stay up in Sunbury all night, or you can stay here all night—the invitation is definitely extended, and the Welcome Mat is always out for you. In fact, why don't you stay all night here? Or, we could drive back to Sunbury that night, and talk Murray into coming up and getting me.

If you don't like any of those suggestions, and would just like to come down Saturday night, I'd gladly come & get you & take you back. But the other idea sounds like more fun. Any Sunday date granted would, of course—also be very much appreciated.

Dearest, please do come down some way or other, anything you say is law with me, and however you want things to be arranged—thus shall it be. However, I wish you would answer this letter right away, as soon as you decide what you're going to do, in order that I can plan with the good brothers, and if you will stay here, so that I can tell mom. Send me a special—I've always wanted to get one anyway.

Well, I've got to get to bed in order to awake bright and cheerful on the morrow, so please accept, and keep, and cherish—All My Love, Always,

Dick

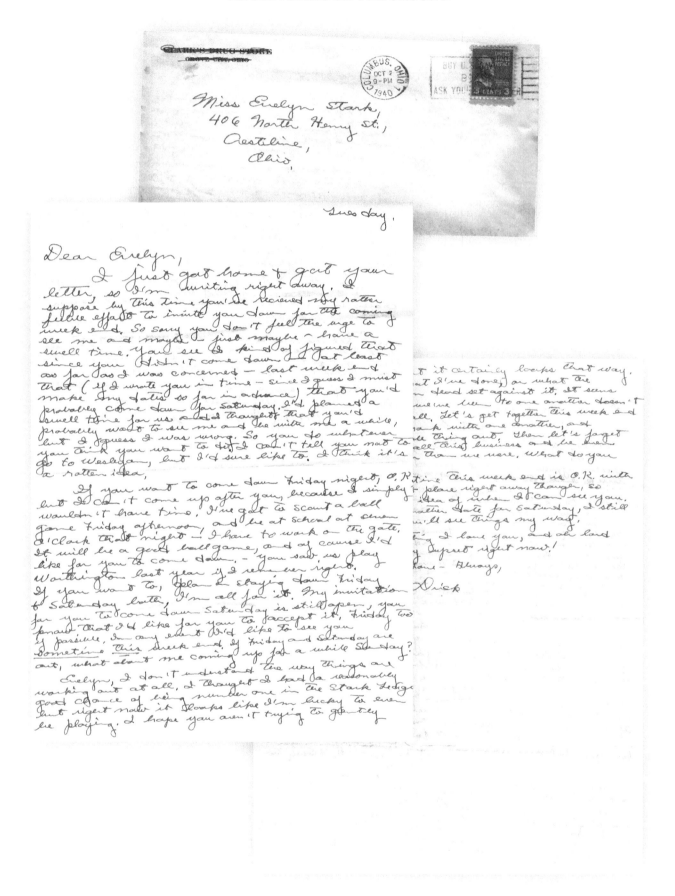

Postmarked Columbus, Ohio—October 2, 1940

Tuesday

Dear Evelyn,

I just got home & got your letter, so I'm writing right away. I suppose by this time you've received my rather feeble effort to invite you down for the coming week end. So sorry you don't feel the urge to see me and maybe—just maybe—have a swell time. You see I kind of figured that since you didn't come down—at least as far as I was concerned—last week end that (if I wrote you in time—since I guess I must make my dates so far in advance) that you'd probably come down for Saturday. I'd planned a swell time for us and I thought that you'd probably want to see me and be with me a while, but I guess I was wrong. So you do whatever you think you want to do. I can't tell you not to go to Wesleyan, but I'd sure like to. I think it's a rotten idea.

If you want to come down Friday night, O. K., but I can't come up after you, because I simply wouldn't have time. I've got to scout a ball game Friday afternoon, and be at school at seven o'clock that night—I have to work on the gate. It will be a good ballgame, and of course I'd like for you to come down. You saw us play Worthington last year if I remember right. If you want to, plan on staying down Friday & Saturday both, I'm all for it. My invitation for you to come down Saturday is still open, you know that I'd like for you to accept it, Friday too if possible. In any event I'd like to see you sometime this week end. If Friday and Saturday are out, what about me coming up for a while Sunday?

Evelyn, I don't understand the way things are working out at all. I thought I had a reasonable good chance of being number one in the Stark League, but right now it looks like I'm lucky to even be playing. I hope you aren't trying to gently fluff me off, but it certainly looks that way. I don't know what I've done, or what the trouble is, but I'm dead set against it. It seems as though everything we've been to one another doesn't mean much after all. Let's get together this week end and be perfectly frank with one another, and straighten the whole thing out. Then let's forget about all this business and be even closer to another than we were. What do you say?

Know that anytime this week end is O.K. with me. Set the time & place right away though, so that I'll have some idea of when I can see you. I'm not getting another date for Saturday, I still have hopes that you'll see things my way!

Despite, everything I love you, and oh lord but I am awfully upset right now!

All My Love—Always,

Dick

Wed eving,

Dear Evelyn,

Since you seem to want it to be that way, I'll come up Friday and be at your house at 6:00. We'll go out for dinner and to the game, and then _talk_! I've got a lot of talking to do I guess.

So sorry you won't change your mind in regard to Saturday. I still wish you would, I'd like to have that date with you particular, but that's up to you. I'm pretty damned disappointed however.

Well, I've got to go to a meeting. I'll see you Friday unless I hear otherwise from you.

Until then —

Dick.

P.S. — Please don't think I don't want to see you Friday, I _do_! I've already made arrangements so that we can go, I detailed you while to scout the ballgame, and I got out of working at the gate. I'd make this letter longer, but I've got such a headache I can hardly see, and I've got this meeting to go to. Besides, I'll say everything when I see you.

Notify me some way or other if you change your mind about Friday, otherwise I'll be up.

POSTMARKED COLUMBUS, OHIO—OCTOBER 2, 1940

Wednesday evening

Dear Evelyn,

Since you seem to want it to be that way, I'll come up Friday and be at your house at 6:00. We'll go out for dinner and to the game, and then talk. I've got a lot of talking to do I guess.

So sorry you won't change your mind in regard to Saturday. I still wish you would, I'd like to have that date with you particularly, but that's up to you. I'm pretty damned disappointed.

Well, I've got to go to a meeting. I'll see you Friday unless I hear otherwise from you.

Until Then—

Dick

P.S. Please don't think I don't want to see you Friday, I do! I've already made arrangements so that we can go. I detailed Tom White to scout the ballgame, and I got out of working on the gate. I'd make this letter longer, but I've got such a headache I can hardly see, and I've got this meeting to go to. Besides, I'll say everything when I see you.

Notify me someway or other if you change your mind about Friday, otherwise I'll be up.

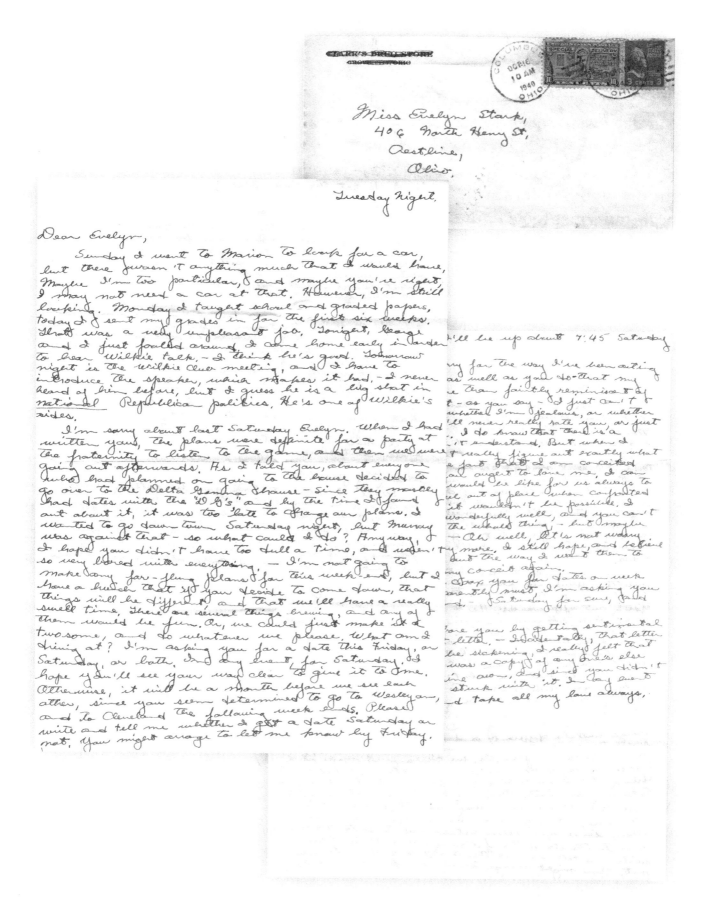

Tuesday Evening

Dear Evelyn,

Sunday I went to Marion to look for a car, but there wasn't anything much that I would have, maybe I'm too particular, and maybe you're right I may not need a car at that. However, I'm still looking. Monday I taught school and graded papers, today I sent my grades in for the first six weeks. That was a very unpleasant job. Tonight, George and I just fooled around. I came home early in order to hear Wilkie talk. I think he's good. Tomorrow night is the Wilkie Club meeting, and I have to introduce the speaker, which makes it bad. I never heard of him before but I guess he is a big shot in national Republican politics. He's one of Wilkie's aides.

I'm sorry about last Saturday Evelyn. When I had written you, the plans were definite for a party at the fraternity to listen to the game, and then we were going out afterwards. As I told you, about every one who had planned on going to the house decided to go over to the Delta Gamma house—since they mostly had dates with the 'DG's," and by the time I found out about it, it was too late to change our plans. I wanted to go downtown Saturday night, but Murray was against that—so what could I do? Anyway, I hope you didn't have too dull a time, and weren't so very bored with everything. I'm not going to make any far-flung plans for this week-end, but I have a hunch that if you decide to come down, that things will be different, and that we'll have a really swell time. There are several things brewing, and any of them would be fun. Or, we could just make it a twosome, and do whatever we please. What am I driving at? I'm asking you for a date this Friday, or Saturday, or both. In any event for Saturday. I hope you'll see your way clear to give it to me. Otherwise, it will be a month before we see each other, since you seem determined to go to Wesleyan, and to Cleveland the following week ends. Please write and tell me whether I get a date Saturday or not. You might arrange to let me know by Friday. If I do get the date, I'll be up about 7:45 Saturday evening. O.K.?

Evelyn, I'm also sorry for the way I've been acting lately. I realize—fully as well as you do—that my behavior has been more than faintly reminiscent of a high-school kid, but—as you say—I just can't help it. I don't know whether I'm jealous, or whether I'm worried for fear I'll never really rate you, or just what is wrong with me. I do know that there is a lot about you that I don't understand. But when I analyze things, I can't really figure out exactly what it is, unless it is the fact that I am conceited enough to think that you ought to love me. I can see so plainly what it would be like for us always to be together, that I feel out of place when confronted with the notion that it wouldn't be possible. I know it would work wonderfully well, and you can't see it. I think that's the whole thing—but maybe it isn't that at all. Oh well, let's not worry about that at all any more. I still hope, and believe that things will work out the way I want them to eventually. Probably my conceit again.

I hate to have to coax you for dates on week ends, but since I apparently must, I'm asking you again for this week end. Saturday for sure, and Friday too, if possible.

Well, I shan't bore you by getting sentimental as I did in my last letter. Incidentally, that letter was not intended to be sickening, I really felt that way, and no part of it was a copy of any one's else handiwork. 'Twas mine own, and since you didn't approve, I guess I'm stuck with it. In any event try and love me, and take all my love always,

Dick

Wed. night.

Dear Evelyn,

When I came home tonight, I was anticipating a letter from you. As a matter of fact, I even asked Murray to wait a minute because I thought I might be able to tell him whether or not we were going to have a date Saturday or not. The result, needless to say was not only no letter, but not even so much as an indication that we have a mailman. To say I was disappointed is an understatement. To be perfectly truthful, I was immediately just as blue as I could be. I'm not asking you why I didn't hear from you, that's up to you. But I am wondering just a little bit more about the status of our relationship. I'm not even asking you to explain that to me now, because I'm afraid to. The fact is, however, that we aren't clicking the way we did for quite a while. I don't know whether it's my fault or yours, or both, or whether it is the natural course of events. Maybe it's just that I have a chip on my shoulder. Possibly you just simply are getting tired of having me around. Probably I've done something to offend you. Believe me, if the latter is true, that I never willingly would do anything to cause you to get peeved. In any event, let's get things back on the track they took this summer and early this fall — up until the last two or three weeks in fact. Let's revive the idea that we're Evelyn and Dick, and that the rest of the world can go hide under a rock someplace. I don't know exactly what I said Saturday night. — I guess I'm out of practice on my beer drinking — I don't know what I did, or failed to do, but I'm truly sorry if you were put out about anything.

Probably tomorrow I'll get a letter and then I'll be sorry I wrote this, but at any rate it's written. What do I want you to do?

1 — Write me oftener; as old as I am you'd think I wouldn't get lonesome, but I do — and just hearing from you helps a lot.

2 — Keep on arranging it so that I can see you about every weekend. If you don't have any desire to see me, that is different. If you do, then let's arrange it and quit this fencing around for dates.

[right column, partial]

...usiastic about us being to try and love me. I'll admit ...at you could love about me, ...e easier to do it that way, than ...y possible reasons why you ...al other things that you might ...in loving you said with the I hope you do is give me one ... Anytime you let me ...want to see you, particularly ...ou the next two week ends I would decide that you wanted

POSTMARKED GROVE CITY, OHIO—OCTOBER 17, 1940

Wednesday Night

Dear Evelyn,

When I came home tonight, I was anticipating a letter from you. As a matter of fact, I even asked Murray to wait a minute because I thought I might be able to tell him whether or not we were going to have a date Saturday or not. The result, needless to say was not only no letter, but not even so much as an indication that we have a mailman. To say that I was disappointed is an understatement. To be perfectly truthful, I was immediately just as blue as I could be. I'm not asking you why I didn't hear from you, that's up to you. But I am wondering just a little bit more about the status of our relationship. I'm not even asking you to explain that to me now, because I'm afraid to. The fact is, however, that we aren't clicking the way we did for quite a while. I don't know whether it's my fault or yours, or both, or whether it is the natural course of events. Maybe it's just that I have a chip on my shoulder. Possibly you are just simply getting tired of having me around. Probably I've done something to offend you. Believe me, if the later is true, that I never willingly would do anything to cause you to get peeved. In any event, let's get things back on the track they took this summer and early this fall—up until the last two or three weeks in fact. Let's revive the idea that we're Evelyn and Dick, and that the rest of the world can go hide under a rock someplace. I don't know exactly what I said Saturday night. I guess I'm out of practice on my beer drinking I don't know what I did, or failed to do, but I'm truly sorry if you were put out about anything.

Probably tomorrow I'll get a letter and then I'll be sorry I wrote this, but at any rate it's written. What do I want you to do?

1. Write me oftener; as old as I am you'd think I wouldn't get lonesome, but I do—and just hearing from you helps a lot.

2. Keep on arranging it so that I can see you about every week end. If you don't have any desireto see me, that is different. If you do, then let's arrange it and quit this fencing around fordates.

3. You might be enthusiastic about us being together, and you might try and love me. I'll admitI don't know exactly what you could love about me, but at least it would be easier to do it thatway, than to think up all of the many possible reasons why you shouldn't love me.

I could think of several other things that you might do, but there's no sense in boring you now with the gory details. One thing I hope you do is give me one or two dates this week end. Any time you let me know is O.K., but I really want to see you, particularly since I won't get to see you the next two week ends after this one—unless you would decide that you wanted to see me.

Goodnight,

Dick

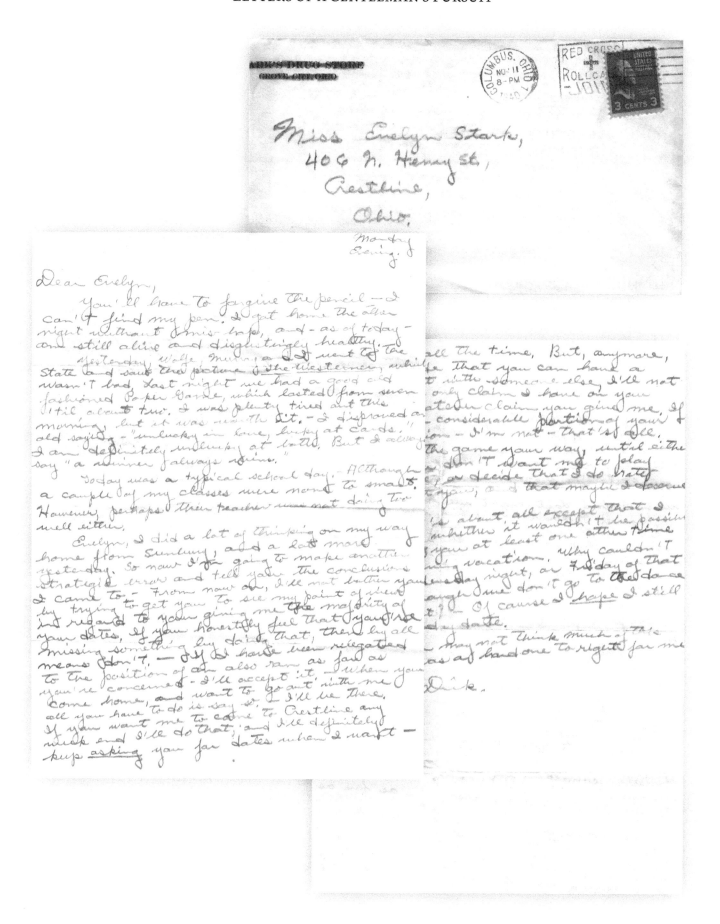

Monday Evening

Dear Evelyn,

You'll have to forgive the pencil—I can't find my pen. I got home the other night without mishap, and—as of today—am still alive and disgustingly healthy.

Yesterday, Wolfe, Murray and I went to the State and saw the picture The Westerner, which wasn't bad. Last night we had a good old fashioned Poker Game, which lasted from seven 'til, about two. I was plenty tired out this morning, but it was worth it. I disproved an old saying—"unlucky in love, lucky at cards." I am definitely unlucky at both. But I always say "a winner always wins."

Today was a typical school day. Although a couple of my classes were none too smart. However, perhaps their teacher was not doing too well either.

Evelyn, I did a lot of thinking on my way home from Sunbury, and a lot more yesterday. So now I'm going to make another strategic error and tell you the conclusions I came to—From now on, I'll not bother you by trying to get you to see my point of view in regard to your giving me the majority of your dates. If you honestly feel that you're missing something by doing that, then by all means don't. If I have been relegated to the position of an also ran as far as you're concerned—I'll accept it. When you come home, and want to go out with me all you have to do is say so. I'll be there. If you want me to come to Crestline any week end I'll do that; and I'll definitely keep asking you for dates when I want—which will be all the time. But, anymore, when you decide that you can have a better time out with someone else, I'll not say anything. The only claim I have on you will be whatever claim you give me. If I'm not worth a considerable portion of your time and affection—I'm not—that's all. So, we'll play the game your way, until either you decide you don't want me to play at all anymore, or decide that I do rate pretty well with you, and that maybe I deserve a few breaks.

Well, that's about all except that I was wondering whether it wouldn't be possible for me to see you at least one other time during Thanksgiving vacation. Why couldn't I see you Wednesday night, or Friday of that weekend, even though we don't go to the dance that Friday night? Of course I hope I still have the Saturday date.

Evelyn, you may not think much of this letter, but it was a hard one to right for me.

Dick

1941

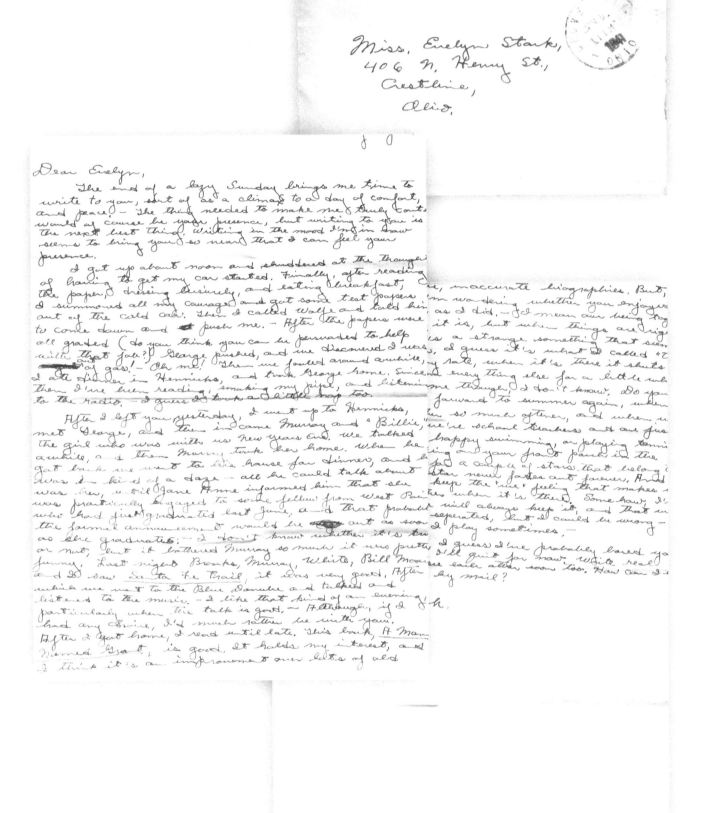

Miss. Evelyn Stark,
406 N. Henry St.,
Crestline,
Ohio.

Dear Evelyn,

The end of a lazy Sunday brings me time to write to you, sort of as a climax to a day of comfort, and peace — The thing needed to make me truly contented would of course be your presence, but writing to you is the next best thing. Writing in the mood I'm in now seems to bring you so near that I can feel your presence.

I got up about noon and shuddered at the thought of having to get my car started. Finally, after reading the paper, dressing leisurely, and eating breakfast, I summoned all my courage and got some test papers out of the cold car. Then I called Wolfe and told him to come down and push me. — After the papers were all graded (do you think you can be persuaded to help with that job?) George pushed, and we discovered I was out of gas! — Oh me! Then we fooled around awhile, I ate dinner in Hennicks, and took George home. Since then I've been reading, smoking my pipe, and listening to the radio. — I guess I took a little nap too.

After I left you yesterday, I went up to Hennicks, met George, and then in came Murray and "Billie," the girl who was with us New Years Eve. We talked awhile, and then Murray took her home. When he got back we went to his house for dinner, and he was in kind of a daze — all he could talk about was her, until Jane Anne informed him that she was practically engaged to some fellow from West Point who had just graduated last June, and that probably the formal announcement would be out as soon as she graduates. — I don't know whether it's true or not, but it bothered Murray so much it was pretty funny. Last night Brooks, Murray, White, Bill Moore and I saw Santa Fe Trail, it was very good. After which we went to the Blue Danube and talked and listened to the music. — I like that kind of an evening, particularly when the talk is good. — Although, if I had any choice, I'd much rather be with you. After I got home, I read until late. This book, A Man Named Grant, is good, it holds my interest, and I think it's an improvement over lots of old

... inaccurate biographies. But, I'm wondering whether you enjoyed it as I did. — I mean our being together ... it is, but when things are right ... is a strange something that seems ... I guess it's what is called "... at any rate, when it's there it shuts out every thing else for a little while ... me though, I don't know. Do you ... forward to summer again, when ... so much better, and when we're school teachers and are just ... happy swimming, or playing tennis ... your front porch in the ... a couple of stars that belong ... star never fades out forever. And ... keep the nice feeling that makes ... when it's there. Somehow, I ... will always keep it, and that in ... separated, but I could be wrong — ... play sometimes, —

I guess I've probably bored you ... I'll quit for now. Write real ... each other soon too. How can I ... by mail?

J. h.

Sunday Night

Dear Evelyn,

The end of a lazy Sunday brings me time to write to you, sort of as a climax to a day of comfort, and peace. The thing needed to make me truly content would of course be your presence, but writing to you is the next best thing. Writing in the mood I'm in now seems to bring you so near that I can feel your presence. I got up about noon and shuddered at the thought of having to get my car started. Finally, after reading the paper, dressing leisurely, and eating breakfast, I summoned all my courage and got some test papers out of the cold car. Then I called Wolfe and told him to come down and push me. After the papers were all graded (do you think you can be persuaded to help with that job?) George pushed, and we discovered I was out of gas! Oh me! Then we fooled around awhile, I ate dinner in Hennicks, and took George home. Since then I've been reading, smoking my pipe, and listening to the radio. I guess I took a little nap too.

After I left you, yesterday, I went up to Hennicks, met George, and then in came Murray and "Billie," the girl who was with us New Years Eve. We talked awhile, and then Murray took her home. When he got back we went to his house for dinner, and he was in kind of a daze—all he could talk about was her, until Jane Anne informed him that she was practically engaged to some fellow from West Point, who had just graduated last June, and that probably the formal announcement would be out as soon as she graduates. I don't know whether it's true or not, but it bothered Murray so much it was pretty funny. Last night Brooks, Murray, White, Bill Moore, and I saw Santa Fe Trail. It was very good. After which we went to the Blue Danube and talked and listened to the music. I like that kind of an evening, particularly when the talk is good. Although, if I had any choice, I'd much rather be with you. After I got home, I read until late. This book, A Man Named Grant, is good. It holds my interest, and I think it's an improvement over lots of old pseudo-sympathetic, inaccurate biographies. But, enough of that, I'm wondering whether you enjoyed yesterday as much as I did. I mean our being together. I don't know why it is, but when things are right between us, there's a strange something that seems to hold us together. I guess it's what I call "the We feeling." At any rate, when it's there it shuts us off completely from every thing else for a little while. Maybe it's just me though, I don't know. Do you know, I'm looking forward to summer again, when we can be together so much oftener, and when we can forget that we're school teachers and are just Evelyn and Dick, happy swimming, or playing tennis, or golfing—or sitting on your front porch in the moonlight looking for a couple of stars that belong to us. I hope the one star never fades out forever. And I hope we can always keep the "we" feeling that makes us so close to one another when it's there. Somehow, I've always felt that we will always keep it, and that we won't ever be really separated, but I could be wrong—look at the horses I play sometimes.

Well, sweetness, I guess I've probably bored you by this time, so I'll quit for now. Write real soon, and let's see each other soon too. How can I ever get you to love me by mail?

Dick

Sunday
About Noon.

Dear "Angel flying on the ground,"

Here it is Sunday and I have just gotten dressed, although I have read the paper and eaten breakfast. Really, I feel remarkably fit today. I've had more sleep over this week end than I've had in quite a spell. I looked at my eyes in the mirror this morning, and there isn't even a trace of a circle.

Since I last wrote, I haven't done an awful lot more than I had then. Wedensday I met "Hot Horse Herbie" Emrich, and we fooled around all evening. Thursday I went down to the Quarterback Club meeting and I saw the pictures of Paul Brown's Massilon team. How those kids could block! I wish Grove City could take a few lessons on that art. Friday I had to go to Groveport and keep score for the Grove City game. Again we got beat. — The thing that bothers me is that I can't figure out how we've managed to win three games. When I got home late Friday night, I found a letter from the originator of the flu epidemic herself. Saturday after I got dressed, bathed, shaved etc, (it was about one o'clock) I met Murray and Tom (Wolfe's girl made him meet her) and we went bowling and shot pool. — That was a pretty profitable venture for me as we were playing loser pays. — I got hot and didn't lose anything. Last night everybody had dates (except Clark, the dateless I wonder) so I came home and read. This reading is allright, but I'm getting a little sick of improving my mind. I'd sort of like to have a date too, just to see what it is like.

I thought maybe Miss Influenza — the girl who is like the angel flying on the ground — I would fall for the very broad hint I put out, and give me a date. But I guess I didn't hint quite strongly enough. I thought about coming up yesterday despite the flue, and then it got slippery and I decided not to. — At least that's the reason I gave myself for not coming up. Actually, I guess I'd have come flu, flue, and everything else notwithstanding, if I had thought you wanted me. But I was afraid — and undoubtedly with reason — that you'd have a date. Oh well, the books I've been reading have been pretty good at that! I guess I'll become a hermit, and learn to know all about everything — except women. What I'd like to know is, how do you ever learn to know anything about them?

Well, sweetness, I guess I'd better quit this foolishness for now. I've got about sixty test papers to grade, and my "studes" will be yelling their heads off if they don't get them by tomorrow. I sure wish you'd hurry up and reach the conclusion that you ought to marry me so that you can help me grade 'em. — No that's not the only reason you ought to reach that conclusion, but you've got to admit it's a reason. I've got some better reasons I could give you, but they require a visible audience, and maybe some practical demonstrations.

Please answer real soon, and tell me all about anything. In case you had decided to believe that stuff about me being a hermit, forget it! I was only fooling, and "by God and by Jesus" I'd like to have a date with you (not somebody else) real soon like this coming week-end, and as many week ends as possible thereafter. Why don't you put the chill on a couple of your boy friends, and be my honey again? I'm a good boy after you get to know me; and you ought to be getting so that you know me don't you think? I've been dreaming about you more than I ever did in my life before, and while they're fine, I need the "Real McCoy."

I heard the operetta Cyrano De Bergerac, last night, and the girl wanted the fellow to figure out some new ways to tell her he loved her. When he couldn't do it, she went angrily into the house. I can't figure out any new ways to tell you either darling, but I guess you know that I do without any invention on my part, so please don't go away in a dither when I say that I think you're the sweetest of them all, and that I miss you, and need you, and will love you always,

Dick,

Sunday About Noon

Dear "Angel flying on the ground,"

Here it is Sunday and I have just gotten dressed, although I have read the paper and eaten breakfast. Really, I feel remarkably fit today. I've had more sleep over this week end than I've had in quite a spell. I looked at my eyes in the mirror this morning, and there isn't even a trace of a circle.

Since I last wrote, I haven't done an awful lot more than I had then. Wednesday I met "Hot Horse Herbie," Emrich, and we fooled around all evening. Thursday I went down to the Quarterback Club meeting and saw the pictures of Paul Brown's Massilon team. How those kids could block! I wish Grove City could take a few lessons on that art. Friday I had to go to Groveport and keep score for the Grove City game. Again we got beat. The thing that bothers me is that I can't figure out how we've managed to win three games. When I got home late Friday night, I found a letter from the originator of the flu epidemic, herself. Saturday after I got dressed, bathed, shaved etc, (was about one o'clock) I met Murray and Tom (Wolfe's girl made him meet her) and we went bowling and shot pool. That was pretty profitable venture for me, as we were playing loser pays. I got hot and didn't lose anything. Last night everybody had dates (except Clark, the dateless wonder) so I came home and read. This reading is alright, but I'm getting a little sick of improving my mind. I'd sort of like to have a date too, just to see what it's like.

I thought maybe Miss Influenza—the girl who is like the angel flying on the ground—would fall for the very broad hint I put out, and give me a date. But I guess I didn't hint quite strongly enough. I thought about coming up yesterday despite the flu, and then it got slippery and I decided not to. At least that's the reason I gave myself for not coming up. Actually, I guess I'd have come flu, ice, and everything else not withstanding, if I had thought you wanted me. But I was afraid—and undoubtedly with reason—that you'd have a date. Oh well, the books I've been reading have been pretty good at that! I guess I'll become a hermit, and learn to know all about everything—except women. What I'd like to know is, how do you ever learn to know anything about them?

Well, sweetness, I guess I'd better quit this foolishness for now. I've got about sixty test papers to grade, and my "studes" will be yelling their heads off if they don't get them by tomorrow. I sure wish you'd hurry up and reach the conclusion that you ought to marry me so that you can help me grade 'em. No that's not the only reason you ought to reach that conclusion, but you've got to admit, it's a reason. I've got some better reasons I could give you, but they require a visible audience, and maybe some practical demonstrations.

Please answer real soon, and tell me all about anything. In case you had decided to believe that stuff about me being a hermit, forget it! I was only fooling, and "by God and by Jesus" I'd like to have a date with you (not somebody else) real soon, like this coming week end, and as many week ends as possible thereafter. Why don't you put the chill on a couple of your boy friends, and be my honey again? I'm a good boy after you get to know me; and you ought to be getting so that you know me don't you think? I've been dreaming about you more than I ever did in my life before, and while they're fine, I need the "Real McCoy."

I heard the operetta Cyrano De Bergerac, last night, and the girl wanted the fellow to figure out some new ways to tell her he loved her. When he couldn't do it, she went angrily in to the house. I can't figure out any new ways to tell you either darling, but I guess you know that I do without any invention on my part, so please don't go away in a dither when I say that I think you're the swellest of them all, and that I miss you, and need you, and will love you always.

Dick

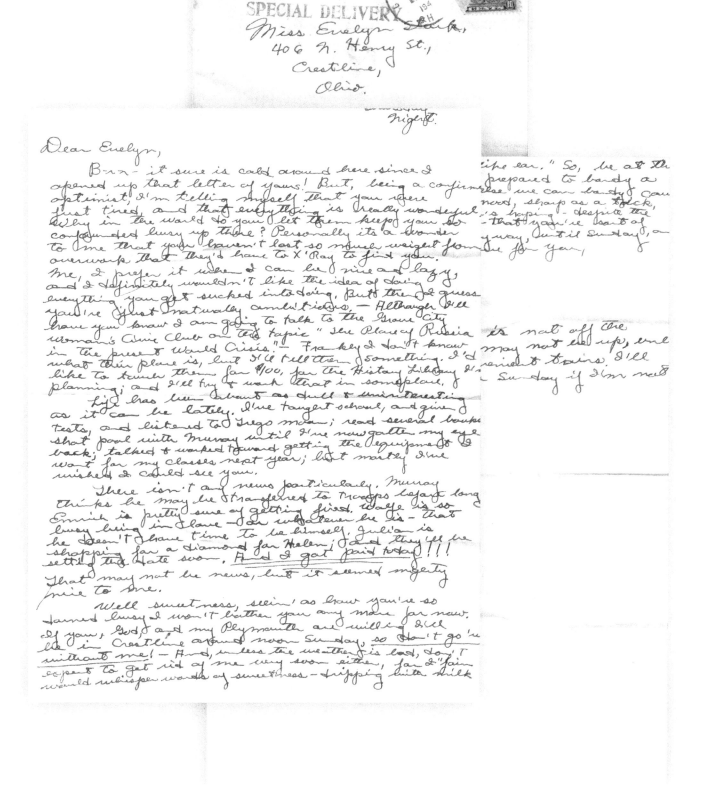

Miss Evelyn Stark,
406 N. Henry St.,
Crestline,
Ohio.

SPECIAL DELIVERY

Monday
Night.

Dear Evelyn,

Brr— it sure is cold around here since I opened up that letter of yours! But, being a confirmed optimist, I'm telling myself that you were just tired, and that everything is really wonderful. Why in the world do you let them keep you so confounded busy up there? Personally its a wonder to me that you haven't lost so much weight from overwork that they'd have to X'Ray to find you. Me, I prefer it where I can be nice and lazy, and I definitely wouldn't like the idea of being everything you get sucked into doing. But then I guess you're just naturally ambitious. — Although I'll have you know I am going to talk to the Grove City Woman's Civic Club on the topic "The Place of Russia in the present World Crisis." — Frankly I don't know what their place is, but I'll tell them something. I'd like to touch them for $100, for the History Library I'm planning; and I'll try to work that in someplace.

Life has been about as dull & uninteresting as it can be lately. I've taught school, and given tests, and listened to Greg's moan; read several books; shot pool with Murray until I've now gotten my eye back; talked & worked toward getting the equipment I want for my classes next year; but mostly I've wished I could see you.

There isn't any news particularly. Murray thinks he may be transferred to Troops before long. Emrich is pretty sure of getting first. Wolfe is so busy being in love — or whatever he is — that he doesn't have time to be himself. Julian is shopping for a diamond for Helen; and they'll be setting the date soon. And I got paid today!!! That may not be news, but it seemed mighty nice to me.

Well sweetness, seein' as how you're so darned busy I won't bother you any more for now. If you, God & my Plymouth are willing I'll be in Crestline around noon Sunday, so don't go without me! — And, unless the weather is bad, don't expect to get rid of me very soon either, for I "fain would whisper words of sweetness — dripping into willing

... tike ear." So, be at the prepared to bandy a sense we can bandy — come next, sharp as a tack, ... 's hoping — despite the ... that you've sort of ... anyway, until Sunday, ...re for you,

... its not off the ... may not be up, but ... remain to trains. I'll ... Sunday if I'm not

Thursday Night

Dear Evelyn,

Br-r-r- it sure is cold around here since I opened up that letter of yours! But, being a confirmed optimist, I'm telling myself that you were just tired, and that everything is really wonderful. Why in the world do you let them keep you so confounded busy up there? Personally it's a wonder to me that you haven't lost so much weight from overwork that they'd have to X-ray to find you. Me, I prefer it when I can be nice and lazy, and I definitely wouldn't like the idea of doing everything you get sucked into doing. But then I guess you're just naturally ambitious. although I'll have you know I am going to talk to the Grove City Woman's Civic Club on the topic "The Place of Russia in the present World Crisis." Frankly, I don't know what their place is, but I'll tell them something. I'd like to touch them for $100, for the History Library I'm planning; and I'll try & work that in someplace.

Life has been about as dull & uninteresting as it can be lately. I've taught school, and given tests, and listened to Trego moan; read several books; shot pool with Murray until I've now gotten my eye back; talked & worked toward getting the equipment I want for my classes next year; but mostly I've wished I could see you.

There isn't any news particularly. Murray thinks he may be transferred to Troops before long. Emrich is pretty sure of getting fired. Wolfe is so busy being in love— or whatever he is—that he doesn't have time to be himself. Julian is shopping for a diamond for Helen; and they'll be setting the date soon. And I got paid today!!! That may not be news, but it seemed mighty nice to me.

Well sweetness, seein' as how you're so darned busy I won't bother you any more for now. If you, God, and my Plymouth are willing I'll be in Crestline around noon Sunday, so don't go 'way without me! And, unless the weather is bad, don't expect to get rid of me very soon either, for I "fain would whisper words of sweetness— dripping with milk and honey into your pearl-like ear." So, be at thy sweetest fair maiden, and be prepared to bandy a lot of sweet nothing & anything else we can bandy, cause "I ain't nuthin' but in the mood, sharp as a tack, and fit & ready to run." Here's hoping—despite the absence of any such assurance—that you're sort of wanting to see me too. Anyway, until Sunday, and always there's—All My Love for You,

Dick

P.S. Friday Morning:

If the snow & ice is not off the roads Sunday morning, I may not be up, unless there are a couple of convenient trains. I'll either wire or phone you Sunday if I'm not coming.

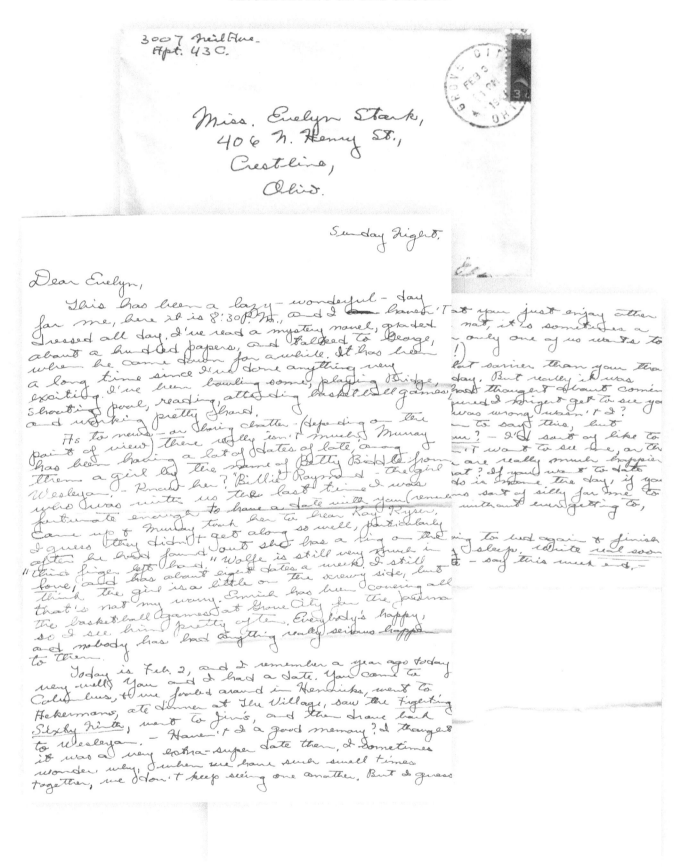

Sunday Night

Dear Evelyn,

This has been a lazy—wonderful—day for me, here it is 8:30 P.M., and I haven't dressed all day. I've read a mystery novel, graded about a hundred papers, and talked to George, when he came down for awhile. It has been a long time since I've done anything very exciting. I've been bowling some, playing Bridge, shooting pool, reading, attending basketball games, and working pretty hard.

As to news—or boring chatter—(depending on the point of view) there really isn't much. Murray has been having a lot of dates of late, among them a girl by the name of Betty Biddle from Wesleyan. Know her? "Billie" Raymond—the girl who was with us the last time I was fortunate enough to have a date with you (remember?) came up & Murray took her to hear Kay Kyser. I guess they didn't get along so well, particularly after he had found out she has a ring on the "third finger left hand." Wolfe is still very much in love, and he has about eight dates a week. I still think the girl is a little on the screwy side, but that's not my worry. Emrich has been covering all the basketball games at Grove City for the Journal so I see him pretty often. Everybody's happy, and nobody has had anything really serious happen to them.

Today is Feb. 2, and I remember a year ago today very well, you and I had a date. You came to Columbus, & we fooled around in Hennicks, went to Ackermans, ate dinner at The Village, saw the <u>Fighting Sixty Ninth</u>, went to Jim's and then drove back to Wesleyan. Haven't I a good memory? I thought it was a very extra-super date then. I sometimes wonder why, when we have such swell times together, we don't keep seeing one another. But I guess the whole thing is that you just enjoy other people more. Believe it or not, it's sometimes a little discouraging when only one of us wants to be with the other (me!)

I'm probably a lot sorrier than you that I didn't get up last Sunday. But really it was awfully bad weather. I had thought about coming on the train, but I figured I might get to see you this week end. I guess I was wrong wasn't I? I should know better than to say this, but <u>when do I get to see you</u>? I'd sort of like to know. Is it that you don't want to see me, or that you've decided that you are really much happier with other people, or what? If you want to date me, all you have to do is name the day, if you don't just say so. It seems sort of silly for me to go on wanting to see you without ever getting to, doesn't it?

Well, honey, I'm going to bed again & finish getting caught upon my sleep. Write real soon, and please give me a date—say this week end.

Dick

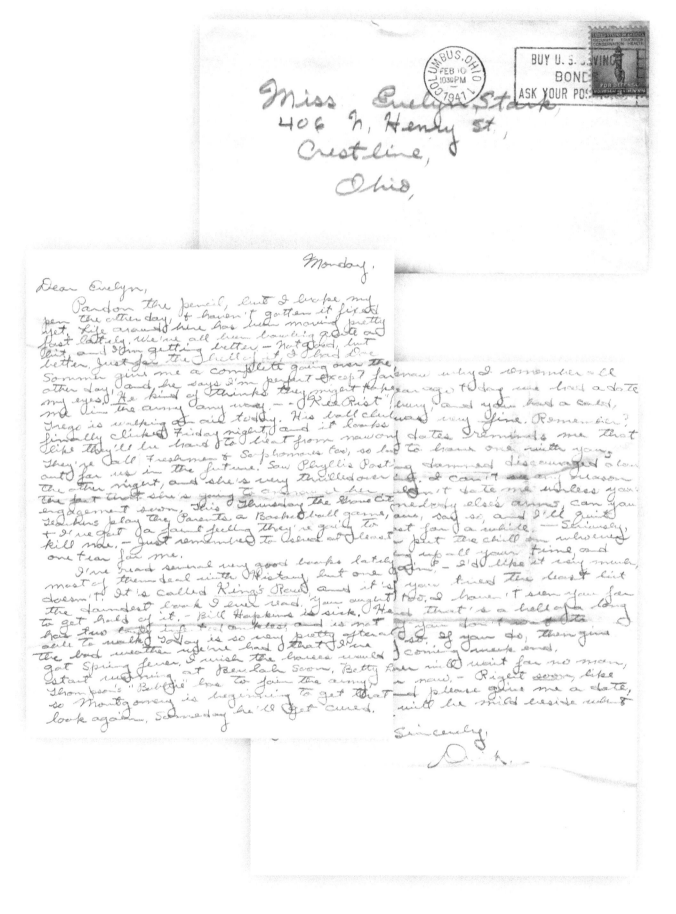

Monday

Dear Evelyn,

Pardon the pencil, but I broke my pen the other day & haven't gotten it fixed yet. Life around here has been moving pretty fast lately. We've all been bowling quite a bit, and I'm getting better. Not good, but better. Just for the hell of it, I had Doc Sommer give me a complete going over the other day, and he says I'm perfect except for my eyes. He kind of thinks they might take me in the army any way. "Kee Rist"! Trego is walking on air today. His ball club finally clicked Friday night, and it looks like they'll be hard to beat from now on. They're all Freshman & Sophomores too, so look out for us in the future. Saw Phyllis Post the other night, and she's very thrilled over the fact that she's going to announce her engagement soon. This Thursday the Grove City Teachers play the Parents a basketball game, & I've got a faint feeling they're going to kill me. Just remember to shed at least one tear for me.

I've read several very good books lately, most of them deal with History, but one doesn't. It's called King's Row, and it's the darndest book I ever read. You ought to get hold of it. Bill Hopkins is sick. He has two lovely infected ankles, and is not able to walk. Today is so very pretty after all the bad weather we've had that I've got spring fever. I wish the horses would start running at Beulah soon. Betty Lou Thompson's "Bobbie" has to join the army, so Montgomery is beginning to get that look again. Someday he'll get cured.

I don't know why I remember all this, but a year ago today we had a date. I came to Sunbury, and you had a cold, and everything was very fine. Remember?

Speaking of dates reminds me that I'd still like to have one with you and I'm getting damned discouraged about the whole thing. I can't see any reason why you shouldn't date me unless you've fallen into somebody else's arms, can you? And if you have, say so, and I'll quit hoping, at least for a while. Seriously, why don't you put the chill on whoever has been taking up all your time, and be my honey again? I'd like it very much, and maybe if you tried the least bit you'd like it too. I haven't seen you for five weeks, and that's a hell of a long time. However, if you don't want to date me please say so. If you do, then give me a date this coming week end.

Well, dinner will wait for no man, so I'll quit for now. Right soon, like right now, and please give me a date, or a spanking will be mild beside what you'll get.

Sincerely,

Dick

1942

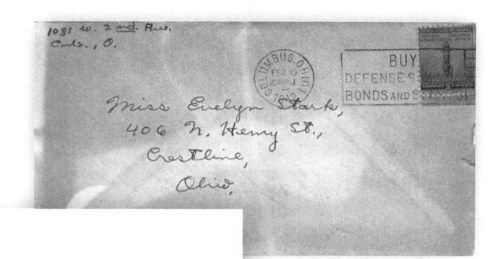

Dear Evelyn,

Here it is Tuesday evening already, for which thank goodness. That means it won't be quite so long until Saturday. — Only three more days to be exact. The weeks really do whiz past, and if it weren't for the fact that I look forward so to the week ends, I would lose all track of time.

There hasn't been much happen lately. Sunday night I came home (I really had no intention of having a date with anyone else) and Tom and Herb came in. We had a bull session until very late. It was an interesting one, we ranged from the war to women. There seemed to be general agreement that the war was the lesser of the two evils. — Ha!

... as really up early ... still out, and it ...ark. However, I ...started in time for ...I discovered that I ...Yes, I was late for ...felt real crazy all ...my kids may have ...I'll bet it ...Last night Tom ...the seventy five ...from him Friday ...but I added another ...collection. Today was ...mediocre days. ...this morning, slush ...in this afternoon. ...knows what it will ...but I don't think ...think I'll stay ...afternoon I've ...of this curriculum ...at the County ...Study group ...office; and Friday is our last

Monday I was really up early. The moon was still out, and it was very very dark. However, I managed to get started in time for school, and then I discovered that I had a flat tire. — Yes, I was late for school again. I felt real crazy all day, and while my kids may have learned something, I'll bet it wasn't history. Last night Tom tried to win back the seventy five cents I won from him Friday shooting pool, but I added another quarter to my collection. Today, was/Tuesday, I guess is one of those dull mediocre days. — We had snow this morning, slush at noon, and rain this afternoon. Heaven only knows what it will be like tonight, but I don't think I'll find out. I think I'll stay home. Tomorrow afternoon I've got a meeting of this curriculum study group in at the County office; and Friday is our last

train.

... I guess is
... Write to me, and
... me, and darn it I
...'d start loving me.
...imagine how bad it
...sure of you. It's an
... to be put off continually.
...an't let me get you
... birthday. ...
...me honey, and at least
... to lose me, because
... will give you

I want you
always — All My Love,
Dick.

Dear Evelyn,

Here it is Tuesday evening already, for which thank goodness. That means it won't be quite so long until Saturday. Only three more days to be exact. The weeks really do whiz past, and if it weren't for the fact that I look forward so to the week ends, I would lose all track of time.

There hasn't been much happening lately. Sunday night I came home (I really had no intention of leaving a date with anyone else) and Tom and Herb came in. We had a bull session until very late. It was an interesting one, we ranged from the war to women. There seems to be general agreement that the war was the lesser of the two evils. Ha!

Monday I was really up early. The moon was still out, and it was very very dark. However, I managed to get started in time for school, and then I discovered that I had a flat tire. Yes, I was late for school again. I felt real crazy all day, and while my kids may have learned something, I'll bet it wasn't history. Last night Tom tried to win back the seventy five cents I won from him Friday shooting pool, but I added another quarter to my collection. Today, was one of those dull mediocre days. We had snow this morning, slush at noon, and rain this afternoon. Heaven only knows what it will be like tonight, but I don't think I'll find out, I think I'll stay home. Tomorrow afternoon I've got a meeting with this curriculum study group in at the County office; and Friday is our last regularly scheduled basketball game of the year. Also Friday I get to eat that steak I won from Goebbel. I think I told you about it.

Honey, what about you? Have you been on your good behavior? Are you still on a liquid diet? Did you get to Crestline in time for your "meeting"? You know when I stop and think about it maybe I acted like a heel this last week end. Anyway, I had a good time, and I only hope you did darling; but I'm afraid you really didn't. I'll try and make it up for you this coming week end—that is if I can still see you. Can I? If so I'll come up or you come down, it doesn't make any difference to me. Only, if the weather is bad and you want me to come up, I may come on the train.

Well sweetness, I guess I'll quit for now. Write to me, and think about me, and darn it I really wish you'd start loving me. You can't imagine how hard it is not to be sure of you. It's an awful feeling to be put off continually. I still wish you'd let me get you a ring for your birthday. Why don't you?

Write to me honey and at least make an effort to love me, because I want you and will give you always—All My Love,

Dick

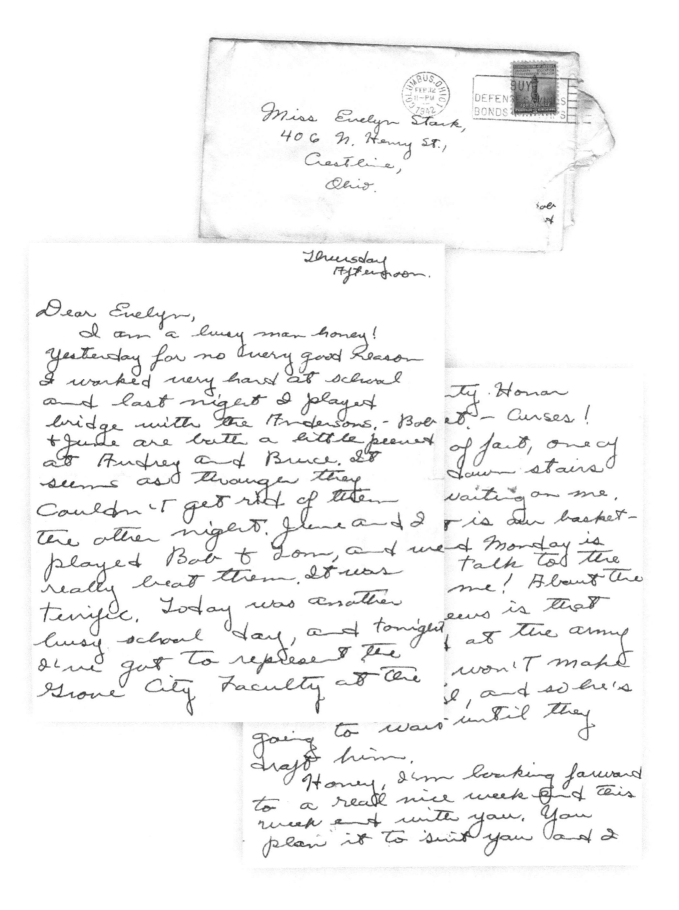

Miss Evelyn Stark,
406 N. Henry St.,
Crestline,
Ohio.

Thursday
Afternoon.

Dear Evelyn,
I am a busy man honey!
Yesterday for no very good Reason
I worked very hard at school
and last night I played
bridge with the Andersons, - Bob
& June are both a little peeved
at Audrey and Bruce. It
seems as though they
couldn't get rid of them
the other night. June and I
played Bob & Tom, and we
really beat them. It was
terrific. Today was another
busy school day, and tonight
I've got to represent the
Grove City Faculty at One

...ty. Honan
et. - Curses!
of fact, one of
down stairs
waiting on me.
is our basket-
& Monday is
talk to the
me! About the
...ews is that
at the army
won't make
, and so he's
going to war until they
draft him.
Honey, I'm looking forward
to a real nice week end this
week end with you. You
plan it to suit you and I

know it will suit me. There's just one thing though, I'm warning you now that — what with It being Valentine's Day and everything — I'm definitely going to be in the mood for love. — Do you mind?

Speaking of love, I know it probably sounds trite, and very much like a broken record for me to keep telling you that I love you, but I do, and I do wish you loved me too. It would be the answer to all my dreams.

Sweetheart, I'll be up Saturday afternoon — unless I hear otherwise from you. — I'll drive up unless the weather is real bad, and I'll get there around five thirty. If the weather

gets bad, I'll take the three o'clock train out of Columbus. But more than likely I'll drive.

So, in the meantime be good, and be prepared — because I warned you, and love me.

All my Love — Always,

Dick

Thursday Afternoon

Dear Evelyn,

I am a busy man honey! Yesterday for no very good reason I worked very hard at school and last night I played bridge with the Andersons. Bob & June are both a little peeved at Audrey and Bruce. It seems as though they couldn't get rid of them the other night. June and I played Bob &Tom, and we really beat them. It was terrific. Today was another busy school day, and tonight I've got to represent the Grove City Faculty at the Franklin County Honor Society Banquet. Curses! As a matter of fact, one of "my boys" is down stairs reading, and waiting on me. Tomorrow night is our basketball game, and Monday is the night I talk to the Hi-Y. Oh me! About the only other news is that Tom is mad at the army because they won't make him a general, and so he's going to wait until they draft him.

Honey, I'm looking forward to a real nice week end this week end with you. You plan it to suit you and I know it will suit me. There's just one thing though, I'm warning you now that—what with it being Valentine's Day and everything. I'm definitely going to be in the mood for love. Do you mind?

Speaking of love, I know it probably sounds trite, and very much like a broken record for me to keep telling you that I love you, but I do, and I do wish you loved me too. It would be the answer to all my dreams.

Sweetheart, I'll be up Saturday afternoon—unless I hear otherwise from you. I'll drive up unless the weather is real bad, and I'll get there around five thirty. If the weather gets bad, I'll take the three o'clock train out of Columbus. But more than likely I'll drive.

So, in the meantime <u>be good</u>, and be prepared—<u>because I warned you</u>, and love me.

All My Love —Always,

Dick

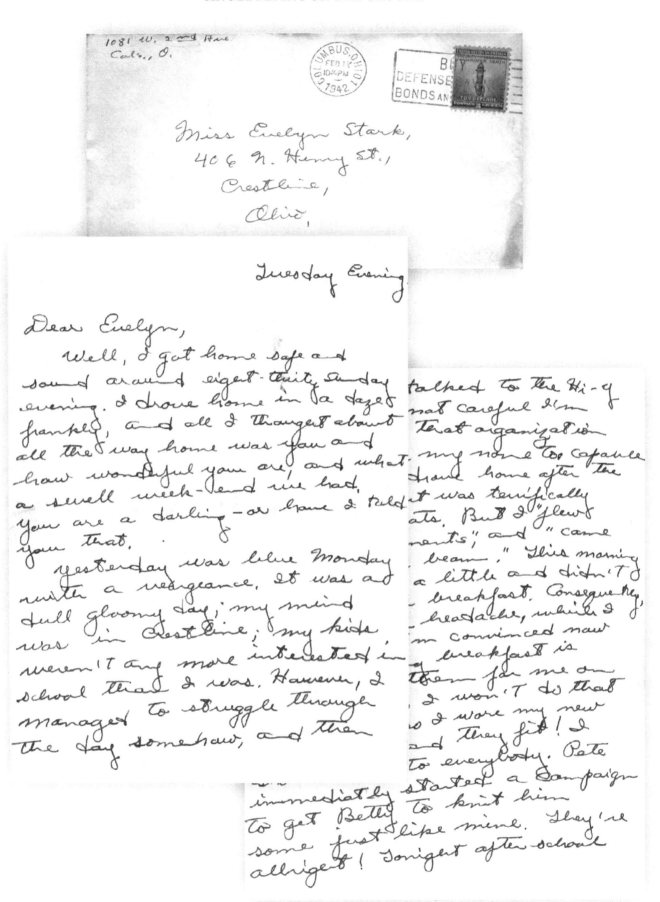

1081 W. 2nd Ave
Cols., O.

COLUMBUS OHIO
FEB 17
10 PM
1942

BUY
DEFENSE
BONDS AN

Miss Evelyn Stark,
406 N. Henry St.,
Crestline,
Ohio,

Tuesday Evening

Dear Evelyn,

Well, I got home safe and
sound around eight-thirty Sunday
evening. I drove home in a daze
frankly, and all I thought about
all the way home was you and
how wonderful you are, and what
a swell week-end we had.
You are a darling — or have I told
you that.

Yesterday was blue Monday
with a vengeance. It was a
dull gloomy day; my mind
was in Crestline; my kids
weren't any more interested in
school than I was. However, I
managed to struggle through
the day somehow, and then

talked to the Hi-Y
not careful I'm
first organization
my none too capable
drove home after the
it was terrifically
cats. But I "flew
rents" and "came
beam." This morning
a little and didn't
breakfast. Consequently,
headache, which I
convinced now
breakfast is
them for me on
I won't do that
so I wore my new
and they fit! I
to everybody. Pete
immediately started a campaign
to get Betty to knit him
some just like mine. They're
allright! Tonight after school

Pete had a practice game against Commercial Paint, and I have never seen a worse team in my life than we were. I finally got so disgusted I came home. If we could ~~—~~ play one of your gym classes we might have a chance of winning a game in the tournament, but the way it is now we couldn't beat a carpet.

Honey, I'm looking forward to Saturday already. I guess maybe the carpet will be laid Saturday, but Mom suggested that we postpone our party for another week or so. However, I still want you to come out Saturday afternoon. Things don't look too bad now. It's your birthday celebration sweetness, so whatever you want to do — we'll do. Write and tell me what it is, and we'll plan it.

never have any ... to than we had ... d. — Not that ... isn't fine, but, ... end was super. ... the time, I'm ... d to have me ... at is unless you ... drive me off. ... ling and if there ... that I can give ... love I'll be ... that maybe ... the tiniest

Dick,

POSTMARKED COLUMBUS, OHIO—FEBRUARY 17, 1942

Tuesday Evening

Dear Evelyn,

Well, I got home safe and sound around eight-thirty Sunday evening. I drove home in a daze frankly, and all I thought about all the way home was you and how wonderful you are, and what a swell weekend we had. You are a darling—or have I told you that.

Yesterday was blue Monday with a vengeance. It was a dull gloomy day; my mind was in Crestline; my kids weren't any more interested in school than I was. However, I managed to struggle through the day somehow, and then last night I talked to the Hi-Y boys. If I'm not careful I'm going to have that organization placed under my name too capable direction. I drove home after the meeting, and it was terrifically foggy in spots. But I "flew by instruments," and "came home on the beam." This morning I over slept a little and didn't have time for breakfast. Consequently, I got another headache, which I still have. I'm convinced now that not eating breakfast is what causes them for me on Saturdays, so I won't do that anymore. Also I wore my new socks today, and they fit! I showed them to everybody. Pete immediately started a campaign to get Betty to knit him some just like mine. They're all right! Tonight after school Peter had a practice game against Commercial Point, and I have never seen a worse team in my life than we were. I finally got so disgusted I came home. If we could play one of your gym classes we might have a chance of winning a game in the tournament, but the way it is now we couldn't beat a carpet.

Honey, I'm looking forward to Saturday, but Mom suggested that we postpone our party for another week or so. However, I still want you to come out Saturday afternoon. Things don't look too bad now. It's your birthday celebration sweetness, so whatever you want to do—we'll do. Write and tell me what it is, and we'll plan it.

Dearest, let's never have any other kind of a date than we had this last week end. Not that every date we have isn't fine, but to me, last weekend was super. I love you more all the time. I'm afraid you're doomed to have me around forever—that is unless you take a club and drive me off.

Write to me darling and if there is anything more that I can give you then all my love I'll be offering, and hoping that maybe you love me just the tiniest bit in return.

Dick

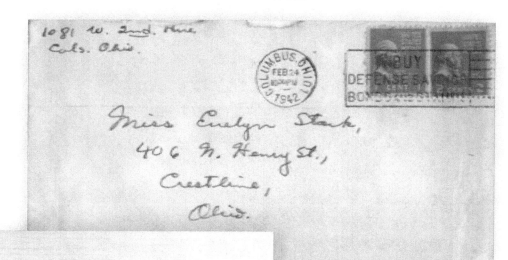

Dearest Evelyn,

Today is a very bad day. All day long I have been grading papers, and getting grades ready for my little dears. Then tonight I came home and figured out my monthly bills. — All I can say is "Boy, my"!

I got home safely Sunday night, and I hope you did too honey. I stopped at Tom's, and he was at Betty's, so I came on home, listened to the radio; and after while Tom came out. We talked awhile, listened to Sherlock Holmes, then he went home and I went to bed. Last night, we fooled around — listened to the president, and talked to a fellow by the name of Jack McGrath. — He's what you could call a "character."

noon, we had a ng, and I got a ked at me, and to head a survey apose means for linary problems, disciplinarian! got a whole up in Monday's in Karl Pauly's editorial page. I'll mail this to bed early for arrow, I'll finish g, and I think we'll play bridge Thursday night is Friday is the boys are engaged in setting up their strategy and it's really something. — They're going to use Groveport's defense against Groveport. Ham's treat for being tricky? I hope it works. Then after Friday comes Saturday again. — The next to the best day in the week. (Sunday of course is my favorite!) Darling, I think George will be home this week end, and if he is I imagine we'll see him too if we play poker Saturday. — I hope we have a Tournament to go to Saturday nite for part of the evening however. But more than anything else, I just want to see my honey. — You still are my honey aren't you sweetness? Darling, I expect if you are to get this letter tomorrow I'd better mail it right away, so be a good girl, and write to me, and honey please love me. I think I love you almost enough for us both, but one sided love

y good thing. So
love me too. – Please?
My Love – Always,
Dick.

e I didn't give
sooner, my phone
University 4901.

Dearest Evelyn,

Today is a very bad day. All day long I have been grading papers and getting grades ready for my little dears. Then tonight I came home and figured out my monthly bills. All I can say is "my, my!"

I got home safely Sunday night, and I hope you did too honey. I stopped at Tom's, and he was at Betty's so I came on home, listened to the radio; and after while Tom came out. We talked awhile, listened to Sherlock Holmes, then he went home and I went to bed. Last night, we fooled around—listened to the president, and talked to a fellow by the name of Jack McGrath. He's what you could call a "character."

Yesterday afternoon, we had a teachers' meeting; and I got a lot of people mad at me, and was appointed to head a survey committee to propose means for handling disciplinary problems. Imagine me a disciplinarian!

Also Toms' dad got a whole column write up in Mondays' Journal. It's in Karl Pauly's column on the editorial page. Tonight I think I'll mail this and then get to bed early for a change. Tomorrow, I'll finish with my grading, and I think tomorrow night we'll play bridge at Andersons. Thursday night is the Operetta, and Friday is the tournament. Pete's boys are engaged in setting up their strategy and it's really something. They're going to use Groveport's defense against Groveport. How's that for being tricky? I hope it works.

Then after Friday comes Saturday again. The next to the best day in the week. (Sunday of course is my favorite!) Darling, I think George will be home this week end, and if he is I imagine we'll see him too if we play poker Saturday. I hope we have a tournament to go to Saturday nite for part of the evening however. But more than anything else, I just want to see my honey. You still are my honey aren't you sweetness? Darling, I expect if you are to get this letter tomorrow I'd better mail it right away, so be a good girl, and write to me, and honey please love me. I think I love you almost enough for us both, but one sided love isn't a very good thing. So darling try and love me too. Please?

All My Love—Always,

Dick

P.S. In case I didn't give it to you sooner, my phone number is University 4901.

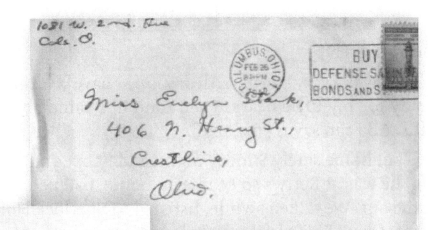

Hi Sweetness,

It's Thursday already! Saturday will be here before we know it. I'm awfully glad you're going to see me Saturday, I don't know what I'd ever do without you on week-ends. — You know honey with all those Japanese attacks on the Pacific Coast, and the possibility of an invasion of the West this summer, I think you had better stay home and take care of me. (Ha!) Yes, I know you said you could just hear me saying that. But Darn it, I'd be like the last sheep without you around, If you want to do something different this summer, why don't you marry me? I'll bet I could be awfully interesting!

—week has been like all —except that there has been —onfusion than there usually —netime. I'm going to grade —pers early and have my —all ready to average when —weeks period ends. Now if —ere around all the time to —e grade them, I'd probably —m done. Plus grading —e've had kids out for —practice, basket ball —, a moving picture, the —a, and gosh only knows —else. Sometimes I don't think I'm very progressive.

Last night Tom and I saw June Swift a minute in Hennick's and found out that George is coming in for sure this week-end. After that, we went up to the Anderson's for a little game of Bridge. Tom & I beat them.

Bob still wants me to buy a Ford, and I might do it if a real bargain comes along and I can get rid of Shasta. Everyone - including me, darling - is glad you're coming down Saturday. Bob said as lucky as you are he didn't think you'd miss a good poker game. I told him that was the only reason you are coming down. Tonight I think I'll stay home and read Random Harvest by James Hilton. It's one of those books I guess I should read but have't done so. Tomorrow night is the Tournament and I guess Tom & Bob are both going. I imagine if we win every body will go up Saturday too.

y morning I think
hunting. I think
to the Appointments
to Dr. La Settels'
to the Columbus Board
ion. Then comes
ternoon which must
getting ready to see
Saturday evening.

Honey, I'll be up about a quarter of six - and I'll really be there then. Whether we go to the tournament or not let's eat out. If you have any other ideas let me know by send, or if you set a different time in your letter we'll go by it. - Last is if I rate another letter - If you're in town Saturday & want me to meet you, call me or write or something. Darling I could write from now on, but I'll save it and talk to man off Sat. - Love me & Take All My Love Dick.

Hi Sweetness,

It's Thursday already! Saturday will be here before we know it. I'm awfully glad you're going to see me Saturday, I don't know what I'd ever do with out you on weekends. You know honey with all those Japanese attacks on the Pacific Coast, and the possibility of an invasion of the West this summer, I think you had better stay home and take care of me. (Ha!) Yes, I know you said you could just hear me saying that. But darn it, I'd be like the lost sheep without you around. If you want to do something different this summer, why don't you marry me? I'll bet I could be awfully interesting!

This week has been like all weeks—except that there has been more confusion than there usually is. Sometime I'm going to grade my papers early and have my grades all ready to average when the six weeks period ends. Now if you were around all the time to help me grade them, I'd probably get them done. Plus grading papers, we've had kids out for operetta practice, basketball practice, a moving picture, the operetta, and gosh only knows what else. Sometimes I don't think I'm very progressive.

Last night Tom and I saw June Swift a minute in Hennicks and found out that George is coming in for sure this weekend. After that, we went up to the Andersons' for a little game of Bridge. Tom & I beat them.

Bob still wants me to buy a Ford, and I might do it if a real bargain comes along and I can get rid of Shasta. Everyone—including me, darling—is glad you're coming down Saturday. Bob said as lucky as you are he didn't think you'd miss a good poker game. I told him that was the only reason you are coming down. Tonight I think I'll stay home and read Random Harvest by James Hilton. It's one of these books I guess I should read but haven't done so. Tomorrow night is the tournament and I guess Tom & Bob are both going. I imagine if we win everybody will go up Saturday too.

Saturday morning I think I'll go job hunting. I think I'll go up to the Appointments office, out to Dr. Lansitels' and down to the Columbus Board of Education. Then comes Saturday afternoon which must be spent getting ready to see my love. Saturday evening, WOW!

Honey, I'll be up about a quarter of six—and I'll really be there then. Whether we go to the tournament or not let's eat out. If you have any other ideas let me know by card, or if you set a different time in your letter we'll go by it. That is if I rate another letter—If you're in town Saturday & want me to meet you, call me or write or something. Darling I could write from now on, but I'll save it and talk an arm off Sat. Love me & take All My Love,

Dick

Dear Evelyn,

Here it is Tuesday, and I have completed two days of another week, while you, you lucky stiff have but lazied away through one. Darling, I don't mind the teaching, but I surely would have liked at least another day with you. Time flies, life is never dull when we're together. What did you do yesterday, honey. Did you wash your car? Did you get to your aunt's? Did you finish your book review? I thought about you all during that perfect spring day; and wished we were together no matter what we were doing. We still haven't had that ice cream cone yet, and we'll have to do that.

Nothing has happened since I saw you. I didn't even miss the little bit of last sleep, and went to school fresh as a daisy. All the teachers wondered whether I played golf - They all went fishing. Last night after school was teacher's meeting - which was like all teacher's meetings. Sometimes I think teachers are a little on the dull side. (Girls physical ed. teachers excepted). I worked on that test all last evening and finally got it completed. The girls ran it off on the mimeograph today. Bob called and wanted me to play cards, but I had too much work to do. He said he didn't have you a convertible yet, but he's working on it. - I still think you ought to save your money for furniture, but maybe you don't like that idea. Today was just another day. I put grades on the grade sheets, and played softball with one of Pete's gym classes. I'm sure not in very good shape. Running around those bases got me. The Shasta had a flat tire, which I "let" a couple of my boys fix for me. I don't know what

right for the rest of the week. Probably work on the article Delno and I are writing. I'll go job hunting as you have requested, I ought to, sweetheart. All the time, though, I'll sure I'll be missing you. Truly, that is what I'll do this week without you. I've told you lots of times that I love you, and it's true, but there are so many different ways. You're not only my sweetheart, but - You're my best friend. I love you - and I want you, because - oh darn it just because, and I've always felt that we belong to one another, something pretty solid behind us, we're just in love.

I don't know that I can tell you why I want you to wear my fraternity pin. Perhaps it's because I'm proud enough to want the world to know that you're mine, maybe it's what the psychologists call "possessiveness." Probably though darling it's because I want to tie some strings to you. I guess I want to be surer of you. - I want to make us last. I honestly believe you know you've got me. You know I love you, but you've never directly said those same words to me. I want you to love me. If you love me I want to know it and I guess I want everyone to know it too. The way things are now I'm pretty sure of you, but I'm not sure you won't suddenly decide to just throw me overboard altogether. If you love me I'd think you'd want me to give you my pin, or a ring, or something. It's really a small thing to ask after all - if you love me. If you don't, then I imagine it's time I found it out. Also, if you don't love me by this time I'm pretty sure you never will, and I might as well start preparing myself for an old age - alone.

I know this is a peculiar letter, but it's an honest one, and I think it's pretty vital that we take inventory of our feelings.

Dick.

Dear Evelyn,

Here it is Tuesday, and I have completed two days of another week, while you, you lucky stiff have but lazed away through one. Darling, I don't mind the teaching, but I surely would have liked at least another day with you. Time flies, life is never dull when we're together. What did you do yesterday, honey? Did you wash your car? Did you get to your Aunts'? Did you finish your book review? I thought about you all during that perfect spring day; and wished we were together no matter what we were doing. We still haven't had that ice cream cone yet, and we'll have to do that.

Nothing has happened since I saw you. I didn't even miss the little bit of last sleep, and went to school fresh as a daisy. All the teachers wondered whether I played golf. They all went fishing. Last night after school was teachers' meeting—which was like all teachers' meetings. Sometimes I think teachers are a little on the dull side. (Girls physical ed. teachers excepted.) I worked on that test all last evening and finally got it completed. The girls ran it off on the mimeograph today. Bob called and wanted me to play cards, but I had too much work to do. He said he didn't have you a convertible yet, but he's working on it. I still think you ought to save your money for furniture, but maybe you don't like that idea. Today was just another day: I put grades on the grade sheets, and played softball with one of Pete's gym classes. I'm sure not in very good shape. Running around those bases got me. Also Shasta had a flat tire, which I "let" a couple of my boys fix for me. I don't know what I'll do tonight or the rest of the week. Probably read and work on the article Delno and I are writing. Saturday I'll go job hunting as you have requested. I know I ought to sweetheart. All the time, though, you can be darned sure I'll be missing you. Truly, I don't know what I'll do this week end without you. I tell you lots of times that I love you, and it's always been true, but there are so many different ways I love you. You're not only my sweetheart, but—even deglamorized—you're my best friend. I love you because I know you, because—oh darn it just because I feel, as I've always felt, that we belong to one another. We've got something pretty solid behind us, we're just Evelyn and Dick.

I don't know that I can tell you why I want you to take my fraternity pin. Perhaps it's because I'm still childlike enough to want the world to know that you're my girl. Maybe it's what the psychologists call "masculine possessiveness." Probably though darling it's just that I want to tie some strings to you. I guess I want to feel surer of you. I want to make us last. After all dearest, you know you've got me. You know that I love you, but you've never directly said those three little words to me. I want you to love me. If you do love me I want to know it, and I guess I want the world to know it too. The way things are now I'm not only not sure of you, but I'm not sure you won't suddenly decide to just throw me overboard altogether. If you do love me I'd think you'd want me to give you my pin, or a ring, or something. It's really a small thing to ask after all—if you love me. If you don't then I imagine it's time I found it out. Also, if you don't love me by this time I'm pretty sure you never will, and I might as well start preparing myself for an old age—alone.

I know this is a peculiar letter, but it's an honest one, and I think it's pretty vital that we take inventory of our feelings.

Dick

Dear Evelyn,

It's Thursday already. Ordinarily I would greet those words with shouts of great joy, but since you're not coming down, it might just as well be Monday again. I don't know what it is, perhaps it's the lousy weather, but I've been awfully gloomy all week. I wish you were around to cheer me up! I haven't done anything worth even talking about. Tuesday night I stayed home and slept, read, and listened to the radio intermittently. Last night I went up to the Anderson's and won a Gin Rummie game. June baked us some Toll house cookies. They were wonderful. If you don't already have a recipe for them you'll have to get one someplace. I told June to give you hers. I got a letter from Tom today, and he tells me that he hasn't liked it, that he has already lost eight pounds, and that he cares a lot more for Betty than he thought he did when he left. Imagine how I'd feel being that far away from you. I'm sure glad I didn't get that job out there. Tonight I'm going to read, tomorrow night I think I'll go to that —— dance out at school, Saturday morning I am going job hunting, and heaven only knows what I'll do after that. One thing I'm sure of is that I'll be wishing you were along with me, and I will miss you - plenty.

School has been about as always. The grades came out yesterday, and I didn't have as

———— ts as I expected, although I —— can't call just as I was starting —— letter last evening. I gave my —— t and picked my team. We had —— ey this afternoon that was pretty —— is in the state contest.

—— after school, Pete & I went over —— some of the horses. Harry Wiener, —— telling you about, has a two year —— full sister to Discovery - one of —— of all time.

—— ng, I expect I'd better close for —— good time in Cleveland (you'd better —— me). Don't do very much "experiment- —— fellows this week-end. Personally —— menting - almost. Write to me real —— etness, please decide in favor of —— next week end. I want you to —— if you don't by this time - I —— out, a nice bridge someplace —— because I don't suppose you ever —— if you don't already.

All my Love - Always,

Dick.

Dear Evelyn,

It's Thursday already. Ordinarily I would greet those words with shouts of great joy, but since you're not coming down, it might just as well be Monday again. I don't know what it is, perhaps it's the lousy weather, but I've been awfully gloomy all week I wish you were around to cheer me up. I haven't done anything worth even talking about: Tuesday night I stayed home and slept, read, and listened to the radio intermittently. Last night I went up to the Anderson's and won a Gin Rummie game. June baked us some Toule house cookies. They were wonderful. If you don't already have a recipe for them you'll have to get one someplace. I told June to give you hers. I got a letter from Tom today, and he tells me that he doesn't like it, that he has already lost eight pounds, and that he cares a lot more for Betty than he thought he did when he left. Imagine how I'd feel being that far away from you. I'm sure glad I didn't get that job out there. Tonight I'm going to read, tomorrow night I think I'll go to that dance out at school, Saturday morning I am going job hunting, and heaven only knows what I'll do after that. One thing I'm sure of is that I'll be wishing you were along with me, and I will miss you—plenty.

School has been about as always. The grades came out yesterday, and I didn't have as many complaints as I expected, although I did have one parent call just as I was starting to read your letter last evening. I gave my scholarship test and picked my team. We had a music assembly this afternoon that was pretty good, our band is in the state contest.

Last night after school, Pete and I went over and looked at some of the horses. Harry Wiener, the Jew I was telling you about, had a two year old that is full sister to Discovery—one of the best horses of all time.

Well darling, I expect I'd better close for now. Have a good time in Cleveland (you'd better after deserting me.) Don't do very much "experimenting" with other fellows this week-end. Personally I've quit experimenting—almost. Write to me real soon, and sweetness please decide in favor of taking my pin next week end. I want you to want me, and if you don't by this time—I might as well go find a nice bridge someplace and jump off, because I don't suppose you ever will love me if you don't already.

All My Love—Always,

Dick

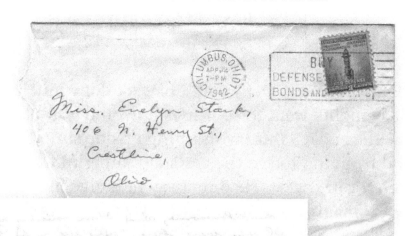

Dear Evelyn,

Today is Sunday, and since I last wrote I haven't done much of anything except read and loaf. Friday night I went to see *Kings Row*, and I was a little disappointed. It was not as good as the book. Saturday morning I made sure that I'd get a date with you next week end by going to see the assistant superintendant of the Columbus schools about a job for next year. He didn't say he'd give me one, but he didn't say he wouldn't either. I imagine that if there are any vacancies I'll get a crack at one. I then went up and saw Dr. Landsittel, and he told me he would help me get in the Columbus system if I wanted in, and hinted that I might possibly get in State as an instructor. — That isn't bad, and we could live on that salary, and have a pretty secure future. The rest of the day I read and worked on the article Delmo and I are writing. Last night I also stayed home — Saturday night I'll have you know, — and wrote Tom a letter. Today so far I've done nothing, and tonight I guess I'll eat dinner with mom and Bill, and listen to the radio. I don't have anything in particular planned for this week except that I'll be looking forward to seeing you. Why can't we have a date this Friday long? — Darn it I really

missing you an awful lot. we could go for a walk, but the old song "It's a is really quite apropos.

is concerned, there isn't much are going to have a baby wish me to something t too. I still think that if you and I ought to get and darling please want to! soon the army would get me. castle in the air I'm building far for what little bit doing. I know I've been over and you've heard everything got a singularly one track ned, and I want you to want you. So darling I'll be week end to take my pin, until I can get you a ring, as is humanly possible. t that just to be talking, I reasonably good position to get I know we will be a year take this pretty seriously, want me the way I

Love — Always,

Dick

POSTMARKED COLUMBUS, OHIO—APRIL, 12, 1942

Dear Evelyn,

Today is Sunday, and since I last wrote I haven't done much of anything except read and loaf. Friday night I went to see <u>Kings Row</u>, and was a little disappointed. It was not as good as the book. Saturday morning I made sure that I'd get a date with you next week end by going to see the assistant superintendent of the Columbus schools about a job for next year. He didn't say he'd give me one, but he didn't say he wouldn't either. I imagine that if there are any vacancies I'll get a crack at one. I then went up and saw Dr. Lansitel, and he told me he would help me get in the Columbus system if I wanted in, and hinted that I might possibly get in State as an instructor. That isn't bad, and we could live on that salary, and have a pretty secure future. The rest of the day I read and worked on the article Delno and I are writing. Last night I also stayed home—<u>Saturday night</u> I'll have you know—and wrote Tom a letter. Today so far I've done nothing, and tonight I guess I'll eat dinner with mom and Bill, and listen to the radio. I don't have anything in particular planned for this week except that I'll be looking forward to seeing you. Why can't we have a date this Friday honey? Darn it I really am lonesome, and I'm missing you an awful lot. If you were here today we could go for a walk, it's a pretty nice day, but the old song "It's a Blue World Without You" is really quite apropos.

As far as other news is concerned, there isn't much except that Murray and Essie are going to have a baby next November. Honey, I wish we'd do something real constructive like that too. I still think that if everything works out all right you and I ought to get married this coming winter, and darling please want to! If I'd lose you, I'd just as soon the army would get me. You're the center of every castle in the air I'm building, and you're the motivating force for what little bit of constructive work I'm doing. I know I've been over everything about us before, and you've heard everything I've got to say, but I've got a singularly one track mind where you're concerned, and I want you to want me as much as I want you. So darling, I'll be asking you again this coming week end to take my pin, to have it mean everything until I can get you a ring, and to get that ring as soon as is humanly possible. I'm not talking any more about that just to be talking, I think that we'll be in a reasonably good position to get married next winter, and I know we will be a year from now; so please dearest, take this pretty seriously, and oh darling love me and want me the way I want you.

All My Love—Always,

Dick

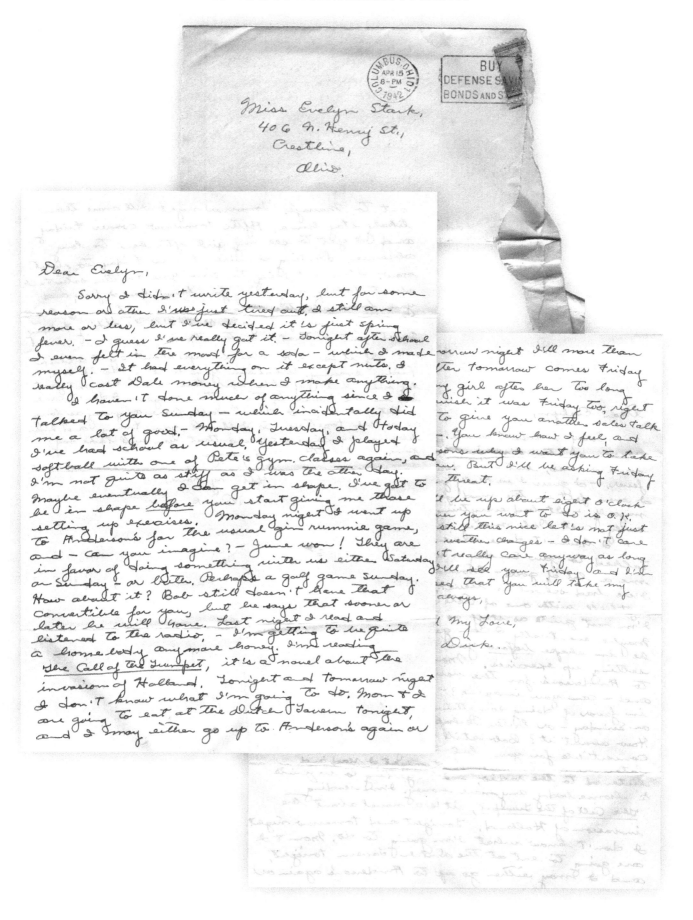

Miss Evelyn Stark,
406 N. Henry St.,
Crestline,
Ohio.

Dear Evelyn,

Sorry I didn't write yesterday, but for some reason or other I was just tired out, I still am more or less, but I've decided it's just spring fever. — I guess I've really got it. — Tonight after school I even felt in the mood for a soda — which I made myself. — It had everything on it except nuts. I really cost Dale money when I make anything.

I haven't done much of anything since I talked to you Sunday — which incidentally did me a lot of good. — Monday, Tuesday, and today I've had school as usual, Yesterday I played softball with one of Pete's gym. classes again, and I'm not quite as stiff as I was the other day. Maybe eventually I can get in shape. I've got to be in shape before you start giving me those setting up exercises. Monday night I went up to Anderson's for the usual gin rummie game, and — can you imagine? — June won! They are in favor of doing something with us either Saturday or Sunday — or both. Perhaps a golf game Sunday. How about it? Bob still doesn't have that convertible for you, but he says that sooner or later he will have. Last night I read and listened to the radio, — I'm getting to be quite a home body any more honey. I'm reading The Call of the Trumpet, it's a novel about the invasion of Holland. Tonight and tomorrow night I don't know what I'm going to do. Mom & I are going to eat at the Dutch Tavern tonight, and I may either go up to Anderson's again or

...tomorrow night I'll more than ...ter tomorrow comes Friday ...y girl after her too long ...wish it was Friday too, right ...to give you another sales talk ...You know how I feel, and ...sons why I want you to take ...w. But I'll be asking Friday ...threat.

...'ll be up about eight o'clock ...en you want to do is O.K. ...still this nice let's not just ...weather changes — I don't care ...t really care anyway as long ...'ll see you Friday and did ...ed that you will take my ...always,

...l My Love,
Dirk.

POSTMARKED COLUMBUS, OHIO—APRIL 15, 1942

Dear Evelyn,

Sorry I didn't write yesterday, but for some reason or other, I was just tired out. I still am more or less, but I've decided it's just spring fever. I guess I've really got it. Tonight after school I even felt in the mood for a soda—which I made myself. It had everything on it except nuts. I really cost Dale money when I make anything.

I haven't done much of anything since I talked to you Sunday—which incidentally did me a lot of good. Monday, Tuesday, and today I've had school as usual. Yesterday I played softball with one of Pete's gym classes again, and I'm not quite as stiff as I was the other day. Maybe eventually I can get in shape. I've got to be in shape before you start giving me those setting up exercises. Monday night I went up to Anderson's for the usual gin rummie game, and—can you imagine? June won! They are in favor of doing something with us either Saturday or Sunday—or both. Perhaps a golf game Sunday. How about it? Bob still doesn't have that convertible for you, but he says that sooner or later he will. Last night I read and listened to the radio. I'm getting to be quite a homebody anymore honey. I'm reading The Call of the Trumpet, it's a novel about the invasion of Holland. Tonight and tomorrow night I don't know what I'm going to do. Mom & I are going to eat at the Dutch Tavern tonight, and I may either go up to Anderson's again or out to Murray's. Tomorrow night I'll more than likely stay home. After tomorrow comes Friday and I get to see my girl after her too long absence. Darling I wish it was Friday too, right now. I'm not going to give you another sales talk about taking my pin. You know how I feel, and you know all the reasons why I want you to take it—So it's up to you. But I'll be asking Friday sweetheart—that's a threat.

If it's O.K. I'll be up about eight o'clock Friday evening. Whatever you want to do is O.K. by me, but if it's still this nice let's not just sit in the house. If the weather changes—I don't care what we do. I don't really care anyway as long as we're together. So I'll see you Friday and I'm keeping my fingers crossed that you will take my pin. Until then and always,

All My Love,

Dick

Miss. Evelyn Stark,
406 N. Henry St.,
Crestline,
Ohio.

Dearest Evelyn,

It's Tuesday already, and soon another week end will be coming around. How I wish it was here! I haven't really done anything so far this week: Sunday night I drove home in a kind of happy daze. I couldn't think of anything except what a wonderful time we'd had all week end. Monday morning was school again, and I was very absent minded; I didn't even remember what I had assigned a couple of my classes. After school we had a teacher's meeting and found out that we're going to have more school than we thought we'd have. — That Griffith is crazier than a bed-bug. I guess we won't finally finish until about the 22 of May; although we won't have classes all of that time. Last night I ~~went~~ went over to the Montgomery's for a while. Essie is feeling better and says that she wants to have us over for dinner as soon as possible. Also, I saw those pictures in Life of the Tulsa schools. They must really be O.K. However, I'm glad I'm here. I don't know how I would have gotten along without you all that time. I haven't done anything today that is even worthy of comment. Tonight I may go up to the Anderson's, but I'm not sure. — It's a good night for the Radio — Fibber McGee, Bob Hope, and Red Skelton are all on. I don't have any plans for the rest of the week either, but I'm hoping to hear that I have dates with my girl Friday, Saturday, and Sunday. Do you think it can be arranged? Honest honey I'll go home

you want me to. As to what week end — that ought to be up to you, decide and let me ... to be doing. As long as ... all that matters to me. ... don't understand what you ... that we're far apart in our ... dislikes. Personally, I think ... If you think I want a ... with social activities you're ... friends. I want us to go ... you to be happy and to go ... you want, because I don't ... with me. But I also ... just you and I and maybe ... us to be able to close our ... tell the rest of the world to go ... darling I just want us to ... as happy together as we have ...

My Love — Always,

Dick,

Dearest Evelyn,

It's Tuesday already, and soon another week end will be coming around. How I wish it was here! I haven't really done anything so far this week: Sunday night I drove home in a kind of happy daze. I couldn't think of anything except what a wonderful time we'd had all week end. Monday morning was school again, and I was very absent minded; I didn't even remember what I had assigned a couple of my classes. After school we had a teacher's meeting and found out that we're going to have more school than we thought we'd have. That Griffith is crazier than a bed-bug. I guess we won't finally finish until about the 22 of May; although we won't have classes all of that time. Last night I went over to the Montgomery's for a while. Essie is feeling better and says that she wants to have us over for dinner as soon as possible. Also, I saw those pictures in Life of the Tulsa schools. They must really be O.K. However, I'm glad I'm here. I don't know how I would have gotten along with out you all that time. I haven't done anything today that is even worthy of comment. Tonight I may go up to the Anderson's, but I'm not sure. It's a good night for the radio—Fibber McGee, Bob Hope, and Red Skelton are all on. I don't have any plans for the rest of the week either, but I'm hoping to hear that I have dates with my girl Friday, Saturday, and Sunday. Do you think it can be arranged? Honest honey I'll go home early Friday if you want me to. As to what we'll do over the weekend—that ought to be up to you darlingest. So you decide and let me know what we're going to be doing. As long as we're together—that's all that matters to me.

Sweetness, I still don't understand what you mean when you say that we're far apart in our wants and our likes and dislikes. Personally, I think we're very close together. If you think I want a life filled to overflowing with social activities you're "off the beam." I want some friends. I want us to go out occasionally. I want you to be happy and to go whenever and wherever you want, because I don't want you to ever get bored with me. But I also want a life filled with just you and I, and maybe a couple of kids. I want us to be able to close our door occasionally and tell the rest of the world to go to hell. But chiefly darling, I just want us to love each other and be as happy together as we have been. How about you?

All My Love—Always,

Dick

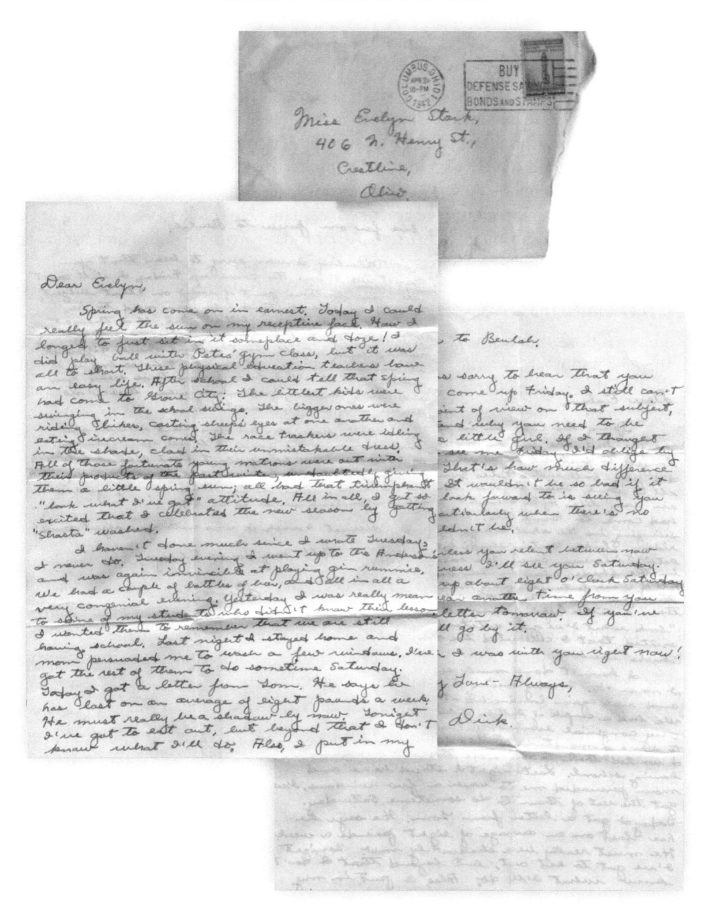

Miss Evelyn Stark,
406 N. Henry St.,
Crestline,
Ohio.

Dear Evelyn,

Spring has come on in earnest. Today I could really feel the sun on my receptive face. How I longed to just sit in it someplace and doze! I did play ball with Pete's gym class, but it was all to short. These physical education teachers have an easy life. After school I could tell that spring had come to Grove City. The littlest kids were swinging in the school swings. The bigger ones were riding bikes, casting sheep's eyes at one another and eating icecream cones. The race trackers were idling in the shade, clad in their unmistakable dress. All of those fortunate young matrons were out with their prospects of the past winter, undoubtedly giving them a little spring sun; all had that triumphant "look what I've got" attitude. All in all, I got so excited that I celebrated the new season by getting "Shasta" washed.

I haven't done much since I wrote Tuesday, I never do. Tuesday evening I went up to the Anderson's and was again invincible at playing gin rummie. We had a couple of bottles of beer, and all in all a very congenial evening. Yesterday I was really mean to some of my students who didn't know their lesson. I wanted them to remember that we are still having school. Last night I stayed home and mom persuaded me to wash a few windows. I've got the rest of them to do sometime Saturday. Today I got a letter from Tom. He says he has lost on an average of eight pounds a week. He must really be a shadow by now. Tonight I've got to eat out, but beyond that I don't know what I'll do. Also, I put in my

...to Beulah.

...was sorry to hear that you ...come up Friday. I still can't ...int of view on that subject, ...and why you need to be ...a little girl. If I thought ...see me Friday I'd delige by ...That's how much difference ...It wouldn't be so bad if it ...look forward to is seeing you ...particularly when there's no ...uldn't be.

...less you relent between now ...uess I'll see you Saturday. ...ep about eight o'clock Saturday ...ear another time from you ...letter tomorrow. If you're ...ll go by it.

...I was with you right now!

Of Love - Always,

Dirk.

POSTMARKED COLUMBUS, OHIO—APRIL 23, 1942

Dear Evelyn,

Spring has come on in earnest. Today I could really feel the sun on my receptive face. How I longed to just sit in it someplace and doze! I did play ball with Petes' gym class, but it was all to short. These physical education teachers have an easy life. After school I could tell that spring had come to Grove City. The littlest kids were swinging in the school swings. The bigger ones were riding bikes, casting sheeps' eyes at one another and eating ice cream cones. The race trackers were idling in the shade, clad in their unmistakable dress. All of those fortunate young matrons were out with their products of the past winter, undoubtedly giving them a little spring sun; all had that triumphant "look what I've got" attitude. All in all, I got so excited that I celebrated the new season by getting "Shasta" washed.

I haven't done much since I wrote Tuesday. I never do. Tuesday evening I went up to the Andersons' and was again invincible at playing gin rummie. We had a couple of bottles of beer, and all in all a very congenial evening. Yesterday I was really mean to some of my students who didn't know their lesson. I wanted them to remember that we are still having school. Last night I stayed home and mom persuaded me to wash a few windows. I've got the rest of them to do sometime Saturday. Today I got a letter from Tom. He says he has lost on an average of eight pounds a week. He must really be a shadow by now. Tonight I've got to eat out, but beyond that I don't know what I'll do. Also, I put in my bid for our passes to Beulah.

Darling I was sorry to hear that you don't want me to come up Friday. I still can't see your mothers' point of view on that subject, and I can't understand why you need to be kept at home like a little girl. If I thought you didn't want to see me Friday I'd oblige by not appearing at all. That's how much difference it makes to me. It wouldn't be so bad if it weren't that all I look forward to is seeing you and being together, particularly when there's no reason why we shouldn't be.

Well honey, unless you relent between now and tomorrow, I guess I'll see you Saturday. If it's O.K. I'll be up about eight o'clock Saturday evening, unless I hear another time from you in (I hope) your letter tomorrow. If you've set another time we'll go by it.

Dearest I wish I was with you right now!

All My Love—Always,

Dick

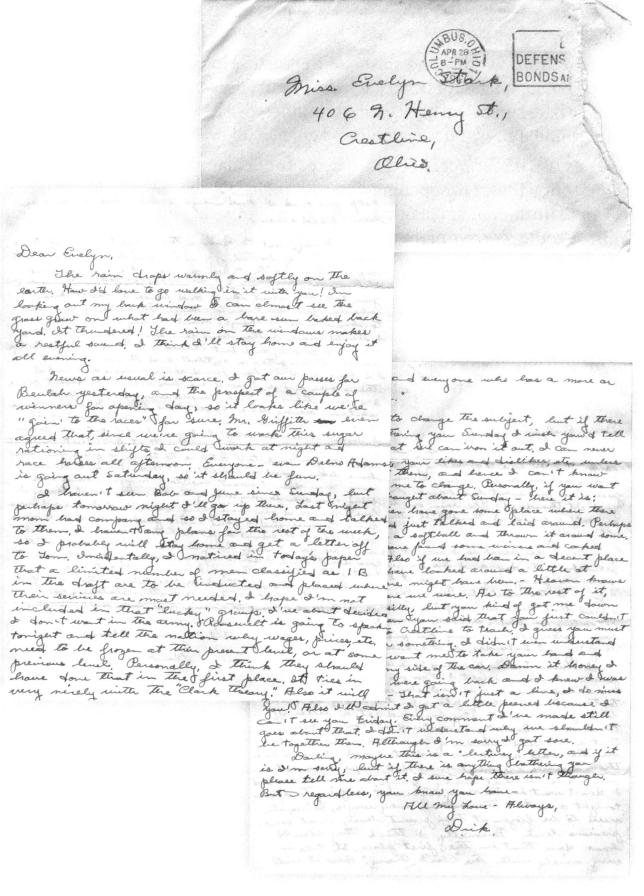

Dear Evelyn,

The rain drops warmly and softly on the earth. How I'd love to go walking in it with you! I'm looking out my back window I can almost see the grass grow on what had been a bare brown baked back yard. It thundered! The rain on the windows makes a restful sound. I think I'll stay home and enjoy it all evening.

News as usual is scarce. I got our passes for Beulah yesterday, and the prospect of a couple of winners for opening day, so it looks like we're "goin' to the races" for sure. Mr. Griffith even agreed that, since we're going to work this sugar rationing in shifts, I could work at night and race horses all afternoon. Everyone — even Delno Adams is going out Saturday, so it should be fun.

I haven't seen Bob and June since Sunday, but perhaps tomorrow night I'll go up there. Last night mom had company and so I stayed home and talked to them. I haven't any plans for the rest of the week, so I probably will stay home and get a letter off to Tom. Incidentally, I noticed in today's paper that a limited number of men classified as 1 B in the draft are to be inducted and placed where their services are most needed. I hope I'm not included in that "lucky" group. I've about decided I don't want in the army. Roosevelt is going to speak tonight and tell the nation why wages, prices, etc. need to be frozen at their present level, or at some previous level. Personally, I think they should have done that in the first place. It ties in very nicely with the "Clark theory." Also it will

and everyone who has a more or ...

to change the subject, but if there ... thering you Sunday I wish you'd tell ... at so I can iron it out. I can never ... your likes and dislikes, etc, unless ... them, and hence I can't know ... me to change. Personally, if you want ... ...ought about Sunday — here it is: ... have gone some place where there ... just talked and laid around. Perhaps ... a softball and thrown it around some, ...me found some wieners and cooked ... Also if we had been in a decent place ... have looked around a little at ... might have been. — Heaven knows ... we were. As to the rest of it, ... silly, but you kind of got me down ... ...en you said that you just couldn't ... Crestline to reach. I guess you must ... ...something. I didn't even understand ... want me to take your hand and ... ...my side of the car, damn it honey I ... were going back and I knew I was ... — That isn't just a line, I do miss ... you. Also I'll admit I got a little peeved because I can't see you Friday. Every comment I've made still goes about that. I don't understand why we shouldn't be together then. Although I'm sorry I got sore.

Darling, maybe this is a "lecture" letter, and if it is I'm sorry, but if there is anything bothering you please tell me about it. I sure hope there isn't though. But regardless, you know you have —

All my Love - Always,

Dick

Dear Evelyn,

The rain drops warmly and softly on the earth. How I'd love to go walking in it with you! I'm looking out my back window I can almost see the grass grow on what had been a bare sun baked back yard. It thundered! The rain on the windows makes a restful sound. I think I'll stay home and enjoy it all evening.

News as usual is scarce. I got our passes for Beulah yesterday, and the prospect of a couple of winners for opening day, so it looks like we're "goin' to the races" for sure. Mr. Griffith even agreed that, since we're going to work this sugar rationing in shifts, I could work at night and race horses all afternoon. Everyone even Delno Adams is going out Saturday, so it should be fun.

I haven't seen Bob and June since Sunday, but perhaps tomorrow night I'll go up there. Last night mom had company and so I stayed home and talked to them. I haven't any plans for the rest of the week, so I probably will stay home and get a letter off to Tom. Incidentally, I noticed in today's paper that a limited number of men classified as 1 B in the draft are to be inducted and placed where their services are most needed. I hope I'm not included in that "lucky" group. I've about decided I don't want in the army. Roosevelt is going to speak tonight and tell the nation why wages, prices, etc. need to be frozen at their present level, or at some previous level. Personally, I think they should have done that in the first place. It ties in very nicely with the "Clark Theory." Also it will help you and I, and everyone who has a more or less "fixed income."

Honey, not to change the subject, but if there was anything bothering you Sunday I wish you'd tell me about it so that we can iron it out. I can never discover your moods, your likes and dislikes, etc. unless you tell me about them, and hence I can't know wherein you want me to change. Personally, if you want to know what I thought about Sunday—here it is: I would much rather have gone some place where there were no people, and just talked and laid around. Perhaps we might have gotten a softball and thrown it around some. I'd have liked to have found some weiners and cooked them over a fire. Also if we had been in a decent place I'd have liked to have looked around a little at whatever scenery there might have been. Heaven knows there was none where we were. As to the rest of it, I know it sounds silly, but you kind of got me down in the dumps when you said that you just couldn't wait to get back to Crestline to teach. I guess you must have been bored or something. I didn't even understand why you didn't want me to take your hand and bring you over to my side of the car. Damn it honey I love you, and you were going back and I knew I was going to miss you! That isn't just a line, I do miss you! Also I'll admit I got a little peeved because I can't see you Friday. Every comment I've made still goes about that. I don't understand why we shouldn't be together then. Although I'm sorry I got sore.

Darling, maybe this is a "lecturey" letter, and if it is I'm sorry, but if there is anything bothering you please tell me about it. I sure hope there isn't though. But regardless, you know you have—

All My Love—Always,

Dick

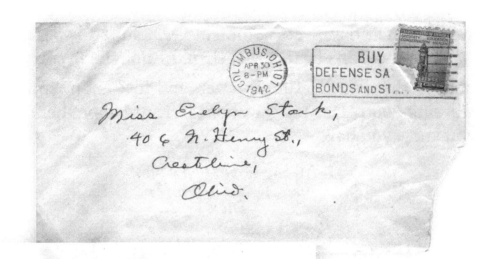

Dearest Evelyn,

As usual – though I admit it this time – I haven't a thought in my head. I'm almost happy, and I'd be completely happy if only you were with me. I'm hot – perhaps I mean warm – but anyway I'm sweating, and I'm writing this preliminary to taking a shower. I taught school this afternoon in my shirt sleeves, and was still uncomfortable. – But I love it. – The heat I mean.

I have been doing about as always: Last night I mowed and raked the yard, and then went over to the Montgomery's for a while. They're going to Beulah Saturday too, and if we picnic Sunday they want to go along unless Essie isn't feeling well. – They must be more to having a baby than I thought. Maybe we ought to only have five. But if you want six I think I can arrange it.

I haven't seen the Anderson's all week. Bob was out of town until yesterday, but I'm going up this evening for a little while. However, I don't think I want to play gin rummie, I got tired of that game. By the way, I noticed they were talking in Johnny Jones' column about those two lonely girls, and Jones was right for once – at least in the case of your failing

...ishing Saturday was here. I'm
...me winners, and maybe
...along that line. At any rate
...out in Grove City tomorrow
...t information I can get, –
...hear that you've changed
...ill let me come up tomorrow

...really a lovely moon this
...hope it's that way Saturday,
...the same way about moons
...ts, and trees and bushes beginning
...o I do. By the way – of course I
...but have soon to me fix
?
...I'll be up Saturday between
...fifteen, and I'll try not to
...hear otherwise from you

my love – Always,

Dick,

POSTMARKED COLUMBUS, OHIO—APRIL 30, 1942

Dearest Evelyn,

As usual—though I admit it this time—I haven't a thought in my head. I'm almost happy, and I'd be completely happy if only you were with me. I'm hot—perhaps I mean warm—but anyway I'm sweating, and I'm writing this preliminary to taking a shower. I taught school this afternoon in my shirt sleeves, and was still uncomfortable. But I love it. The heat I mean.

I have been doing about as always: Last night I mowed and raked the yard, and then went over to the Montgomery's for a while. They're going to Beulah Saturday too; and if we picnic Sunday they want to go along unless Essie isn't feeling well. They're must be more to having a baby than I thought. Maybe we ought to only have five. But if you want six I think I can arrange it.

I haven't seen the Anderson's all week. Bob was out of town until yesterday, but I'm going up this evening for a little while. However, I don't think I want to play gin rummie. I got tired of that game. By the way, I noticed they were talking in Johny Jones' column about those two lovely girls, and Jones was right for once—at least in the case of you darling.

I'm really wishing Saturday was here. I'm trying to get us some winners, and maybe we'll be all set along that line. At any rate I think I'll stay out in Grove City tomorrow night and see what information I can get. That is unless I hear that you've changed your mind and will let me come up tomorrow night.

Honey there is really a lovely moon this week, and I really hope it's that way Saturday, and that you feel the same way about moons and soft spring nights, and trees and bushes beginning to bud and bloom as I do. By the way—of course I'm not hinting—but how soon do we fix up the porch swing?

Well darlingest I'll be up Saturday between twelve and twelve fifteen, and I'll try not to be late, so unless I hear otherwise from you I'll see you then.

All My Love—Always,

Dick

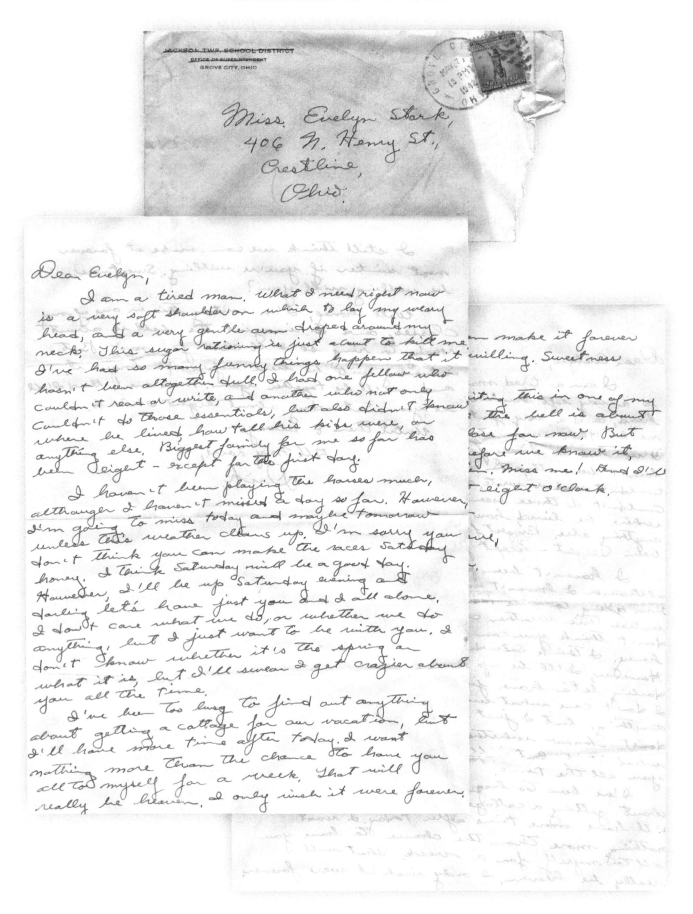

JACKSON TWP. SCHOOL DISTRICT
OFFICE OF SUPERINTENDENT
GROVE CITY, OHIO

Miss. Evelyn Stark,
406 N. Henry St.,
Crestline,
Ohio.

Dear Evelyn,

I am a tired man. What I need right now is a very soft shoulder on which to lay my weary head, and a very gentle arm draped around my neck. This sugar rationing is just about to kill me. I've had so many funny things happen that it hasn't been altogether dull. I had one fellow who couldn't read or write, and another who not only couldn't do those essentials, but also didn't know where he lived, how tall his kids were, or anything else. Biggest family for me so far has been Feigert - except for the first day.

I haven't been playing the horses much, although I haven't missed a day so far. However, I'm going to miss today and maybe tomorrow unless this weather clears up. I'm sorry you don't think you can make the races Saturday honey. I think Saturday will be a good day. However, I'll be up Saturday evening and darling let's have just you and I all alone. I don't care what we do, or whether we do anything, but I just want to be with you. I don't know whether it is the spring or what it is, but I'll swear I get crazier about you all the time.

I've been too busy to find out anything about getting a cottage for our vacation, but I'll have more time after today. I want nothing more than the chance to have you all to myself for a week. That will really be heaven. I only wish it were forever.

POSTMARKED GROVE CITY, OHIO—MAY 7, 1942

Dear Evelyn,

I am a tired man. What I need right now is a very soft shoulder on which to lay my weary head, and a very gentle arm draped around my neck. This sugar rationing is just about to kill me. I've had so many funny things happen that it hasn't been altogether dull. I had one fellow who couldn't read or write, and another who not only couldn't do those essentials, but also didn't know where he lived, how tall his kids were, or anything else. Biggest family for me so far has been eight—except for the first day.

I haven't been playing the horses much, although I haven't missed a day so far. However, I'm going to miss today and maybe tomorrow unless this weather clears up. I'm sorry you don't think you can make the races Saturday honey. I think Saturday will be a good day. However, I'll be up Saturday evening and darling let's have just you and I all alone. I don't care what we do, or whether we do anything, but I just want to be with you. I don't know whether it's the spring or what it is, but I'll swear I get crazier about you all the time.

I've been too busy to find out anything about getting a cottage for our vacation, but I'll have more time after today. I want nothing more than the chance to have you all to myself for a week. That will really be heaven. I only wish it were forever.

I still think we can make it forever next winter if you're willing. Sweetness be willing, will you?

Well honey, I'm writing this in one of my classes, and I imagine the bell is about ready to ring so I'll close for now. But Saturday will be here before we know it, and we'll be together again. Miss me! And I'll see you Saturday about eight o'clock.

Until then & always—

All My Love,

Dick

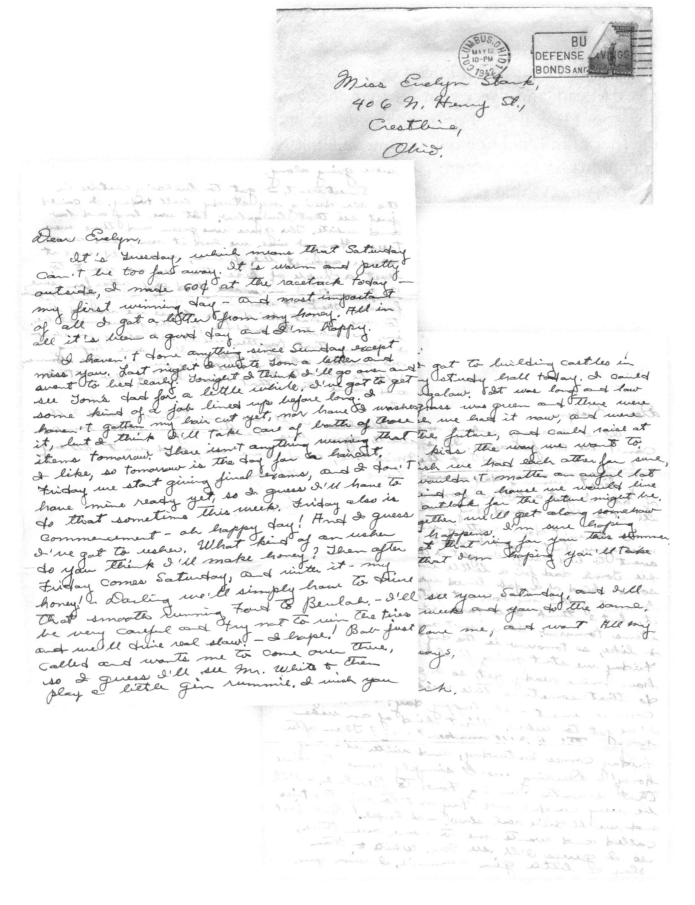

Dear Evelyn,

It's Tuesday, which means that Saturday can't be too far away. It's warm and pretty outside, I made 60¢ at the racetrack today—my first winning day—and most important of all I got a letter from my honey. All in all it's been a good day and I'm happy.

I haven't done anything since Sunday except miss you. Last night I wrote Tom a letter and went to bed early. Tonight I think I'll go over and see Tom's dad for a little while. I've got to get some kind of a job lined up before long. I haven't gotten my hair cut yet, nor have I washed it, but I think I'll take care of both of those items tomorrow. There isn't anything running that I like, so tomorrow is the day for a haircut. Friday we start giving final exams, and I don't have mine ready yet, so I guess I'll have to do that sometime this week. Friday also is commencement—oh happy day! And I guess I've got to usher. What kind of an usher do you think I'll make honey? Then after Friday comes Saturday, and with it—my honey! Darling we'll simply have to drive that smooth running Ford to Beulah. I'll be very careful and try not to ruin the tires and we'll drive real slow. I hope! Bob just called and wants me to come over there, so I guess I'll see Mr. White & then play a little gin rummie. I wish you were going along.

Sweetheart, I got to building castles in the air during my study hall today. I could just see that bungalow. It was long and low and white. The grass was green and there were trees. Honey I wish we had it now, and were secure against the future, and could raise at least a couple of kids the way we want to. But mostly I wish we had each other for sure, forever. Then it wouldn't matter an awful lot to me what kind of a house we would live in, or what the outlook for the future might be. I know that together we'll get along somehow no matter what happens. I'm sure hoping I'll be able to get that ring for you this summer, and more than that I'm hoping you'll take it.

Darling, I'll see you Saturday, and I'll write again this week and you do the same. Miss me, and love me, and want

All My Love—Always,

Dick

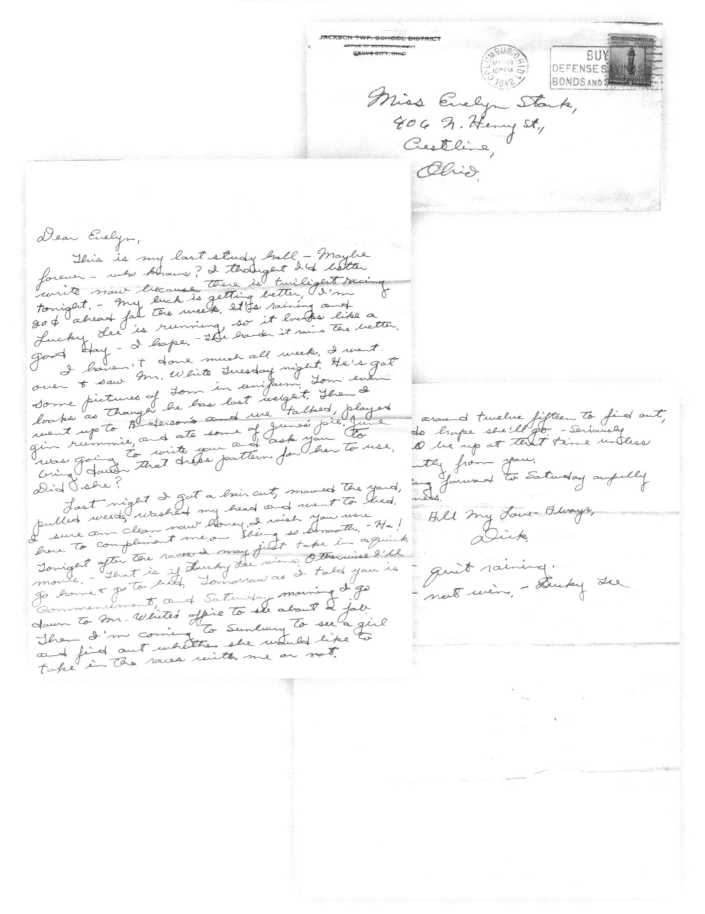

Miss Evelyn Stark,
406 N. Henry St.,
Crestline,
Ohio.

Dear Evelyn,

This is my last study hall – Maybe forever – who knows? I thought I'd better write now because there is twilight racing tonight. – My luck is getting better, I'm 80¢ ahead for the week. It is raining and Lucky Lee is running so it looks like a good day – I hope. – The harder it rains the better.

I haven't done much all week. I went over & saw Mr. White Tuesday night. He's got some pictures of Tom in uniform. Tom even looks as though he has lost weight. Then I went up to Anderson's and we talked, played gin rummie, and ate some of June's pie. June was going to write you and ask you to bring down that dress pattern for her to use. Did she?

Last night I got a hair cut, mowed the yard, pulled weeds, washed my head and went to bed. I sure am clean now honey, I wish you were here to compliment me on being so smooth. – Ha! Tonight after the races I may just take in a quick movie. – That is if Lucky Lee wins. Otherwise I'll go home & go to bed. Tomorrow as I told you is Commencement, and Saturday morning I go down to Mr. White's office to see about a job. Then I'm coming to Sunbury to see a girl and find out whether she would like to take in the races with me or not.

around twelve fifteen to find out. Do hope she'll go. – Seriously be up at that time unless ntly from you.

ing forward to Saturday awfully ness.

All My Love – Always,
Dick.

– quit raining.
– not win. – Lucky Lee

Dear Evelyn,

This is my last study hall—Maybe forever—who knows? I thought I'd better write now because there is twilight racing tonight. My luck is getting better, I'm 20¢ ahead for the week. It's raining and Lucky Lee is running so it looks like a good day—I hope. The harder it rains the better.

I haven't done much all week. I went over and saw Mr. White Tuesday night. He's got some pictures of Tom in uniform. Tom even looks as though he has lost weight. Then I went up to Anderson's and we talked, played gin rummie, and ate some of Junes' pie. June was going to write you and ask you to bring down that dress pattern for her to use, Did she?

Last night I got a hair cut, mowed the yard, pulled weeds, washed my head and went to bed. I sure am clean now honey, I wish you were here to compliment me on being so smooth. Ha! Tonight after the races I may just take in a quick movie. That is if Lucky Lee wins otherwise I'll go home & go to bed. Tomorrow as I told you is commencement, and Saturday morning I go down to Mr. White's office to see about a job. Then I'm coming to Sunbury to see a girl and find out whether she would like to take in the races with me or not.

I'll be up around twelve fifteen to find out, and I sure do hope she'll go. Seriously darling, I will be up at that time unless I hear differently from you.

I'm looking forward to Saturday awfully much sweetness.

All My Love—Always

Dick

P.S. It quit raining. He might not win. Lucky Lee I mean.

JACKSON TWP. SCHOOL DISTRICT
OFFICE OF SUPERINTENDENT
GROVE CITY, OHIO

Miss Evelyn Stark,
406 N. Henry St.,
Crestline,
Ohio.

Dear Evelyn,

It's Tuesday morning and I'm giving my next to last final to about 60 "bright" young students. They all look puzzled, they all would like to cheat, and probably will before they get out of here. Thank God this is the last week for me, I'm slowly getting to be a mere shadow of my former self.

Again, there isn't much news. I went in yesterday to see Mr. White, but I found that he was making a series of speeches and wouldn't be in the office until Wednesday. Last night I went up to Bob and June's a little while, but came home early and went to bed. I was tired. Now Bob doesn't know whether he'll get his vacation or not. — If we go on this trip — what with all the complications likely to arise — it will be a miracle.

I ate dinner in Hennick's last night and saw June Swift. She told me that George gets a five day furlough - starting tonight - and that he's pretty sure this time that he made officers training school. Maybe they'll be at Beulah Saturday for the big race. Pete applied for a commission in the Navy yesterday in this physical fitness program, and he thinks he stands a good chance

Before long I really will be left, and if they get me I chance at getting a commission. weather looks wonderful. I'm you in a golf game Sunday way. It won't be long before ming, and play tennis, ces that are air cooled. all for it, the heck with

ss, I guess I'd better take children's papers, - I won't that I didn't even mention etter. That's so you won't love with the horses and day. You're really first ength, Darling, and you My Love — Always,

Dick,

Dear Evelyn,

It's Tuesday morning and I'm giving my next to last final to about 60 "bright" young students. They all look puzzled, they all would like to cheat, and probably will before they get out of here. Thank God this is the last week for me, I'm slowly getting to be a mere shadow of my former self.

Again, there isn't much news. I went in yesterday to see Mr. White, but I found that he was making a series of speeches and wouldn't be in the office until Wednesday. Last night I went up to Bob and June's a little while, but came home early and went to bed. I was tired. Now Bob doesn't know whether he'll get his vacation or not. If we go on this trip—what with all the complications likely to arise—it will be a miracle.

I ate dinner in Hennicks' last night and saw June Swift. She told me that George gets a five day furlough—starting tonight—and that he's pretty sure this time that he made officers training school. Maybe they'll be at Beulah Saturday for the big race. Pete applied for a commission in the Navy yesterday in this physical fitness program, and he thinks he stands a good chance of getting it. Before long I really will be the only one left, and if they get me I won't stand any chance at getting a commission.

Honey, the weather looks wonderful. I'm already to wallop you in a golf game Sunday if it stays this way. It won't be long before we can go swimming, and play tennis, and look for places that are air cooled. Personally I'm all for it, the heck with this cold weather.

Well sweetness, I guess I'd better take a look at my children's papers, I want you to notice that I didn't even mention horses in this letter. That's so you won't think I'm in love with the horses and that you're secondary. You're really first by plenty of lengths darling, and you do have

—All My Love—Always,

Dick

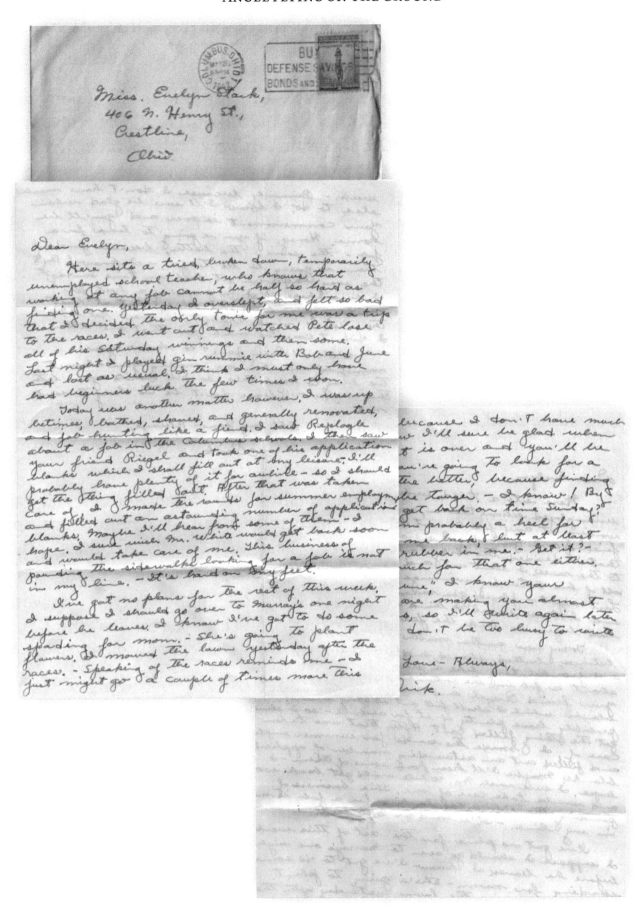

Dear Evelyn,

Here sits a tired, broken down, temporarily unemployed school teacher, who knows that working at any job cannot be half so hard as finding one. Yesterday I overslept, and felt so bad that I decided the only tonic for me was a trip to the races. I went out and watched Pete lose all of his Saturday winnings and then some. Last night I played gin rummie with Bob and June and lost as usual. I think I must only have had beginners luck the few times I won.

Today was another matter however, I was up betimes, bathed, shaved, and generally renovated, and job hunting like a fiend. I saw Replogle about a job in the Columbus schools. I then saw your friend Riegel and took one of his application blanks which I shall fill out at my leisure — so I should probably have plenty of it for awhile — so I should get the thing filled out. After that was taken care of I made the rounds for summer employment and filled out an astounding number of application blanks. Maybe I'll hear from some of them — I hope. I sure wish Mr. White would get back soon and would take care of me. This business of pounding the sidewalks looking for a job is not in my line. — It's hard on my feet.

I've got no plans for the rest of this week. I suppose I should go over to Murray's one night before he leaves. I know I've got to do some spading for mom. — She's going to plant flowers. I mowed the lawn yesterday after the races. — Speaking of the races reminds me — I just might go a couple of times more this

because I don't have much ___ I'll sure be glad when ___ is over and you'll be ___ you're going to look for a ___ the better, because finding ___ the tougher. — I know! By ___ get back on time Sunday? ___ probably a heel for ___ me back, but at least ___ rubber in me. — Get it? — ___ much for that one either.

___ me," I know your ___ are making you almost ___ so I'll write again later ___ don't be too busy to write

Love — Always,

Nick.

POSTMARKED COLUMBUS, OHIO—MAY 26, 1942

Dear Evelyn,

Here sits a tired, broken down, temporarily unemployed school teacher, who knows that working at any job cannot be half so hard as finding one. Yesterday I overslept, and felt so bad that I decided the only tonic for me was a trip to the races. I went out and watched Pete lose all of his Saturday winnings and then some. Last night I played gin rummie with Bob and June and lost as usual. I think I must only have had beginners luck the few times I won.

Today was another matter however, I was up betimes; bathed, shaved, and generally renovated and job hunting like a fiend. I saw Replogle about a job in the Columbus schools. I then saw your friend Riegel and took one of his application blanks which I shall fill out at my leisure. I'll probably have plenty of it for awhile—so I should get the thing filled out. After that was taken care of, I made the rounds for summer employment and filled out an astounding number of application blanks. Maybe I'll hear from some of them—I hope. I sure wish Mr. White would get back soon and would take care of me. This business of pounding the sidewalk looking for a job is not in my line. It's hard on my feet.

I've got no plans for the rest of this week. I suppose I should go over to Murray's one night before he leaves. I know I've got to do some spading for mom. She's going to plant flowers. I mowed the lawn yesterday after the races. Speaking of the races reminds me—I just might go a couple of times more this week. Primarily because I don't have much else to do. I know I'll sure be glad when your commencement is over and you'll be home. Honey, if you're going to look for a job—the sooner the better, because finding them is going to be tough. I know! By the way did you get back on time Sunday? I sure hope so. I'm probably a heel for making you bring me back, but at least there isn't much rubber in me. Get it? I didn't care too much for that one either.

Well, "Daisy June," I know your manifold activities are making you almost too busy to read this, so I'll write again later this week. Please don't be too busy to write me.

All My Love—Always,

Dick

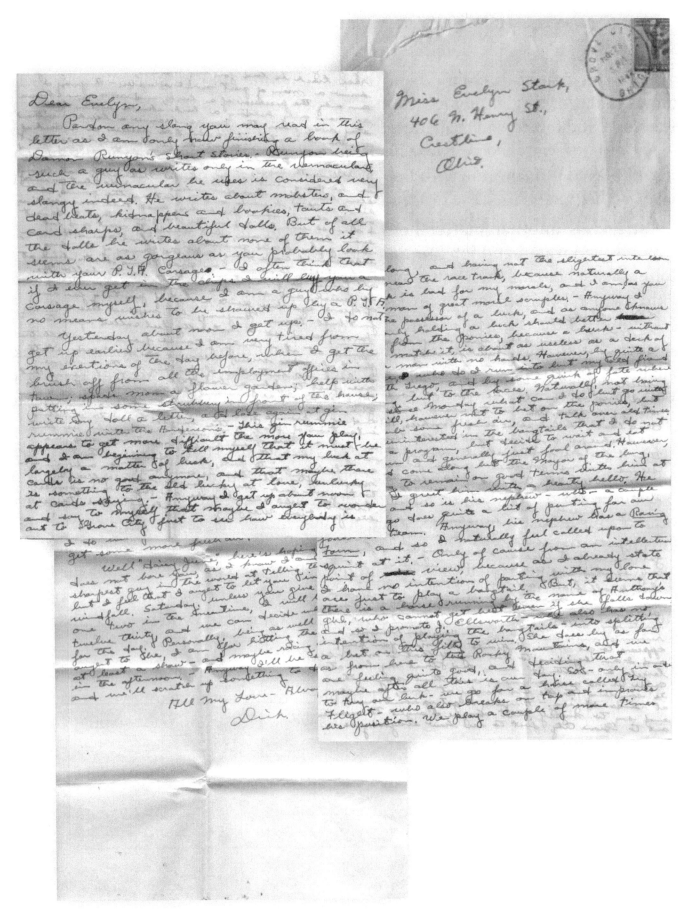

Dear Evelyn,

Pardon any slang you may read in this letter as I am only now finishing a book of Damon Runyon's short stories. Runyon being such a guy as writes only in the vernacular and the vernacular he uses is considered very slangy indeed. He writes about mobsters, and dead beats, kidnappers and bookies, tarts and card sharps, and beautiful dolls. But of all the dolls he writes about none of them it seems are as gorgeous as you probably look with your P.T.A. Corsage—I often think that if I ever get in the chips I will buy you a corsage myself, because I am a guy who by no means wishes to be showed up by the P.T.A.

Yesterday about noon I got up. I do not get up earlier because I am very tired from my exertions of the day before, when I get the brush off from all the employment offices in town; spade mom a flower garden; help with putting in some shrubbery in front of the house; write my doll a letter, and lose again at gin rummie with the Andersons' This gin rummie appears to get more difficult the more you play, and I am beginning to tell myself that it must be largely a matter of luck, and that my luck at cards is no good anymore, and that maybe there is something to the old lucky at love, unlucky at cards saying. Anyways I get up about noon and say to myself that maybe I ought to wander out to Grove City just to see how everybody is getting along, and having not the slightest intention of going near the race track, because naturally a race track is bad for morals, and I am, as you know a man of great moral scruples. Anyway I am only the possessor of a buck, and as anyone knows a man only holding a buck should better stay away from the ponies, because a buck—without another to match it, is about as useless as a deck of cards to a man with no hands. However, by quite a coincidence, who do I run into but my old friend J. Ellswoth Trego, and by some quirk of fate where is he going but to the races. Naturally, not having seen him since Monday what can I do but go with him? Still, however not to bet on the ponies, but only to absorb some fresh air, and talk over old times. I am so uninterested in the bangtails that I do not even buy a program, but decide to wait and eat some popcorn and generally just fool around. However who should come along but the Mayor of the burg, and wishing to remain on good terms with him at all times I greet him with a hearty hello. He is jovial, and so is his nephew—who—a couple of years ago does quite a bit of punting for our football team. Anyway, his nephew has a Racing Form, and so I naturally feel called upon to squint at it. Only of course from an intellectual point of view, because as I already state I have no intention of parting with my lone ace just to play a bangtail. But, it seems that there is a horse running by the name of Anthony's girl, who cannot get beat even if she falls down, and so I promote J.

127

Ellsworth—who also has no intention of playing the bangtails—into splitting a bet on this filly to win. She does by as far as from here to the Rocky Mountains, and we are feeling quite good, and deciding that maybe after all this is our day. So—only in order to try our luck—we go for a horse called Fry Flight—who also breaks on top and improves his position. We play a couple of more times and come home, and my ace is stretched into a ten spot, and I am feeling very good indeed. Especially as I am told by a couple of guys who should know that False Card and Bobbys' Son—who is no son at all, but older than I am—are going to win today. Naturally, with a couple of hot cookies like those running, and with my new ten spot, and with pay day today, what can I do but go out and eat some more popcorn, and get some more fresh air?

Well "Daisy June," here's hoping this tale does not bore you, as I know I am not the sharpest guy in the world at telling the tale but I feel that I ought to let you in on my windfall. Saturday, unless you give me the old one two in the meantime, I will be up about twelve thirty, and we can decide what to cook up for the day. Personally, being as well heeled as I ought to be, I am for hitting the high spots—at least a show—and maybe racing a few horses in the afternoon. Anyway I'll be seeing you and we'll scratch up something to do.

All My Love—Always,

Dick

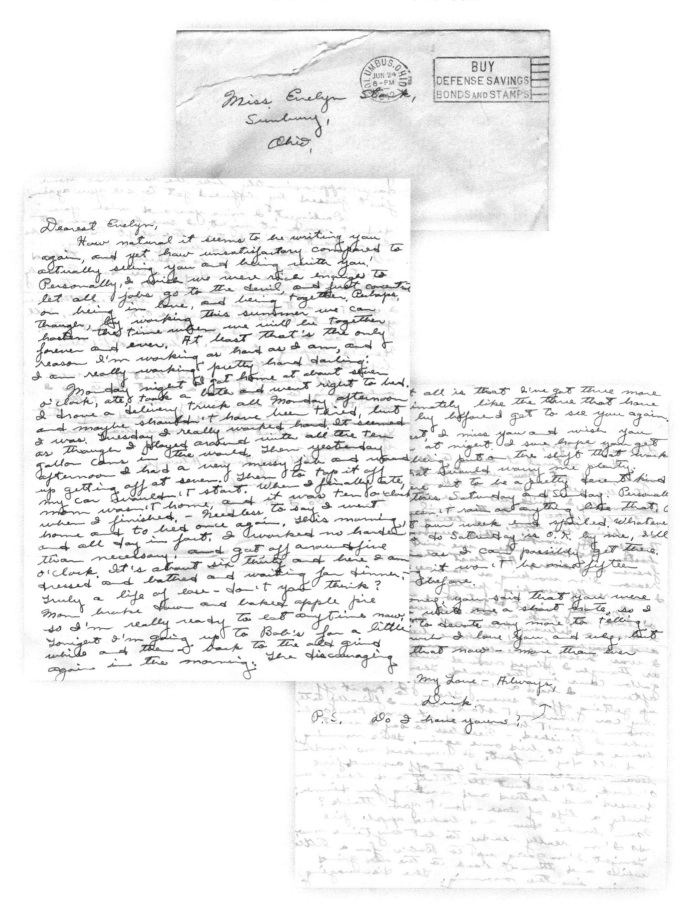

Postmarked Columbus, Ohio—June 24, 1942

Dearest Evelyn,

How natural it seems to be writing you again, and yet how unsatisfactory compared to actually seeing you and being with you! Personally, I wish we were rich enough to let all jobs go to the devil, and first concentrate on being in love, and being together. Perhaps though, by working this summer we can hasten the time when we will be together forever and ever. At least that's the only reason I'm working as hard as I am, and I am really working pretty had darling: Monday night I got home at about seven o'clock, ate, took a bath and went right to bed. I drove a delivery truck all Monday afternoon and maybe shouldn't have been tired, but I was. Tuesday I really worked hard. It seemed as though I played around with all the ten gallon cans in the world. Then yesterday afternoon I had a very messy job and wound up getting off at seven. Then to top it off my car wouldn't start. When I finally ate, mom wasn't home, and it was ten o'clock when I finished. Needless to say I went home and to bed once again. This morning and all day in fact, I worked no harder than necessary, and got off around five o'clock. It's about six thirty and here I am dressed and bathed and waiting for dinner. Truly a life of ease—don't you think? Mom broke down and baked apple pie so I'm really ready to eat anytime now. Tonight I'm going up to Bob's for a little while and then—back to the old grind again in the morning. The discouraging part about it all is that I've got three more days approximately like the three that have just passed by before I get to see you again.

Darlingest, I miss you and wish you didn't work at night. I sure hope you get by without being put on the shift that works all night. That would worry me plenty. Sweetness, there ought to be a pretty decent kind of a moon this Saturday and Sunday. Personally, I sure hope it doesn't rain or anything like that. I don't want our week end spoiled. Whatever you want to do Saturday is O.K. by me. I'll be up as soon as I can possibly get there. Here's hoping it won't be nine fifteen like it was before.

Well honey, you said that you were only going to write me a short note, so I won't "bother" to devote any more to telling you how much I love you and why, but you know that now—more than ever you have—

All My Love—Always,

Dick

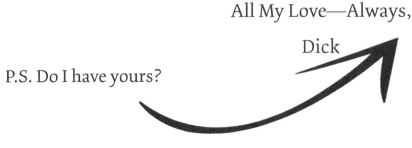

P.S. Do I have yours?

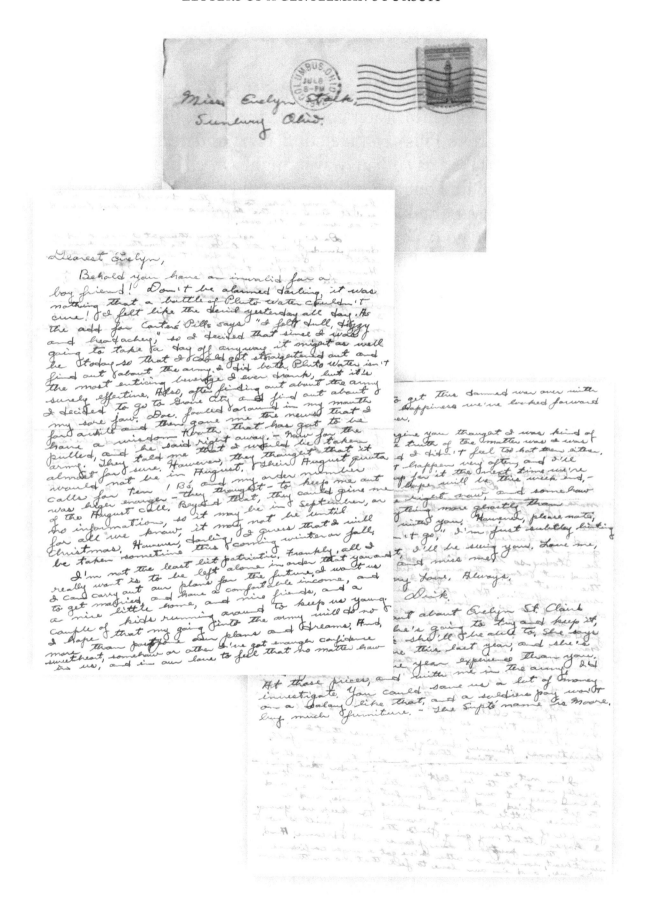

POSTMARKED COLUMBUS, OHIO—JULY 8, 1942

Dearest Evelyn,

Behold you have an invalid for a boy friend! Don't be alarmed darling, it was nothing that a bottle of Pluto Water couldn't cure! I felt like the devil yesterday all day. As the ad for Carters' Pills says "I felt dull, dizzy and heartachey," so I decide that since I was going to take a day off anyway it might as well be today so that I could get straightened out and find out about the army. I did both, Pluto Water isn't the most enticing beverage I ever drank, but it's surely effective. Also, after finding out about the army I decided to go to Grove City and find out about my sore jaw. Doc. fooled around in my mouth for awhile and then gave me the news that I have a wisdom tooth that has got to be pulled, and he said right away. Now for the army. They told me that I would be taken almost for sure. However, they thought that it would not be in August. Their August quota calls for ten 1 B's, and my order number was high enough—they though —to keep me out of the August call. Beyond that, they could give me no information, so it may be in September, or for all we know, it may not be until Christmas. However, darling, I guess that I will be taken sometime this coming winter or fall.

I'm not the least bit patriotic. Frankly, all I really want is to be left alone in order that you and I can carry out our plans for the future. I want us to get married, and have a comfortable income, and a nice little home, and nice friends, and a couple of kids running around to keep us young. I hope that my going into the army will do no more than postpone our plans and dreams. And, sweetheart, somehow or other I've got enough confidence in us, and in our love to feel that no matter how long it may take to get this damned war over with we'll have all the happiness we've looked forward to as soon as it's over.

Darling, I imagine you thought I was kind of dopey Sunday, but the truth of the matter was I was still very tired, and I didn't feel too hot then either. However, that doesn't happen very often, and I'll guarantee to make up for it the next time we're together—which I hope will be this week end. I'm pretty lonesome right now, and somehow I can't imagine anything more ghastly than missing a weekend with you. However, please note, I'm not saying "don't go," I'm just subtlety hinting.

Well sweetheart, I'll be seeing you. Love me, and write to me, and miss me.

All My Love, Always,

Dick

P.S. I found out about Evelyn St. Claires job at Girard. She's going to try and keep it, but doesn't think she'll be able to, she says she got $1,750 there this last year, and she's had just one more year experience than you. At those prices, and with me in the army, I'd investigate. You could save us a lot of money on a salary like that, and a soldiers pay won't buy much furniture. The Supts' name is Moore.

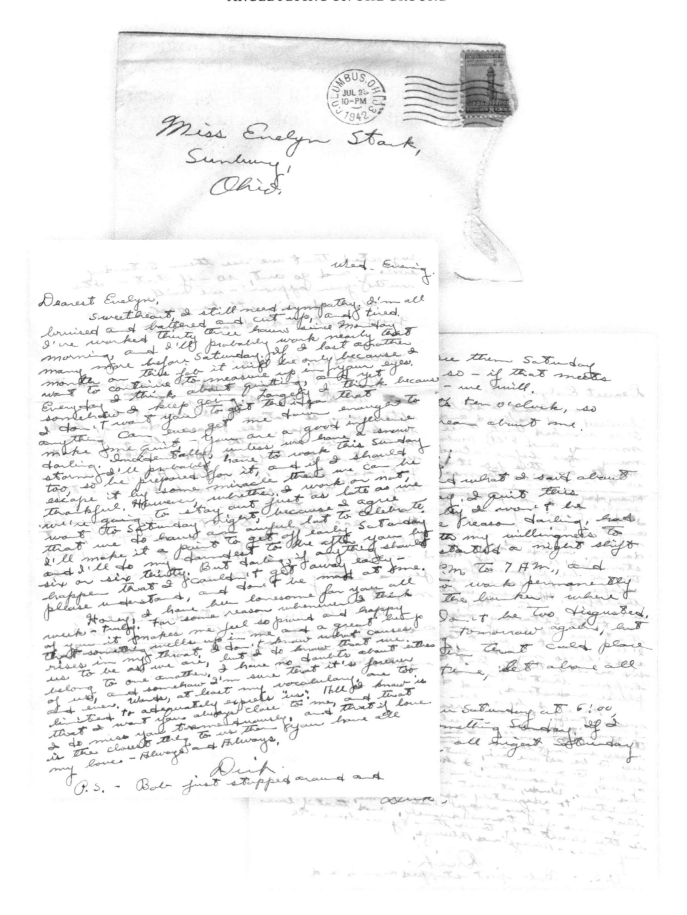

Wed. Evening

Dearest Evelyn,

Sweetheart, I still need sympathy. I'm all bruised and battered and cut up, and tired. I've worked thirty three hours since Monday morning, and I'll probably work nearly that many more before Saturday. If I last another month on this job it will be only because I want to continue to measure up in your eyes. Every day I think about quitting, and yet somehow I keep going. Largely I think because I don't want you to get the idea that anything can ever get me down enough to make me quit. You are a good influence darling. Incidentally, unless we have a snow storm I'll probably have to work this Sunday too, so be prepared for it, and if I should escape it by some miracle then we can be thankful. However, whether, I work or not, we're going to stay out just as late as we want to Saturday night, because I agree that we do have an awful lot to celebrate. I'll make it a point to get off early Saturday and I'll do my darndest to be after you by six or six thirty. But darling, if anything should happen that I couldn't get away early—please understand, and don't be mad at me.

Honey, I have been lonesome for you all week—truly! For some reason whenever I think of you it makes me feel so proud and happy that something wells up in me and a great lump rises in my throat. I don't know what causes us to be as we are, but I do know that we belong to one another. I have no doubts about either of us, and somehow I'm sure that it's forever and ever. Words, at least my vocabulary, are too limited to adequately express "us." All I know is that I want you always close to me, and that I do miss you tremendously, and that if love is the closest thing to us then you have all my love.

Always and Always,

Dick

P.S. Bob just stopped around and suggested that we see them Saturday evening and go out, so—if that meets with your approval—we will.

Well darling its ten o'clock, so good night, and dream about me.

Thursday Evening:

Honey disregard what I said about working Sunday. I quit this afternoon, so naturally I won't be working Sunday. The reason darling, had nothing to do with my willingness to work, but they started a night shift yesterday from 7P.M. to 7A.M., and they wanted me to work permanently—every night in the bunker—where it's 20° below. Don't be too disgusted. I'll go job hunting tomorrow again, but I wouldn't work in that cold place permanently any time, let alone all night.

So, I'll see you Saturday at 6:00, and we can do something Sunday. If I were invited to stay all night Saturday night I'd accept.

Love,

Dick

POSTMARKED COLUMBUS, OHIO—JULY 29, 1942

Dearest Evelyn,

Excuse the pencil honey, but mom used my pen last, and life is too short to worry over where she puts things. If this letter sounds dopier than usual put it down to the fact that I just had a little nap, and haven't yet gotten clear awake. I haven't done a thing since I saw you Sunday except stand around on my new job. Some of those guys down there call it work, but I feel like I'm on vacation. It's just like the bridge painting job I had, only there isn't any nice cool bridge to sleep under. Also, I must say I'm loafing in good company: Besides my superintendent there are two other superintendents, and a good round number of school principals, plus a varied assortment of teachers running around. Then too, a couple of the boys who quit at Telling's before I did are out there. And I ran into an old friend by the name of Ollie Haskins, who has worked himself up—how I don't know, knowing him—to be Assistant Chief of Warehouses. He said if I wanted to work from two thirty till eleven he'd give me a job at 85¢ an hour, and all I'd need to do would be follow him around. I declined with thanks. However, I guess when they get really busy you do have to work overtime, and unless I'm pretty lucky, I'll have to work some Sunday's. But maybe I'll be lucky.

Darling, there's something I've been wondering about, and that is what you meant Sunday when you talked about my kidding you. Whatever was bothering you, forget it. Just because I told you a little white lie about my going to the bookies doesn't mean that I make a habit of it. And I've never fibbed to you about anything important. There's one thing I know is no kidding, and that is that I love you more and more all the time, and that I miss you, and wish that we could be together more than we get to, I sure hope you don't have to work any more on that night shift I also hope I get to see you sometime this week end. Have you decided yet how you're going to work it about meeting Rita, and going to the wedding etc? Sweetheart, if you can, please try and work me in some place in your plans for the weekend. I'm lonesome now. What will I be by the time I see you if it isn't soon?

Well honey, I haven't eaten yet, so—love me—and want

All My Love—Always,

Dick

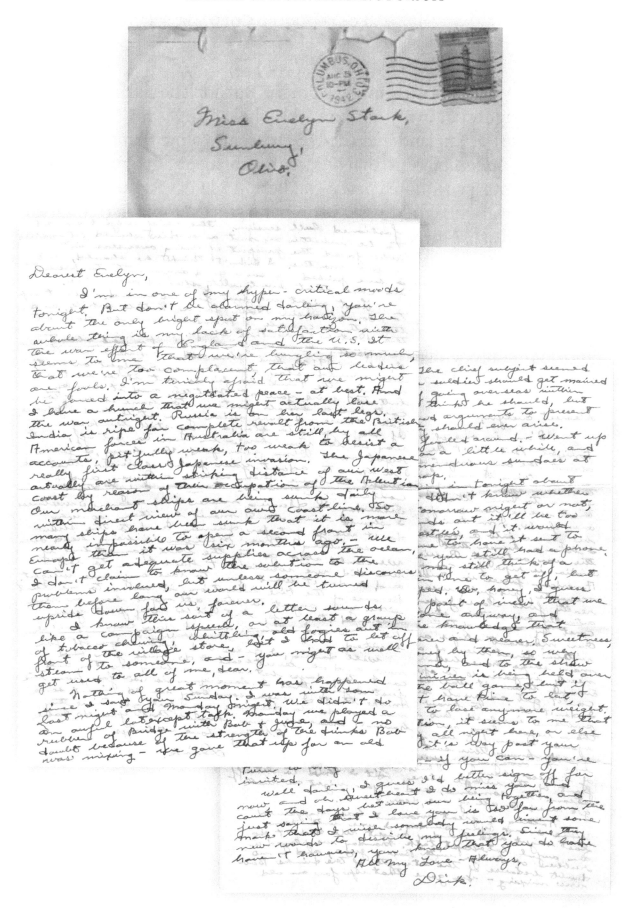

Dearest Evelyn,

I'm in one of my hyper-critical moods tonight. But don't be alarmed darling, you're about the only bright spot in my horizon. The whole thing is my lack of satisfaction with the war effort of England and the U.S. It seems to me that we're bungling so much, that we're too complacent, that our leaders are fools. I'm terribly afraid that we might be forced into a negotiated peace—at best. And I have a hunch that we might actually lose the war outright. Russia is on her last legs. India is ripe for complete revolt from the British. American forces in Australia are still by all accounts pitifully weak, two weak to resist a really first class Japanese invasion. The Japanese actually are within striking distance of our West Coast by reason of their occupation of the Aleutians. Our merchant ships are being sunk daily within direct view of our own coast line. So many ships have been sunk that it is more nearly impossible to open a second front in Europe than it was six months ago. We can't get adequate supplies across the ocean, I don't claim to know the solution to the problems involved, but unless someone discovers them before long our world will be turned upside down for us, forever.

I know this sort of letter sounds like a campaign speech, or at least a group of tobacco chewing, whittling old fogies out in front of the village store, but I had to let off steam to someone, and—you might as well get used to all of me, dear.

Nothing of great moment has happened since I saw you Sunday. I was with Tom last night and Monday night. We didn't do an awful lot except talk. Monday we played a rubber of bridge with Bob & June, and—no doubt because of the strength of the drinks Bob was mixing—we gave that up for an old fashioned bull session. The chief subject seemed to be whether or not a soldier should get married who faced the prospect of going overseas within a few months. I didn't think he should, but I sure picked up some good arguments to present in case that eventuality should even arise.

Last night we just fooled around. Went up to Toms' cousin Don's for a little while, and then ate a couple of tremendous sundaes at the Dutch chocolate shop.

Betty Geraw is coming in tonight about 8:30 or 9:00, but Tom didn't know whether she would stay over tomorrow night or not, and by the time he finds out it'll be too late to wire you at Nestle's, and it would cost me a small fortune to have it sent to your house. I sure wish you still had a phone. If she's going to stay, I may still think of a way to let you know in time to get off, but right now I'm stumped. So, honey, I guess I'll have to adopt your point of view that we ought to leave them alone anyway, and content myself with the knowledge that Saturday is drawing nearer and nearer. Sweetness, I should have some money by then, so why don't we go out for dinner, and to the show or something? <u>Mrs. Miniver</u> is being held over. We could also go to the ball game, but if we did we wouldn't have time to eat, and I don't want you to lose anymore weight. Because of the tire situation, it seems to me that either you ought to stay all night here, or else I should stay up, but it's way past your turn to stay down, so—if you can—you're invited.

Well darling, I guess I'd better sign off for now, and oh sweetheart I do miss you and count the days between our being together, and just saying that I love you is so far from the mark that I wish somebody would invent some new words to describe my feelings. Since they haven't however, you know that you do have,

All My Love—Always

Dick

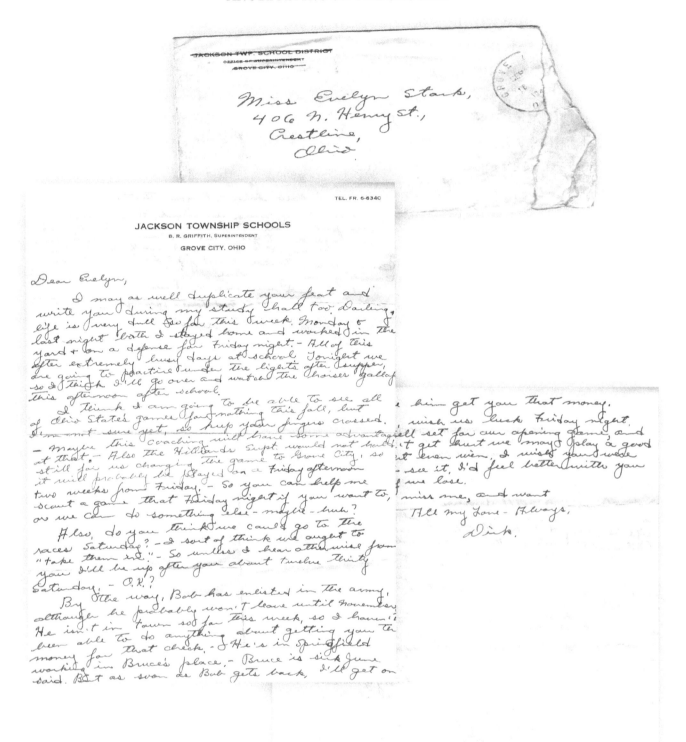

Miss Evelyn Stark,
406 N. Henry St.,
Crestline,
Ohio.

JACKSON TOWNSHIP SCHOOLS
B. R. GRIFFITH, SUPERINTENDENT
GROVE CITY, OHIO

TEL. FR. 6-8340

Dear Evelyn,

I may as well duplicate your feat and write you during my study hall too. Darling, life is very full so far this week. Monday to last night both I stayed home and worked in the yard + on a defense for Friday night. — All of this after extremely busy days at school. Tonight we are going to practice under the lights after supper, so I think I'll go over and watch the horses gallop this afternoon after school.

I think I am going to be able to see all of Ohio State's games, fat, nothing this fall, but I'm not sure yet, so keep your fingers crossed. — Maybe this coaching will have some advantage after all. — Also the Hilliards Supt. would not hear of that. it will probably be played on a Friday afternoon still for us changing the game to Grove City, so two weeks from Friday. — So you can help me scout a game that Friday night if you want to, or we can do something else — maybe — huh?

Also, do you think we could go to the races Saturday? — I sort of think we ought to "take them in." — So unless I hear otherwise from you I'll be up after you about twelve thirty Saturday. — O. K.?

By the way, Bob has enlisted in the army, although he probably won't leave until November. He isn't in town so far this week, so I haven't been able to do anything about getting you the money for that check. — He's in Springfield working in Bruce's place. — Bruce is sick June said. But as soon as Bob gets back, I'll get on

him get you that money. wish us luck Friday night. all set for our opening game, and if I get hurt we may. I play a good but even then, I wish you were see it, I'd feel better with you if we lose. miss me, and want

All my Love — Always,
Dick.

POSTMARKED GROVE CITY, OHIO—SEPTEMBER 16, 1942

Dear Evelyn,

I may as well duplicate your feat and write you during my study hall too. Darling, life is very dull so far this week. Monday & last night both I stayed home and worked in the yard and on a defense for Friday night. All of this after extremely busy days at school. Tonight we are going to practice under the lights after supper, so I think I'll go on over and watch the horses gallop this afternoon after school.

I think I am going to be able to see all of Ohio State's games for nothing this fall, but I'm not sure yet, so keep your fingers crossed. Maybe this coaching will have some advantages at that. Also the Hilliards Supt. would not hold still for us changing the game to Grove City, so it will probably be played on a Friday afternoon two weeks from Friday. So you can help me scout a game that Friday night if you want to, or we can do something else—maybe—huh?

Also, do you think we could go to the races Saturday? I sort of think we ought to "take them in." So unless I hear otherwise from you I'll be up after you about twelve thirty Saturday. O.K.?

By the way, Bob has enlisted in the army. Although he probably won't leave until November. He isn't in town so far this week, so I haven't been able to do anything about getting you the money for that check. He's in Springfield working in Bruce's place. Bruce is sick June said. But as soon a Bob gets back, I'll get on him and have him get you that money.

Well honey, wish us luck Friday night. We're pretty well set for our opening game, and if our boys don't get hurt we may play a good game, and might even win. I wish you were coming down to see it. I'd feel better with you consoling me—if we lose.

Write, and miss me, and want

All My Love—Always,

Dick

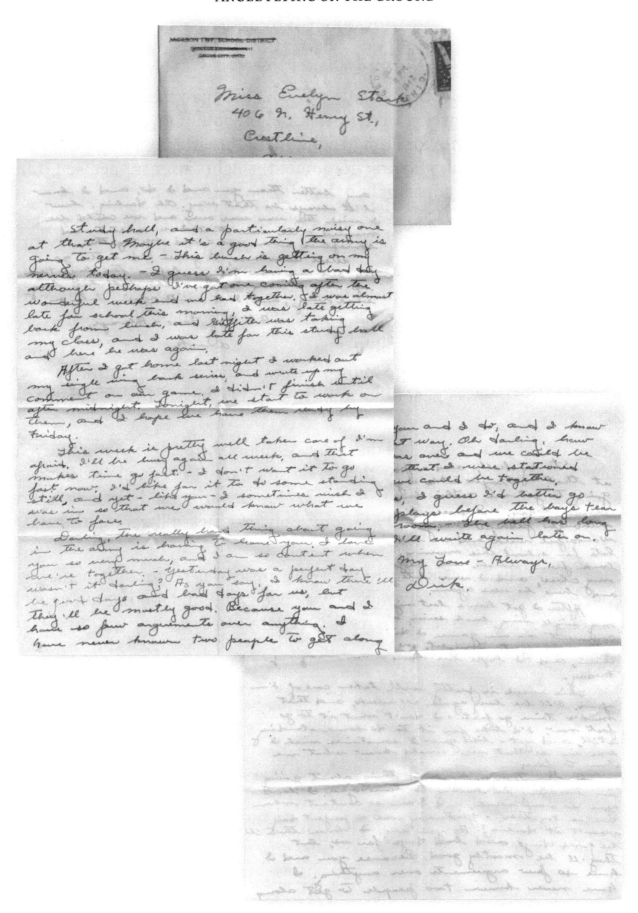

study hall, and a particularly noisy one
at that — Maybe it's a good thing the army is
going to get me — This lunch is getting on my
nerves today. — I guess I'm having a bad day,
although perhaps I've got one coming after the
wonderful week end we had together. I was almost
late for school this morning, I was late getting
back from lunch, and Wiffiter was taking
my class, and I was late for this study hall
and here he was again.

After I got home last night I worked out
my single wing book series, and wrote up my
comment on our game. I didn't finish until
after midnight. Tonight, we start to work on
them, and I hope we have them ready by
Friday.

This week is pretty well taken care of I'm
afraid. I'll be busy again all week, and that
makes time go fast. — I don't want it to go
fast now. I'd like for it to do some standing
still, and yet — like you — I sometimes wish I
was in so that we would know what we
have to face.

Darling, the really bad thing about going
in the army is having to leave you. I love
you so very much, and I am so content when
we're together. — Yesterday was a perfect day
wasn't it darling? As you say, I know there'll
be good days and bad days for us, but
they'll be mostly good. Because you and I
have so few arguments over anything. I
have never known two people to get along

you and I do, and I know
[...] way. Oh darling, how
[...] was over and we could be
[...] that I were stationed
[...] we could be together,
[...] I guess I'd better go
[...] plays before the boys team
[...] room. — See will last long
[...] I'll write again later on.

My Love — Always,

Dick.

(Note: Seems to be missing a page)

Study hall, and a particularly noisy one at that. Maybe it's a good thing the army is going to get me. This lunch is getting on my nerves today. I guess I'm having a bad day although perhaps I've got one coming after the wonderful week end we had together. I was almost late for school this morning, I was late getting back from lunch, and Griffith was taking my class, and I was late for this study hall and here he was again.

After I got home last night I worked out my single wing back series, and wrote up my comment on our game. I didn't finish until after midnight. Tonight, we start to work on them, and I hope we have them ready by Friday.

This week is pretty well taken care of I'm afraid. I'll be busy again all week, and that makes time go fast. I don't want it to go fast now. I'd like for it to do some standing still, and yet—like you— I sometimes wish I was in so that we would know what we have to face.

Darling, the really hard thing about going in the army is having to leave you, I love you so very much, and I am so content when we're together—yesterday was a perfect day wasn't it darling? As you say, I know there'll be good days and bad days for us, but they'll be mostly good. Because you and I have so few arguments over anything. I have never known two people to get along any better than you and I do, and I know it'll always be that way, Oh darling, how I wish the war was over and we could be married. Or even that I were stationed someplace where we could be together.

Well sweetness, I guess I'd better go try out my new plays before the boys tear up the dressing room. The bell has long since rung, and I'll write again later on.

All My Love—Always,

Dick

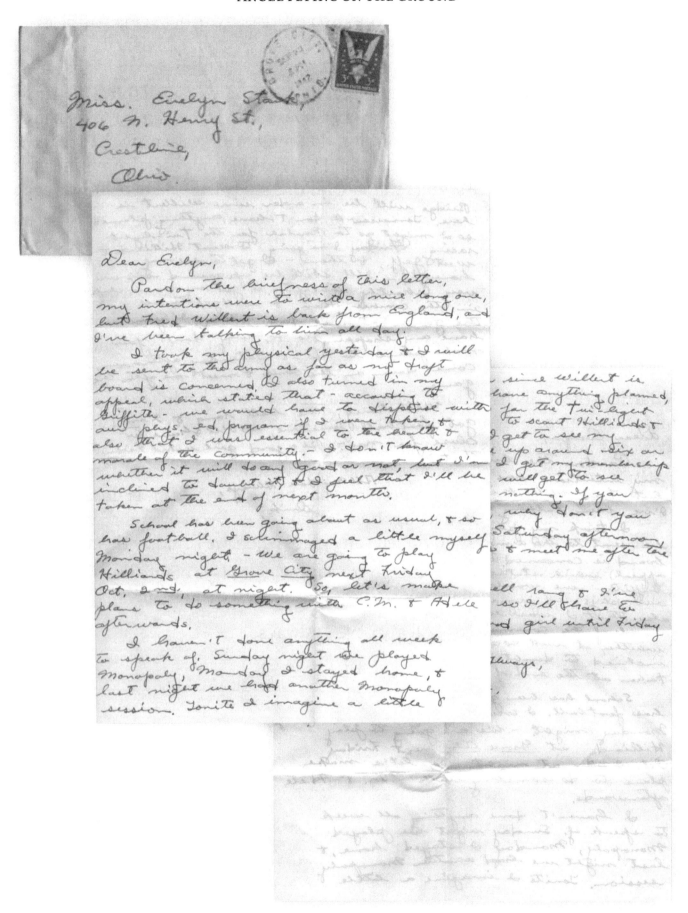

Dear Evelyn,

Pardon the briefness of this letter, my intentions were to write a nice long one, but Fred Willert is back from England, and I've been talking to him all day.

I took my physical yesterday and I will be sent to the army as far as my draft board is concerned. I also turned in my appeal, which stated that—according to Griffith—we would have to dispense with our phys. ed. program if I were taken, and also that I was essential to the health and morale of the community. I don't know whether it will do any good or not, but I'm inclined to doubt it, and I feel that I'll be taken at the end of next month.

School has been going about as usual, and so has football. I scrimmaged a little myself Monday night. We are going to play Hilliards at Grove City next Friday Oct. 2nd, at night. So, let's make plans to do something with C. M. & Adele afterwards.

I haven't done anything all week to speak of, Sunday night we played Monopoly, Monday I stayed home, and last night we had another Monopoly session. Tonite I imagine a little Bridge will be in order since Willert is here. Tomorrow I don't have anything planned, so I might go to Beulah for the twilight racing. Friday I'm going to scout Hilliards & West Jeff., and then—I get to see my honey!! I'll still be up around six or very shortly thereafter. I got my membership to the coaches assn. and will get to see the game Saturday for nothing. If you have any shopping to do, why don't you make plans to do it Saturday afternoon, come down on the bus & meet me after the game?

Well honey, the bell rang and I've got football practice, so I'll have to close for now. Be a good girl until Friday that is.

All My Love—Always,

Dick

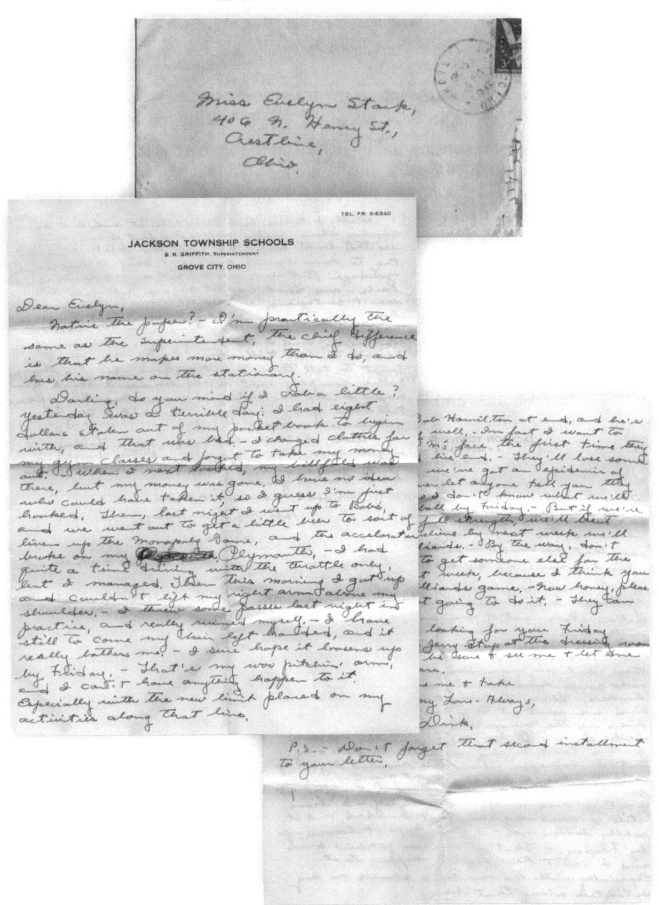

POSTMARKED GROVE CITY, OHIO—SEPTEMBER 30, 1942

Dear Evelyn,

Notice the paper? I'm practically the same as the Superintendent, the chief difference is that he makes more money than I do, and has his name on the stationary.

Darling, do you mind if I crab a little? Yesterday was a terrible day: I had eight dollars stolen out of my pocket book to begin with, and that was bad. I changed clothes for my gym classes and forgot to take my money out. When I next looked, my billfold was there, but my money was gone. I have no idea who could have taken it, so guess I'm just hooked. Then, last night I went up to Bob's and we went out to get a little beer to sort of liven up the Monopoly Game, and the accelerator broke on my Plymouth. I had quite a time driving with the throttle only, but I managed. Then this morning I got up and couldn't lift my right arm above my shoulder. I threw some passes last night in practice, and really ruined myself. I have still to comb my hair left handed, and it really bothers me. I sure hope it loosens up by Friday. That's my woo pitchin' arm and I can't have anything happen to it. Especially with the new limit placed on my activities along that line.

Well, I tried Bob Hamilton at end, and he's coming along pretty well. In fact I want to see the look on C.M's face the first time they try to run around his end. They'll lose some yardage. But now, we've got an epidemic of boils—and don't even let anyone tell you they aren't contagious, so I don't know who we'll have ready to play ball by Friday. But if we're anyways near at full strength, we'll beat Worthington, and I believe by next week we'll be able to beat Hilliards. By the way, don't forget to tell them to get someone else for the game you play next week, because I think you ought to see the Hilliards game. Now honey, please tell them you're not going to do it. They can get someone else.

Well, I'll be looking for you Friday night honey. Have Jerry stay at the dressing room, or if you're late, be sure and see me and let me know where you are.

Be good, and love me and take

All My Love —Always,

Dick

P.S. Don't forget that second installment to your letter.

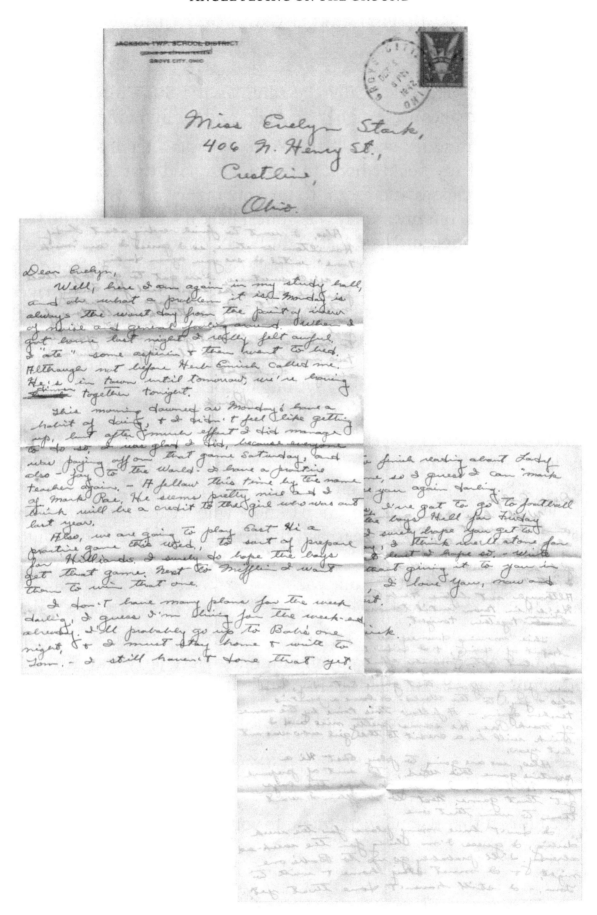

Dear Evelyn,

Well, here I am again in my study hall, and oh what a problem it is. Monday is always the worst day from the point of view of noise and general fooling around. When I got home last night I really felt awful. I "ate" some aspirin & then went to bed. Although not before Herb Emich called me. He's in town until tomorrow; we're having dinner together tonight.

This morning dawned as Monday's have a habit of doing, & I didn't feel like getting up, but after much effort I did manage to do so. I was glad I did, because everyone was paying off on that game Saturday, and also — Joy to the World! I have a practice teacher again. — A fellow this time by the name of Mark Rae. He seems pretty nice and I think will be a credit to the girl who was out last year.

Also, we are going to play East Hi a practice game this week, to sort of prepare for Hilliards. I surely do hope the boys get that game. Next to Mifflin I want them to win that one.

I don't have many plans for the week darling, I guess I'm living for the week-end already. I'll probably go up to Bob's one night, & I must stay home & write to Tom. — I still haven't done that yet.

[...] finish reading about Lady [...] me, so I guess I can mark [...] you again darling.

[...] I've got to go to football [...] the boys Hall for Friday [...] surely hope you get to [...], I think we'll atone for [...] least I hope so. — Write [...] giving it to you in [...] I love you, now and [...].

Dear Evelyn,

Well, here I am again in my study hall, and oh what a problem it is. Monday is always the worst day from the point of view of noise and general fooling around. When I got home last night I really felt awful. I "ate" some aspirin and then went to bed, although not before Herb Emrich called me. He's in town until tomorrow, we're having dinner together tonight.

This morning dawned as Monday! have a habit of doing, I didn't feel like getting up, but after much effort I did manage to do so I was glad I did, because everyone was paying off on that game Saturday, and also Joy to the World—I have a practice teacher again. A fellow this time by the name of Mark Rowe. He seems pretty nice and I think will be accredit to the girl who was out last year.

Also, we are going to play East Hi a practice game this Wed., to sort of prepare for Hilliards. I surely do hope the boys get that game. Next to Mifflin I want them to win that one.

I don't have many plans for the week darling, I guess I'm living for the week-end already. I'll probably go up to Bob's one night, and I must stay home and write to Tom. I still haven't done that yet.

Also, I want to finish reading about Lady Hamilton sometime, so I guess I can "mark time" until I see you again darling.

Well sweetness, I've got to go to football practice and give the boys hell for Friday nite's effort. I surely hope you get to come down Friday. I think we'll atone for past sins then, at least I hope so. Write to me, and without giving it to you in two installments, I love you, now and always, darlingest.

Dick

Dear — I a— not a Cider Press, — Evelyn,

Forgive the pencil and the typing paper darling, but I'm giving a test and this is all I' have available.

There isn't much more news than usual I was out with Herb Monday evening and we did a lot of talking. He left for Chicago Tuesday, but hopes to be back for the game Saturday. — If he is, we may go out with them Sat. night.

Yesterday football practice went very badly. I don't know what is wrong with them, I've made all the changes I told you about, and even moved Goose out of the starting lineup — trying for some speed. That Hamilton is a mighty sweet end, and I don't believe they'll be able to run around us this week.

I stayed home last night, and wrote Tom a letter, and read, and ate more than a pint of icecream. — As a result I had quite a dream — it seems as though you were putting on a strip tease — I think I'll eat some more tonight!

My practice teacher is a pretty nice fellow I'm glad, because I thought that girl last year was a pill. — Now I only have three classes — soft huh?

going to have a practice this & Reserve Team, so learn their blocking a little on edge, want that game, me again tonight and Larry Hamilton. She's now night I'm ____ anderson's. — They game last Saturday too to the one this week. I'll see a real game night we have a game pe you can get off, I can, I'll be up thirty. — That I give before the game.

it's time for me so I'll see you if not then, Saturday miss you too, and I forward to that time with me for always.

All my Love,
Dick.

Dear—I am not a Cider Press. Evelyn,

Forgive the pencil and the typing paper darling, but I'm giving a test and this is all I have available.

There isn't much more news than usual. I was out with Herb Monday evening, and we did a lot of talking. He left for Chicago Tuesday, but hopes to be back for the game Saturday. If he is, we may go out with them Sat. night.

Yesterday football practice went very badly. I don't know what is wrong with them. I've made all the changes I told you about, and even moved Goose out of the starting lineup—trying for some speed. That Hamilton is a mighty sweet end, and I don't believe they'll be able to run around us this week.

I stayed home last night, and wrote Tom a letter, and read, and ate more than a pint of ice cream. As a result I had quite a dream—it seems as though you were putting on a strip tease —! etc, I think I'll eat some more tonight! My practice teacher is a pretty nice fellow. I'm glad, because I thought that girl last year was a pill. Now I only have three classes soft huh?

Tonight we're going to have a practice game with East Hi's reserve team, so that the boys will learn their blocking assignments, and get a little on edge for Hilliards. We want that game! I think I'll stay home again tonight and finish reading about Lady Hamilton. She's quite a gal. Tomorrow night I'm going up to the Anderson's. They went to the State game last Saturday too, and I guess are going to the one this week. I've got a hunch we'll see a real game again honey. Friday night we have a game, and darling I sure hope you can get off. If I hear that you can, I'll be up after you about five—thirty. That'll give us time to eat before the game.

Well sweetheart it's time for me to eat right now, so I'll see you Friday I hope, and if not then, Saturday at noon. Honey I miss you too, and I really am looking forward to that time when you'll be with me for always.

All My Love,

Dick

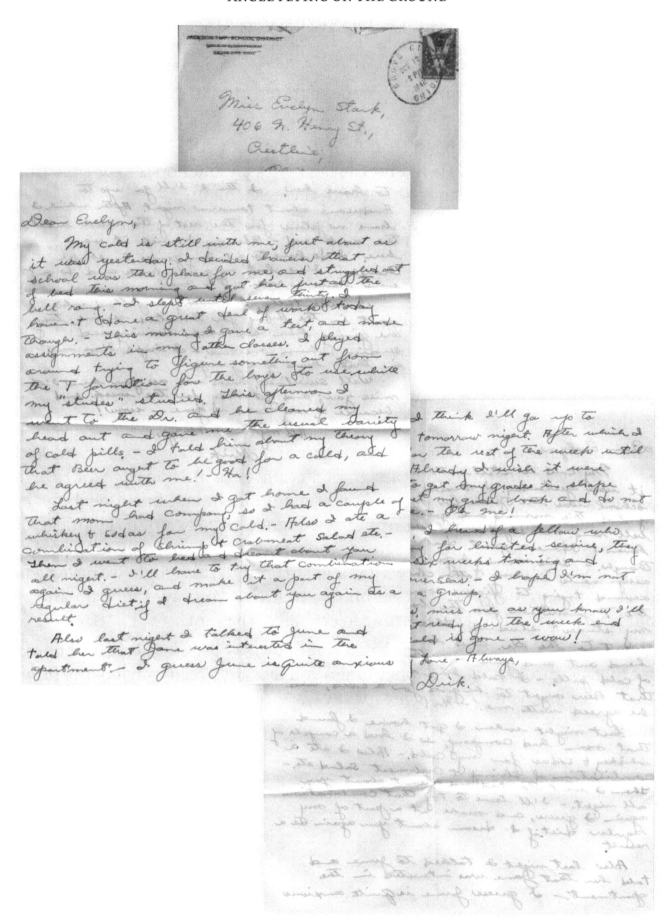

Dear Evelyn,

My cold is still with me, just about as it was yesterday. I decided however that school was the place for me, and struggled out of bed this morning and got here just as the bell rang. I slept until seven thirty. I haven't done a great deal of work today though. This morning I gave a test, and made assignments in my other classes. I played around trying to figure something out from the T formation for the boys to use while my "studes" studied. This afternoon I went to the Dr. and he cleaned my head out and gave me the usual variety of cold pills. I told him about my theory that Beer ought to be good for a cold, and he agreed with me! Ha!

Last night when I got home I found that mom had company, so I had a couple of whiskey & sodas for my cold. Also I ate a combination of shrimp & crabmeat salad etc. Then I went to bed and dreamt about you all night. I'll have to try that combination again I guess, and make it a part of my regular diet if I dream about you again as a result.

Also last night I talked to June and told her that Jane was interested in the apartment—I guess June is quite anxious to have her. I think I'll go up to Andersons' about tomorrow night. After which I have no plans for the rest of the week until the week end. Already I wish it were here. I do have to get my grades in shape though. I've lost my grade book and do not even have a roll. Oh me!

Incidentally, I heard of a fellow who went in the Army for limited service, they are giving him six weeks training and sending him overseas. I hope I'm not in that kind of a group.

Well sweetness, miss me as you know I'll miss you; and get ready for the week end because if my cold is gone—wow!

All My Love—Always,

Dick

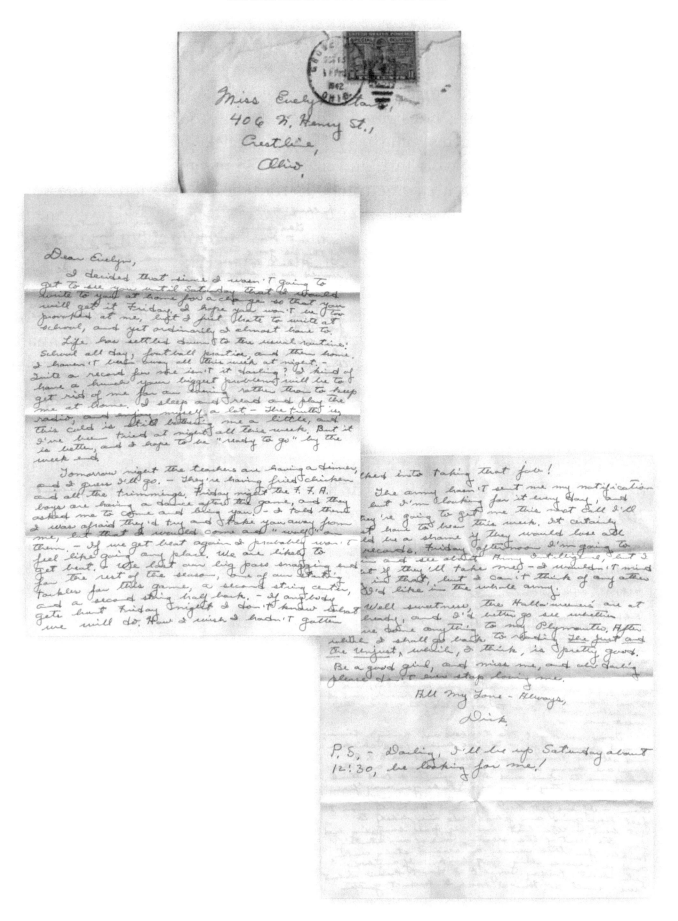

POSTMARKED GROVE CITY, OHIO—OCTOBER 13, 1942

Dear Evelyn,

I decided that since I wasn't going to get to see you until Saturday that I would write to you at home for a change so that you will get it Friday. I hope you won't be too provoked at me, but I just hate to write at school, and yet ordinarily I almost have to.

Life has settled down to the usual routine; school all day, football practice, and then home. I haven't been away all this week at night. Quite a record for me isn't it darling? I kind of have a hunch your biggest problem will be to get rid of me for an evening rather than to keep me at home. I sleep and read and play the radio, and enjoy myself a lot. The truth is, this cold is still bothering me a little, and I've been tired at night all this week. But it is better, and I hope to be "ready to go" by the weekend.

Tomorrow night the teachers are having a dinner, and I guess I'll go. They're having fried chicken and all the trimmings. Friday night the F.F.A. boys are having a dance after the game, and they asked me to come and bring you. I told them I was afraid they'd try take you away from me, but that I would come and "wolf" on them. If we get beat again I probably won't feel like going any place. We are likely to get beat. We lost our big pass snagging end for the rest of the season, one of our starting tackles for this game, a second string center, and a second string half back. If anybody gets hurt Friday night I don't know what we will do. How I wish I hadn't gotten talked into taking that job!

The army hasn't sent me my notification yet, but I'm looking for it every day, and if they're going to get me this next call I'll almost have to hear this week. It certainly would be a shame if they would lose all my records. Friday afternoon I'm going to go in and see about Army Intelligence, but I doubt if they'll take me. I wouldn't mind being in that, but I can't think of any other job I'd like in the whole army.

Well sweetness, the Hallo'weeners' are at it already, and I'd better go see whether they've done anything to my Plymouth. After which I shall go back to reading The Just and The Unjust, which, I think, is pretty good. Be a good girl, and miss me, and oh darling please don't ever stop loving me.

All My Love—Always,

Dick

P.S. Darling, I'll be up Saturday about 12:30, be looking for me.

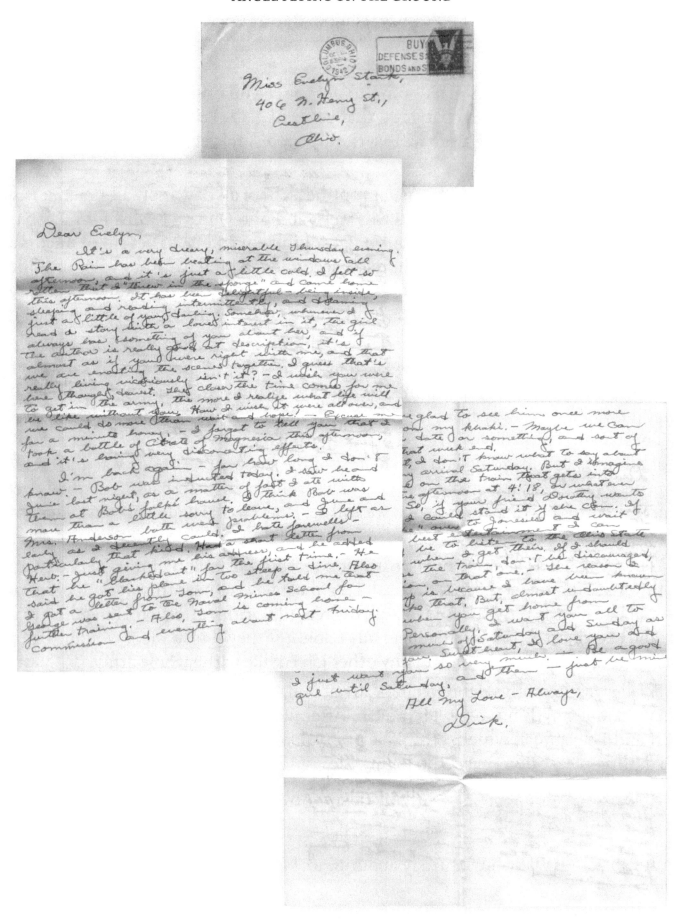

POSTMARKED COLUMBUS, OHIO—OCTOBER 22, 1942

Dear Evelyn,

It's a very dreary, miserable Thursday evening. The rain has been beating at the windows all afternoon, and it's just a little cold. I felt so rotten that I "threw in the sponge" and came home this afternoon. It has been delightful—being inside, sleeping and reading intermittently, and dreaming just a little of you darling. Somehow, whenever I read a story with a love interest in it, the girl always has something of you about her, and if the author is really good at description, it's almost as if you were right with me, and that we are enacting the scenes together. I guess that's really living vicariously isn't it? I wish you were here though, dearest. The closer the time comes for me to get in the army, the more I realize what life will be like without you. How I wish it were all over, and we could do more than wait and hope! Excuse me for a minute honey—I forgot to tell you that I took a bottle of Citrate of Magnesium this afternoon, and it's having very disconcerting effects.

I'm back again—for how long I don't know—Bob was inducted today. I saw he and June last night. As a matter of fact I ate with them at Bob's folks' house. I think Bob was more than a little sorry to leave, and June and Mrs. Anderson both were problems. I left as early as I decently could. I hate farewells—particularly that kind. Had a short letter from Herb. Just giving me his address, and he added that he "blacked out" for the first time. He said he got his plane in too steep a dive. Also I got a letter from Tom, and he told me that George was sent to the Naval Mines School for further training. Also, Tom is coming home—commission and everything about next Friday.

I'll really be glad to see him once more before I put on my khaki. Maybe we can fix him up a date or something, and sort of do the town that week end.

Sweetheart, I don't know what to say about the time of my arrival Saturday. But I imagine I'd better come on the train that gets into Crestline in the afternoon at 4:18, or whatever that time is. So, if your friend Dorothy wants to meet me, I could stand it if she can. If not I'll "hike" over to Joneses and wait for you. The best entertainment I can think of would be to listen to the Ohio State game though when I get there. If I should happen to miss the train, don't be discouraged, I'll be at Galion on that one. The reason I brought that up is because I have been known to do things like that. But, almost undoubtedly I'll be there when you get home from "play day."

Personally, I want you all to myself for as much of Saturday and Sunday as I can have you. Sweetheart, I love you and I just want you so very much. Be a good girl until Saturday, and then—just be mine.

All My Love—Always,

Dick

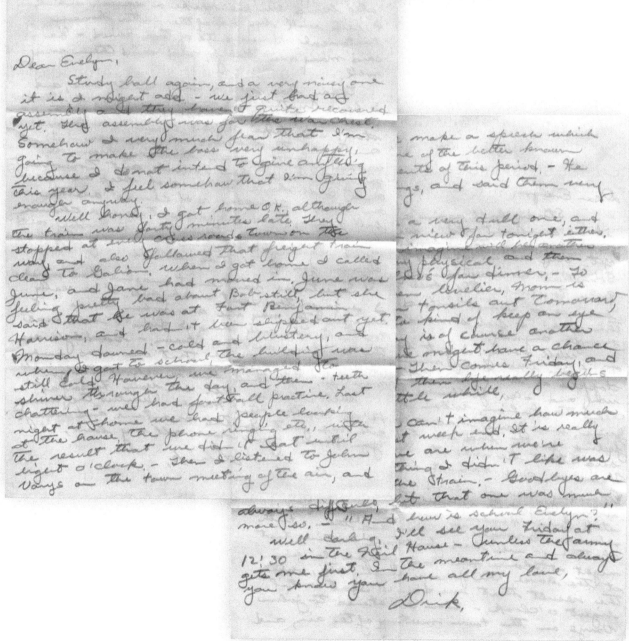

Dear Evelyn,

Study hall again, and a very noisy one it is I might add. We just had an assembly and they haven't quite recovered yet. The assembly was for the War Chest. Somehow I very much fear that I'm going to make the boss very unhappy because I do not intend to give anything this year. I feel somehow that I'm giving enough anyway.

Well honey, I got home O.K. although the train was forty minutes late. They stopped at every crossroad town on the way, and also followed that freight train clear to Galion. When I got home I called June, and Jane had moved in. June was feeling pretty bad about Bob still, but she said that he was at Fort Benjamin Harrison, and hadn't been shipped out yet. Monday dawned—cold and blustery, and when I got to school the building was still cold. However, we managed to shiver through the day, and then—teeth chattering—we had people looking at the house, the phone ringing etc.. with the result that we didn't eat until eight o'clock. Then I listened to John Varys on the town meeting of the air, and also heard Wilkie make a speech which I feel will be one of the better known historical documents of this period. He said many new things, and said them very well.

Today has been a very dull one, and I have nothing in view for tonight either. Tomorrow though I imagine will be another story. I take my physical and then am going to Delno's for dinner. To make matters even livelier, Mom is going to have her tonsils out tomorrow, and I'll have to kind of keep an eye on her. Thursday is of course another ball game, and we might have a chance in this one. Then comes Friday, and you darling, and then life really begins again for a little while.

Sweetness, you can't imagine how much I enjoyed the last week end. It is really amazing the way we are when we're together. The only thing I didn't like was the waiting on the train. Goodbyes are always difficult, but that one was much more so. "And how is school Evelyn?"

Well darling, I'll see you Friday at 12:30 in the Neil House—unless the army gets me first. In the meantime and always you know you have all my love,

Dick

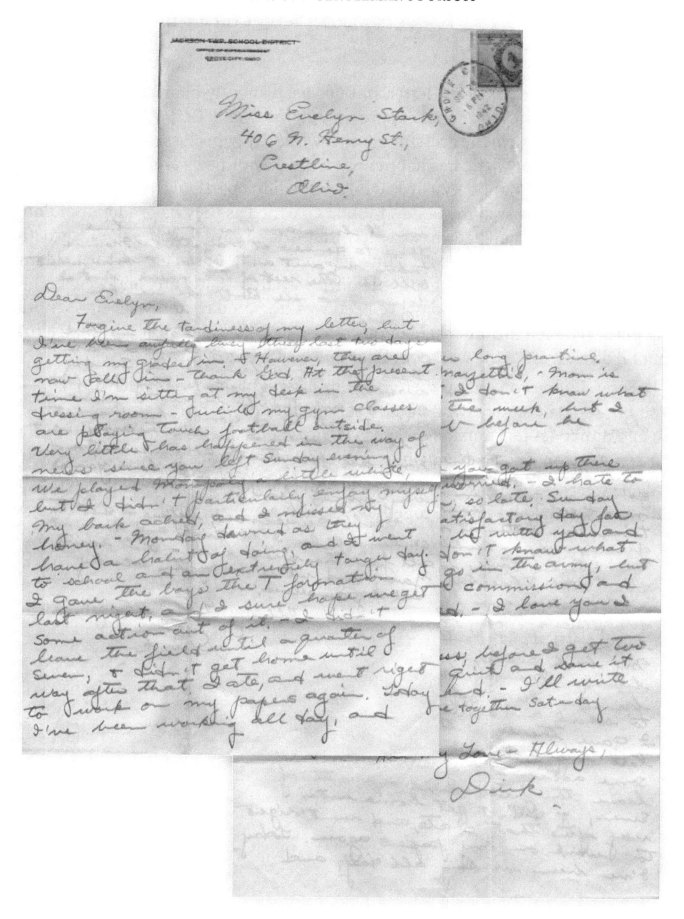

Dear Evelyn,

Forgive the tardiness of my letter, but I've been awfully busy these last two days getting my grades in. However, they are now all in—thank God. At the present time I'm sitting at my desk in the dressing room—while my gym classes are playing touch football outside. Very little has happened in the way of news since you left Sunday evening. We played Monopoly a little while, but I didn't particularly enjoy myself. My back ached, and I missed my honey. Monday dawned as they have a habit of doing, and I went to school and had an extremely tough day. I gave the boys the T formation last night, and I sure hope we get some action out of it. I didn't leave the field until a quarter of seven, and didn't get home until way after that. I ate, and went right to work on my papers again. Today I've been working all day, and we'll have another long practice. Then to dinner at Marzetti's. Mom is taking my Aunt out. I don't know what I'll do the rest of the week, but I do want to see Bob before he leaves.

Darling, I hope you got up there O.K. Sunday night. I worried. I hate to have you go so far, so late. Sunday wasn't a very satisfactory day for me. I wanted to be with you and didn't get to. I don't know what I'll do when I go in the army, but I'm all for that commission, and us getting married. I love you I very much fear.

Well sweetness, before I get too sentimental I'll quit and save it all for the week end. I'll write you, and we'll be together Saturday all by ourselves.

All My Love—Always,

Dick

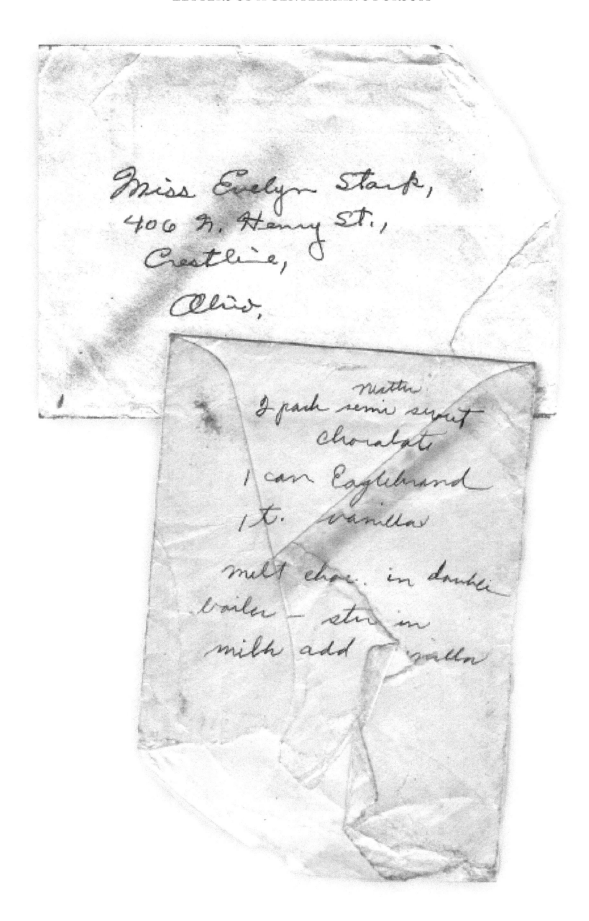

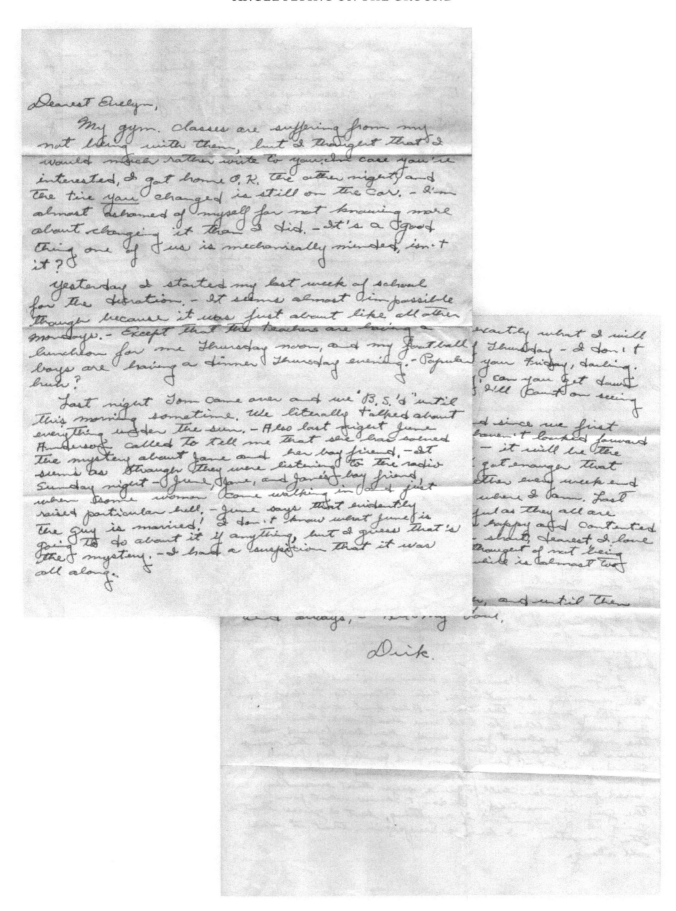

Dearest Evelyn,

My gym. classes are suffering from my not being with them, but I thought that I would much rather write to you. In case you're interested, I got home O.K. the other night, and the tire you changed is still on the car. — I'm almost ashamed of myself for not knowing more about changing it than I did. — It's a good thing one of us is mechanically minded, isn't it?

Yesterday I started my last week of school for the duration. — It seems almost impossible though because it was just about like all other mondays. — Except that the teachers are having a luncheon for me Thursday noon, and my football boys are having a dinner Thursday evening. — Payment ...

Last night Tom came over and we "B.S.'d" until this morning sometime. We literally talked about everything under the sun. — Also last night June Anderson called to tell me that she had solved the mystery about Jane and her boy friend. — It seems as though they were listening to the radio Sunday night — June, Jane, and Jane's boy friend, when some woman came walking in and just raised particular hell. — June says that evidently the guy is married! I don't know what June is going to do about it if anything, but I guess that's the mystery. — I had a suspicion that it was all along.

... exactly what I will ... Thursday — I don't ... your Friday, darling. ... can you get down ... I'll count on seeing ... since we first ... haven't looked forward ... it will be there ... got enough that ... other every week and ... where I am. Last ... ful as they all are ... happy and contented ... short, dearest I love ... thought of not being ... while is almost too ...

... and until then ... and always, — loving you,

Dick.

Dearest Evelyn,

My gym classes are suffering from my not being with them, but I thought that I would much rather write to you. In case you're interested, I got home O.K. the other night, and the tire you changed is still on the car. I'm almost ashamed of myself for not knowing more about changing it than I did. It's a good thing one of us is mechanically minded, isn't it?

Yesterday I started my last week of school for the duration. It seems almost impossible though because it was just about like all other Mondays. Except that the teachers are having a luncheon for me Thursday noon, and my football boys are having a dinner Thursday evening. Popular huh?

Last night Tom came over and we "B.S.'d" until this morning sometime. We literally talked about everything under the sun. Also last night June Anderson called to tell me that she has solved the mystery about Jane and her boy friend. It seems as though they were listening to the radio Sunday night—June, Jane, and Janes' boy friend when some woman came walking in and just raised particular hell. June says that evidently the guy is married! I don't know what June is going to do about it if anything, but I guess that's the mystery. I had a suspicion that it was all along.

Tonight, I don't know exactly what I will do, or—with the exception of Thursday—I don't have anything to do until I see you Friday, darling. By the way, speaking of Friday, can you get down by about six o'clock? O.K. I'll count on seeing you about that time honey.

This is the first weekend since we first started going together that I haven't looked forward to seeing you. You know why—it will be the last one. But darling, we've got enough that we'll always—really be together every week end and every week, no matter where I am. Last week end was just as wonderful as they all are though, and I was just as happy and contented as I could possibly be. I'm short, dearest I love you so very much that the thought of not being able to be with you for awhile is almost too much.

I'll see you Friday though, and until then and always,

All My Love,

Dick

*Editor's Note: Research and story line shows that this was written on Tuesday, November 3, 1942.

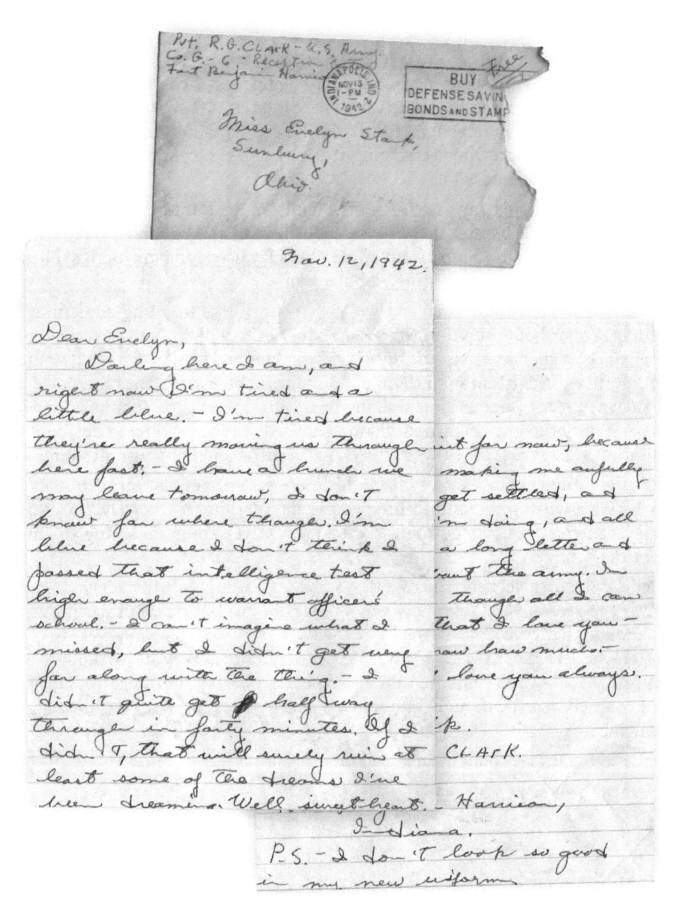

Nov. 12, 1942

Dear Evelyn,

Darling here I am, and right now I'm tired and a little blue. I'm tired because they're really moving us through here fast. I have a hunch we may leave tomorrow, I don't know for where though. I'm blue because I don't think I passed that intelligence test high enough to warrant officers' school. I can't imagine what I missed, but I didn't get very far along with the thing. I didn't quite get half way through in forty minutes. If I didn't that will surely ruin at least some of the dreams I've been dreaming. Well sweetheart, I'm going to quit for now, because writing you is making me awfully blue. When I get settled, and know what I'm doing, and all, I'll write you a long letter and tell you all about the army. In the meantime though all I can tell you is that I love you—you'll never know how much.

And that I'll love you always,

Dick

Pvt. Richard G. Clark
Co G-6
Fort Benjamin Harrison, Indiana

P.S. I don't look so good in my new uniform.

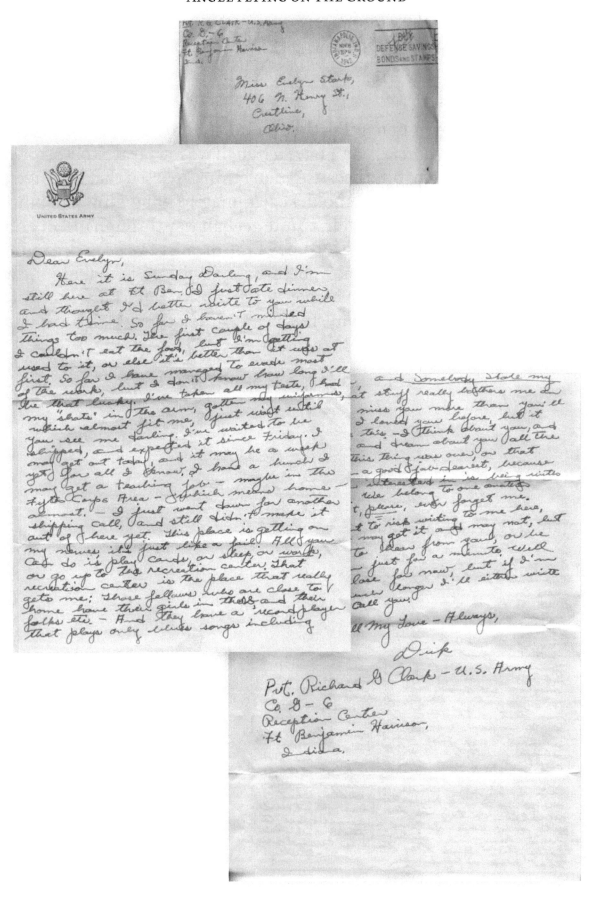

Dear Evelyn,

Here it is Sunday Darling, and I'm still here at Ft Ben. I just ate dinner and thought I'd better write to you while I had time. So far I haven't minded things too much. The first couple of days I couldn't eat the food, but I'm getting used to it, or else it's better than it was at first. So far I have managed to evade most of the work, but I don't know how long I'll be that lucky. I've taken all my tests, had my "shots" in the arm, gotten my uniforms, which almost fit me, just wait until you see me darling. I've waited to be shipped, and expected it since Friday. I may get out today, and it may be a week yet for all I know. I have a hunch I may get a teaching job — maybe in the Fifth Corps Area — which means home — almost. — I just went down for another shipping call, and still didn't make it out of here yet. This place is getting on my nerves its just like a jail! All you can do is play cards, or sleep, or work, or go up to the recreation center. That recreation center is the place that really gets me; those fellows who are close to home have their girls in there, and their folks etc. — And they have a record player that plays only blues songs including

... and somebody stole my
... stuff really bothers me an
... miss you more than you'll
... I loved you before, but it
... ties — I think about you, and
... and dream about you all the
... this thing was over, on that
... a good job dearest, because
... interested in its being until
... we belong to one another
... please, ever forget me.
... to risk writing to me here,
... may get it and may not, but
... to hear from you, or be
... just for a minute. Well
... close for now, but if I'm
... much longer I'll either write
... call you.

all my Love — Always,

Dick

Pvt. Richard G Clark — U.S. Army
Co. B — 6
Reception Center
Ft Benjamin Harrison,
Indiana.

POSTMARKED INDIANAPOLIS, INDIANA—NOVEMBER 16, 1942

Dear Evelyn,

Here it is Sunday Darling, and I'm still here at Ben. I just ate dinner and thought I'd better write to you while I had time. So far I haven't minded things too much. The first couple of days I couldn't eat the food, but I'm getting used to it, or else it's better than it was at first. So far I have managed to evade most of the work, but I don't know how long I'll be that lucky. I've taken all my tests, had my "shots" in the arm, gotten my uniforms, which almost fit me, just wait until you see me, darling. I've waited to be shipped, and expected it since Friday. I may get out today, and it may be a week yet for all I know. I have a hunch I may get a teaching job—maybe in the Fifth Corps Area—which means home—almost. I just went down for another shipping call, and still didn't make it out of there yet. This place is getting on my nerves; it's just like a jail. All you can do is play cards, or sleep or <u>work</u>, or go up to the recreation center. That recreation center is the place that really gets me: Those fellows who are close to home have their girls in there, and their folks etc. And they have a record player that plays only blues songs including <u>I Cried For You</u>, and <u>Somebody Stole My Gal</u>. Honey, that stuff really bothers me an awful lot I miss you more than you'll even know, and I loved you before, but it was never like this. I think about you, and talk about you, and dream about you all the time. I wish this thing was over, or that I was settled in a good job dearest, because all I really am interested in is being with you always. We belong to one another and honey don't, <u>please</u>, ever forget me.

If you want to risk writing to me here, go ahead, but I may get it and may not, but I'd surely love to hear from you, or be with you even just for a minute. Well darling I'll close for now, but if I'm here very much longer I'll either write you again or call you.

All My Love—Always,

Dick

Pvt. Richard G. Clark – U.S. Army
Co. G-6
Reception Center
Ft. Benjamin Harrison, Indiana

Nov. 19, '42.

Dear Evelyn,

Forgive me for not writing sooner, but I've really been awfully busy. We got here yesterday about 9:00 A.M., after a forty-three hour train ride in a day coach with no water or anything else. We were very tired, but we had to work at one thing or another until nine last night, which is "lights out time". — Down here it is also a blackout all night from then until daylight.

We are living in a very fine resort hotel right on Miami Beach. — I'm in the penthouse. — Everything is very beautiful here: The palm trees, the coconuts, the blue ocean, etc., but outside of the scenery this is no picnic. I've made beds, rolled socks, fixed & re-fixed my drawer, swept floors, emptied trash, and cleaned, and cleaned, and cleaned. — Also, this morning we began to drill. — We marched two miles to the drill field, drilled, took calisthenics, then double timed until I at least was ready to drop. — After which we marched back another two miles, listened to a lecture — very brief and to the point — if you know what I mean. —

The food here is not very good and they are in such a temporary stage that we have to eat out of mess kits, which "ain't good."

I don't know how long I'll be here, or where I'll go next, or what I'll be in, but I do know it will be in some part of the Air Corps. We start processing tomorrow, to determine what we go into, I don't know but I would guess that I will be in administration of some sort, I should know before long however.

Darling, if I live through of this, I know it will be good; but I'm not really [sure] I'll live through it. — [things] are bothering me plenty [right] now. — Personally, I [wish] I was back home with [you] dearest. — You have no [idea how] much more you mean to [me] now than ever before. I [real]ly do miss you, and long [for the] day when I am perfectly [won]derful [to]gether. — You sounded [kin]d of cold over the phone [the other] day, and I've worried ev[er] since. — Sweetness, don't e[ver]

honey, and don't ever change.

Write to me right away — a nice long letter, and remember that I love you and I always will.

Dick.

Pvt. R.G. Clark. - U.S.A.
1130 T.S.S. — Sq. - 42.
Miami Beach Schools, 1st District
Special Training Unit.
Miami Beach,
Fla.

Nov. 19, 1942

Dear Evelyn,

Forgive me for not writing sooner, but I've really been awfully busy. We got here yesterday about 9:00 A.M., after a forty-three hour train ride in a day coach with no water or anything else. We were very tired, but we had to work at one thing or another until nine last night, which is "lights out time." Dear, here it is also a blackout all night from then until daylight.

We are living in a very fine resort hotel right on Miami Beach. I'm in the penthouse. Everything is very beautiful here: the palm trees, the coconuts, the blue ocean, etc., but outside of the scenery this is no picnic. I've made beds, rolled socks, fixed & re-fixed my drawer, swept floors emptied trash, and cleaned and cleaned, and cleaned. Also, this morning we began to drill. We marched two miles to the drill field, drilled, took an hours calisthenics, then double timed until I at least was ready to drop. After which we marched back another two miles, listened to a lecture—very brief and to the point—if you know what I mean.

The food here is not very good and they are in such a temporary stage that we have to eat out of mess kits, which "ain't good."

I don't know how long I'll be here, or where I'll go next, or what I'll be in, but I do know it will be in some part of the Air Corps. We start processing tomorrow, to determine what we go into, I don't know but I would guess that I will be in administration of some sort, I should know before long however.

Darling, if I live through all of this, I know it will do me good; but I'm not really sure I'll live through it. My feet are bothering me plenty right now. Personally, I wish I was back home with you dearest. You have no idea how much more you mean to me now than ever before. I really do miss you, and long for one of our perfectly wonderful days together. You sounded kind of cold over the phone Sunday, and I've worried ever since. Sweetness, don't ever really get cold to me. Love me, now and always, please honey and don't ever change.

Write to me right away—a nice <u>long</u> letter, and remember that I love you and I always will.

Dick

Pvt. R.G.Clark. – U.S.A.
1130 T.S.S. – Sq. – 42
Miami Beach Schools, 1st District
Special Training Unit
Miami Beach, FLA

Sunday
Morning.

Dear Evelyn,

The reason I haven't written since Thursday is that I have been kept entirely too busy. We get up every day at 5:30 A.M., & stand reveille (?) at five of six. — Then we eat and come back to our rooms and clean them up, and I mean they really have to be immaculate. — I'm sure getting plenty of good training in keeping house lately. — Then we march to the drill field and drill and exercise until eleven. — Then back to lunch, then out on the drill field again until four. Then we should be through

but Friday night we had to learn our "general orders", and that took all evening.

Saturday was a repetition of Friday except that it was hotter, and the drill and exercises were stiffer. Saturday night was the first time we were allowed out, and we got out until ten o'clock. I didn't do much except eat a great big meal "with everything". I was too tired, and so I was in bed well before we had to be in.

The town, the ocean, everything is beautiful, — even the drill field, which was a very fine golf course. There are palm trees and coconuts, and everything you've ever heard about Florida.

Last night after I undressed I went out on the roof porch of our penthouse and looked at the ocean in the moonlight. The ocean breeze was blowing and the tide was in. The palm trees were swaying and everything was very peaceful. You can imagine what I was wishing, and dreaming about, can't you? Honey, all that was needed to make the thing perfect was for you to be with me. How wonderful it would be! Sometime I hope we can come here, just us, and enjoy it together. Darling, I try not to miss you

take eight or ten weeks to get. It's the stiffest training that any of them get. I still don't know what I'll be doing, or where I'll be stationed, we haven't been processed yet. I think I'll know by next week sometime though. — I sure wish they'd either send me to Dayton, or else to this officer's school down here.

Darling, I imagine you're tired of hearing all this twaddle, so I'll quit for now. Write, and write, and keep on writing to me; and honey keep on loving me too. As long as I know that you're

still mine I can go through all of this, and come out on top. — Don't forget to keep in touch with mom, and tell me how she is, and don't forget that I love you, and that I will forever and ever.

Dick.

note address
↘

Pvt. R. G. CLARK, — U.S. Army,
1130 T.S.S. (Sp) — Flight 42.
Miami Beach Schools, 1st
District,
Special Training Unit.
Miami Beach, Fla.

POSTMARKED MIAMI, FLORIDA—NOVEMBER 22, 1942

Sunday Morning

Dear Evelyn,

The reason I haven't written since Thursday is that I have been kept entirely too busy: We get up every day at 5:30 A.M., & stand revellerie (?) at five of six. Then we eat and come back to our rooms and clean them up, and I mean they really have to be immaculate. I'm sure getting plenty of good training in keeping house darling. Then we march to the drill field and drill and exercise until eleven. Then back to lunch, then out on the drill field again until four. Then we should be through but Friday night we had to learn our "general orders," and that took all evening.

Saturday was a repetition of Friday except it was hotter, and the drill and exercises were stiffer. Saturday night was the first time we were allowed out, and we got out until ten o'clock. I didn't do much except buy a great big meal "with everything." I was too tired and so I was in bed well before we had to be in.

The town, the ocean, everything is beautiful, even the drill field, which was a very fine golf course. There are palm trees and coconuts, and everything you've ever heard about Florida.

Last night after I undressed I went out on the roof porch of our penthouse and looked—at the ocean in the moonlight. The ocean breeze was blowing and the tide was in. The palm tree were swaying and everything was very peaceful. You can imagine what I was wishing, and dreaming about, can't you? Honey, all that was needed to make the thing perfect was for you to be with me. How wonderful it would be! Sometime I hope we can come here, just us, and enjoy it together. Darling I try not to miss you but I do. I want you and need you right now, and always. Sweet, I've had the darndest dreams. It seems as though I'm losing you, and I don't ever want that to happen, I sure hope they've been just bad dreams.

I expect you're wondering about how the army and I are getting along by now, so I'll tell you as well as I can: My feet have been giving me a lot of trouble, and I'm stiff and sore all over. However, I imagine that I'll be much better off physically before long. In fact, I'll come back to you a mere shadow of my former self. In three weeks we get the same training that the other branches of the service take eight or ten weeks to get. It's the stiffest training that any of them get. I still don't know what I'll be doing, or where I'll be stationed, we haven't been processed yet. I think I'll know by next week sometime though. I sure wish they'd either send me to Dayton, or else to this officer's school down here.

Darling, I imagine you're tired of hearing all this twaddle, so I'll quit for now. Write, and write, and keep on writing to me; and honey keep on loving me too. As long as I know that you're still mine I can go through all of this, and come out on top. Don't forget to keep in touch with mom, and tell me how she is, and don't forget that I love you, and that I will forever and ever.

Dick

Note address
Pvt. R.G.CLARK, U.S. Army,
1130 T.S.S. –(SP) – Flight 42.
Miami Beach Schools, 1st district
Special Training Unit
Miami Beach, Fla.

Tuesday
Evening
Nov. 24, '42

Dearest Evelyn,

The U. S. Army Air Corps and I are still going 'round & 'round. Yesterday I did all of my running and marching, and exercises without drawing a deep breath, and felt so good that I went out and drank a little beer. — It was Budweiser and it tasted awfully good. Sunday night I played a little poker and came out "about even." Last night, after we got back from the bar, and went out on the roof & sang & held a bull session about our respective girl friends until

Tomorrow we really do get classified, & maybe the next letter you get from me will tell you more nearly what I'll be doing, and where.

Darling, I don't know whether you haven't gotten my letters, or whether you just haven't taken time to write, but I haven't heard from you or mom either yet. — Please send me an old cancelled stamp with a letter on it. — I'm really a little homesick, and lovesick, & awfully anxious to hear from a certain young lady whom I love —

that we went to bed and dreamt of home, and you — I dreamt about you again darling, but it was a better dream. You weren't exactly giving me the go by, and I woke up feeling awfully happy.

Today I got my first army job. — We had to pitch hay, and you can imagine what a success I was at that, can't you? — It turned out to be very similar to a W.P.A. group. No one really did anything. This afternoon we got some more "shots," & both of my arms are awfully sore tonight. Since you last saw me, I've been vaccinated for Small Pox, Typhoid & Lockjaw, & there is more to follow I guess.

is going to give me my calisthenics for the rest of my life. — You are, aren't you darling? — There's a roommate of mine from the heart of the Bluegrass in Ky. who is betting that when I get home you won't be waiting. I've been giving him plenty of back talk on that subject though.

Dearest write a long, long letter to me & tell me — just anything. — I miss you and I love you for now and for always.
Dick.

Pvt. R.G. Clark,
1130th T.S.S. (SP) Flight 42.
Miami Beach Schools 1st district
special training unit,
Miami Beach Fla.

Tuesday Evening, Nov. 24, 1942

Dearest Evelyn,

The U.S. Army Air Corps and I are still going 'round and 'round. Yesterday I did all of my running and marching, and exercises without drawing a deep breathe, and felt so good that I went out and drank a little beer. It was Budweiser and it tasted awfully good. Sunday night I played a little poker and came out "about even." Last night after we got back from the beer joint, and went out on the roof and sang, and held a bull session about our respective girl friends until we got so darned homesick that we went to bed and dreamt of home, and yes—I dreamt about you again darling, but it was a better dream. You weren't exactly giving me the go by, and I woke up feeling awfully happy.

Today I got my first army job. We had to pitch hay, and you can imagine what a success I was at that, can't you? It turned out to be very similar to a W.P.A. group. No one really did anything. This afternoon we got some more "shots," and both of my arms are awfully sore tonight. Since you last saw me, I've been vaccinated for small pox, typhoid & lockjaw, and there is more to follow I guess.

Tomorrow we really do get classified, and maybe the next letter you get from me will tell you more nearly what I'll be doing, and where.

Darling, I don't know whether you haven't gotten my letters, or whether you just haven't taken time to write, but I haven't heard from either you or mom yet. Please send me an old cancelled stamp with a letter on it. I'm really a little homesick, and lovesick, and awfully anxious to hear from a certain young lady who—I hope—is going to give me my calisthenics for the rest of my life. You are, aren't you darling? There's a roommate of mine from the heart of the Bluegrass in Ky.who is betting that when I get home you won't be waiting. I've been giving him plenty of back talkon that subject though.

Dearest write a long, long, letter to me and tell me—just anything. I miss you and I love you for now and for always,

Dick

Pvt. R.G.CLARK
1130th T.S.S. (Sp.) Flight 42
Miami Beach Schools, - 1st District
Special Training Unit
Miami Beach, Fla.

Mr. R. E. CLARK
1130 T.S.S. (Sp) T.S. 42
BT. C. #9
A.A.F.T.T.C.
Miami Beach, Fla.

BUY
WAR SAVINGS
BONDS and STAMPS

Miss. Evelyn Stark,
406 N. Henry St.,
Crestline,
Ohio.

-1-

Friday
Evening
Nov. 27, '42.

Dear Evelyn,

I surely was glad to hear from you. I never got any letters that I appreciated more than the two I got from you. No kidding, it was really wonderful. In answer to your question about coming to Florida for X'mas, I'm not absolutely sure, but I think I'll be here for the duration and then some. And, darling, without hinting or anything, I can think of no Christmas present in the world that I would rather have than a visit from you. I miss you all the time, and I'm ___ you all the time ___

wiggle a transfer north to my honey, I may be right here for the duration. I'll tell you more about this when I know more about it, so stand by for further details.

I'm awfully glad that you and Mom are going to stay together. I want you two to become very close while I'm gone. — I think it will do you both good, and also it will help you two to remember me. That may be a little hard to do after a while, so — well, just don't forget me either of you.

I got a letter from Bob today, & he was telling me all about life in the infantry. Maybe I don't have it so

and I want you with me for always. Christmas will be just a sample of how I'll be from now on with you darling, so be prepared. We can work out details later, but honestly sweetheart, I do want to see you so very much. — Everything else in this world pales by comparison with my desire for you. How glad I'll be when we can be together always. — One room, or no room, or a mansion will be all the same to me, just so I know you're mine forever + that nothing can ever separate us as long as we live. Are you beginning to get the idea that I do want you for Christmas?

-5-

tougher at that, although it is tough enough to suit me right now. — I do think I'll have an easy job by Christmas though.

Darling, since I last wrote you, I have done nothing except stand in line & drill. We are being classified, and are just finding out where we can best get into this army. — It isn't thrilling! and hasn't been, and won't be. It's just dull and rather mixed up, so don't get the idea that I'm a hero, or that most of the rest of the army ___

-3-

Sweetness, I am, as I said pretty sure of remaining here for six months at least, I guess — from what I found out today — that I'm slated to be a lecturer, on what subjects I can't imagine. I may go to school for awhile and I may not, but in all probability I'll be down here teaching something or other. Also, I found out that I am eligible for O.C.S., so if I make it, — which in the air corps, is a little tough, I'll be down here three months after my first three months, and if I don't, and can't

we're all just a bunch of "handcuffed volunteers," who want to go back to our women and our jobs as God intended we should. I'll do my part, but at best it will be very little.

Well, honey, it's long since time for lights out, and we're on a new schedule — we get up at five o'clock again — so I'd better close and get to bed. Goodnight sweetness, I love you, now and always, and oh how I wish you were here for me to say that to — with gestures — if you know what I mean.

All My Love,

Dick

Friday Evening, Nov 27, 1942

Dear Evelyn,

I surely was glad to hear from you. I never got any letters that I appreciated more than the two I got from you. No kidding, it was really wonderful. In answer to your question about coming to Florida for X-Mas, I'm not absolutely sure, but I think I'll be here for the duration and then some. And, darling, without hinting or anything, I can think of no Christmas present in the world that I would rather have than a visit from you. I miss you all the time, and think about you all the time, and I want you with me for always. Christmas will be just a sample of how I'll be from now on with you darling, so be prepared. We can work out details later, but honestly sweetheart, I do want to see you so very much. Everything else in the world pales by comparison with my desire for you. How glad I'll be when we can be together always. One room or no room, or a mansion will be all the same to me, just so I know you're mine forever and that nothing can ever separate us as long as we live. Are you beginning to get the idea that I do want you for Christmas?

Sweetness, I am, and I said pretty sure of remaining here for six months at least. I guess—from what I found out today—that I'm slated to be a lecturer, on what subjects I can't imagine. I may go to school for awhile and I may not, but in all probability I'll be down here teaching something or other. Also, I found out that I am eligible for O.C.S., so if I make it—which in the air corps, is a little tough—I'll be down here three months after my first three months. And if I don't, and can't wiggle a transfer North to my honey, I may be right here for the duration. I'll tell you more about this when I know more about it, so stand by for further details.

I'm awfully glad that you and Mom are going to stay together. I want you two to become very close while I'm gone. I think it will do you both good, and also it will help you two to remember me. That may be a little hard to do after a while, so—well, just don't forget me either of you.

I got a letter from Bob today, and he was telling me all about life in the infantry. Maybe I don't have it so tough at that, although it is tough enough to suit me right now. I do think I'll have an easy job by Christmas though.

Darling, since I last wrote you, I have done nothing except stand in line & drill. We are being classified, and are just finding out where we can best fit into this army. It isn't thrilling, and hasn't been, and won't be. It's just drill and rather mixed up, so don't get the idea that I'm a hero, or that most of the rest of the army are hero's. We're all just a bunch of "handcuffed volunteers," who want to go back to our women and our jobs as God intended we should. I'll do my part, but at best it will be very little.

Well, honey, it's long since time for lights out, and we're on a new schedule—we get up at five o'clock again—so I'd better close and get to bed. Goodnight sweetness, I love you, now and always, and oh—how I wish you were here for me to say that to—with gestures—if you know what I mean.

All My Love,

Dick

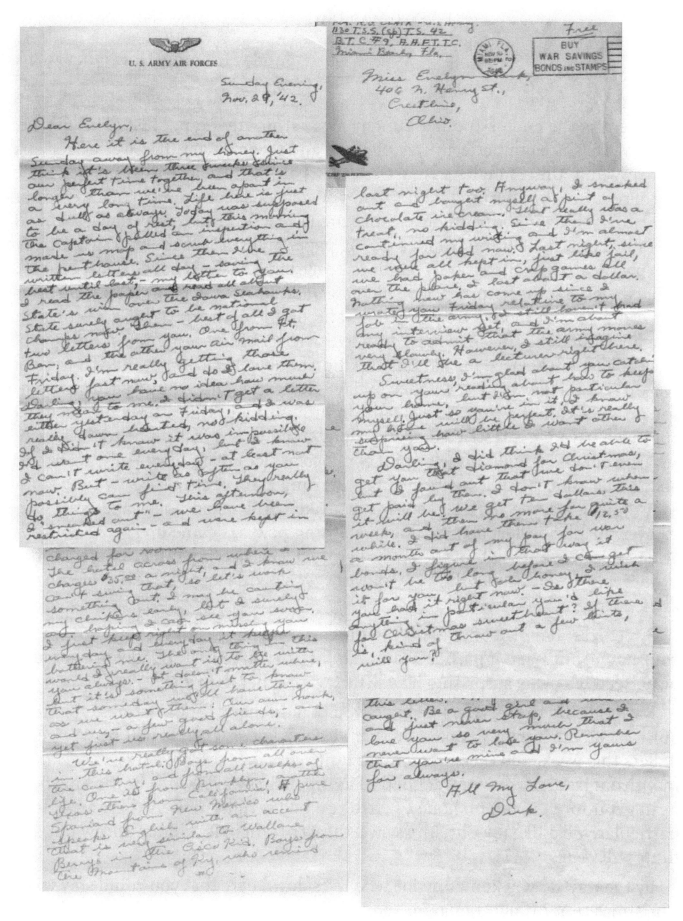

Sunday Evening, November 29, 1942

Dear Evelyn,

Here it is the end of another Sunday away from my home. Just think it's been three weeks since our perfect time together, and that's longer than we've been apart in a very long time. Life here is just as dull as always. Today was supposed to be a day of rest, but this morning the Captain pulled an inspection and made us mop and scrub everything in the penthouse. Since then I've written letters all day—saving the best until last, my letter to you. I read the paper and read all about State's win over the Iowa Seahawks. State surely ought to be national champs now. Then—best of all I got two letters from you. One from Ft. Ben, and the other your air mail from Friday. I'm really getting those letters fast now, and do I love them. Darling, you have no idea how much they mean to me. I didn't get a letter either yesterday or Friday, and I was really down hearted, no kidding. If I didn't know it was impossible I'd want one every day, but I know I can't write everyday—at least not now. But—write as often as you possibly can find time. They really do things to me. This afternoon, I "sneaked out"—we have been restricted again—and were kept in last night too. Anyway, I sneaked out and bought myself a pint of chocolate ice cream. That really was a treat, no kidding. Since then I've continued my writing and I'm almost ready for bed now. Last night, since we were all kept in, just like jail, we had poker and crap games all over the place. I lost about a dollar. Nothing new has come up since I wrote you Friday relative to my job in the army. I still haven't had my interview yet, and I'm about ready to admit that the army moves very slowly. However, I still imagine that I'll be a lecturer right here.

Sweetness, I'm glad about you catching up on your reading about how to keep your home, but I'm not particular myself. Just so you're in it. I know my home will be perfect. It's really surprising how little I want other than you.

Darling, I did think I'd be able to get you that diamond for Christmas, but I found out that we don't even get paid by then. I don't know when it will be. We get ten dollars this week, and then no more for quite a while. I did have them take $12.50 a month out from my pay for war bonds. I figure in that way it won't be too long before I can get it for you, but oh honey, I wish you had it right now. Is there anything in particular you'd like for Christmas sweetheart? If there is, kind of throw out a few hints will you?

By the way, do you know anyone who lives down here that you could stay with at Christmas time? If not, I imagine mom and I can contact some friends and fix you up. There are some people from Grove City who just came here, and also a very old friend of moms' lives here. The reason I asked is because I understand that some of the prices charged for rooms are out of sight. The hotel across from where I am charges $35.00 a night, and I know we can't swing that, so let's work something out. I may be counting my chickens early, but I surely am hoping I can see you soon. I just keep right on missing you everyday and everyday it keeps bothering me. The only thing in this world I really want is to be with you, always. It doesn't matter where, but it's something just to know that someday we'll have things as we want them: Our own nook, and us, a few good friends, and yet just us really all alone.

We've really got some characters in this hotel: Boys from all over the country, and from all walks of life. One is from Brooklyn, another Texas, others from California, a pure Spaniard from New Mexico who speaks English with an accent that is very similar to Wallace Berrys' in the Cisco Kid; boys from the Mountains of Ky., who remind me daily of the song about the Martins and the Cays being reckless Mountain boys. Nearly everyone of them wants to be a gunner in one of those bombers. Then there is the boy from Kentucky farm that I told you about—he says now for me to wait a while and then see what you say. I just missed him with my messkit. But really, I'm getting quite an education about living with different people. We all get along well together. We all crab, we all would like to be home; we bother one another continually, and it's almost impossible to keep out of a bull session. I had to hide in order to write to you they kept bothering me so much. They have nicknamed me "Teach," because they know I was a teacher. But I guess I've made some pretty good friends at that.

Well dearest, I'm going to close now and try and sneak out to mail this letter. Hope I don't get caught. Be a good girl and love me and just never stop, because I love you so very much that I never want to lose you. Remember that you're mine and I'm yours for always.

All My Love,

Dick

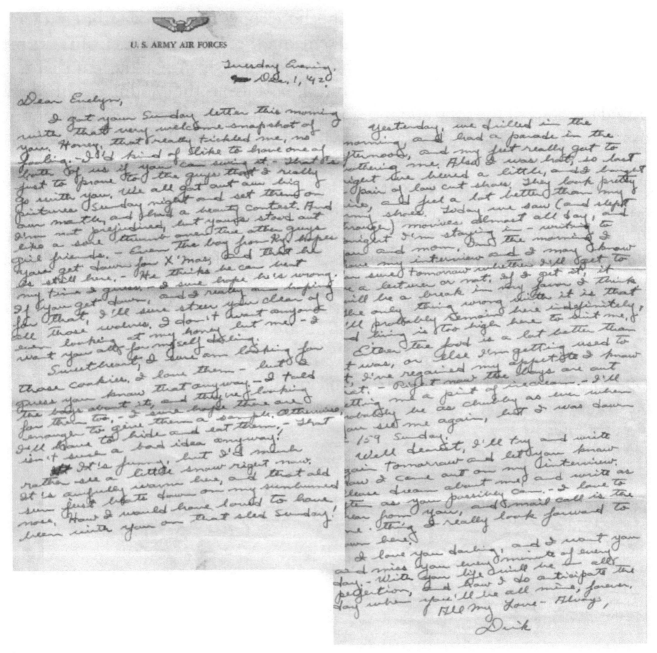

Tuesday Evening, Dec. 1, 1942

Dear Evelyn,

I got your Sunday letter this morning with that very welcome snapshot of you. Honey, that really tickled me, no fooling. I'd kind of like to have one of both of us if you can swing it. That's just to prove to the guys that I really go with you. We all got out our big pictures Sunday night and set them on our mantle, and had a beauty contest. And I'm not prejudiced, but you stood out like a sore thumb over the other guys girl friends. Even the boy from Ky. hopes you get down for X-Mas, and that he is still here. He thinks he can beat my time I guess. I sure hope he's wrong. If you get down, and I really am hoping for that, I'll sure steer you clear of all those wolves. I don't want anyone even looking at my honey but me. I want you all for myself darling.

Sweetheart, I sure am looking for those cookies. I love them—but I guess you know that anyway. I told the boys about it, and they're looking for them too. I sure hope there are enough to givethem a sample. Otherwise, I'll have to hide and eat them. That isn't such a bad idea anyway!

It's funny, but I'd much rather see a little snow right now. It's awfully warm here, and that old sun just beats down on my sunburned nose. How I would have loved to have been with you on that sled Sunday!

Yesterday, we drilled in the morning, and had a parade in the afternoon, and my feet really got to bothering me. Also I was hot, so last night we beered a little, and I bought a pair of low cut shoes. They look pretty nice, and feel a lot better than my army shoes. Today we saw (and slept through) movies almost all day, and tonight I'm staying in—writing to you and mom. In the morning I have my interview and I may know for sure tomorrow whether I'll get to be a lecturer or not. If I get it, it will be a break in my favor I think. The only thing wrong with it is that I'll probably remain here indefinitely, and living is too high here to suit me.

Either the food is a lot better than it was, or else I'm getting used to it, I've regained my appetite I know that. Right now the boys are out getting me a pint of ice cream. I'll probably be as chubby as ever when you see me again, but I was down to 159 Sunday.

Well dearest, I'll try and write again tomorrow and let you know how I came out on my interview. Please dream about me, and write as often as you possibly can. I love to hear from you, and mail call is the one thing I really look forward to down here.

I love you darling, and I want you and miss you every minute of every day. With you life will be—all perfection, and how I do anticipate the day when you'll be all mine, forever,

All My Love—Always,

Dick

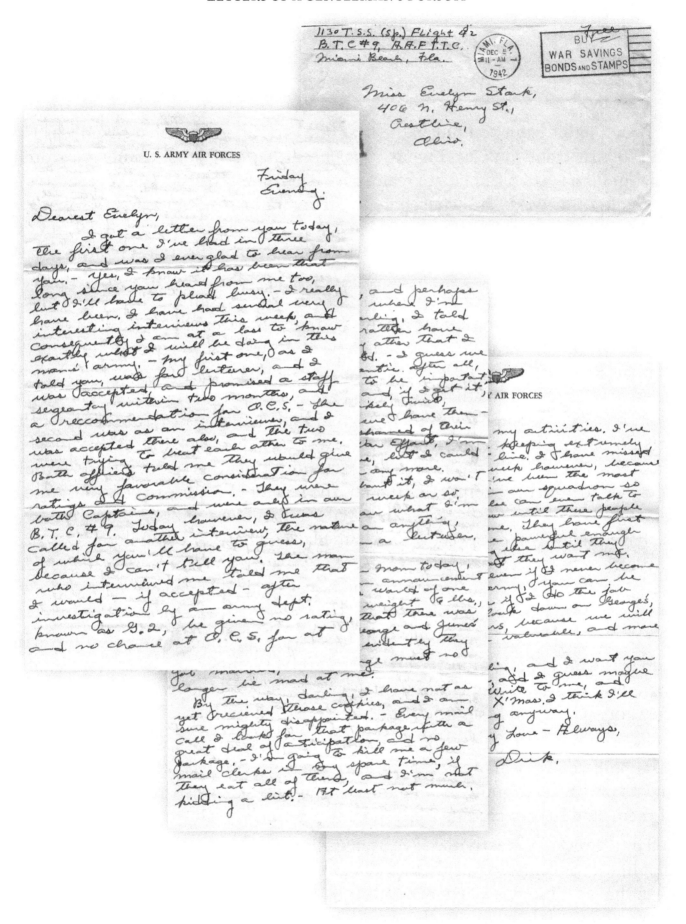

1130 T.S.S. (Sp.) Flight #2
B.T.C. #9, A.A.F.T.C.
Miami Beach, Fla.

BUY
WAR SAVINGS
BONDS AND STAMPS

Miss Evelyn Stark,
406 N. Henry St.,
Crestline,
Ohio.

U. S. ARMY AIR FORCES

Friday
Evening.

Dearest Evelyn,

I got a letter from you today, the first one I've had in three days, and was I ever glad to hear from you. — Yes, I know it has been that long since you heard from me too, but I'll have to plead busy. — I really have been. I have had several very interesting interviews this week, and consequently I am at a loss to know exactly what I will be doing in this man' army. — My first one, as I told you, was for Lecturer, and I was accepted and promised a staff sergeantcy within two months, and a recommendation for O.C.S. — The second was as an interviewer, and I was accepted there also, and the two were trying to beat each other to me. Both officers told me they would give me very favorable consideration for ratings & commission. — They were both Captains, and were only in our B.T.C. #9. Today however, I was called for another interview, the nature of which you'll have to guess, because I can't tell you. The man who interviewed me told me that I would — if accepted — after investigation by an army dept. known as G.2, be given no rating, and no chance at O.C.S. for at least...

By the way, darling, I have not as yet received those cookies, and I am sure mighty disappointed. — Every mail call I look for that package with a great deal of anticipation, and no package. — I'm going to kill me a few mail clerks in my spare time, if they eat all of them, and I'm not kidding a bit! — At least not much.

[right column fragments]

... and perhaps ... where I'm ... darling, I told ... rather have ... after that I ... — I guess we ... entic. after all, ... to be important, ... and, if I get it, ... isely finish, ... we have them — ... ashamed of their ... Effort, I'm ... list I could ... any more. ... bout it, I won't ... week or so ... what I'm ... anything, ... a lecturer.

... mom today, ... announcement ... word of one ... weight to lbs., ... that there was ... eorge and James ... sidently they ... ge must no

... my activities. I've ... keeping extremely ... ive. I have missed ... week however, because ... be been the most ... in our squadron so ... lse can even talk to ... w until these people ... me. They have first ... e powerful enough ... elie until they ... t they want me. ... even if I never become ... army, you can be ... if I do the job ... look down on George's, ... rs, because we will ... valuable, and more

... ling, and I want you ... add I guess maybe ... write to me, and ... X'mas. I think I'll ... g anyway.

y Love — Always,

Dick.

189

POSTMARKED MIAMI, FLORIDA—DECEMBER 5, 1942

Friday Evening

Dearest Evelyn,

I got a letter from you today, the first one I've had in three days, and was I ever glad to hear from you. Yes, I know it has been that long since you heard from me too, but I'll have to plead busy. I really have been. I have had several very interesting interviews this week, and consequently I am at a loss to know exactly what I will be doing in this mans' army. My first one, as I told you, was for lecturer, and I was accepted, and promised a staff sergeantry within two months, and a recommendation for O.C.S. The second was as an interviewer, and I was accepted there also, and the two were trying to beat each other to me. Both officers told me they would give me very favorable consideration for ratings and commission. They were both Captains, and were only in our B.T.C. #9. Today however, I was called for another interview, the nature of which you'll have to guess, because I can't tell you. The man who interviewed me told me that I would—if accepted—after investigation by an army dept. known as G.2., be given no rating, and no chance at O.C.S. for at least three months, and perhaps never, depending on where I'm placed. However, darling, I told them that I would rather have such a job than any other that I know of, and I would. I guess we all are a little romantic after all, and have some desire to be important. The job is important, and if I get it, which I more than likely will, our children—when we have them—will not need to be ashamed of their father's part in the War effort. I'm sorry to be so secretive, but I could be shot if I told you any more. However, don't worry about it, I won't know for sure for a week or so. If anyone even asks you what I'm doing, or trying for, or anything, tell them that I am a lecturer. I may be yet.

I got a letter from mom today, and she sent me an announcement of the arrival into this world of one Judith Ann Rafferty weight 6 lbs., 6 oz., also mom said that there was an announcement of George and Junes' wedding sent out, so evidently they got married, and George must no longer be mad at me.

By the way, darling, I have not as yet received those cookies, and I am sure mighty disappointed. Every mail call I look for that package with a great deal of anticipation, and no package. I'm going to kill me a few mail clerks in my spare time, if they eat all of them, and I'm not kidding a bit. At least not much.

For the rest of my activities. I've been drilling, and keeping extremely busy along that line. I have missed calisthenics all week however, because of my interviews. I've been the most interviewed man in our squadron so far, but no one else can even talk to me about a job now until these people are through with me. They have to first call on me, and are powerful enough to hold up everything else until they decide whether or not they want me. Once again darling, even if I never become an officer in this army, you can be kind of proud of me if I do the job well, and we can look down on Georges', Toms' & Murrays' bars, because we will have done a more valuable, and more trustworthy job.

I love you darling, and I want you to be proud of me, and I guess maybe you can be now. Write to me, and plan to come here X-Mas. I think I'll be here that long anyways.

All My Love—Always,

Dick

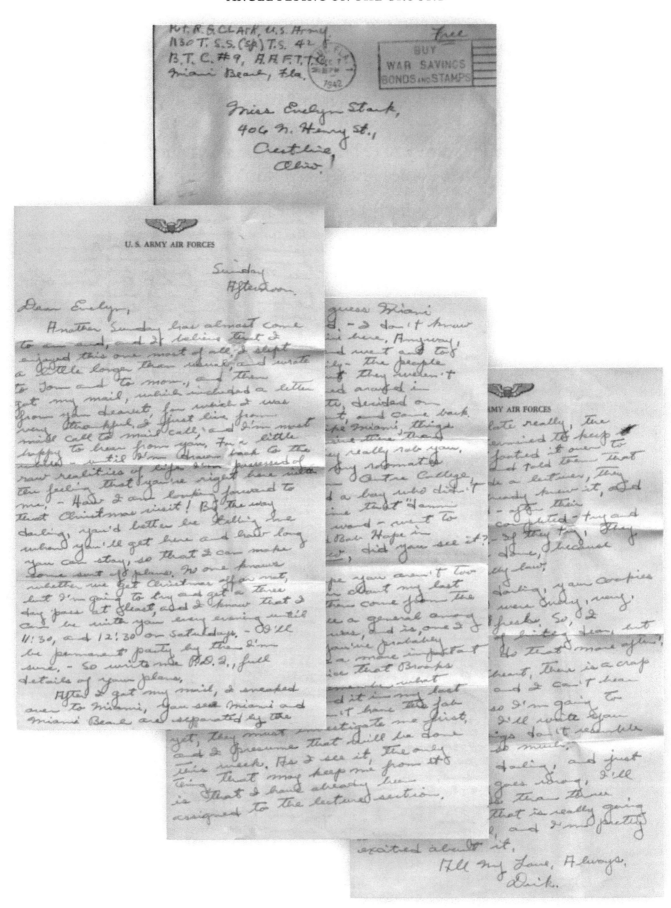

Postmarked Miami, Florida—December 7, 1942

(Note: One Year Anniversary of Pearl Harbor)

Sunday Afternoon

Dear Evelyn,

Another Sunday has almost come to an end, and I believe that I enjoyed this one most of all. I slept a little longer than usual, and wrote to Tom and to mom, and then got my mail, which included a letter from you dearest, for which I was very thankful. I just live from mail call to mail call, and I'm most happy to hear from you. For a little while—until I'm drawn back to the raw realities of life I'm possessed of the feeling that you're right here with me. How I am looking forward to that Christmas visit! By the way darling, you'd better be telling me when you'll get here and how long you can stay, so that I can make some sort of plans. No one knows whether we get Christmas off or not, but I'm going to try and get a three day pass at least, and I know that I can be with you every evening until 11:30, and 12:30 on Saturdays. I'll be permanent party by then I'm sure. So write me P.D.Q., full details of your plans.

After I got my mail, I sneaked over to Miami, you see Miami and Miami Beach are separated by the ocean, actually I guess Miami Beach is an Island. I don't know for sure—I just live here. Anyway, I went to Miami and went out to see the Bella family—the people from Grove City—but they weren't at home, so I wandered around in down town Miami, ate, decided on your Christmas present, and came back. I think I would like Miami, things are much less expensive there than here. Out here they really rob you.

Last night one of my roommates and I—he's from Center College, a horse player, and a boy who didn't know for a long time that "damn yankee" wasn't one word—went to see Bing Crosby and Bob Hope in The Road to Morocco, did you see it?

Sweetheart, I hope you aren't too much up in the air about my last letter. I had just then come from the interview, I did see a general among others, and the job was, and is, one I really would love. You've probably guessed what, it is a more important part of the same service that Brooks was in—if you remember what that was. You'll find it in my last letter. However, I don't have the job yet, they must investigate me first, and I presume that will be done this week. As I see it, the only thing that may keep me from it is that I have already been assigned to the lecture section.

They were too late really, the lecturers are determined to keep me, but I had floated it over to this other place and told them that I had been made a lecturer, they told me they already knew it, and that they would—after their investigation is completed—try and get me out of it. If they try, they can get the job done, because their word is really law.

By the way darling, your cookies came, and they were very, very, good, and still fresh. So, I wouldn't think of biting dear, but why don't we do that more often?

Well sweetheart, there is a crap game going on, and I can't hear myself think, so I'm going to quit for now, I'll write you more when things don't resemble a madhouse so much.

I love you darling, and just think, if nothing goes wrong, I'll see you in less than three weeks. Honey that is really going to be wonderful, and I'm pretty excited about it.

All My Love, Always,

Dick

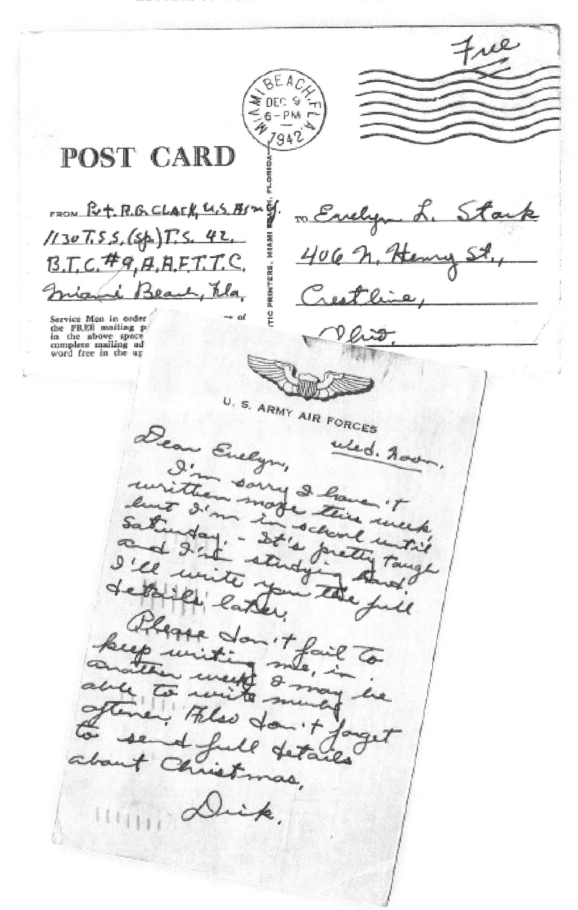

POST CARD

FROM Pvt. R.G. Clark, U.S. Army
1130 T.S.S. (Sp) T.S. 42,
B.T.C. #9, A.A.F.T.T.C.
Miami Beach, Fla.

Service Men in order
the FREE mailing p
in the above space
complete mailing ad
word free in the up

TO Evelyn L. Stark
406 N. Henry St.,
Crestline,
Ohio.

MIAMI BEACH, FLA.
DEC 8
6—PM
1942

Free

U. S. ARMY AIR FORCES

Wed. Noon,

Dear Evelyn,

I'm sorry I haven't written more this week but I'm in school until Saturday. — It's pretty tough and I've studying. And I'll write you the full details later.

Please don't fail to keep writing me, in another week I may be able to write much oftener. Also don't forget to send full details about Christmas,

Dick.

Wednesday Afternoon

Dear Evelyn,

I'm sorry I haven't written more this week but I'm in school until Saturday. It's pretty tough and I'm studying hard. I'll write you the full details later.

Please don't fail to keep writing me; in another week I may be able to write more often. Also don't forget to send full details about Christmas.

Dick

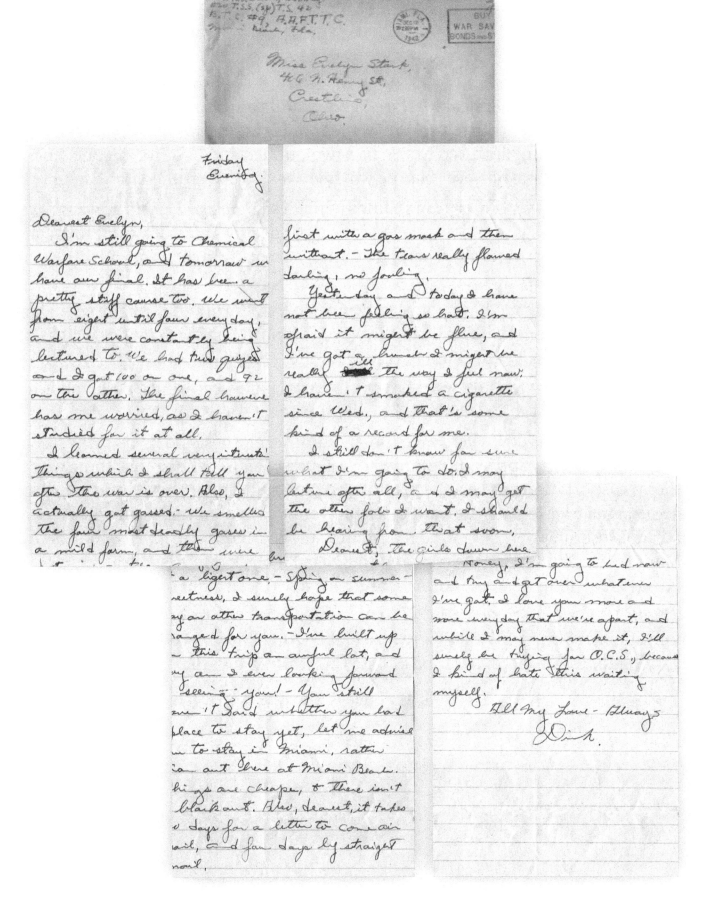

Friday
Evening.

Dearest Evelyn,

I'm still going to Chemical Warfare School, and tomorrow we have our final. It has been a pretty stiff course too. We went from eight until four every day, and we were constantly being lectured to. We had two quizes and I got 100 on one, and 92 on the other. The final however has me worried, as I haven't studied for it at all.

I learned several very interesting things which I shall tell you after the war is over. Also, I actually got gassed. We smelled the four most deadly gases in a mild form, and then were [ ] [ ] [ ]

first with a gas mask and then without. — The tears really flowed darling, no fooling.

Yesterday and today I have not been feeling so hot. I'm afraid it might be flue, and I've got a hunch I might be really ill the way I feel now. I haven't smoked a cigarette since Wed., and that's some kind of a record for me.

I still don't know for sure what I'm going to do. I may lecture after all, and I may get the other job I want. I should be hearing from that soon.

Dearest, the girls down here

a light one. — Spring or summer sweetness, I surely hope that some way or other transportation can be arranged for you. — I've built up this trip an awful lot, and boy am I even looking forward seeing you! — You still [ ]'t said whether you had place to stay yet, let me advise to stay in Miami, rather ia out here at Miami Beach. hings are cheaper, & there isn't blackout. Also, dearest, it takes days for a letter to come air ail, and four days by straight mail.

Honey, I'm going to bed now and try and get over whatever I've got. I love you more and more everyday that we're apart, and while I may never make it, I'll surely be trying for O.C.S., because I kind of hate this waiting myself.

All My Love — Always
Dick.

POSTMARKED MIAMI, FLORIDA—DECEMBER 12, 1942

Friday Evening

Dearest Evelyn,

I'm still going to Chemical Warfare School, and tomorrow we have our final. It has been a pretty stiff course too. We went from eight until four every day, and we were constantly being lectured to. We had two quizzes and I got 100 on one, and 92 on the other. The final however has me worried, as I haven't studied for it at all.

I learned several very interesting things which I shall tell you after the war is over. Also, I actually got gassed. We smelled four most deadly gases in a mild form, and then were put in a tear gas chamber first with a gas mask and then without. The tears really flowed darling, no fooling.

Yesterday and today I have not been feeling so hot. I'm afraid it might be flu, and I've got a hunch I might be really ill the way I feel now. I haven't smoked a cigarette since Wed., and that's some kind of record for me.

I still don't know for sure what I'm going to do. I may lecture after all, and I may get the other job I want. I should be hearing from that soon.

Dearest, the girls down here wear mostly summer clothes, and if you bring a coat, make it a light one. Spring or summer—Sweetness, I surely hope that some way or other transportation can be arranged for you. I've built up for this trip an awful lot, and boy am I ever looking forward to seeing you! You still haven't said whether you had a place to stay yet. Let me advise you to stay in Miami, rather than out here at Miami Beach. Things are cheaper, and there isn't a black out. Also, dearest, it takes two days for a letter to come air mail, and four days by straight mail.

Honey, I'm going to bed now and try and get over whatever I've got. I love you more and more every day that we're apart, and while I may never make it, I'll surely be trying for O.C.S., because I kind of hate this waiting myself.

All My Love—Always,

Dick

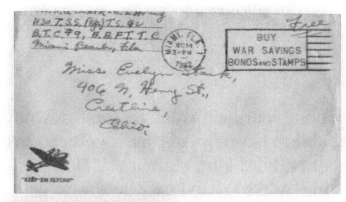

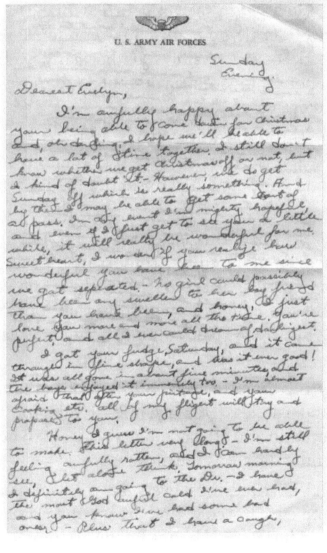

POSTMARKED MIAMI, FLORIDA—DECEMBER 14, 1942

Sunday Evening

Dearest Evelyn,

I'm awfully happy about your being able to come down for Christmas and, oh darling, I hope we'll be able to have a lot of time together. I still don't know whether we get Christmas off or not, but I kind of doubt it. However, we do get Sunday off which is really something. And by then I may be able to get some sort of a pass. In any event I'm mighty hopeful, and even if I just get to see you a little while, it will really be wonderful for me. Sweetheart, I wonder if you realize how wonderful you have been to me since we got separated. No girl could possibly have been any sweller to her boy friend than you have been, and honey, I just love you more and more all the time. You're perfect, and all I ever could dream of, darlingest.

I got your fudge, Saturday, and it came through in fine shape, and was it ever good! It was all gone in about five minutes, and the boys enjoyed it immensely too. I'm almost afraid that after your picture, and your cooking etc. all of my flight will try and propose to you.

Honey I guess I'm not going to be able to make this letter very long. I'm still feeling awfully rotten, and I can hardly see, let alone think. Tomorrow morning I definitely am going to the Dr. I have the most God awful cold I've ever had, and you know I've had some bad ones. Plus that I have a cough, some chest irritation, and some temperature. Don't worry, I'll be O.K., but I really feel bad right now, and I want to be O.K. for Christmas. In fact I want to be in A-1 shape, why? You guess?

There is not much more news than I wrote the other day. I think I did pass my Chemical Warfare Course pretty high, and—at least for a while—I imagine I'll lecture, and on that subject. Yesterday afternoon and all day today I've spent in bed, trying to cure my cold. I've been nervous and irritable as the dickens too.

Sweetness, I'm going to quit for now, but I'll write almost every day this week, and that's a promise. I'm going to bed again, and cure my cold, and dream of your dear. If you know where you're going to stay down here, you'd better let me know at once in case I can't meet you when you get in, and also—I stay at the Croydon Arms Hotel

(I shouldn't tell you that)—It's at 38th & Collins—Miami Beach. I could be called at noon, or in the evening around six o'clock. Just in case we can't get connected any other way. Write and tell me your suggestion right away.

Goodnight darling, I'll see you and I love you—now and forever,

Dick

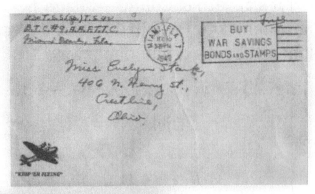

U. S. ARMY AIR FORCES

Monday
Evening
Dec. 14, '42.

Dearest Evelyn,

If you and mom aren't really too wonderful to me. I got your Christmas present today, and it is really perfect. It is the nicest watch I ever saw, and I really do appreciate it. You're just too good to me, you'll spoil me, and after we're married I'll be just awfully hard to handle. Darling, not only does this year will surely my present to you, but please believe that it doesn't measure up, and I don't want it to, and — it isn't that a present coming sometime you will have this year that I hope you'll like. You know what it is and as soon as I can accumulate enough it'll sure be forthcoming.

Honey I do love you so very much, you're really wonderful to me, and I only hope I can spend my life being good to you, and taking care of you, and just being happy with you. You're mine and I'm yours, and I'm so happy.

There isn't anything new with me that you don't already know except that I think the flu has left me, and now all I have is a rotten cold, and I surely hope I'm over that by Christmas, because I'm awfully likely to kiss you, cold and all, and I wouldn't want

you aunt to catch cold.

Sweetheart, it has been mighty cold here the last couple of days. You'd better bring a wool dress, and maybe one coat. Of course it'll probably be hot again when you get here. Also, bring a bathing suit, we may not go swimming, but we might want to. — You may get to even if I don't have time.

Well honey, here it is about time for lights out again, so goodnight, and remember I think about you always, and I love you always too. — Dream about me, for I know I'll dream of you.

Goodnight,
Dick.

P.S. — Don't fail to tell me where you're going to stay so that we can make connections. P.S.2.

Love
Dick.

POSTMARKED MIAMI, FLORIDA—DECEMBER 15, 1942

Monday Evening Dec 14, 1942

Dearest Evelyn,

If you and mom aren't really too wonderful to me. I got your Christmas present today, and it's really perfect. It's the nicest watch I ever saw, and I really do appreciate it. You're just too good to me, you'll spoil me, and after we're married I'll be just awfully hard to handle. Darlingest, my present to you this year will surely not measure up, but please believe that it isn't that I don't want it to, and—you will have a present coming sometime this year that I hope you'll like. You know what it is, and as soon as I can accumulate enough it'll sure be forthcoming!

Honey I do love you so very much, you're really wonderful to me, and I only hope I can spend my life being good to you, and taking care of you, and just being happy with you. You're mine and I'm yours, and I'm so happy.

There isn't anything new with me that you don't already know except that I think the flu has left me, and now all I have is a rotten cold. I surely hope I'm over that by Christmas, because I'm awfully likely to kiss you, auntie and all, and I wouldn't want your aunt to catch cold.

Sweetheart, it has been mighty cold here the last couple of days. You'd better bring a wool dress, and maybe one coat. Of course it'll probably be hot again when you get here. Also, bring a bathing suit, we may not go swimming, but—we might want to. You may get to even if I don't have time.

Well honey, here it is about time for lights out again, so goodnight, and remember I think about you always, and love you always too. Dream about me, for I know I'll dream of you.

Goodnight,

Dick

P.S. Don't fail to tell me where you're going to stay so that we can make connections P.D.Q.

Love

Dick

U. S. ARMY AIR FORCES

Thursday
Evening.

Dearest Evelyn,

In another week you'll be just about in Georgia someplace, watching the red clay roads pass by, and seeing the picaninnies, half clothed and starving. Every minute of that time you'll be speeding closer and closer to me darling. I'll be awfully anxious, and my heart will speed as fast as the train wheels turn. — I'm really just beginning to realize that you are coming sweetheart.

The reason I haven't written since Monday is that time has been working against me again, and today is the first that I have really had time to do anything. Yesterday I drilled all day, and last night I made an illicit trip to Miami and got your Christmas present under control. Tuesday too I drilled and Tuesday night our room was "gigged" and we had to stay in and clean it. By the time it was inspected it was time for lights out, and to bed again.

Honey, I'm sorry about opening my Christmas present, but I had! & yet recieved your letter telling me not to open it, and if you have ever recieved a registered package, you'll know how curious I was. I had no idea what was in it, and believe me darling, I'm so proud of

my watch that it will still be new to me and very wonderful Christmas day. Anyway, you're really all the Christmas present I'll need to make things seem like Christmas.

Darling, today everything happened at once. All three of my possibilities for jobs came through; they wanted me for interviewer, lecturer, and for S 2. S 2 had the authority to take me away from the other two, and so I'll be definitely in that finest branch of the service there is, and if I'm successful they'll almost automatically make an officer out of me. By summer I ought to be a cinch darling, and you know what that means to you and I.

Well sweetheart, I know this is short and there is just one more thing I want to tell you I may not be at the Copter Arms next week this time, so it's awfully important that I know where you're going to stay. Let me know right away if you can. If not, I will — if I'm off — try and meet your train Friday morning. Otherwise, I'm going to refer you to the Bellens. They live at ☒☒ N. E. 5th Ave, Miami. Go there and let 6522 them know where you are, or call Walter Bellen at the Naval Recruiting office and tell him. If that doesn't work, and we haven't made connections by then, meet me at 7:30 P.M. Friday evening in Walgreen's at their soda fountain. This is at the corner of E. Flagler and (?), it's about two blocks away from Miami Ave., which is the center of town.

Write, and All My Love — Always,

Dick

POSTMARKED MIAMI, FLORIDA—DECEMBER 18, 1942

Thursday Evening

Dearest Evelyn,

In another week you'll be just about in Georgia someplace, watching the red clay roads pass by, and seeing the picaninnies, half clothed and starving. Every minute of that time you'll be speeding closer and closer to me darling. I'll be awfully anxious, and my heart will speed as fast as the train wheels turn. I'm really just beginning to realize that you are coming sweetheart.

The reason I haven't written since Monday is that time has been working against me again, and today is the first that I have really had time to do anything. Yesterday I drilled all day, and last night I made an illicit trip to Miami and got your Christmas present under control. Tuesday too I drilled and Tuesday night our room was "gigged" and we had to stay in and clean it. By the time it was inspected it was time for lights out, and to bed again.

Honey, I'm sorry about opening my Christmas present, but I hadn't yet received your letter telling me not to open it; and if you have ever received a registered package, you'll know how curious I was. I had no idea what was in it, and believe me darling, I'm so proud of my watch that it will still be new to me and very wonderful Christmas day. Anyways, you're really all the Christmas present I'll need to make things seem like Christmas.

Darling, today everything happened at once. All three of my possibilities for jobs came through; they wanted me for interviewer, lecturer and for S2. S2 had the authority to take me away from the other two, and so I'll be definitely in that finest branch of the service there is, and if I'm successful they'll almost automatically make an officer out of me. By summer I ought to be a cinch darling, and you know what that means to you and I.

Well sweetheart, I know this is short, and there is just one more thing I want to tell you. I may not be at the Croydon Arms next week this time, so it's awfully important that I know where you're going to stay. Let me know right away if you can. If not, I will—if I am off—try and meet your train Friday morning. Otherwise, I'm going to refer you to the Bellars. They live at 6522 N.E. 5th Ave, Miami. Go there and let them know where you are, or call Walter Bellar at the Naval Recruiting Office and tell him.

If that doesn't work, and we haven't made connections by then, meet me at 7:30 P.M. Friday Evening in Walgreen's at their soda fountain. This is at the Corner of E.Flagler and (?), it's about two blocks away from Miami Ave., which is the center of town.

Write, and All My Love—Always,

Dick

U. S. ARMY AIR FORCES

Friday Evening.

Dearest Evelyn,

A week from tonight we'll be together darling, and I'll be the happiest man alive. The moon should be full, and Miami will be a very beautiful place to be — with you. Honey, I'll almost certainly be here at the Dayton Arms just in case we miss connections otherwise. You can call me here. However, I'll more than likely be able to meet your train Friday morning. I'm going to try to anyway. But don't forget about meeting me at Walgreens at 7:30 Friday evening if all other connections fail. If possible let me know where you're staying ahead of time. — I may have an even surer way of getting in touch with me by then though, and if I do I'll write you air mail tomorrow night. I don't want to make any false statements, but by the time you get here, I'll probably have a pass allowing me to stay out as late as I please, in which case we can really be together in the evenings — Everything is breaking our way Sweets.

Sweetheart, I started to work on my new job today. I can't tell you the nature of the work because I'm sworn to secrecy, and could be executed if I told you any of the details. But I am in S2, or Air Corps Intelligence, which is army secret service. You can tell that to anyone you want to

... me, although "be careful and ... that the Nazis get hold of it." Ha! ... make good, I will be given ... training in about three months. ... means, unless something happens, ... about June I'll get some ... But let's not count on them ... they are actually on my shoulders. ... really never knows in the army. ... make it, you know that I ... you to truly (loyally) be mine ... and ever. — Now you've got ... dawn! — Ha! Well ... it's time for "lights out," so ... see for now. I may write ... tomorrow and then I'll look ... to seeing you and won't ... anymore. I love you ... with all my heart, and ... night, and I always shall.

All My Love — Always,

Dick.

Wire me if you have a ... in plans, or find out ... you're going to stay.

Friday Evening

Dearest Evelyn,

A week from tonight we'll be together darling, and I'll be the happiest man alive. The moon should be full, and Miami will be a very beautiful place to be—with you. Honey, I'll almost certainly be here at the Croydon Arms just in case we miss connections otherwise. You can call me here. However, I'll more than likely be able to meet your train Friday morning, I'm going to try to anyway. But don't forget about meeting me at Walgreens at 7:30 Friday evening if all other connections fail. If possible, let me know where you're staying ahead of time. I may have an even surer way of getting in touch with me by then though, and if I do I'll write you an air mail tomorrow night. I don't want to make any false statements, but by the time you get here, I'll probably have a pass allowing me to stay out as late as I please. In which case we can really be together in the evenings. Everything is breaking our way dearest.

Sweetheart, I started to work on my new job today. I can't tell you the nature of the work because I'm sworn to secrecy, and could be executed if I told you any of the details. But I am in S2, or Air Corps Intelligence, which is Army Secret Service. You can tell that to anyone you want to at home, although "be careful and don't let the Nazi's get hold of it." Ha!

If I make good, I will be given officer training in about three months. Which means, unless something happens, that about June I'll get some gold bars.But let's not count on them until they are actually on my shoulders. One really never knows in the army. If I do make it, you know that I want you to truly (legally) be mine forever and ever. Now you've got me pinned down! Ha! Well darling it's time for "lights out," so I'll close for now. I may write again tomorrow, and then I'll look forward to seeing you and won't write anymore. I love you dearest with all my heart, and soul, and might, and I always shall,

All My Love—Always,

Dick

P.S. Wire me if you have a change in plans or find out where you're going to stay.

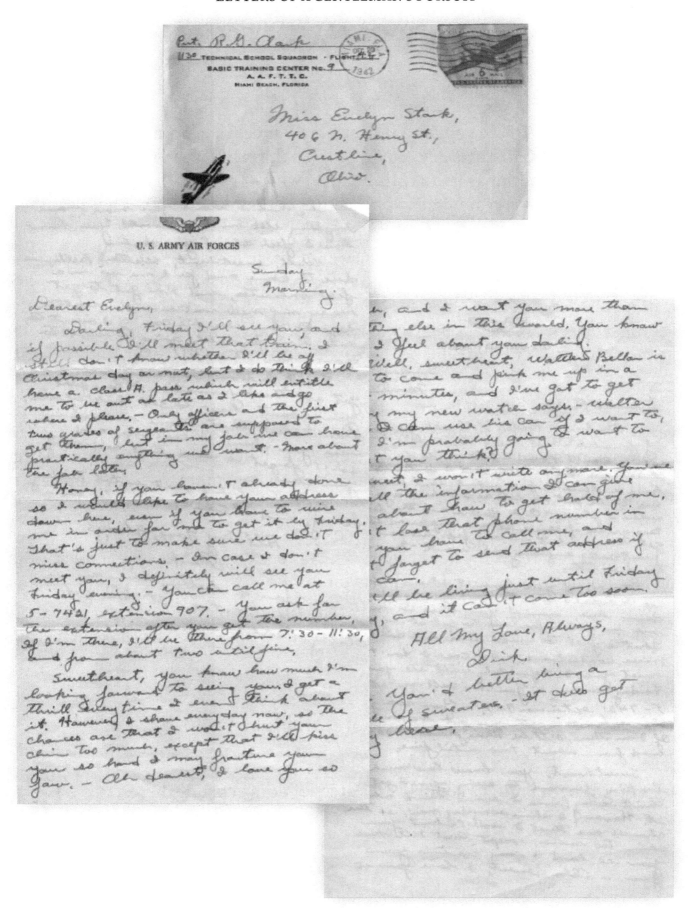

U. S. ARMY AIR FORCES

Sunday
Morning.

Dearest Evelyn,

Darling, Friday I'll see you, and if possible I'll meet that train. I still don't know whether I'll be off Christmas day or not, but I do think I'll have a class A. pass, which will entitle me to be out as late as I like and go where I please, — Only officers and the first two grades of sergeants are supposed to get them, but in my field we can have practically anything we want. — More about the pass later.

Honey, if you haven't already done so I would like to have your address down here, even if you have to wire me in order for me to get it by Friday. That's just to make sure we don't miss connections. — In case I don't meet you, I definitely will see you Friday evening. — You can call me at 5-7421, extension 907. — You ask for the extension after you get the number, if I'm there, I'll be there from 7:30 - 11:30, and from about two until five.

Sweetheart, you know how much I'm looking forward to seeing you, I get a thrill everytime I even think about it. However I shave everyday now, so the chances are that I won't hurt your chin too much, except that I'll kiss you so hard I may fracture your jaw. — Oh dearest, I love you so

——, and I want you more than any else in this world. You know I feel about you darling.

Well, sweetheart, Walter Bellar is to come and pick me up in a minutes, and I've got to get my new watch says, — Walter I can use his car if I want to, I'm probably going to want to what you think?

——, I won't write anymore. You all the information I can give about how to get hold of me, lose that phone number in have to call me, and forget to send that address if can.

I'll be living just until Friday and it can't come too soon.

All My Love, Always,
Dick.

You + better bring a lot of sweaters. — It does get y here.

Sunday Evening

Dearest Evelyn,

Darling, Friday I'll see you, and if possible I'll meet that train. I still don't know whether I'll be off Christmas day or not, but I do think I'll have a Class A pass which will entitle me to be out as late as I like and go where I please. Only officers and the first two grades of sergeants are supposed to get them but in my job we can have practically anything we want. More about the job later.

Honey, if you haven't already done so I would like to have your address down here, even if you have to wire me in order for me to get it by Friday. That's just to make sure we don't miss connections. In case I don't meet you, I definitely will see you Friday evening. You can call me at 5-7421, extension 907. You ask for the extension after you get the number. If I'm there, I'll be there from 7:30–11:30, and from about two until five.

Sweetheart, you know how much I'm looking forward to seeing you. I get a thrill every time I even think about it. However, I shave everyday now, so the chances are that I won't hurt your chin too much, except that I'll kiss you so hard I may fracture your jaw. Oh dearest, I love you so much, and I want you more than anything else in this world. You know how I feel about you darling.

Well, sweetheart, Walter Bellar is due to come and pick me up in a few minutes, and I've got to get ready my new watch says. Walter says I can use his car if I want to, and I'm probably going to want to don't you think?

Sweet, I won't write anymore. You've got all the information I can give you about how to get hold of me. Don't lose that phone number in case you have to call me, and don't forget to send that address if you can.

I'll be living just until Friday honey, and it can't come too soon.

All My Love, Always,

Dick

P.S. You'd better bring a couple of sweaters. It does get chilly here.

1943

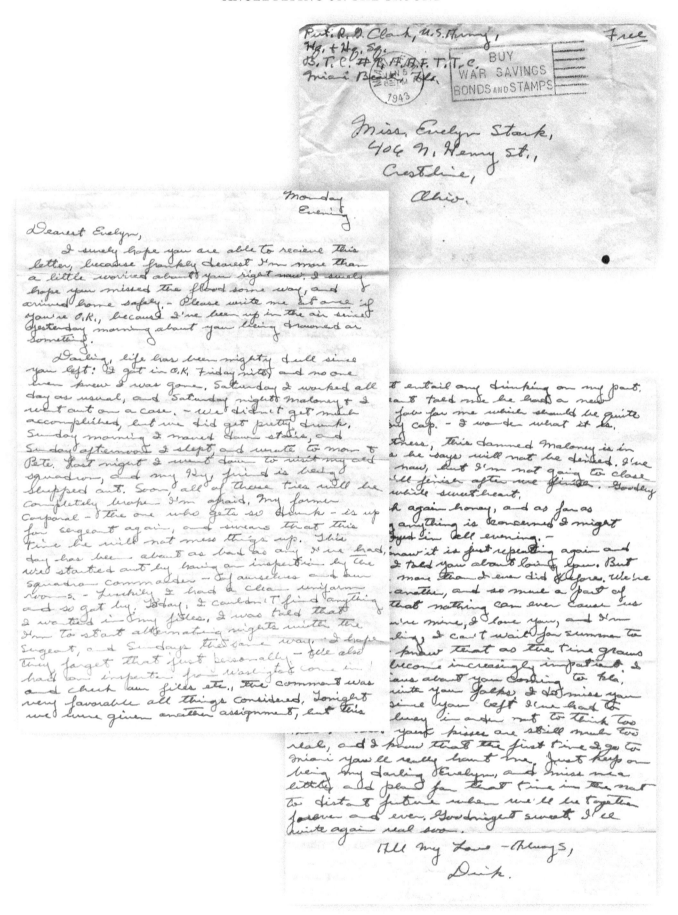

POSTMARKED MIAMI, FLORIDA—JANUARY 5, 1943

Monday Evening

Dearest Evelyn,

I surely hope you are able to receive this letter, because frankly dearest I'm more than a little worried about you right now, I surely hope you missed the flood some way, and arrived home safely—Please write me <u>at once</u> if you're O.K., because I've been up in the air since yesterday morning about you being drowned or something.

Darling, life has been mightly dull since you left: I got in O.K. Friday nite, and no one even knew I was gone. Saturday I worked all day as usual, and Saturday night Malone and I went out on a case. We didn't get much accomplished, but we did get pretty drunk. Sunday morning I moved downstairs, and Sunday afternoon I slept, and wrote to mom & Pete. Last night I went down to visit my old squadron, and my KY friend is being shipped out. Soon, all of those ties will be completely broken I'm afraid. My farmer corporal—the one who gets so drunk—is up for sergeant again, and swears that this time he will not mess things up. This day has been about as bad as any I've had. We started out by having an inspection by the squadron commander —of ourselves and our rooms. Luckily I had a clean uniform and so got by. Today, I couldn't find anything I wanted in my files. I was told that I'm to start alternating nights with the sergeant, and Sundays the same way. I hope they forget that personally We also had an inspector from Washington come in and check our files etc., the comment was very favorable all things considered. Tonight we were given another assignment, but this one will not entail any drinking on my part. Also, the sergeant told me he had a new every morning job for me which should be quite a feather in my cap—I wonder what it is.

Well, sweetness, this damned Maloney is in again, and as he says will not be denied. I've got to go for now, but I'm not going to close this letter. I'll finish after we finish. Goodbye for a little while sweetheart.

I'm back again honey, and as far as accomplishing anything is concerned I might better have stayed in all evening.

Honey, I know it is just repeating again and again what I told you about loving you. But I do, I think more than I ever did before. We're so sure of one another, and so much a part of one another that nothing can ever cause us to change. You're mine, I love you, and I'm yours. Oh darling, I can't wait for summer to come, and I know that as the time grows shorter I'll become increasingly impatient. I still am serious about you coming to Fla. this winter with your folks. I do miss you sweet, and since you left

I've had to keep myself busy in order not to think too much—But your kisses are still much too real, and I know that the first time I go to Miami you'll really haunt me. Just keep on being my darling Evelyn, and miss me a little, and plan for that time in the not too distant future when we'll be together forever and ever. Goodnight sweet, I'll write again real soon.

All My Love—Always,

Dick

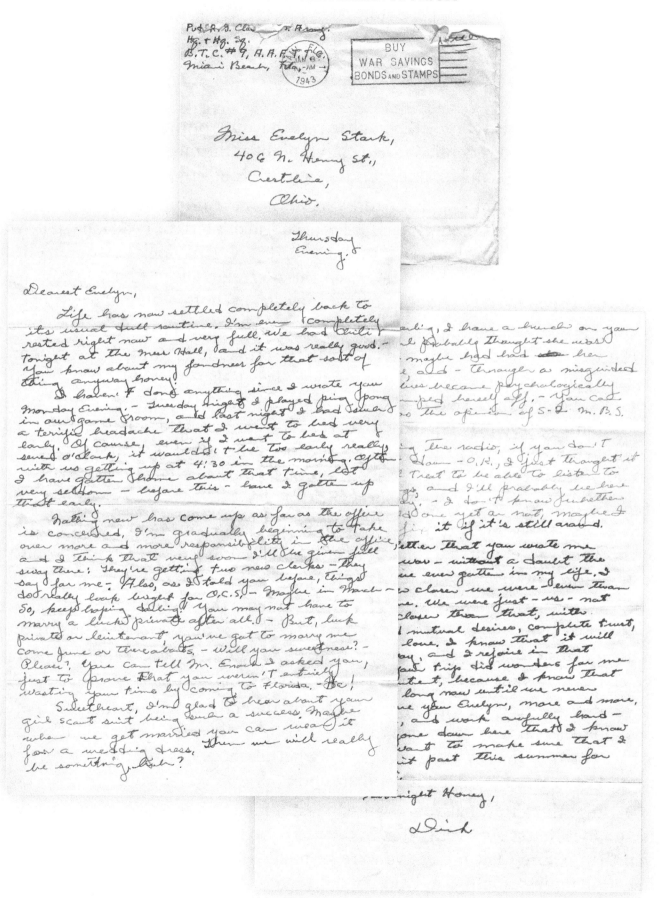

Thursday Evening

Dearest Evelyn,

Life has now settled completely back to its usual dull routine. I'm even completely rested right now and very full. We had chili tonight at the mess hall, and it was really good. You know about my fondness for that sort of thing anyway honey.

I haven't done anything since I wrote you Monday evening. Tuesday night I played ping pong in our game room, and last night I had such a terrific headache that I went to bed very early. Of course, even if I went to bed at seven o'clock, it wouldn't be too early really, with us getting up at 4:30 in the morning. Often I have gotten home about that time, but very seldom—before this—have I gotten up that early.

Nothing new has come up as far as the office is concerned, I'm gradually beginning to take over more and more responsibility in the office, and I think that very soon I'll be given full sway there: They're getting two new clerks—they say for me. Also, as I told you before, things do really look bright for O.C.S. Maybe in March So, keep hoping darling! You may not have to marry a luck private after all. But, luck private or lieutenant, you've got to marry me come June or thereabouts. Will you sweetness? Please? You can tell Mr. Enoch I asked you, just to prove that you weren't entirely wasting your time by coming to Florida. Ha!

Sweetheart, I'm glad to hear about your girl scout suit being such a success. Maybe when we get married you can wear it for a wedding dress. Then we will really be something, huh?

By the way darling, I have a hunch on your suicide that the girl probably thought she was pregnant, or else—maybe had had her first sex experience, and—through a misguided sense of moral values became psychologically unstrung and bumped herself off. You can pass that along as the opinion of S – 2 M.B.S. Fla. Ha!

Honey, regarding the radio, if you don't want to send it down—O.K., I just thought it would be a real treat to be able to listen to one in the evenings, and I'll probably be here two months anyway. I don't know whether mom has our old one yet or not; maybe I can get her to fix it if it's still around.

Darling, the letter that you wrote me last Sunday night was—without a doubt the grandest letter I've ever gotten in my life. I too felt how much closer we were— even than before I left home. We were just—us—not two people, but closer than that, with understanding, and mutual desires, complete trust, and faith—and love. I know that it will be ever that way, and I rejoice in that feeling. Dearest, your trip did wonders for me too. Now I am content, because I know that it won't be too long now until we never part again. I love you Evelyn, more and more I plan and hope, and work awfully hard—harder than anyone down here that I know just because I want to make sure that I don't have to wait past this summer for you sweetheart.

Goodnight Honey,

Dick

Sunday
Afternoon,

Dearest Evelyn,

Today is like one of our early fall Sundays at home. Cool, much cooler than when you were down. My jacket feels good today. How I wish we were home with no war, and no gas rationing! On a day like this darling, we're going to take a trip down in the hills, getting up early, eating breakfast in Lancaster and then driving on clear to the river, stopping at some very wonderful place for dinner on the way. — Just you and I darling, the kids can stay at one of their grandmothers.

Life is going on here very much as always. I have been continuing taking on new things in the office, and I have also been out about three times this week on night assignment. Had it not been for that, I would have had to work today. Nothing very interesting developed in anything we were assigned, but we did by luck run into a Communist Party Leader whom we will probably have the goods on before too long.

One change did take place yesterday that may develop into something either very good or very bad. Our lieutenant was notified yesterday by wire that he is being sent to Washington at once, and so consequently the chances and that whatever amount of good feeling has been built up around him towards my chances for O.C.S. may vanish under a new officer. On the other hand, the guy may be O.K., and things could be even better than they are. — Here's hoping! Also, I found out that a new school is opening up, and I surely am interested. It's a school for Post War Administration in European conquered nations. If we can get that dearest, we'll see Europe, and also have a pretty good future in store for us. Would you like that sort of a set up? — It's just an idea now of course, but as lucky as I am, I might be able to do it.

... Bob yesterday, and he ... about another month of ... before the O.C.S. board, ... them as to whether he ...

... so unreal to me right ... that I was home and ... towards raising that ... seen that ... we're going to ... now represents seeing you ... here was wonderful, it ... as nearly long enough. It ... to me, and I can't ... here at all. All that is ... four thirty, mess kits, ... files, files, files, ... from home — spies, ... who never did ... enough to come to ... and palm trees etc., that ... else too is unreal! — Home ... a Shangri La, ... that happiness of being home! ... our old gang together ... and separation staring ... if Bob and Tom and ... and Brooks and Willett, ... will all get back ... a series of partings I guess, ... is stable and set ... now. Finally, after ... has proven fruitless I ... by a dynamic society. ... as I have never known ... life is you, a couple ... the kind of home life ...

I know we ultimately will have; friends — close friends — our friends now with the inevitable additions — leading a life that to many would seem drab and uninteresting, but our life together — with roots.

All my Love — Always and Always,
Dick.

POSTMARKED MIAMI, FLORIDA—JANUARY 10, 1943

Sunday Afternoon

Dearest Evelyn,

Today is like one of our early fall Sundays at home. Cool, much cooler than when you were down. My jacket feels good today. How I wish we were home with no war, and no gas rationing! On a day like this darling, we're going to take a trip down in the hills, getting up early, eating breakfast in Lancaster and then driving on clear to the river, stopping at some very wonderful place for dinner on the way. Just you and I darling, the kids can stay at one of their grandmothers.

Life is going on here very much as always. I have been continuing taking on new things in the office, and I have also been out about three times this week on night assignment. Had it not been for that, I would have had to work today. Nothing very interesting developed in anything we were assigned, but we did by luck run into a Communist Party Leader whom we will probably have the goods on before too long.

One change did take place yesterday that may develop into something either very good or very bad. Our lieutenant was notified yesterday by wire that he is being sent to Washington at once, and so consequently the chances are that whatever amount of good feeling has been built up around him towards my chances for O.C.S. may vanish under a new officer. On the other hand, the guy may be O.K., and things could be even better than they are. Here's hoping! Also, I found out that a new school is opening up and I surely am interested. It's a school for Post War Administration in European conquered nations. If we can get that dearest, we'll see Europe, and also have a pretty good future in store for, us. Would you like that sort of a set up? It's just an idea now of course, but as lucky as I am, I might be able to do it.

I got a letter from Bob yesterday, and he tells me that he has about another month of training before he goes before the O.C.S. board. Then of course it's up to them as to whether he makes it or not.

Darling, everything seems so unreal to me right now. I do wish very much that I was home and that we had a good start towards raising that quarterback and campus queen that we're going to turn out. Home to me now represents seeing you and mom. Your trip down here was wonderful, but I don't think it was nearly long enough. It does seem like a dream to me, and I can't really be sure you were here at all. All that is real is my getting up at four thirty, mess kits, soldiers and more soldiers, files, files, files, letters—dictation—letters from home—spies, saboteurs, communists, foreigners who never did anything except be smart enough to come to America; and the sun and palm trees etc., that is Miami. Everything else too is unreal! Home is like a mythical fairyland, a Shangri La.

How I long to regain that happiness of being home! How I would like to have our old gang together without the shadow of war and separation staring us all in the face. I wonder if Bob and Tom and George and Murray and Herb and Brooks and Willet, and Bill Moore and Pete will all get back safely again. Life is simply a series of partings I guess, and nothing is real, nothing is stable and set and fixed in life, and least not now. Finally, after the efforts of several professors has proven fruitless, I do realize what is meant by a dynamic society.

I know now dearest as I have never known before that all I want from life is you, a couple of kids, a nice home, and the kind of home life I know we ultimately will have; friends—close friends—our friends now with the inevitable additions—leading a life that to many would seem drab and uninteresting, but our life together—with roots.

All My Love—Always and Always,

Dick

Pvt. R. G. Clark, U. S. Army
Hq. + Hq. Sq. B.T.C.*
A.A.F.T.T.C.
Miami Beach * Florida

Miss. Evelyn Sterk,
406 N. Henry St.

Dear Evelyn,

Are you ever surprised to get a letter from me written on a
typewriter, or are you. I have been in the office all evening
working on my OCS application, and I have finally gotten it
to the point where I can send it in to the commanding officer,
with the approval of my officer. I don't know yet that I will
make the grade. The big problem is to get passed the examining
board, and if I can do that, I will be in for sure, probably in
the March class. My three choices were U.S. Army Administration,
Air Corps Administration, and Medical Corps Administration. If
all goes well, I will get assigned to the U.S. Army Administration
I don't particularly want either of the others. I don't want
Air Corps because it is located here, and I don't think I have
any particular aptitude for the Medical Corps end of it. I have
gotten some good connections, my Lt. is pulling for me, and
one of our privates is a personal friend of my commanding officer,
and the Lt. said he would get me before the board immediatly upon
completion of everything that goes on in the preliminary stage.
Then if I get the approval of the board, our Sergeant knows a guy
who can fix it up so that I can make school pretty quickly. So
as I said before, the board is the big problem.

Not much news as far as my work here is concerned. Sunday I
did go out to see the Bellars, and had an enjoyable afternoon and
evening. I'M going out there again this coming Sunday.

They enjoyed you so much, and were quite hopeful that you and I
would be stationed here for the duration.

Last night, I worked on my application, and heard a very interesti[
lecture by one of our boys, Painter by name, who is - by his own
admission- the worlds elading authority on homosexual relations.
No fooling, I guess he really is. He has written, andpublished,
a couple of books on the subjedt, and has travelled all over the
world to study it. Isn't that the damndest subject to be a specialist
in- I really got an education however, as did a couple of other
boys in the office. He is not one himself, but became interested
while in college because his room mate was. He is a minister, and
is a graduate of Ya le, and of Union Theological Seminary. When we
run out of conversational matter- about twenty or thirty years hence-
I'll tell you all about it.

Tonight, Dick Taylor, the boy who is from Ha rvard, Middlebury,
and the State Department, and I blew ourselves again, and went out
to dinner at this Francis K Powells here on the Beach. We had a
wonderful meal, better thaN Marzettis, and they were so nice to us
that they kept bringing us seconds of everything, and three kinds
of desert. They really go all out for a uniform, probably because
only colonels etc. eat there ordinarily, and a buck private is a
rarity.

There isn't much else of a newsy nature to write. The weather
is getting positively schorching now, and it must be around ninety
in this room I'M in.

Darling did you go down to mon's last week end- How is she, and what was the general trend of the conversation between you- What did you talk about, as if I didn't know. Write and tell me all about it. I got your letter with the pictures in it, and I'm having them developed right away. Also, just as kind of a hint, how are the Stark cookies coming along- My roomates, and the boys in the office are always bringing stuff around, and I keep telling them I'm just an orphan, and that I sure am glad they're not.

Sweetheart, the moon is very beautiful down her now. I really wish you were here to help me enjoy it. A moon isn't much fun without you around to explain it all to me, and to lend thy soft presence to make the scene really perfect. Deares, when we do get together again, I'll never let you go, you wait and see. I hope we can work out a deal whereby I can be home in March before O.C.S. anytime I see you is a good time. And if I do get home, you had better take time off to be with me, or I won't kiss you in front of the alter. I'll stick my tongue out, and make faces at you right in front of who ever marries us. You wait and see.

Well dearest, your little soldier boy is sleepy, and must get to bed right away. So goodnight darling, and I love you more and more, and anticipate the time when we can be together once again, and the time when it will be for keeps. What a wonderful day that will be. I'll be so nervous that I won't know what to do. We'd better get married with no one else around.

      All MY LOVE ALWAYS,   DICK.

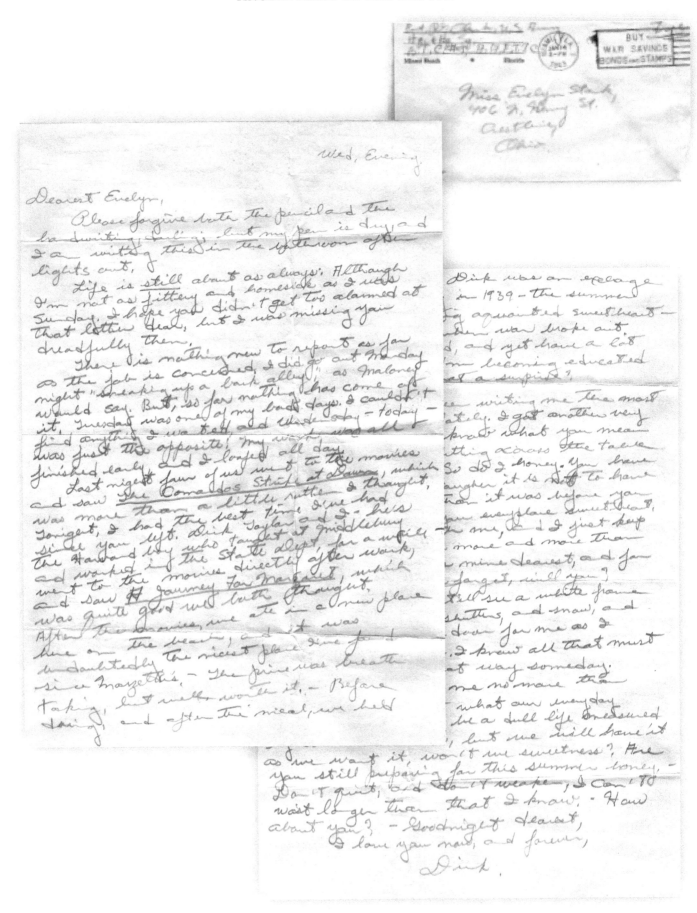

Wed, Evening

Dearest Evelyn,

Please forgive both the pencil and the handwriting, darling, but my pen is dry, and I am writing this in the bathroom after lights out,

Life is still about as always. Although I'm not as jittery and homesick as I was Sunday. I hope you didn't get too alarmed at that letter then, but I was missing you dreadfully then,

There is nothing new to report as far as the job is concerned, I did go out Monday night "sneaking up a back alley," as Maloney would say. But, so far nothing has come of it. Tuesday was one of my bad days. I couldn't find anything I was after, and Wednesday — today — was just the opposite, my work was all finished early and I loafed all day

Last night four of us went to the movies and saw The Commandos Strike at Dawn, which I thought, was more than a little rather I thought, Tonight, I had the best time I've had since you left. Dick Taylor and I — he's the Harvard boy who taught at Middlebury and worked in the State dept for a while — went to the movies directly after work, and saw A Journey for Margaret, which was quite good we both thought.

After the movies, we ate in a new place here on the beach, and it was undoubtedly the nicest place since you — since Mayette's — The price was breath taking, but well worth it, — Before taking, and after the meal, we held

Dick was an average in 1939 — the summer — ty acquainted sweetheart — — war broke out, —, and yet have a lot — becoming educated — a surprise?

— writing me the most — ately. I got another very — know what you mean — thing across the table — So do I honey. You have — rather it is not to have — than it was before you — new airplane sweetheart, — me, and I just keep — more and more than — mine dearest, and for — forget, will you? — tell me a white frame — shutters, and snow, and — door for me as I — I knew all that must — at my someday. — me no more than — what our everyday — be a full life dressed — , but we will have it as we want it, won't we sweetness? Are you still preparing for this summer honey, — Don't quit, and don't weaken, I can't wait longer than that I know, — How about you? — Goodnight dearest, I love you now, and forever, Dick,

Wednesday Evening

Dearest Evelyn,

Please forgive both the pencil and the handwriting, darling; but my pen is dry, and I am writing this in the bathroom after lights out.

Life is still about as always, although I'm not as jittery and homesick as I was Sunday. I hope you didn't get too alarmed at that letter dear, but I was missing you dreadfully then.

There is nothing new to report as far as the job is concerned. I did go out Monday night "sneaking up a back alley," as Maloney would say. But, so far nothing has come of it. Tuesday was one of my bad days. I couldn't find anything I wanted, and Wednesday—today—was just the opposite! My work was all finished early and I loafed all day.

Last night, four of us went to the movies and saw The Commandos Strike at Dawn, which was more than a little rotten I thought. Tonight, I had the best time I've had since you left. Dick Taylor and I—he's the Harvard boy who taught at Middlebury and worked in the State Dept. for awhile—went to the movies directly after work, and saw Journey for Margaret, which was quite good we both thought. After the movies, we ate in a new place here on the beach, and it was undoubtedly the nicest place I have found since Marzettti's. The price was breath taking, but well worth it. Before during, and after the meal, we held quite a bull session. Dick was an exchange student in Germany in 1939—the summer you and I were getting acquainted sweetheart—and he was there when the war broke out. We talked and talked, and have a lot more yet to do. I'm becoming educated yet honey! Isn't that a surprise?

Dear, you've been writing me the most wonderful letters lately. I got another very super one today. I know what you mean about missing that sitting across the table from one another. So do I honey. You have no idea how much tougher it is not to have you with me now than it was before you came down. I see you every place sweetheart. You are always with me, and I just keep right on loving you more and more than ever before. You are mine dearest, and for always. Don't ever forget, will you?

Somehow, I can still see a white frame house with green shutters, and snow and you waiting at the door for me as I come up the walk. I know all that must come true just that way someday. Heaven could give me no more than that. I even know what our everyday will be like: It may be a dull life measured by some standards, but we will have it as we want it, won't we sweetness? Are you still preparing for this summer honey, Don't quit, and don't weaken, I can't wait longer than that I know. How about you? Good night dearest, I love you now, and forever,

Dick

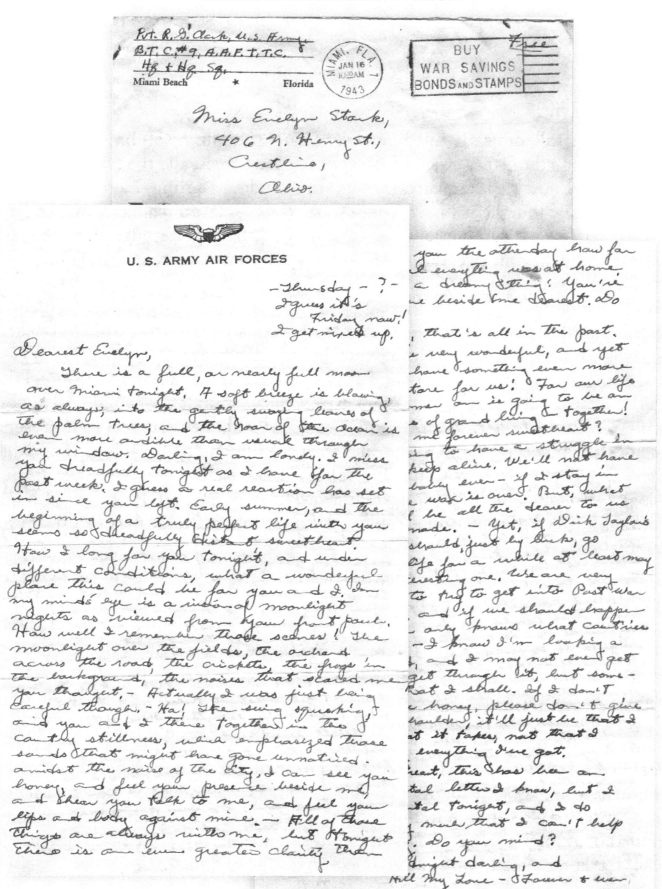

U. S. ARMY AIR FORCES

— Thursday — ? —
I guess it's
Friday now!
I get mixed up.

Dearest Evelyn,

There is a full, or nearly full moon over Miami tonight. A soft breeze is blowing as always, into the gently swaying leaves of the palm trees, and the roar of the ocean is even more audible than usual through my window. Darling, I am lonely. I miss you dreadfully tonight as I have for the past week. I guess a real reaction has set in since you left. Early summer, and the beginning of a truly perfect life with you seems so dreadfully distant sweetheart. How I long for you tonight, and under different conditions, what a wonderful place this could be for you and I. In my mind's eye is a vision of moonlight nights as viewed from your front porch. How well I remember those scenes! The moonlight over the fields, the orchard across the road, the crickets, the frogs in the background, the noises that scared me you thought, — Actually I was just being careful though. — Ha! the swing squeaking, and you and I there together in the country stillness, which emphasized those sounds that might have gone unnoticed. amidst the noise of the city, I can see you honey, and feel your presence beside me, and hear you talk to me, and feel your lips and body against mine. — All of those things are always with me, but tonight there is an even greater clarity than

you the other day how far away everything was at home a dreamy thing! You're beside me dearest. Do

that's all in the past. very wonderful, and yet have something even more store for us! For our life men are is going to be an of grand living together! me forever sweetheart? to have a struggle to keep alive. We'll not have bally even — if I stay the war is over. But, what be all the dearer to us made. — Yet, if Dick Taylor's should, just by luck, go life for a while at least may everlasting one. We are very to try to get into Post War and if we should happen only knows what countries — I know I'm losing a and I may not even get get through it, but some that I shall. If I don't honey, please don't give couldn't, it'll just be that I at it takes, not that I everything I've got.

heart, this has been an tal letter I know, but I tal tonight, and I do much, that I can't help Do you mind?

tonight darling, and All my Love — Forever & ever,

Dick.

POSTMARKED MIAMI, FLORIDA—JANUARY 16, 1943
Thursday - ? = I guess its Friday now!
I get mixed up.

Dearest Evelyn,

There is a full, or nearly full moon over Miami tonight. A soft breeze is blowing, as always, into the gently swaying leaves of the palm trees, and the roar of the ocean is even more audible than usual through my window. Darling, I am lonely. I miss you dreadfully tonight as I have for the past week. I guess a real reaction has set in since you left. Early summer, and the beginning of a truly perfect life with you seems so dreadfully distant, sweetheart. How I long for you tonight, and under different conditions, what a wonderful place this could be for you and I. In my minds' eye is a vision of moonlight nights as viewed from your front porch. How well I remember those scenes! The moonlight over the fields, the orchard across the road, the crickets, the frogs in the background; the noises that scared me, you thought. Actually I was just being careful though. Ha! The swing squeaking, and you and I there together in the country stillness, which emphasized those sounds that might have gone unnoticed amidst the noise of the city. I can see you honey, and feel your presence beside me, and hear you talk to me, and feel your lips and body against mine. All of those things are always with me, but tonight there is an even greater clarity than usual. I told you the other day how far away, how unreal everything was at home. Tonight it isn't a dreamy thing! You're almost right here beside me dearest. Do you mind?

But darling, that's all in the past. Those days were very wonderful, and yet I feel that we have something even more wonderful in store for us! For our life from this summer on is going to be an unbroken series of grand living—together! Can you stand me forever sweetheart? I know we're going to have a struggle in order to just keep alive. We'll not have any money—probably even—if I stay in teaching after the war is over. But, what we do get will be all the dearer to us for the effort made. Yet, if Dick Taylor's and my plans should, just by luck, go through, your life for awhile at least may be a pretty interesting one. We are very definitely going to try to get into Post War Administration, and if we should happen to do it heaven only knows what countries you may see. I know I'm looking a long way ahead, and I may not ever get into O.C.S., or get through it, but somehow I think that I shall. If I don't make the grade honey, please don't give me the cold shoulder, it'll just be that I haven't got what it takes, not that I won't be giving everything I've got.

Well sweetheart, this has been an awfully sentimental letter I know, but I feel very sentimental tonight, and I do love you so very much, that I can't help being that way. Do you mind?

Good night darling, and All My Love—Forever & ever,

Dick

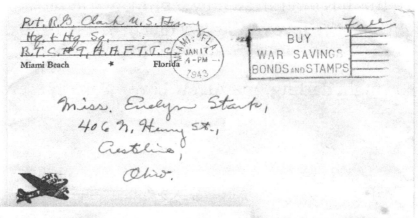

Pvt. R.G. Clark U.S. Army
Hq. + Hq. Sq.
B.T.C. #9, A.A.F.T.C.
Miami Beach   *   Florida

MIAMI, FLA.
JAN 17
4 - PM
1943

BUY
WAR SAVINGS
BONDS and STAMPS

Miss. Evelyn Stark,
406 N. Henry St.,
Crestline,
Ohio.

U. S. ARMY AIR FORCES

Sunday
Afternoon.

Dearest Evelyn,

I'm going to make this a short letter darling, because I'm going to go over and call on the Bellars. — I haven't been over since you left, and I think I ought to go.

As usual, there isn't much news. Last night I went to Miami with some of the boys, had a huge steak, went to the movies and saw China girl, which was not so hot, and then drank beer. We got in after hours, but as usual, nothing was either said or done. You and I could have stayed out a lot longer together, had I only known about how easy it is to do.

The Lt. who had been an Assistant Officer was promoted and took complete charge of our office. — This is very good, because it means that things will stack up about the same as before with regard to school, etc. I'm going to try and make the March class if it is at all possible. The Post War Problems is out as far as we're concerned I'm afraid. They want older

honey, you talk about my
draving comments, you ought
what they say about yours. I
burst with pride, and boy do
it when they tell me how pretty
, or that you look like a
. — You are a real girl darling,
're mine, and I'll never never
go. I just love you and miss
want you so hard that it
to even think about it. I
but you at night, and day
all day dearest.
te to me real often, I so love
from you, short letters or long
be no difference. You're
and hearing from you helps

All My Love — Always Sweetheart,
Dick.

POSTMARKED MIAMI, FLORIDA—JANUARY 17, 1943

Sunday Afternoon

Dearest Evelyn,

I'm going to make this a short letter darling, because I'm going to go over and call on the Bellars. I haven't been over since you left, and I think I ought to go.

As usual, there isn't much news. Last night I went to Miami with some of the boys, had a huge steak, went to the movies and saw China Girl, which was not so hot, and then drank beer. We got in after hours, but as usual, nothing was either said or done. You and I could have stayed out a lot longer together had I only known about how easy it is to do.

The Lt. who had been our Assistant Officer was promoted and took complete charge of our office. This is very good, because it means that things will stack up about the same as before with regard to school, etc, I'm going to try and make the March class if it is at all possible. The Post War Programs is out as far as we're concerned I'm afraid. They want older men.

Well honey, you talk about my picture drawing comments, you ought to hear what they say about yours. I really do burst with pride, and boy do I love it when they tell me how pretty you are, or that you look like a real girl. You are a real girl darling, and you're mine, and I'll never never let you go. I just love you and miss you, and want you so hard that it hurts me to even think about it. I dream about you at night, and day dream all day dearest.

Write to me real often, I do love to hear from you; short letters or long ones make no difference. You're just it, and hearing from you helps a lot.

All My Love—Always Sweetheart,

Dick

PT. R.G CLARK, U.S Army.
Hq. & Hq. Sq. BTC #7
T.B.F.T.C.
Miami Beach ＊ Florida

BUY
WAR SAVINGS
BONDS AND STAMPS

Miss. Evelyn Stark,
406 N. Henry St,
Crestline,
Mo.

Dearest Evelyn,

    Yes, I'm at the typewriter again, which indicates that I have been
working in the office all evening, and have just now gotten
finished. Darling; everything has been sort of topsy turvy
for me this last week. I have really been busy, particularly
so today. We really got out a lot of work. Earlier in
the week I was busy getting my application for OCS in shape.
Today, I gave it to my Lt. for his rating, and tomorrow it goes
to my commanding officer for his approval or rejection.
I think that he will approve it allright, from what I can gather
from the Lt.'s secretary, it was a real recommendation. It
may even be good enough to carry me past the examing board
without very much trouble at all. I surely hope so. Honey, that
damned application is all that I have had on my mind for the last
week. I want school so badly, and I want that commision even
more badly. Why- for just one reason really. You ought
to know what that reason is. I want to graduate in June, and
then take up a little matter with a girl I know relative to
the pros, and cons of getting married. I guess you may have
heard something of that story before, but I just don't want you to
forget about it. Let's keep our fingers crossed for the next
few weeks s weetheart. If I get in the damned school no power on
earth is going to get me out of it without a commission.

    As far as outside activities are concerned, I ahave done
nothing all week. Monday andTuesday, I worked late in the office
on my application, Wed. our whole hotel was restricted for having
dirty rooms, andThursday- last night- I want over to see the
Sergeant- my immediate boss for a little while, and then went
back to the hotel, and took a bath- which is forbidden now
because of a great shortage of water, and went to bed early.
This morning I didn't fall out for drill, and so far haven't heard
anything about it. Whether I do or not I don't know, but I was really
sleepy this morning, and whatever the punishment, it willbe
worth it. Tonight, we worked, and most of the other boys have
gone home except Maloney and I, he too is writing a letter to his
girl, and I'LL bet is really spreading it. He deesn't have a
girl like MINE, and he has to give her a line- he thinks; I used
to kind of do the same thing didn't I- so did you.

    T omorrow night my plans are very indefinite, I may just stay home
again, but Sunday I'm going out to Bellars again. Beyond that
you can't figure in this army. By the way, I read the letter you
wrote the Bellars, when I wasout there last Sunday, and it was
a might nice one.

I'm really glad that you went down home last week end, and had a
good time. I really enjoyed finding out about mom from a
reliable source. I do write mom just about as often as I do you,
but honey, it is really impossible to write every day, or even
every couple of days. I just simply have too much to do. You know
that it isn't that I don't want to write either of you. As to
telling her about my associates, I did do that. But I couldn't
tell her in a letter very much about what my duties are except in
a general way. I'm under oath not to. I relied on you to
transmit that information to her persona ly. I got a letter
from her today, and she remarked ablut how much she enjoyed having you
down- Why don't you two get together again before too long.

I'm glad you are going down to June's this week end. Soemhow,
I feel that B ob, and I will be with you both, drinking beer,
playing gin rummie, and eating and talkin talking our heads off.
I got a letter from Bob this week, and he had been up before the
board for OCS, but didn't know as yet how hecame out. From what he
said, the infantry must be a rea;lly tough branch. You will
probably know more about his making OCS than I will by the time
you get my letter. How about writing, and telling me all about it*
Also, what about Jane, and her boy friend- Are they still at it-

Well darlingest, it is now way past my bedtime, and I must get
up in the morning as alwyys, and get to work. I'm going to knock off
for now, but I'll be writing again real soon. I love to get your
letters sweetness. Every noon, I hurry over to the hotel to
see whether or not anything has come from you. How glad I will be
when I can rush home every noon just to see you, and find out
whether or not you still love me, and don't regret your bargain.
I surely hope that you never will be sorry for marrying me, sweet.
Will you be as glad as I shall be if I do make OCS, and get a
commission in Jane, or sooner-

Be a good girl honey, and write to me, and keep on loving
me, as I am keeping on loving you, more and more all the time.
All I really am living for now is that day this coming summer
when I can take you in my arms, and say you're really mine now
darling f orever and ever.

                    All My L ove- Always,

                    DICK.

Pvt. R. G Clark, U. S. Army.
Hq. & Hq. Sq.
B. T. C. #9, B.M.F.T.C.
Miami Beach   *   Florida

Miss. Evelyn Stark,
406 N. Henry St.
Crestline,

MIAMI, FLA
JAN 25
1943

BUY
WAR SAVINGS
BONDS and STAMPS

                                          Monday

Dearest Evelyn,

        It is almost lunch time again, and my work is all caught up,
so I figured that now would be an excellent time to write my
honey.

        Friday night I worked in the office as I told you, and
Saturday was a pretty light one, comparatively speaking, I
loafed the day away. Saturday night, I went to Miami, and ate at
the Miami hangers out special place: The M&M restuarant. The
Food was really marvelous. That's one that we missed, darling.
After that, I went to a perfectly charming beer garden with
one of the boys from the office, and remained for the evening.
Budweiser was on tap, and we only had to buy about one round for
ourselves. The customers were setting them up for the soldiers.
They had a waitress there who used to sing- many years ago- in
German opera, and every now and then she would sing for us. The
Bartender put on a couple of acts, as did the customers. Bob
would really have enjoyed himself had he been there. To top
it all off, a man and his wife who were there decided that
gas rationing, and the elimination of pleasure driving or not,
we were not going to get back to the Beach any other way than
in their car. Sunday, I went out to Bellars, and we took a ride out t
to Oppa Loca, took some pictures, and generally fooled around.
Last night we ate at Harveys, and I came back and went to bed early.

        This morning was inspection again, and I passed, our room and
our floor were about the best in the hotel apparently. After
struggling through my OCS application, I found out that I would have
to do it all over because of about two mistakes. I persuaded
our typists to type it for me this time however. Everything
is ok except passing the board. I'll get before them pretty
rapidly, I worked out a deal witha guy on that. And if I get
passed the board, I'll get to school quickly because we have
a deal cooking there too. So we still have to keep out fingers
crossed. I should know one way or the other in a couple of weeks
if all goes well.

        Well darling, how was June, and what is the news from Bob.
Tell me all about your week end. You're surely an old week end
gad about, aren't you? When are you going to stay home, and
write your honey a letter twenty pages long, and also when are you
going to come up with some more of that wonderful candy, or those
Toll House cookies? I'm getting awfully hungry. I wouldn't
hint understand, I'm above that. Ha .

        Sweet, I'm going to knock off now, and go to lunch. I love
you and miss you more than you know. One of our boys wife is
coming down today, and I surely wish that it was you coming back.
Have you figured out how long it is

until June. It isn't too long, and yet it's awfully far away from
my point of view. Love miss and want me sweet, because I really
have got that yen for you.

         All My Love- Always,

              Dick.

PVT. R.G. CLARK, U.S. Army
Hq & Hq Sq., B.T.C. #9
A.A.F.T.T.C.
Miami Beach, Fla.

MIAMI, FLA
JAN 23
1943

BUY
WAR
BONDS AND STAMPS

Miss Evelyn Stark,
406 N. Henry St,
Crestline,
Ohio.

Thursday

Dearest Evelyn,

Today is about as blue a day as I have had in the army. Never was I more homesick, and never did I have a greater desire to see you and be home with you. The letter you wrote Sunday may have something to do with it — undoubtedly does — but if I don't get to go to O.C.S. very shortly, I'm going to ask to be transferred out of here. We're not really rendering a great deal of service to the war effort in my judgement, and this place is very reminiscent of a boy scout camp. I honestly feel that I was of more service to the country when I was teaching than I am now.

Darling, I guess all of this grumbling is just indicative of the tremendous fact of my love for you. How happy I'll be when June comes! And how very much I hope that I'll be in a position to properly take care of you sweetheart. This being away from you is hard, but as you say, it does really make us realize how very lucky we really were, and how much we did have together, and how

... really is. I've told you time and ... to love you, but all I can do now ... grows stronger and stronger by the ... memories of us together dearest, and ... beautiful ones. I could go ahead and ... after page, and hour after hour; for ... with me. There composite total ... soul and spirit, religion, and pride ... Sweetheart, you are truly everything ... all else either led up to, my meeting ... been spun like a spider's web ... you have been, and are, to me.

Now as to what little news there is: I have done very little of any importance all week. I had to do my O.C.S. application all over again because of about three very minor mistakes. However, I did finally get it right, and got an excellent recommendation from my commanding officer — whom I never saw before in my life. — I sold him a bill of goods I guess. — I also really got a wonderful rating plus a letter from my own officer, so I guess it's entirely up to the O.C.S. Board now.

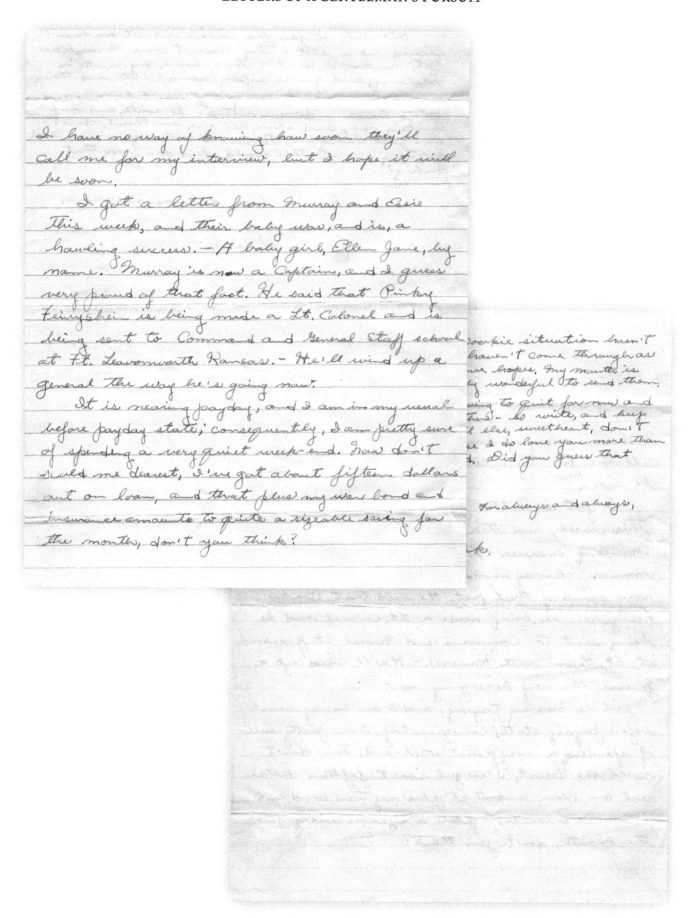

I have no way of knowing how soon they'll call me for my interview, but I hope it will be soon.

I got a letter from Murray and Essie this week, and their baby was, and is, a howling success. — A baby girl, Ellen Jane, by name. Murray is now a Captain, and I guess very proud of that fact. He said that Pinky Feinyshin is being made a Lt. Colonel and is being sent to Command and General Staff school at Ft. Leavenworth Kansas. — He'll wind up a general the way he's going now.

It is nearing payday, and I am in my usual before payday state; consequently, I am pretty sure of spending a very quiet week-end. Now don't scold me dearest, I've got about fifteen dollars out on loan, and that plus my war bond and insurance amounts to quite a sizeable saving for the month, don't you think?

rookie situation hasn't haven't come through as we hopes. My mother is ly wonderful to send them.

ing to quit for now and this — to write, and keep else, sweetheart, don't I do love you more than d. Did you guess that

For always & always,

k.

Thursday

Dearest Evelyn,

Today is about as blue a day as I have had in the army. Never was I more homesick, and never did I have a greater desire to see you and be home with you. The letter you wrote Sunday may have something to do with it—undoubtedly does—but if I don't get to go to O.C.S. very shortly, I'm going to ask to be transferred out of here. We're not really rendering a great deal of service to the war effort in my judgment, and this place is very reminiscent of a boy scout camp. I honestly feel that I was of more service to the country when I was teaching than I am now.

Darling, I guess all of this grouching is just indicative of the tremendous fact of my love for you. How happy I'll be when June comes! And how very much I hope that I'll be in a position to properly take care of you sweetheart. This being away from you is hard, but as you say, it does really make us realize how very lucky we really were, and how much we did have together, and how strong our love really is. I've told you time and time again that I love you, but all I can do now is say that it grows stronger and stronger by the day. I too have memories of us together dearest, and they are all beautiful ones. I could go ahead and recall them page after page, and hour after hour; for they are always with me. There composite total forms whatever soul and spirit, religion, and pride that I have. Sweetheart, you are truly everything in my life. All else either led up to my meeting you, or else has been spun like a spiders' web out of everything you have been, and are, to me.

Now as to what little news there is: I have done very little of any importance all week. I had to do my O.C.S. application all over again because of about three very minor mistakes. However, I did finally get it right, and got an excellent recommendation from my commanding officer—whom I never saw before in my life. I sold him a bill of goods I guess. I also really got a wonderful rating plus a letter from my own officer, so I guess it's entirely up to the O.C.S. Board now. I have no way of knowing how soon they'll call me for my interview, but I hope it will be soon.

I got a letter from Murray and Essie this week, and their baby was, and is, a howling success. A baby girl, Ellen Jane, by name. Murray is now a Captain, and I guess very proud of that fact. He said that Pinky Feiryshein is being made a Lt. Colonel and is being sent to Command and General Staff school in Ft. Leavenworth Kansas. He'll wind up a General the way he's going now.

It is nearing payday, and I am in my usual before payday state; consequently, I am pretty sure of spending a very quiet weekend. Now don't scold me dearest, I've got about fifteen dollars on loan, and that plus my war bond and insurance amounts to quite a sizeable saving for the months, don't you think?

Dearest, so far the cookie situation hasn't cleared up a bit—they haven't come through as yet, however I do still have hopes. My mouth is watering, and you're awfully wonderful to send them.

Well sweetheart, I'm going to quit for now and go to lunch—dinner rather—so write, and keep writing me, and above all else, sweetheart, don't ever quit loving me. Because I do love you more than anything else in this world. Did you guess that darling?

All My Love, For always and always,

Dick

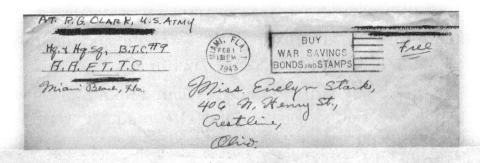

Dearest Evelyn,

I'm now more firmly convinced than ever that I have the most
wonderful, and the swellest girl in all the world. So too are
my roommates, and the boys at the office. The cookies were
wonderful, and we all really enjoyed them a lot darling. I
never could choose which brand I like best, because I like them
both very much. If you have any other recipes that you want
to try out on me now, go ahead, and perhaps that will make some
difference as to my final opinion on the matter. No sweet, I
wouldn't hint for the world.

Life around here follows a definite pattern anymore. It is now
Sunday, but I even came to the office today- although all I am
going to do is write my honey. I think I spend more time here,
and with the boys who work with me than I do anywhere else.
Last night Maloney and I wnent out and had a few beers, and
spent a very enjoyable evening lieing to one another, and generally
fanning the breeze about every subjedt under the sun. We got
home around twelve in a very jovial frame of mind, and then I
slept until noon- we had no revielle this morning- when I was
awakened by my roommate bringing in a letter from my sweetheart.
Next to being awakened by her in person, it was wonderful to
be awakened by the presence of a letter from her. All day today,
we have loafed around. We went out for dinner- Taylor's father
sent him fifty dollars, and so I was enlisted to help him spend
it. Then I helped him write a letter which has been bothering
him for some time. It seems that he can't get a commission in
the Army because of the fact that he is accused of being a Nazi.
Imagine a man working in our office accused of anything like that.
It obviously is based on rumor, and so I outlined his course
of action for him. Never a dull day around here. Almost everyone
in the office has something sensational connected with them,
I sometimes think that I am too much the average man.

Friday night you would have loved had you been here. We went
accross the 41 st. bridge- the narrow one, and to the drug store
on the corner, where I met you in the evenings dearest, and had
a sandwich. While on the way over there, we got caught in the
most torrentiaa downpour of rain it has ever been my misfortune
to even see. We were soaked to the skin, and my only clean
uniform was ruined. After getting dried off somewhat, we decided
to brave the storm, and cross the street to the movie. However,
the water was then up to our knees, and was coming in the front
of the drug store. So we rolled up our pants legs, took off
our GI shoes, and waded accross the street. Imagine the amount
of attention we receeved as we walked down the aisle of the
theatre, shoes in hand, and barefoot as we could be. The movie
was well worth it however, it was one of the Andy Hakdy series.
And I really get a kick out of those things.

My OCS application goes on apace: As I told you the other day, I did get the approval of my commanding officer, and a swell rating from the head of our department. The application came through to me, and I investigated myself, and wasted now time about it either. It is now back in the hands of the OCS office, and all that remains is the interview with the Board. The sooner I get before them the better, but it may be this week, in fact, I may have been before them by the time you get this letter. The new Lt. whom I told you about- the one who is the Georgia politician- swears that I'll get put in ahead of all the others, or else he will donothing to expidite investigation on the men the OCS office want to make the grade. I think that he will look out for me rather well. He is really a wonderful fellow, and I couldn't ask for a better break than to work under him. He's a gambler of the old school, and this week we are going to the dog races together. He "guarantees" that I will make plenty of money. The other night he wanted me to go down for him, and play them on a percentage basis, because he had to go to a meeting, I didn't, and the next day he was mad as hell at me, because he figured that we could have made- had we played the dogs he wanted to- a bout a hundred dollars apiece. When I see you, I can tell you story after story abo ut him. He's one of the few real "characters that Damon Runyon has missed writing about.

Well sweetheart, if I don't make OCS, I have decided to go to Cryptography school, with Maloney, and learn all about codes. I think that if I do that, I might get a chance to go over seas in that capacity, and if I don't get to school, I think that is where I want to go. Maloney leaves in two weeks.

Darling, I wish that you could be here with me. That letter β of discontent that I wrote the other day was indicative of only one thing really. That is that I love you, and miss you terribly. You're my honey dearest, and I love you so very much that it hurts me not to have you right with me all the time. Love me, and if I don't get approval of the Board for OCS, don't decide that we can't get married until the war is over. I think that we ought to get married no matter what. I would like to have your opinion on that score sweet. Write and give me your ideas please. It's important.

Honey, I'm going to quit for now, but I'll write often this week, and tell you how everything is coming along. Keep your fingers crossed for me, and don't ever stop loving me, no matter what may happen. Write, and keep on writing. Getting letters from you every day or so is wonderful, and believe me when I tell you that the only reason I don't do likewise is because I've got so many other things to do in such a very short time. It certainly isn't because I don't think about you, because I think about you all the time. I have found the most wonderful place for day dreaming, and I occupy it constantly.

                                        All of my   Love   Always,
                                                     Dick.

Dearest Evelyn,

Imagine how wonderful it was to me to recieve two letters from
my honey on the same day, and one of them a wonderful ten page
affair. How I wish that I could have been there to help you
write it. And HOW I would have LOVED to have been with you for
last week end. The wheel whole thing sounded marvelous. Tell
me, was the chicken that you had the one that I tried to run over
one Sunday afternoon just before I left, in order that we might
have chicken for Sunday evening'S snack? Yes darling, we would
most certainly have chased your brother off the lounge, but as to
whether or not we would have gotten much reading done- I wonder.
Those Sundays, as I have doubtless told you a million times were
the greatest delight I had of all the many delights I had with you.
For then it was just us, and no one else in the wonld mattered a
damn. I know in my mind and heart that that is the way it will
be for us always, and I very much fear that you will have to
really prod me to get me to move from your immediate vicinity
to go visit anyone, or to do very much of anything else except
have perpetual Sundays with you the rest of my life. Do you mind?

The S-2 section of B.T.C# 9 is just as it always is. We work ah
awhile, and then loaf an even longer time, crab at one another
constantly by day, and then are inseperable by night. Tonight
is typical: Maloney, Taylor and I went out to dinner together,
and had a wonderful chat about everything under the sun, including
a further lecture on little old New York a dministered by Maloney,
and a discussion by Taylor on South American oddities- he's an
authority on South America. Now the three of us have come back
to the office, and are each occupying a typewriter, busily engaged
in writing letters.

In answer to your question about Maloney, his first name is Melvin,
and the middle one is Daniel. He has worked on almost every paper
in New York, and has also held about a million other jobs. When
the war is over, you and I are going to New York, and visit him.
I think that he can really show us the city, as it is not given
to very many from the mid west to see it, unless they live there
a long time. He says that his tour will definitely not be a
sightseeing one from the top of a bus. Incidently, he is leaving
us either this week or next, unless we can persuade him to change
his mind, and return to New York to attend Cryptography school.
If my other plans don't work out, I may soon follow him.

Speaking of my other plans, and I know I speak of nothing else,
I may possibly go before the Board before you get this letter.
Possibly tomorrow night. I don't have too much confidence in
myself darling. Not only is this Board intrinsicly tough, but
only recently the quotas for almost all schools have been greatly
lowered, and consequently, the standards have increased considerably.

I'm telling you this not as an alibi, because I think that I
should still pass with flying colors, but it is the truth.
If I don't get by them, I still have a good set up right here.
I have no doubt that before too long, I'll have a good sergeantcy,
with charge of this office entirely. That was what ehy intimated
today, in an effort to get me to change my mind about leaving.
with Maloney in the event that my OCS doesn't go as planned.

Darling, today should have been the happiest of all days in the
month for me, because it was payday, but for some reason or other,
I only got fourteen dollars, and fifteen cents. I don't know
why, but I do know that the finance department and I are going to
confer ~~tomorrro~~ tomorrow on the subject. It was just luck that
I had saved about ten dollars out of last months pay, or I would
really have been in a sad fix. Not that I'm now anyway. I guess
that all the stories that I have heard about the Army pay methods
are true. Damn it?*-¢@.

The most important other bit of news right now is that mom is coming
to Miami this month for sure. I got a wire from her todgy, telling
me that she is leaving Columbus the eleventh of this month, unless
my plans are suddenly changed. Will I ever be glad to see her.

Sweet, just to think that it has now been over a month since I have
last seen you, and then only for that short, wonderful week. How
glad I shall be for a furluugh, and how I will enjoy coming home
onee more. I don't know when it will be, but I do know that it
can't be to far away. The last of April, or the first of May at
the outside. Will you be happy then? Boy I really will.

Write to me dearest, and love me, andn never stop. I love you,
and miss you tremendously. And, on how I hope that I get by that
Board, so that we can take care of a little matrimonial matter.

                        All My Love...Always,

                              Dick.

Dearest Evelyn,

I'M pretty excited right now, because I have just been before the
OCS Board, and I think that I made it. I'm not sure that I did
however. But, at any rate, tomorrow morning I ought to know whether
I'm man or mouse. If I did make it, it ws probably for any of
three schools: Army Administration, Intelligence, or Medical
Administrative. Of the three I would guess that they send me to
Medical Administrative. There is a class that starts in that
on Washington's Birthday, and I guess that it is only an eight
weeks course. If I go to it, and if I get through it- and they
are both big ifs, I will probably be a Lt. in April. But don't
get your hopes to aroused. I might not make it in any of the
three branches. Or in any thing else for that matter. As a rule
the Board tells the men whther or not they made it almost immediatly
after they leave the room. However, when the officer came in to
call for the next candidate, all he did was look at me and grin.
I don't know whether it was an encouraging grin, or whether it
was an attempt to smother a laugh. But, I've got to know by
tomorrow surely. I f I find out that I did make it, I'll more
than likely send you a wire. Otherwise, I'll write you the bad news.
So, if you haven't already found out by the time you get this letter,
you'll know that I didn't do too well. In which case, I'll find
out definitely what the score is with regard to my taking over the
running of the S-2 office, and if the chances aren't too good, I'll
turn casual, and get shipped to some other post.

Oh darling, I do hope I make it, not only for my sake, because I'd
get along allright as an enlisted man, but rather for the sake
of our being together for ever and ever. The sooner that I get to
school, and get a commission, the sooner you and I can be together
for always, and I want that very much. Do you? -I guess that is a
silly question, come to think of it. But I love to here you tell
me that you love me. If I don't ever get to be anofficer, please
don't ever forsake me. You know that I tried with everything that
I've got.

Well sweetheart, this is a very peculiar letter I know, and I'll
write yo a much longer one later, but I've got to get out of here
now, I'm too excited- still to stay in one place very long.

                    All My Love - Always, and Always,

                        Dick.

WESTERN UNION

1204

CLASS OF SERVICE

This is a full-rate Telegram or Cablegram unless its deferred character is indicated by a suitable symbol above or preceding the address.

R. B. WHITE
PRESIDENT

NEWCOMB CARLTON
CHAIRMAN OF THE BOARD

J. C. WILLEVER
FIRST VICE-PRESIDENT

SYMBOLS

DL = Day Letter

NT = Overnight Telegram

LC = Deferred Cable

NLT = Cable Night Letter

Ship Radiogram

The filing time shown in the date line on telegrams and day letters is STANDARD TIME at point of origin. Time of receipt is STANDARD TIME at point of destination

3 FA BI CK 5
aiami Beach Fla 133 PM Feb 5
    Miss Evelyn Stark
    Care Hardin Jones
    406 N Henry St
    Crestline O

        Have made CCS medical administration will write full detatils

        LOVE

                                Dick

                            220 pm.

THE COMPANY WILL APPRECIATE SUGGESTIONS FROM ITS PATRONS CONCERNING ITS SERVICE

Pvt. R. G. Clark U.S. Army,
Hq. & Hq. Sq.
B.T.C. #9, A.A.F.T.T.C.
Miami Beach, Fla.

Miss. Evelyn Stark,
406 N. Henry St.,
Crestline,
Ohio.

Dearest Evelyn,

This is the hardest letter that I have ever had to write: I'm
not going to beat around the bush- I flunked my OCS physical
this morning. It seems that if there is no vision in one eye,
the other must be correctible to 20/20. Mine corrected- according
to the Medics- to 20/30. Consequently, I can't go to school
now or ever, unless I can find some army Dr. who will give me
a break. My officers, and in fact almost every officer here at
headquarters including the new colonel thied to get something
accomplished for me. But all was to k now avail.

I took my oral exam as I told you Thursday night, and passed as
I wired you Friday, but this physical was something I could do
nothing about. The order which prevented me from going was a
new one, and these officers didn't even know anything about it.
As a matter of actual fact, I had a very high mark from the
OCS Board here. High enough to jump me over about a hundred
other men who had also passed the Board earlier, and get me
sent to school in the next shipment of men. I qualified for
all three schools that I applied for, and placed high in all
three of them. I was slated to go to Pennsylvania the 19th
of this month. By next week this time, I would probably have
been home in your arms. But I guess that's out now. The school
was Medical Administration, and there was a good chance that
from there I would have been sent directly to another school
in Harrisburg Pa. in Intelligence, and commissioned a First Lt.
Those were the plans here.

I'm sitting tight right now, hoping that something good will
come of this. I may be able eventually to talk somebody into
letting me get by on that -*-* eye chart. I also am writing
Murray asking for all of the influence that he can get including,
of course, his father. If I can think of any other angles I'm
going to play them. Including- probably before I'm finished-
the former Governor oaf Georgia, the senator from the same state,
and of course all of the Ohio Republicans in Ohio.

If I can't get any action that way, I'm going to have two possibili
ties left: First, if I stay here, eventually- probably about
1980, but eventually, I will probably be able to get a commission
direct, without going to school or anything else. The other
possibility is that I do nothing more to get a commission. I'll
probably be made a Sergeant before long, and by summer, I might
be a Tech Sergeant at least. So darling, the chances of our
getting married are for a moment at least, knocked into a cokked
hat, unless you want to be poor, and the wife of an enlisted
man, rather than an officer. I'm sorry, sorrier than you'll
ever know. But that's the way things arenow. I love you dearest,

more than you'll ever realize. I know that this won't make
any difference in the way things are with us, but I guess
any plans for this summer are out now, unless something happens
rather quickly. Love me, and believe in me, and maybe everything will come out OK. Can you love a sergeant sweetheart?

All My love Always and Always,

Dick.

Cpl. R.G. Clark, U.S. Army.
Hq. & Hq. Sq.
B.F.C. #9, A.A.F.T.T.C.
Miami Beach, Fla.

Miss. Evelyn Stark,
404 N. Henry St,
Aurline,
Ohio.

Dearest Evelyn,

I was pretty surprised to get the reaction I did from you regarding my rather silly question about your feelings on the subject of our getting married. Darling, of course I'm sure that's what I want. There's nothing else that I've been planning on and looking forward to since that New Years Eve when I first told you that I loved you. There hasn't been any other girl for me all during that time, and there never will be. If I had thought that you would have married me last summer, or this fall before I was inducted; or when you were down here, we wouldn't have any such problems to worry about now. But always when I asked you, you would say wait! What else could I do?

I felt all along that by summer I would have a commission in the Army. I knew that if I did, we could be married and could live comfortably without any worries of a financial nature. I looked forward to that day because I didn't want you to have to worry, or live in a little dumpy apartment and

things going. In short, I ... that would cause even a little ... will be a perfect marriage. ... ces of ever getting a chance to ... on whether I can ever pass ... the chance that they ... ttle. If they don't, I'll just ... f getting enough of a rating ... d heaven only knows how ... . It will mean, even if I'm lucky, that we'll have to struggle to make ends meet. But darling, if you'll have me, I'd marry you tomorrow standing naked in a snow drift. — It's going to be whenever and wherever you say.

I'm disappointed in not getting sent to O.C.S. only because I wanted it for you, and for what it would mean to us. If you don't care whether I make it or not, and if you'll still marry me. Then I don't care either.

As to my going to Crypt. school, I shouldn't even have mentioned it. I guess that was just what

Maloney was leaving — he has ... it sounded darned interesting. ... eal, a chance to go anyplace ... was all there was to that. ... y, and very hard to figure out, ... mmary of my feelings as I ... ue, and I'm very, very sure. ... ready — forgive that letter, and get ready to marry me. If you want to quit teaching and come here now, there's nothing I'd rather have than that.

Write to me, and love me, and tear up that application for physical therapy school.

All My Love, Always,

Dick

Dearest Evelyn,

I was pretty surprised to get the reaction I did from you regarding my rather silly question about your feelings on the subject of our getting married. Darling, of course I'm sure that's what I want. There's nothing else that I've been planning on and looking forward to since that New Years Eve when I first told you that I loved you. There hasn't been any other girl for me all during that time, and there never will be. If I had thought that you would have married me last summer, or this fall before I was inducted; or when you were down here, we wouldn't have any such problems to worry about now. But always when I asked you, you would say <u>wait</u>! What else could I do?

I felt all along that by summer I would have a commission in the Army. I knew that if I did, we could be married and could live comfortably without any worries of a financial nature. I looked forward to that day because I didn't want you to have to worry, or live in a little dumpy apartment and have to skimp to keep things going. In short, I wanted to avoid anything that would cause even a little cloud over what I know will be a perfect marriage.

Now, however, my chances of ever getting a chance to become an officer depend on whether I can even pass that eye examination, or on the chance that they may relax standards a little. If they don't I'll just have to take my chances of getting enough of a rating as an enlisted man. And heaven only knows how good those chances may be. It will mean, even if I'm lucky, that we'll have to struggle to make ends meet. But darling, if you'll have me, I'd marry you tomorrow standing naked in a snow drift. It's going to be whenever and wherever you say.

I'm disappointed in not getting sent to O.C.S. only because I wanted it for you, and for what it would mean to us. If you don't care whether I make it or not, and if you'll still marry me, then I don't care either.

As to my going to Crypt. School, I shouldn't even have to mention it. I guess that was just what you'd call soldier talk. Maloney was leaving—he has left now—and I thought it sounded darned interesting. To any soldier here on the Beach, a chance to go any place different seems good. That was all there was to that. Maybe I'm incoherent darling, and very hard to figure out, but that's as clear a summary of my feelings as I can give you.

I love you, and want you, and I'm very, very sure. So please—whenever you're ready—forgive that letter, and get ready to marry me. If you want to quit teaching and come here now, there's nothing I'd rather have than that.

Write to me, and love me, and tear up that application for physical therapy school.

All My Love, <u>Always</u>,

Dick

Dearest Evelyn,

Yes, this is the second letter today, but I just felt like talking
to you, so here I am.

Sweetheart, I'm mighty blue tonight. Nothing seems to go right
for me anyplace right now. I don't know what to do honey, and I
need your advice. I had only planned to stay in Miami until I
passed the Board for OCS, and got sent to school. Now, I doubt
really whether we'll ever be able to figure out a way to get me
past that damned physical. Consequently, my original goal is shot.
I don't know now whether the sergeant in charge of our office
is going to leave, but I'M beginning to think that all of his talk
along that line was just hot air. At any rate, now that Maloney
has gone, I'm being moved out of the office, and into his job of
actual investigation. I was told that it was only to give me
experience for the big job of running the office, but I wonder
now whether that isn't a good way to side track me. There has
been a lot of talk about my being made a corporal or a sergeant
yet this month, but so far, that is just talk. If I stay here,
I may not be among the first three grades of sergeants by spring,
and if I'm not, we wouldn't be allowed to live together, unless
plenty of strings were pulled. All in all, things don't look
as rosy as they seemed to all along. If I ask to leave here,
I may be kept anyway in Miami Beach as a lecturer. Had I gone
into that in the first place, and forgotten about this being
"the most honorable branch of the service" I would be a sergeant
now, with excellent chances for advancement in the near future.
If I do get shipped out, I more than likely would be placed in
the same kind of work I'm now doing, wherever I go. However,
furloughs would probably be much easier to get, and I could be
home oftener. The way things are here now, I would only be eligible
for my first furlough as an enlisted man at the end of six months.
In other words, I still would have three months to go. Also, I
might- if I leave- find a set up, where the sergeant in charge
was due to leave, and I could possibly fall into a good job quick.
All In all, I guess the story is that I'm disgusted over not
passing my physical, and want to get away from here as fast as
possible. What should I do?

Darling, I miss you so very much right now. I need you here to
cheer me up. I'm so ashamed of not getting to go to school, and
so disappointed on your account. I guess that's the only real
reason why I wanted it all so badly. Now that the bubble has
burst there, I have got to make a fresh start as far as plans are
concerned for my Army future.---- Oh, forget about it sweetheart.
I'll struggle through it someway, and make you proud of me yet.

Last Sunday morning I was awakened by Pete Trego yelling at me.
He had come in from Bocca Raton,

and we really spent the day talking everything over. He's about
in the same boat that I am. He has been through two schools, and
is still a private, with prospects none to good of being anything
else for quite a while. We got last falls football schedule played,
and agreed that wewould have a really fine team when we get back.
Also, we wondered about our basketball team, and why it isn't
doing so well. Pete says that Heskett is the third high point
man in the state so far this year. I guess we really can turn
them out, even if they do leave, and go elsewhere. Also, he thought
and I agreed that you and Betty ought to come down here for good,
as soon as school is out, even though neither of us have any
ratings of any kind. We could at least be together in the
evenings, and all day Sundays, and we could get by somehow.
Maybe you could even get a teaching job down here. It mightn't
be as interesting as physical therapy school, but it would be
a whole lot more interesting to me. Damn it, we just can't
wait any longer honey. When school is out, I'll ask for my first
furlough, no matter whether I stay here or where I am, and we'll
-- I forgot, you didn't want to discuss that subject any further.
But, we will anyway; if you'll have me.

Oh dearest, it's almost Valentine's day, and although I can't
do much more than send you a Valentine this year, don't think that
my love for you isn't deeper than it ever was. It increases
with every disappointment, because I realize just how much I'm
counting on having you . You're my Valentine, and I surely want
to be yours, not only on Valentine's day, but forever, throughout
all the years to come. I'm very humble right now, and on my knees
to you, begging you and coaxing you not to ever think of anything
but us for always. There aren't any new ways of saying the old
wordsof love, but even if there were, I should still use the ones
now in existence. I love you Evelyn. Ilove no one else in the
whole world but you, and I want nothing else but you near to me.
If you'll have me, I don't care whether we live in one room or
in a mansion. I don't even care whether we ever leave Grove City
or not after the War. If I can make you happy there, then that
shall be all I want. On the other hand, if you want the moon,
I'll try and get a step ladder someplace, and climb after it for
you.

I imagine that this is an even more incoherent letter than was the
one that drew your wrath down upon my head, but it isn't that my
thinking is incoherent regarding you. It's just that the only
clear thing in my mind right now is my wanting you so much, and
not seeing any sure way of accomplishing my aim right now.
Understand me as you always do sweetness, and don't for a minute
forget me, or forget us together. I'll be all right, and so will
will everything regarding our future.

                    All My Love- Forever, and Ever,

                         Dick.

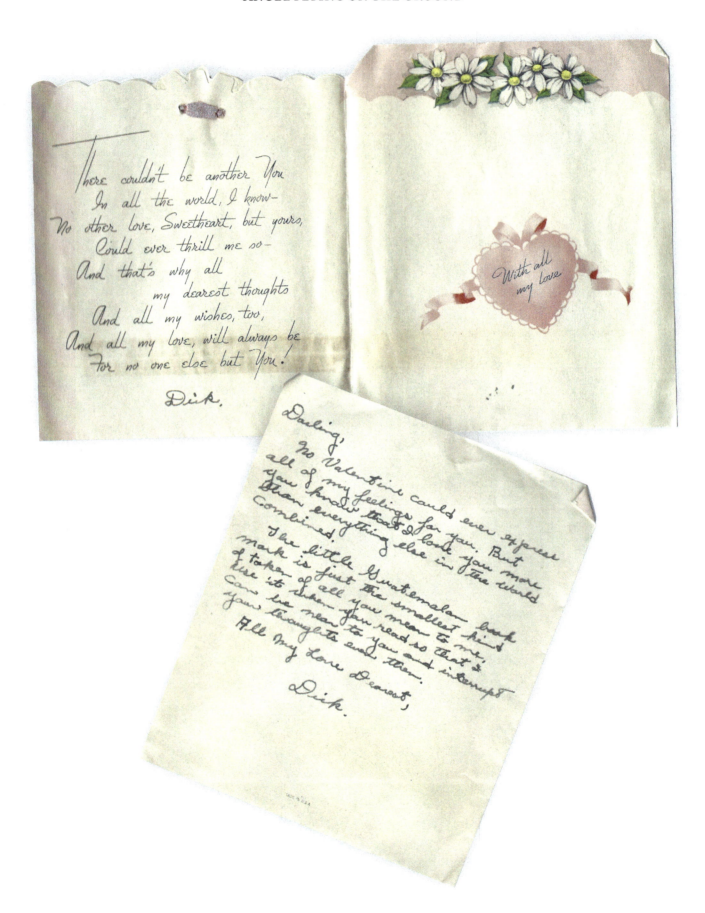

There couldn't be another You
In all the world, I know—
No other love, Sweetheart, but yours,
Could ever thrill me so—
And that's why all
my dearest thoughts
And all my wishes, too,
And all my love, will always be
For no one else but You!

Dick.

With all
my love

Darling,
No Valentine could ever express
all of my feelings for you. But
you know that I love you more
than everything else in the world
combined.
The little Guatemalan book
mark is just the smallest hint
of taken of all you mean to me,
Use it when you read so that it
can be near you when interupt
your thoughts even then.
All My Love Dearest,

Dick.

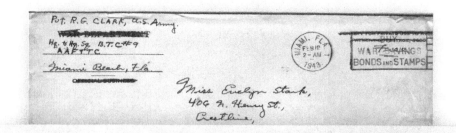

Thursday Evening

Dearest Evelyn,

Honey, I hope that you don't mind my writing you all the time on
the typewriter, but it really is a lot more comfortable to sit
here, and peck away than it is to lie on my bed at the hotel under
a very poor light, and scribble away. Speaking of writing, I have
only gotten one letter from you all week, plus your very nice
telegram of congratulations. Are you really mad at me darling?
Please don't be. I really have felt bad ever since I got that
letter from you the other day.--That on top of everything else
that has happened in the last week have made life pretty miserable
for me, no kidding.

I started on my new job of sleuthing yesterday with a vengeance.
When we listen to Sherlock Holmes, Ellery Queen etc. we should
be able to really dope them out. I think that I will like this
much better than general office work. I get to go practically
any place I want to at any time, and so that makes just one less
restriction that I have to put up with in this mans army. There
is a new table of organization out, which I have as yet not seen,
but the rumor has it that there is a Tech Sergeant, two sergeants,
a corporal, and innumerable PFC ratings included. I figure that
if that is the case, I will probably be given the corporals stripes,
because we have a couple of fellows who have been here longer thhan
I have who will most likely be made sergeants, and we already have
a tech sergeant. However, the chances of my eventually getting
the tech stripes are pretty good. All three of those men are 1A
and are likely to be shipped out at any time. Certainly if I sit
tight I should have things my own way by the end of summer.
However, I still don't know what to do. I'm awaiting a reply to
the letter I wrote you the other night asking for advice. A new
possibility opened up this afternoon: If I can be assigned to
CIC school, (counter intelligence corps) I can be made at least
a staff sergeant to begin with, upon completion of the course.
In that case, I would get to go back into civilian clothes.
Probably somewhere in Ohio. The big question along that line is
whether or not we can get them to waive on my eyes. The director
of our division was here this afternoon, and my Lt. spoke to him
about the idea of my getting a crack at it, and the comments-
after an interview with me were rather favorable. But, anymore,
I'm not predicting anything until it happens. By the way, we are
still working on the idea of getting me past that eye examination,
and ultimately, something favorable may develop. One thing sure,
I have gotten a lot of people interested in me who otherwise would
never have heard of me. The Board which recommended me for school
have all written requesting my appointment to school anyway. I
don't know how much weight that will carry though. I guess all
I can do about anything is just wait, and hope that something

good eventually happens to me in this damned mess. At least
though I can console myself with the idea that I did make school
on every ground except something that I couldn't ehlp. But that
is not a great deal of consolation, is it?

I haven't done a whole lot this week. MOnday night, I wne went
over to see the Bellars, and they have moved just this week. Walter
has changed jobs, and is now in Shore Patrol, I think as a Chief
Petty Officer. So, I guess that his ambition has been realized.
Tuesday night I wrote you a letter, and Wedensday night I was
Charge of Quarters at the hotel. I had to work until midnight
last night. Tomorrow I think that I will go over to Miami, and
find out whether Willert is staying at the Columbus Hotel. He
wrote me, and said that he thought he would be there- with his
new wife- this week end. I'm anxious to see him, and her to for
that matter. He then is going up to Bocca Raton to teach, which
may turn out to be a break for Pete. I got a nice piece of mail
this week: The Grove City Library sent me a new book THE LAST
TIME I SAW PARIS. I started it last night, and found it to be
really quite good. I think that after I finish this letter to
you I'll go back to my room, and read.

Mom gets here Saturday morning, and I think that I will probably
be able to get off to go and meet her. I hope that her train isn't
as late as yours was, on my boss will be very unhappy. But wait
I shall nevertheless. I'll really be glad to see her, and I know
it will make me feel a lot better about everything than I do right
now. While she is here, I think that I'll go and have my eyes
checked by an eye specialist to see whether anything can be done
to correct my eyes for just long enough to pass one physical exam.
That would really be worth a lot of money to me, no kidding.

Darling, I have been in the army for three months today. In some
ways it seems like three years though. At times I still have the
feeling that it is all a horrible dream, and that when I wake up
it will be Sunday morning, and you are bending over me getting
me to come down stairs for dinner. I thought that a t the end
of three months I would be sitting pretty, and now everything is
still just as uncertain as it ever was for me. I've learned a lot
however. I've learned how to be neat about my clothes, which is
something that I surely didn't know before. I don't think that
you'll have nearly as much trouble with me along that line as you
might have had otherwise. I even pick things up off the floor now,
but I could lapse there very easily. It is only because of fairly
rigid inspections that I do that. I have learned how to set up
a filing system, how to dictate correspondance, and now I'm learning
how to be an investigator. I have yet to really learn how to conduct
an interview, but eventually that will come too. Also, I have learned
how to walk just a little more as one should, and as I know you
want me to. So, all and all the experience has proven valueable.

The most important thing that I have learned however sweetheart,
is how much you really mean to me. I write you letters and tell

you how much you mean to me, and maybe they sound to you as though
I'm not sure, but- however they sound- I do love you more than
anything else in this world. I want you all the time, and I miss
you all the time. Every day that we're apart you are just that
much dearer to me. I know now pretty much what life is. It is
a quiet evening with you in our home, perhaps with a couple of
kids to put to bed, perhaps with some problem to be solved by both
of us together, perhpas with friends to entertain, and places to
go occasionally. It's getting up in the morning to fix the fire
while you are still warm and peaceful in bed. It's going to my
job whatever it may be, and wherever it is, with a new zest for
work, because I'll know that I'm not just working to give myself
food, and clothing, and pleasure, but rather to provide things for
you and I together. Life is coming home again in the evening and
you at the door of whatever we call home- waiting for me. It's
a lot of other things too, but they are all tied up with you and
I in the picture together somewhere. It's happiness, and love
and sorrow, and disappointment shared with you. That's what I
know life really is forme. It isn't fame, or a lot of money, or
brilliance in any way. It is just a simple quiet sort of life,
but if you will help me live it, it will be all that any man
can ask.

Goodnight darling, write to me, and miss me a little, and want me
just as hard as I 'm wanting you this minute.

        All My Love for always,

                DICK.

Darling,

It's Sunday morning, and a very cold one at that. Yesterday and today have
been the coldest days that we have had since I've been down here. I slept
with two blankets last night, and nearly froze to death. However, the sun
is out now, and I have hopes that it will get back to normal. As long as
I have tolive in Florida, I think that I ought to get the benefit of all
the warm weather I can. After I once get away from here, I don't ever
plan on coming back.

Mother got in yesterday morning, and her train was only an hour late, which
I thought was really pretty good, considering the fact that yours was so
awfully late when you came down. She looked grand, and I was really glad to
see her. She and Frances spent most of the day together, and last night
she and I went out to dinner, and had a really wonderful time just talking
to one another. I think that she is going to stay about two weeks, which
is plenty all right with me. As you said, she couldn't have come at a
better time. I hope that it gets warmer for her than it is now, this is
November Ohio weather right now.

In one sense however, she picked a bad time to come. For some reason,
my hotel is finally getting really strict, and I'm liable to be restricted
almost any time. That would be really awful, to plan to meet her some
place, and then not be able to get out. We even had to clean our rooms
this morning, and were not allowed to go back to bed. And even the rookies
get out of that on Sunday. Dick Taylor was restricted last night because
there was a little dust on the windowsill, so you can see what it's like.
Honey, I'll stay home and keep house, you get the job- I really ought to be
good at it when this is all over.

Friday night, I spent with Willert and his new wife, who is rather nice,
but awfully young. However they are crazy about one another, and that is
really all that matters. She is only going to have two weeks with him,
and then is going back to New Jersey. He thinks that his new assignment
is going to call for him to be shipped overseas. He is a First Lt. now,
and soon will be a Captain.

Honey, there isn't a thing new in my case. All I'm doing now is waiting
to see what finally happens to me. If nothing good ever does, I will
ask to be sent somewhere else. But not until I wait a reasonable length
of time. The Lt. just told me that he still didn't know what he would
be allowed to give out in the way of ratings. And added that it would be
as good as he could possibly give. So, again, I guess that I will just
have to wait and see. I still would like to either get to OCS by hook
or crook, or else get shipped out of here to some other Base.

Yesterday, I heard that a fellow by the name of Frank Gaines is down here,
and I think that I will have to look him up. He is Betty Lou Burnett's
husband.- She is one of the kids that I grew up with. I don't understand
why he was drafted, I thought that he was in the FBI, if they're drafting
them now, then it won't be too long until they start taking Congressmen

Farmers, old women, and men in wheel chairs. Truly, I ran across a case the other day where a man who was drawing a dis-ability pension from the Government for injury recieved in the last war is down here in the army, a draftee.

Sweetheart, the letter I got from you Friday was the most wonderful letter I ever got from anyone. I knew that you would feel the way you do about my missing out on OCS, and I know how much it would mean to be able to tell all your friends that your boy friend is going to be an officer. I'm awfully sorry that I ever wired you at all honey, because I know how disappointed you must have been too. From now on, until anything is actually completely accomplished, I'm not going to wire you, or get you all excited about it. Maybe nothing else good will ever even look like it is going to happen though. But, at any rate, dear, I know more and more how really wonderful you are, and I'm just that much more in love with you. You're the most wonderful girl in all the world, and I love you so very much. If you'll have me, we surely will get married this summer. I don't know what we'll live on, or even- at thismoment how I'll ever get you back down here- if I'm still here- but, I want you so much that I'm not going to let my pride stand in the way, if you'll take me the way I am. It will mean probably that you will have to work, and it will mean a lot of incomvenience for you, in other words it will really be a struggle, but if you will take me as I am, there is nothing in this world I want more. I want you right now as far as that is concerned. How I wish that you were right here beside me and I could tell you allthe things you mean tome, in every way I know of. Honey, I did write you as soon as I heard the news about missing out on going to school. Mom must have mis-understood what I meant. Iwanted her to call you Sunday and tell you. I hated to make the phone call. I was afraid that I wouldn't be able to talk, and I wanted you to know as soom as possible. Am I forgiven?

Darling, your cup cakes arrived, much to the satisfaction of my entire floor, they must have known that some sort of food came to me, and they all came down to investigate. After those cookies, and the cup cakes, I'd better get you really married, and really safe from wolves, because I think they all are planning to come to Ohio, and propose to you.

Well honey, I'm going to quit for now, and go out and see mother. I may not write as often as usual while she is here, but I'll write as often as I can.

                    All My Love- Always and Always,
                            DICK.

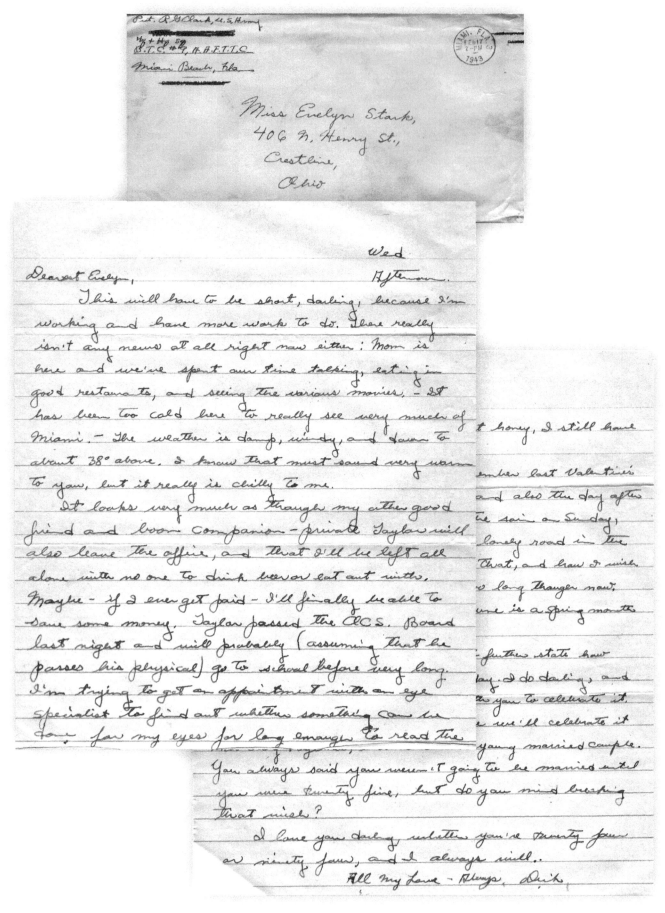

POSTMARKED MIAMI, FLORIDA—FEBRUARY 17, 1943

Wednesday Afternoon

Dearest Evelyn,

This will have to be short, darling, because I'm working and have more work to do. There really isn't any news at all right now either: Mom is here and we've spent our time talking, eating in good restaurants, and seeing the various movies. It has been too cold here to really see very much of Miami. The weather is damp, windy, and down to about 38° above. I know that must sound very warm to you, but it really is chilly to me.

It looks very much as though my other good friend and boon companion—Private Taylor will also leave the office, and that I'll be left all alone with no one to drink beer or eat out with. Maybe—if I ever get paid—I'll finally be able to save some money. Taylor passed the OCS Board last night and will probably (assuming that he passes his physical) go to school before very long. I'm trying to get an appointment with an eye specialist to find out whether something can be done for my eyes for long enough to read the chart. Don't give up on me yet honey, I still have hopes and I'm still fighting.

Sweet, you know that I remember last Valentine's day as though it were yesterday, and also the day after too. Remember the snow and the rain on Sunday, and the two of us alone on a lovely road in Plymouth? How I long for all of that, and how I wish for it all again! It won't be too long though now. Spring is just a month away, and June is a spring month dear.

Evelyn, primarily this letter is to further state how much I wish you a happy birthday. I do darling, and again I wish that I could be with you to celebrate it. Next year for your Birthday I hope we'll celebrate it not only together but as a nice young married couple. You always said you weren't going to be married until you were twenty-five, but do you mind breaking that wish?

I love you darling, whether you're twenty-four or ninety-four, and I always will.

All My Love—Always,

Dick

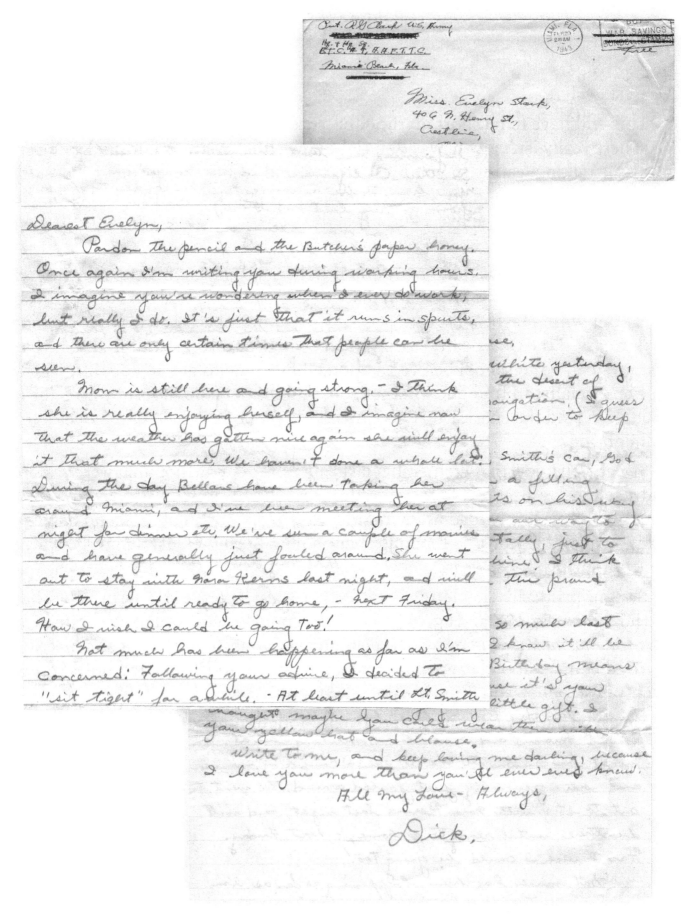

Dearest Evelyn,

Pardon the pencil and the Butcher's paper honey. Once again I'm writing you during warping hours. I imagine you're wondering when I ever do work, but really I do. It's just that it runs in spurts, and there are only certain times that people can be seen.

Mom is still here and going strong. - I think she is really enjoying herself, and I imagine now that the weather has gotten nice again she will enjoy it that much more. We haven't done a whole lot. During the day Bellans have been taking her around Miami, and I've been meeting her at night for dinner etc. We've seen a couple of movies and have generally just fooled around. She went out to stay with Nora Kerns last night, and will be there until ready to go home, - next Friday. How I wish I could be going too!

Not much has been happening as far as I'm concerned: Following your advice, I decided to "sit tight" for a while. - At least until Lt. Smith

... white yesterday, ... the desert of ... navigation. (I guess ... order to keep

... Smith's car, got ... a filling ... ts on his way ... out way to ... tally, just to ... him. I think ... the proud

... so much last ... I know it'll be ... Birthday means ... use it's your ... little gift. I

... nought maybe you could wear the ... your yellow hat and blouse.

Write to me, and keep loving me darling, because I love you more than you'll ever ever know.

All My Love - Always,

Dick.

Dearest Evelyn,

Pardon the pencil and the Butcher's paper honey. Once again I'm writing you during working hours. I imagine you're wondering when I ever do work, but really I do. It's just that it runs in spurts, and there are only certain times that people can be seen.

Mom is still here and going strong. I think she is really enjoying herself, and I imagine now that the weather has gotten nice again she will enjoy it that much more. We haven't done a whole lot. During the day the Bellars have been taking her around Miami, and I've been meeting her at night for dinner etc. We've seen a couple of movies and have generally just fooled around. She went out to stay with Nora Kerns last night, and will be there until ready to go home, next Friday. How I wish I could be going too!

Not much has been happening as far as I'm concerned: Following your advice, I decided to "sit tight" for awhile. At least until Lt. Smith gets us transferred to another Base.

I got a letter from Mrs. White yesterday, informing me that Tom is in the desert of Southern California studying Navigation. (I guess you have to be a navigator in order to keep from getting lost out there.)

I'm now sitting in Lt. Smith's car, God only knows how far away from a filling station—out of gas! The Lt. is on his way after some now. We were on our way to do a little work, and incidentally, just to take a nice ride in the sunshine. I think eventually that we'll become the proud processors of a Jeep.

Dearest, I did miss you so much last Sunday (Valentine's Day) and I know it'll be that way tomorrow too. Your Birthday means a lot to me honey, just because it's your Birthday. I hope you enjoy my little gift. I thought maybe you could wear them with your yellow hat and blouse.

Write to me, and keep loving me darling, because I love you more than you'll ever ever know!

All My Love—Always,

Dick

Dearest Evelyn,

This will have to be another shorty honey: It is Sunday, and I'm
Supposed to be working today. We have a little re-organizing to do,
and I've been kept busy all morning, and am due to go out again as soon
as I finish writing you. We had the best meal this noon that I have
ever eaten in a mess hall: Turkey, Mashed Potatos, Corn, Peas, Salad,
Ice Cream and pie. It was really all right. I guess that this is the
first anniversary of the founding of the Miami Beach Schools. We even
had a Jute Box going during the meal. If that sort of thing keeps
up, I'll eat in the Mess Hall more often, and save considerable
money by so doing.

Mom is still here, and going strong. I had planned to stay out at
Kerns' house last night, but when I found out that I had to work,
there was no soap. We played Poker, and again I lost. I haven't
had any luck playing cards since I came in the army. I hope though
that the old slogan of unlucky at cards- lucky at love still holds
true though. If it does, I'll give up the idea of playing cards.
I've heard- through the Kerns family that jobs here, good ones,
are not too hard to get, and so maybe if a certain young lady ever
decides that this is the place for her to live, for one reason or another
it might be possible for her to make out all right, if she wants
to work for a time. I have been hearing rumors to the effect that it
won't be two weeks before I'm wearing Sergeants stripes. If that is true,
I'll really be happy, because it will mean that by summer, I'll
probably have enough stipes, and the corresponding amount of pay, to
adequately take care of any NEW DEPENDANT that I might pick up.

Darling, if you think that I'm going to come home in May, you're
sadly mistaken, I811 be home in June, and if you'll stop and think,
you'll know why I'm putting it off the extra month. You will still
be teaching school in May won't you, or has the war caused the schools
to shut down early?

Well honey, I know that this isn't even a letter, but I have got to
get busy again, or else those stripes won't loom so large, so I'll
write you more when I have more time. After Mom leaves, I will do
a lot better, I promise.

                    All My Love- Always,

                         . DICK

Pvt. R.G. Clark, U.S. Army
Hq + Hq Sq.
B.T.C.#4, A.B.F.T.T.C.
Miami Beach, Fla.

MIAMI FLA.
FEB 26
7-PM
1943

Miss Evelyn Stark,
406 N. Henry St.,
Crestline,
Ohio.

MAiL

Friday,

Darling,

I'm awfully, terribly, terrifically sorry that I haven't written this week, but honestly I just haven't had any time at all: I've been working very hard this week, and I've - of course been with Mom every night. We played cards a couple of times, and "did" Miami - as far as eating is concerned. Also, we went to the Dog Races last Friday night, and while I didn't lose much, I ran true to form, if you know what I mean, - Mom is going home tonight at ten o'clock, and then I'll be desolate again. How I wish I were leaving with her!

Honey, there isn't a great deal of good news, although there is some news: The Squadron commander wouldn't sign my promotion to Sergeant, and so we sent in (our office) a request that I be made Corporal, and he wouldn't sign that either, saying that I didn't work in the Squadron, and therefore since he needed ratings for his own men - he didn't see his way clear. - Eventually, we'll get something, but it will have to be over his head.

Also, I went to an eye specialist yesterday and he told me that he couldn't even correct my vision to the place where I could read a 20/20 line. - So, the only chance I have is to fake the exam, or else wait for the army to lower their requirements, in order for me to become an officer.

— I guess I'm just very unlucky, that's all I can figure out as a solution. — Nothing seems to be going right for me at present. I

I do is wail to you about
and maybe sometime I'll
Penelope into a griper.
was slated to go to Infantry
Ga., if he's in Camp Hood, the
unit. - That, in my book,
used to be a suicide outfit.
home at all, it will be
When do you get through
to make sure you're
Think about coming home.
definite intentions of
or wherever I am then,
my intentions, how about
you'll be in the mood for
new job? - the four of

write you a great long letter
the meantime, please forgive
I haven't written
most important, keep loving
me and waiting me darling.

All My Love, Always,

Dick.

POSTMARKED MIAMI, FLORIDA—FEBRUARY 26, 1943

Friday

Darling,

I'm awfully, terribly, terrifically sorry that I haven't written this week, but honestly I just haven't had any time at all: I've been working very hard this week, and I've—of course been with mom every night. We played cards a couple of times, and "did" Miami—as far as eating is concerned. Also, we went to the Dog Races last Friday night, and while I didn't lose much, I ran true to form, if you know what I mean. Mom is going home tonight at ten o'clock, and then I'll be desolate again. How I wish I were leaving with her.

Honey, there isn't a great deal of good news, although there is some news: the squadron commander wouldn't sign my promotion to Sergeant, and so we sent in (our office) a request that I be made Corporal, and he wouldn't sign that either, saying that I didn't work in the squadron, and therefore—since he needed ratings for his own men—he didn't see his way clear. Eventually, we'll get something, but it will have to be over his head.

Also, I went to an eye specialist yesterday and he told me that he could not even correct my vision to the place where I could read a 20/20 line. So, the only chance I have is to take the exam, or else wait for the army to lower their requirements, in order for me to become an officer.

I guess I'm just very unlucky, that's all; I can figure out as a solution. Nothing seems to be going right for me at present. It seems that all I do is wail to you about all my troubles darling, and maybe sometime I'll quit. I guess I've just developed into a griper.

I thought that Bob was slated to go to Infantry O.C.S. at Ft. Benning Ga., if he's in Camp Hood, he is in a Tank Destroyer unit. That, in my book, isn't good. That's supposed to be a suicide outfit. Honey, I imagine if he gets home at all, it will be about the last of May. When do you get through school anyway? I want to make sure you're through before I even think about coming home. Because I have very definite intentions of not going back to Miami, or wherever I am then, by myself. Those are my intentions, how about you? Do you think you'll be in the mood for a little trip, and a new job? The job of taking care of me!

Well dearest, I'll write you a great long letter Sunday, I promise. In the meantime, please forgive me, and understand why I haven't written oftener this week, and most important, keep loving me and wanting me darling.

All My Love, Always,

Dick

Darling,

Life goes on as it has a habit of doing, and I'm no smarter than I was whenI wrote you Saturday. I still have recieved no officialwor d as to when I shall go to school, or where, all that I have in the way of tangible information is what Lt. Smith told me Saturday afternoon. So, maybe you'll have an officer in June, and maybe not. In any event, eventually I feel sure that I will get to go to school. Perhaps it would be a break if I don't get to go to Medical Administration because I here that for one who has no background in medicine it is right tough, and if I miss it, I will get to go to the next class in Army Administration, which is what I really want.

I have done very little of any imporiance since Ilast wrote you. Saturday night, I stayed in my room, and slept. Sunday I worked all morning, helping to move the office, and slept all afternoon. Then last night I want to Miami with Jim Flynn, and drank some beer. Tonight I'm catching up on my correspondence again. I don't really have any plans for this week at all, of for that matter, I don't have any social engagements lined up until June, or possibly the first part of July.

Lt. Smith took a troop train, and won't be back until Wed. and in the meantime, I'm acting for him in running our end of the S-2 office. It has really been fun today. Tomorrow morning I'm going to talk to a portugese by means of an interpreter. That should prove to be an interesting experience. -Something new and different every day.

Did I tell you that I got a letter from Tom last week? He is at Portsmouth Va. and I have a hunch that he is getting ready to ship accross, although he didn't say so. Did you see June this past week end? And if so, is Bob at Camp Hood Texas in the Tank destroyer unit? I really hope that that is only a rumor, as that outfit is known as the suicide squad. I don't know what they do exactly, but I do know that it is supposed to be dangerous. If possible, get his address from her, and find out where in Texas Camp Hood is.

I'm glad to here that Jerome is so nicely situated. I'll bet your mother is greatly relieved to find that he is so near home, and living in such nice surroundings. God when I think of her last summer when she thought that he would have to go in just as a buck private, I shudder. Remember how she used to come out on the front porch and bother us when we definitely wanted to be alone? We even wasted some moonlight on account of her didn't we darling?

Well sweetheart, I guess that you will just have to sit tight until I find out more definitely what the score is on me. However, unless I should get lucky and get to go to sbhool in Pa. or Iowa, I doubt very much that I will get home. So don't count on that now. Boy, I surely would like to though. Goodnight honey, and remember that I just keep on loving you dearest. The letter I got from you about my passing my physical was the nicest thing that I ever recieved- next to the one you wrote when I didn't pass the first one. You just steadily grow in my estimation, and I seem to learn to love you more and more all the time, when I long ago didn't think that more love was possible.

                    Goodnight Darling,

                            Dick.

Dearest Evelyn,

I came over to the office about three hours ago, intent upon
writing you a long letter- which I still want to do- and also
I had in mind writing several other letters too. However, I got
here, and the Lt. put me to work as soon as he saw me. I guess
that in the army ones life is not ones own. Now, I guess that Illl
have to let them go for another week. But not my little sugar plum.

Things here are about the same as always. Every day something new
comes up in the way of rumors, but nothing definite is ever given
out. I heard last Tuesday that I was going to be sent out on
a Cadre, to Bocca Raton- where Pete and Willert are. But they decided
that they couldn't let me go right now. Later on, I may be put
on Cadre somewhere. Where I don't know. Also there are the usual
run of rumors that this camp is going to be disbanded as far as
enlisted men are concerned. I don't believe that either. I have
a hunch that when the war is over, unless I do something about it,
I'll be sent home from Miami Beach. Probably- I hope- with my
wife, and four or five kids. What about that?

I told you that I didn't get any Sergeants stripes, nor corporals
either, because of what this damned squadron commander did. Eventually
that will be corrected, and I will get something, but when or what
I don't know. Honey, I have finally solved my problem as to what
to do. I am going to stay here another month, or until the first
of April, in the meantime unless I make OCS definitely, or am made
a Warrant Officer, or get a definite promise that by the first of
June I'll be made at least a Staff Sergeant, or get a chance at CIC
by then, I'm going to ask to be transferred out of here. I don't
know whether I can get sent closer to home or not, but I imagine
that I probably can. Perhaps I might even get a chance to go to
Dayton, or Lockbourne Air Base. At any rate, I'll try and get as
near home as I possibly can. Perhaps I'll remain in this work, and
perhaps I'll be put in something else. But there isn't really
any sense in my staying here if I don't get any place. It isn't
that any one else is getting anyplace ahead of me. I'm still the
fair haired boy, but that doesn't produce the ratings that I feel
I am entitled to. What do you think about my ideas? That is
the way I propose to handle it, unless you object.

Mom went home Friday night, and should be there safely by this
time. I really hated to see her leave. It was wonderful having
her down. Perhaps the next time you go to Columbus you might call
her up, that is if you are interested in what your honey is doing,
and how he is. Are you?

Darling, you have no idea how glad I was to get those letters from
you today. I hadn't heard from you but once this week, and I began
to wonder whether something was wrong. I imagined all kinds of
things. In fact, I think that I thought of everything except the
rationing. Please don't scare me like that very often though.
I really got low. I'm afraid that you mean an awful lot more to
me than I would like to admit. In fact, I guess that you are the
only girl in the world as far as I'm concerned. I love you so very
much, and every day I realize it more. There isn't an hour of the
day that passed but that I don't think about you, and wonder what
you're doing, and picture you in some pose or other, and hear your
voice, and feel your arms around me. Truly dearest you are wonderful,
do you know that? I want that day to roll around real soon when
I'll have eye you with me forever. If you'd only quit teaching
and come down right now, I'd be perfectly happy. In fact, that is
isn't such a bad idea. You never did say anything more about
coming down for the rest of the winter with your folks. What ever
happened to that idea any way? To make a long story short sweetheart
I would give anything in the world to see you this very minute, and
to hold you real close, and tell you how very much you mean to me,
and then I would never take my arms from around you as long as I
live.

Well honey, I guess that I will quit for now, and try and catch up
on my correspondence. I haven't written anyone but you for the
last two weeks. Write to me, and love me, and plan and hope and
pray for June to come, as I am doing.

                    All My Love-Always,

                        DICK.

WESTERN UNION

1204

CLASS OF SERVICE

This is a full-rate Telegram or Cablegram unless its deferred character is indicated by a suitable symbol above or preceding the address.

R. B. WHITE
PRESIDENT

NEWCOMB CARLTON
CHAIRMAN OF THE BOARD

J. C. WILLEVER
FIRST VICE-PRESIDENT

SYMBOLS

DL = Day Letter

NT = Overnight Telegram

LC = Deferred Cable

NLT = Cable Night Letter

Ship Radiogram

The filing time shown in the date line on telegrams and day letters is STANDARD TIME at point of origin. Time of receipt is STANDARD TIME at point of destination

7 FARV   9

Miami Beach Flo 148 PM Mar 2nd

Evelyn Stark
Hardin Mones,
406 N.Henry St
Crestline, Ohio.

Passed OCS physical will write details later Darling love.

Dick

310 PM.

THE COMPANY WILL APPRECIATE SUGGESTIONS FROM ITS PATRONS CONCERNING ITS SERVICE

271

Pvt. R.G. Clark — U.S. Army
Hq & Hq Sq
B.T.C. 9
A.A.F.T.T.C.

MIAMI, FLA.
MAR 3
7:30 PM
1943

Miss. Evelyn Stark,
406 N. Henry St.,
Crestline,

AiR MAiL

Wed, Afternoon

Dearest Evelyn,

I'm very happy right now: I'm happy that I got by that physical and am going to O.C.S. — I'm happy for myself, but I think I'm happier for _us_, because it will make our dream come true a little easier than it might have otherwise.

Naturally, I really didn't pass the thing. I never will know what the 20/20 line of that chart was, but they did let me through (which was all that was really necessary.) Now, I'll promise to work real hard, and be very sure to get through no matter how tough it may be. — It will still be June, darling! — Then we'll be together for always!

I'm not real sure now as to what school I'll go to, but it will be either Army Administration, or Medical Administration — probably Medical, in Texas and without a furlough. I don't know how near I'll be to Baby, but at least we'll be in the same state. — You can become as bad as June R/C "your officer" (I hope!) because I'll

y a soldier as possible —
e lately anyway. Taylor and
s leaving for A.A.F. O.C.S.
that Sat. nite, and
e're going to celebrate
Last night I met
er husband for dinner
g about old times.
I leave, which will be
shall do will be to
teh up on all of the
e leaving.

til next time —

Love — Always & Always,

Dick.

POSTMARKED MIAMI, FLORIDA—MARCH 3, 1943

Wednesday Afternoon

Dearest Evelyn,

I'm very happy right now: I'm happy that I got by that physical and am going to OCS. I'm happy for myself, but I think I'm happier for us, because it will make our dream come true a little easier than it might have otherwise.

Naturally, I really didn't pass the thing. I never will know what the 20/20 line of that chart was, but they did let me through (which was all that was really necessary.) Now, I'll promise to work real hard, and be very sure to get through no matter how tough it may be. It will still be June, darling! Then we'll be together for always!

I'm not real sure now as to what school I'll go to, but it will be either Army Administration, or Medical Administration—probably Medical, in Texas and without a furlough. I don't know how near I'll be to Bob, but at least we'll be in the same state. You can become as bad as June R/E "your officer" (I hope!) because I'll try to be as sharp looking a soldier as possible—just for you, sweetheart.

Life has not been dull lately anyway. Taylor and I have been celebrating his leaving for A.H.F. O.C.S. tomorrow—We celebrated that Sat. nite, and Monday, and tonight we're going to celebrate my passing my physical. Last night I met Betty Lou Burnett and her husband for dinner and an evening of chatting about old times.

After tonight, until I leave, which will be fairly soon all that I shall do will be to write my honey, and catch upon all of the things I need to do before leaving.

So for now, and until next time—

All My Love—Always & Always,

Dick

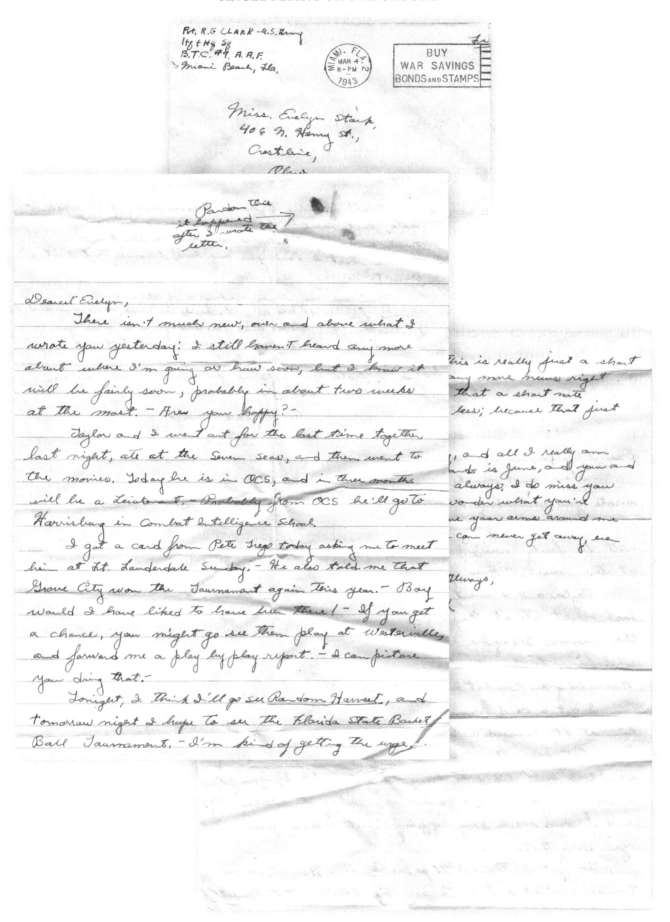

Pvt. R.G CLARK - U.S. Army
Hq & Hq Sq
B.T.C. #7, A.A.F.
Miami Beach, Fla.

MIAMI, FLA.
MAR 4
8-PM
1943

BUY
WAR SAVINGS
BONDS AND STAMPS

Miss. Evelyn Stark,
406 N. Henry St.,
Crestline,
Ohio

Pardon this
it happened
after I wrote the
letter.

Dearest Evelyn,

There isn't much new, over and above what I wrote you yesterday: I still haven't heard any more about where I'm going or how soon, but I know it will be fairly soon, probably in about two weeks at the most. — Aren't you happy? —

Taylor and I went out for the last time together, last night, ate at the Seven Seas, and then went to the movies. Today he is in OCS, and in three months will be a Lieutenant. — Probably from OCS he'll go to Harrisburg in Combat Intelligence School.

I got a card from Pete Trego today asking me to meet him at Ft. Lauderdale Sunday. — He also told me that Grove City won the Tournament again this year. — Boy would I have liked to have been there! — If you get a chance, you might go see them play at Westerville, and forward me a play by play report. — I can picture you doing that. —

Tonight, I think I'll go see Random Harvest, and tomorrow night I hope to see the Florida State Basket Ball Tournament. — I'm kind of getting the urge.

This is really just a short
any more means right
that a short note
less; because that just

, and all I really am
lands is June, and you and
always; I do miss you
wonder what you've
e your arms around me
can never get away, ea

llways,

**Pardon this --->
it happened after I wrote the letter.

Dearest Evelyn,

There isn't much new, over and above what I wrote you yesterday: I still haven't heard any more about where I'm going or how soon, but I know it will be fairly soon, probably in about two weeks at the most. Are you happy?

Taylor and I went out for the last time together last night, ate at the Seven Seas, and then went to the movies. Today he is in OCS, and in three months will be a Lieutenant. Probably from OCS he'll go to Harrisburg in Combat Intelligence School.

I got a card from Pete Trego today asking me to meet him at Ft. Lauderdale on Sunday. He also told me that Grove City won the Tournament again this year. Boy would I have liked to have been there! If you get a chance, you might go see them play at Westerville, and forward me a play by play report. I can picture you doing that.

Tonight, I think I'll go see <u>Random Harvest</u>, and tomorrow night I hope to see the Florida State Basketball Tournament. I'm kind of getting the urge.

Well darling, I know this is really just a short note, but there just isn't any more news right now, and I don't get the idea that a short note means that I love you any less; because that just ain't so.

You are my honey, darling, and all I really am living for, and working towards is June, and you and I together for then and for always. I do miss you and dream about you, and wonder what you're doing, and I surely long to have your arms around me and to hold you so close you can never get away, even for a little while.

All My Love—Always,

Dick

Dearest Evelyn,

Today is the most springlike day we've had in Miami. It reminds me of late April at home. Consequently, spring is in my heart too, and I wish, even more than usual, that I were with you. We could take a nice ride, or a leisurely walk in weather like this. — A walk up the mud road would really be wonderful to me. All of which means that I miss you terribly today. Darling, last night I saw Random Harvest, and as usual you were the heroine to my "Smithy." I couldn't help but shudder at the possibility — however slim — of anything like that standing between the complete fruition of our love. Then I dreamt of you last night, and it was a terribly bad dream. You had decided that after all we weren't really meant for one another, and had told me that you would never see me again. When I awoke this morning I was sad, and I've had a lost feeling in the pit of my stomach all day. Darling, please don't ever really do anything like that to me, or I know that my life will be completely shot. I love you so very much, and want you more than you'll ever ever know.

Well, I got reasonably definite word today that my papers are being made out for OCS in Medical Administrative. The school is located at Camp Barcley, Texas, which is located at Abilene in the heart of the cow country. — Yipee! I think the school starts on the 19th of this month, which means that I will leave either the end of next week, or the first of the following one. — About the fourteenth, or very close thereto. From all I can gather, the school is a stiff one, and there are about

Dearest Evelyn,

Today is the most spring like day we've had in Miami: It reminds me of late April at home. Consequently, spring is in my heart too, and I wish, even more than usual, that I were with you. We could take a nice ride, or a leisurely walk in weather like this. A walk up the mud road would really be wonderful to me. All of which means that I miss you terribly today. Darling, last night I saw <u>Random Harvest</u>, and as usual you were the heroine to my "Smith." I couldn't help but shudder at the possibility —however slim—of anything like that standing between the complete fruition of our love. Then I dreamt of you last night, and it was a terribly bad dream: You had decided that after all we weren't really meant for one another, and had told me that you would never see me again. When I awoke this morning I was sad, and I've had a lost feeling in the pit of my stomach all day. Darling, please don't ever really do anything like that to me, or I know that my life will be completely shot. I love you so very much, and want you more than you'll ever ever know.

Well, I got reasonably definite word today that my papers are being made out for OCS in Medical Administrative. The school is located at Camp Barcley Texas, which is located at Abilene in the heart of the cow country. Yipee! I think the school starts on the 19th of this month, which means that I will leave either the end of next week, or the first of the following one. About the fourteenth, or very close there to. From all I can gather, the school is a stiff one, and there are about forty percent who do not get through it. Add to that the fact that I'm not in any way qualified for such a school, having only a very negative knowledge of Medical Terminology, and you can see what I'll be up against. However, honey, some way I'm going to get through the course and get a commission pretty close to June the 19th. So make plans accordingly.

You asked me, before we knew about my really getting a crack at OCS, whether I really thought we could make it, or whether I was only dreaming. My answer is—of course we could have made it, and if I get a commission we'll be a cinch to do so. But, if anything should keep me from it, we'll still get along somehow—that is if you'd have me under such circumstance. I know that no matter how tough things could ever get we'll get along somehow, because I know that we've got enough love for one another, and enough faith to take us through anything.

All My Love—Always,

Dick

Cmd. R. D. Clark, U.S. Army.
C. C., Class 17,
O.C.S. M.R.T.C.
Camp Barkeley, Texas.

Miss. Evelyn Stark,
406 N. Henry St.,
Crestline,

Darling,

I never have been more discouraged in my life. It is awfully muddy here to begin with. It is worse than the middle of Beulah Park in a pouring rain, and we march in it, walk in it, eat in it, and drink it. We don't wash in it because we very seldom wash. We have only cold water here and have to wade through mud and jump a couple of trenches to get to the latrine. Our Hutments leak, and yesterday my bed was wet. I haven't changed underwear or taken a shower since I got here. Already, about thirty men have resigned, and there will be more. Old tough regular army infantry men swear it's the hardest living they've ever done, and you can imagine what it's like for me.

The classes are not so hard, but you don't have time to study your assignments. In short, if the exams are very hard, I may not get through them. Then too there is a course given called Logistics, which deals with motors and machinery, and you know how I am about that sort of thing. Also, they give grades on military bearing, which I don't have, and on the ability to kill men, which I never have done. The fact is, if I get through this course I will be very surprised. — However, I'm not quitting, they'll have to throw me out. So, don't tell anybody I'm in OCS, and just pray that I'm lucky enough to get through.

Honey, I have never missed you more, or longed for you more in my life. I only hope I can make it here so that we can be together. But please dearest if I don't get through don't disown me, I'm giving it all I've got. I'd better quit now, but keep writing often, and know that even if I don't answer every time, I'm thinking of you every minute, and working only for you.

All my love, Always
Dick.

POSTMARKED CAMP BARKLEY, TEXAS—MARCH 10, 1943

Darling,

I have never been more discouraged in my life: It is awfully muddy here to begin with. It is worse than the middle of Beulah Park in a pouring rain, and we march in it, walk in it, eat in it, and drink it. We don't wash in it because we very seldom wash. We have only cold water here and have to wade through mud and jump a couple of trenches to get to the latrine. Our Hutments leak, and yesterday my bed was wet. I haven't changed underwear or taken a shower since I got here. Already, about thirty men have resigned, and there will be more. Old tough regular army infantry men swear it's the hardest living they've even done, and you can imagine what it's like for me.

The classes are not so hard, but you don't have time to study your assignments. In short, if the exams are very hard, I may not get through them. Then too there is a course given called Logistics, which deals with motors and machinery, and you know how I am about that sort of thing. Also, they give grades on military bearing, which I don't have, and on the ability to drill men, which I never have done. The fact is, if I get through this course I will be very surprised. However, I'm not quitting, they'll have to throw me out. So, don't tell anybody I'm in OCS, and just pray that I'm lucky enough to get through.

Honey, I have never missed you more, or longed for you more in my life. I only hope I can make it here so that we can be together. But please dearest if I don't get through, don't disown me. I'm giving it all I've got. I'd better quit now, but keep writing often, and know that even if I don't answer every time, I'm thinking of you every minute and working only for you.

All My Love, Always,

Dick

Cand R. D. Clark
O.C.S., M.R.T.C.
C.C. Class 17.
Camp Barkeley, Texas

Miss Evelyn Stark,
406 N. Henry St.,
Crestline,
Ohio.

Thursday.

Darling

    Things are not quite as busy as usual tonight, and so I'm taking time out to write you. I should be studying I suppose, but I just can't keep at it all the time. I'll give you a review of the past week to give you an idea of how things are going:

    I told you about the mud I guess. — It quit raining Friday, and by Sunday it was just as dry as it could possibly be. Saturday we moved to some other hutments, and then spent all day Sunday cleaning them. — To make a long story short, I just haven't had a free moment. We have our first formation at six fifteen in the morning, and our last one at nine at night. Between nine and ten we must shine shoes, and get on the ball generally. Lights are out at ten, and we shave after that. Then up at five fifteen and at it again, — cleaning up the barracks etc. — I wanted to write you Sunday, but I just didn't have the time.

    The academic end of it is coming along a little better now. — I think I can get through that part of it all right. We just started drill this week, which is also very important, and so far I have gotten that

we're just in
, and I've never
— We were out
yesterday in a
ked the mud
that is happened
way my not
I've gotten six
looks out of line,
, etc. I'm not
can have, but
still trying
still hoping I
weren't for you
go back to my old
, if it wouldn't

you and long for
all I want and I
me by June. I
ways, and I love
you more than you can possibly ever know.
Love me darling, whether I make it here or not
and keep rooting for me.
    All My Love, Always — Dick

POSTMARKED CAMP BARKLEY, TEXAS—APRIL 3, 1943

Thursday

Darling,

Things are not quite as busy as usual tonight, and so I'm <u>taking</u> time out to write you. I should be studying I suppose, but I just can't keep at it all the time. I'll give you a review of the past week to give you an idea of how things are going:

I told you about the mud I guess. It quit raining Friday, and by Sunday it was just as dry as it could possibly be. Saturday we moved to some other hutments, and then spent all day Sunday cleaning them. To make a long story short, I just haven't had a free moment. We have our first formation at six fifteen in the morning, and our last one at nine at night. Between nine and ten we must shine shoes, and get on the ball generally. Lights are out at ten, and we shave after that. Then up at five fifteen and at it again, cleaning up the barracks etc. I wanted to write you Sunday, but I just didn't have the time.

The academic end of it is coming along a little better now. I think I can get through that part of it all right. We just started drill this week, which is also very important, and so far I have gotten that without any trouble. But we're just in the beginning stages of drill, and I've never drilled any men in my life. We were out for three hours day before yesterday in a dust storm; I think I like the mud better. The worst thing that's happened so far from the point of view of my not making it is that I've gotten six demerits for things like "books out of line, pack not properly rolled, etc." I'm not sure how many of those I can have, but I'm afraid not many. I'm still trying as hard as I know how, I'm still happy I make it, but darling, if it weren't for you I think I would quit and go back to my old job at Miami. Except for you, it wouldn't be worth it to me.

Honey, I do think of you and long for you all the time. You're all I want and I just have to have you with me by June. I want you for always and always, and I love you more than you can possibly ever know. Love me darling, whether I make it here or not and keep rooting for me.

All My Love, Always

Dick

Cpl. R. B. Clark,
Co. C. Class 17
O.C.S. M.R.I.C.
Camp Barkely, Texas.

Free

Miss Evelyn Stark,
406 N. Henry St.
Crestline,
Ohio.

Darling,

Sunday has rolled around again, and with it time to write a letter to you, and then — study. I have four exams this coming week. One tomorrow in Sanitation, and the big one Friday in Logistics, — that's the course on motors and motor maintenance that I am expecting so much trouble with. Also, I have one on Service Records, and one in Military Courtesy.

Yesterday, I was really a tired boy: We took a hike yesterday morning that was about five miles long, and we did it with a full field pack in just a little over an hour. After that, we crawled in and out of fox holes and trenches in simulated battle maneuvers. Then came the real tough one, we crawled on our stomachs threw a maze of barbed wire. I did it, but it wasn't a bit easy. This morning I was really stiff. — One thing dearest, if I live through it, you'll have a honey who is really in shape.

I got my first grade on my first exam. — it was an A. There were about a hundred and eighty who flunked the thing, so I felt pretty good about that. However, I still have so awfully much to get through, that I have a lot of doubt about my making the grade. I told you that I got six demerits I guess. They count quite a bit if you get too many of them. So — I may become a Lt. some day, and I may not. If not, I think I'll either try C. I. C., or else Army Specialist Corps. — The Army Specialists Corps has set up schools in both Military Government and Intelligence.

Sweetheart, don't ever get the idea that I don't look forward to your letters, because I really do. They and you keep me going. Without that combination, I would be lost. You are it for me my dearest, and I love you and miss you so much. It's spring at home I know, and home with you is where I belong. — I know I do. I know I need you to walk with me, and to be close to me. I want to talk to you and look at you and tell you

love you. You asked me ... I was sure I loved you and ... forever with you. — To raise ... our home and our life together ... need to ask that question, ... and of course I've been sure ... — Darling, I can hardly wait ... that I get my commission ... Hoping that, whether I get a ... you'll marry me then. — I ... much more if I had you right ... but you know how I feel ... keep on writing just as

I love Always and Always,

Dick.

Postmarked Camp Barkley, Texas—April 5, 1943

Darling,

Sunday has rolled around again, and with it time to write a letter to you, and then —study. I have four exams this coming week: one tomorrow in Sanitation, and the big one Friday in Logistics. That's the course on motors and motor maintenance that I am expecting so much trouble with. Also, I have one on Service Records, and one in Military Courtesy.

Yesterday, I was really a tired boy: We took a hike yesterday morning that was about five miles long, and we did it with a full field pack in just a little over an hour. After that, we crawled in and out of fox holes and trenches in simulated battle maneuvers. Then came the real tough one, we crawled on our stomachs throw a maze of barbed wire. I did it, but it wasn't a bit easy. This morning I was really stiff. One thing dearest, if I live through it, you'll have a honey who is really in shape.

I got my first grade on my first exam—it was an A. There were about a hundred and eighty who flunked the thing, so I felt pretty good about that. However, I still have so awfully much to get through that I have a lot of doubt about my making the grade. I told you that I got six demerits I guess. They count quite a bit if you get too many of them. So—I may become a Lt. someday, and I may not. If not, I think I'll either try C. L. C., or else Army Specialist Corps. The Army Specialists Corps has set up schools in both military Government and Intelligence.

Sweetheart, don't ever get the idea that I don't look forward to your letters, because I really do. They and you keep me going. Without that combination, I would be lost. You are it for me my dearest, and I love you and miss you so much. Its spring at home I know, and home with you is where I belong. I know I do. I know I need you to walk with me, and to be close to me. I want to talk to you and look at you and tell you how very much I love you. You asked me the other day whether I was sure I love you and wanted to settle down forever with you. To raise our children, to have our home and our life together. Honey, you didn't even need to ask that question. Of course, I'm sure, and of course I've been sure for such a long time. Darling, I can hardly wait until June—assuming that I get my commission then. And I'm still hoping that, whether I get a commission or not, you'll marry me then. I could tell you so much more if I had you right here with me. But you know how I feel darling. Love me, and keep on writing just as often as you can.

All My Love Always and Always,

Dick

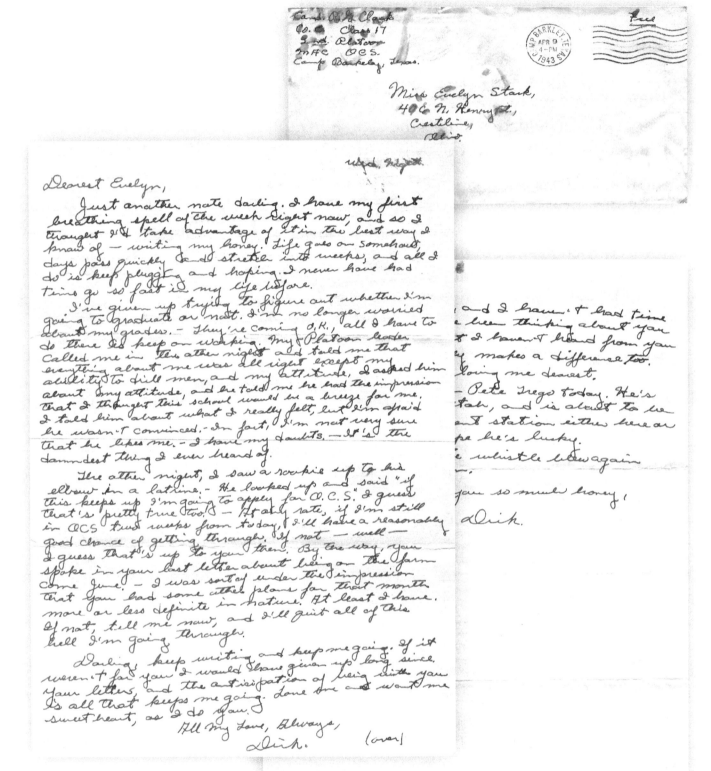

Wednesday Night

Dearest Evelyn,

Just another note darling. I have my first breathing spell of the week right now, and so I thought I'd take advantage of it in the best way I know of— writing my honey. Life goes on somehow, days pass quickly and stretch into weeks, and all I do is keep plugging and hoping. I never have had time go so fast in my life before.

I've given up trying to figure out whether I'm going to graduate or not. I'm no longer worried about my grades. They're coming O.K., all I have to do there is keep on working. My Platoon leader called me in the other night and told me that everything about me was all right except my ability to drill men, and my attitude, I asked him about my attitude, and he told me he had the impression that I thought this school would be a breeze for me. I told him about what I really felt, but I'm afraid he wasn't convinced. In fact, I'm not very sure that he likes me. I have my doubts. It's the damndest thing I ever heard of.

The other night, I saw a rookie up to his elbow in a latrine. He looked up and said, "if this keeps up I'm going to apply for O.C.S." I guess that's pretty true too! At any rate, if I'm still in OCS two weeks from today, I'll have a reasonable good chance of getting through. If not—well—I guess that's up to you then. By the way, you spoke in your last letter about being on the farm come June. I was sort of under the impression that you had some other plans for that month more or less definite in nature. At least I have. If not, tell me now, and I'll quit all of this hell I'm going through.

Darling, keep writing and keep me going. If it weren't for you I would have given up long since. Your letters, and the anticipation of being with you is all that keeps me going. Love me and want me sweetheart, as I do you.

All My Love, Always,

Dick

P.S. It's Thursday, and I haven't had time yet to mail this. I've been thinking about you all day as usual, but I haven't heard from you in two days. It really makes a difference too. Please keep writing & loving me dearest.

I got a card from Pete Trego today. He's at Salt Lake City, Utah, and is about to be assigned his permanent station either here or overseas. I sure hope he's lucky.

Well sweet, the whistle blew again and I've got to run.

I love you so much honey,

Dick

Cand. R. D. Clark
Co. C, Class 17
2 nd. Platoon,
M. A. C. O. C. S.
Camp Barkeley, Texas.

Miss Evelyn Stark,
404 N. Henry St.,
Crestline,
Ohio.

Darling,

Sunday once more dearest, and the only day of peace I have. How I do look forward to that day! Darling, do you know it was just five months ago today that I got in the army. — That really seems like a long time ago doesn't it? How I wish it was all over and I could go home again for good! Day after day I hate this place more than I did the day before. It is like nothing I ever saw before, and I would never go through it if it weren't for you. If I knew that at the end of three months I would get a commission, I wouldn't mind it at all, but I have the feeling that I'm not going to get through it. My grades are coming along all right, but nothing else is. I guess I'm just not a soldier. There is to be a great amount of kicking out at the end of this week, and again two weeks later. If I make those two, I might get through. In other words, the next three weeks will pretty definitely tell the tale, and even then I can't be sure. — The class which graduates this coming week has one platoon with only fourteen men left in it. — Fourteen out of an original fifty four. Things like that get me a little discouraged.

So darling, that's the way it is. I just don't think I'll make it. Probably had I gone to Air Forces, or Army Administrative things would have been a little different, and I know — in the case of the Air Corps — a whole lot easier. I haven't quit trying yet, but I get sorely tempted sometimes.

I only hope that if I don't make it you won't give up on me. I think that anything like that would cause me to be pretty completely washed up. When I don't hear from you for a couple of days, even that bothers me a great deal. It's hell to want someone as I want you, and not be able to do anything about it. Sometimes I can't think of anything else but you, and of being with you and talking to you, and holding you close. Oh sweetheart, how I long for our Sundays together, — walking over the

spring come over the countryside, ... in love. That's all I'm hoping ... to be with you again! — But ... ... rein the streams I have of ... that if I don't get through here ... lose some of the pride you have ... it won't really make any difference

... I'm so blue that I just don't ... anymore today. But I'll try and ... sometime, and please dearest ... ... , I need you so much ... don't stop loving me no matter ... — I'll make it up to you

... my Love, Always and Always,

Dick.

Postmarked Camp Barkeley, Texas—April 12, 1943

Darling,

Sunday once more dearest, and the only day of peace I have. How I do look forward to that day! Darling, do you know it was just five months ago today that I got in the army. That really seems like a long time ago doesn't it? How I wish it was all over and I could go home again for good! Day after day I hate this place more than I did the day before. It is like nothing I ever saw before, and I would never go through it if it weren't for you. If I knew that at the end of three months I would get a commission, I wouldn't mind it at all, but I have the feeling that I'm not going to get through it. My grades are coming along all right, but nothing else is. I guess I'm just not a soldier. There is to be a great amount of kicking out at the end of this week, and again two weeks later. If I make those two, I might get through. In other words, the next three weeks will pretty definitely tell the tale, and even then I can't be sure. The class which graduates this coming week has one platoon with only fourteen men left in it. Fourteen out of an original fifty-four. Things like that get me a little discouraged.

So darling, that's the way it is. I just don't think I'll make it. Probably had I gone to Air Forces, or Army Administrative things would have been a little different, and I know—in the case of the Air Corps—a whole lot easier, I haven't quit trying yet, but I get sorely tempted sometimes.

I only hope that if I don't make it you won't give up on me. I think that anything like that would cause me to be pretty completely washed up. When I don't hear from you for a couple of days, even that bothers me a great deal. It's hell to want someone as I want you, and not be able to do anything about it. Sometimes I can't think of anything else but you, and of being with you and talking to you, and holding you close. Oh sweetheart, how I long for one of our Sundays together—walking over the fields, and watching spring come over the countryside, and just being together in love. That's all I'm hoping and living for. Just to be with you again! But honey, don't let anything ruin the dreams I have of us together. I know that if I don't get through here it will cause you to lose some of the pride you have in me, but I hope it won't really make any difference to you. Will it?

Well, honey, I'm so blue that I just don't think I can write anymore today. But I'll try and write during the week sometime, and please dearest keep writing real often. I need you so much right now. And don't stop loving me no matter what happens here. I'll make it up to you somehow.

All My Love, Always and Always,

Dick

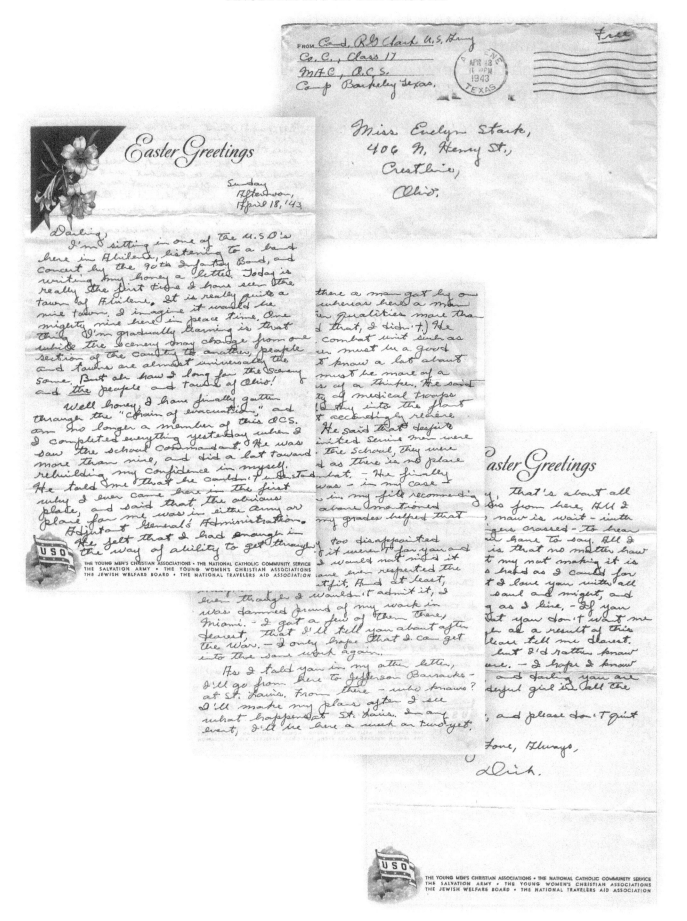

POSTMARKED ABILENE, TEXAS—APRIL 18, 1943

Sunday Afternoon

Darling,

I'm sitting in one of the U.S.O's here in Abilene, listening to a band concert by the 90th Infantry Band, and writing my honey a letter. Today is really the first time I have seen the town of Abilene. It is really quite a nice town. I imagine it would be might nice here in peace time. One thing I'm gradually learning is that while the scenery may change from one section of the country to another, people and towns are almost universally the same. But oh how I long for the scenery and the people and towns of Ohio!

Well honey, I have finally gotten through the "chain of evacuation," and am no longer a member of this O.C.S. I completed everything yesterday when I saw the school commandant. He was more than nice, and did a lot toward rebuilding my confidence in myself. He told me that he couldn't understand why I even came here in the first place, and said that the obvious place for me was in either Army or Adjutant General's Administration. He felt that I had enough in the way of ability to get through. He said that there a man got by on ability to think, whereas here a man must have other qualities more than brains. (He said that, I didn't.) He said that in a combat unit such as this is, an officer must be a good drill man, must know a lot about the army, and must be more of a soldier and less of a thinker. He said that the majority of medical troops go with the Infantry into the front lines, and must accordingly receive Infantry training. He said that despite the fact that Limited Service men were being admitted to the school, they were not really wanted as there is no place for them in combat. He finally stated he was—in my case—enclosing a letter in my file recommending me for the two above mentioned schools. I guess my grades helped that much at least.

I'm not really too disappointed about all this. If it weren't for you and I, and our plans, I would not miss it at all. I never have even respected the insignia of this outfit. And at least, even though I wouldn't admit it, I was damned proud of my work in Miami. I got a few of them there, dearest, that I'll tell you about after the War. I only hope that I can get into the same work again. As I told you in my other letter, I'll go from here to Jefferson Barracks—at St. Louis. From there—who knows? I'll make my plans after I see what happens at St. Louis. In any event, I'll be here a week or two yet.

Honey, that's about all the news from here. All I can do now is wait—with my fingers crossed—to hear what you have to say. All I can tell you is that no matter how you feel about my not making it is that I tried as hard as I could for you, and that I love you with all my heart and soul and might, and I will as long as I live. If you should feel that you don't want me anymore though as a result of this business here, please tell me dearest. It would hurt, but I'd rather know than not be sure. I hope I know already though, and darling you are the most wonderful girl in all the World.

Write to me, and please don't quit loving me.

All My Love, Always,

Dick

Cand. R. B. Clark, U.S. Army.
Co C, Class 17
M.B.C., O.C.S.
Camp Barkeley, Texas.

CAMP BARKELEY TEXAS
APR 20
6-PM
1943

free

Miss Evelyn Stark,
406 N. Henry St,
Crestline,
Ohio.

Monday night
April 19, 1943.

Dearest Evelyn,

I got the letter that you wrote Thursday, today, and sweetheart ever since then I've been tingling all over, and my heart is still going like a sledge hammer, and my heart is reeling. Oh darling, I want you so very much right with me in person right now, as you are now and always in my thoughts. I've told you for almost four years that I love you, and I've said it a million times to you and to myself. When I first started saying it, I didn't know quite what love was, but I knew I felt differently about you than I ever had about anyone else. When I got a smile from you it did something to me, and a little teasing encouragement was all I needed to keep me working and trying to win you. The first time you decided not to see me again was more a blow to my pride than anything else - for awhile - and then the idea dawned on me that I really missed you. When we had that first new years out together, that added to it all. - I meant it even then when I gave you my pin, and persuaded you it was a joke. Then — through the whole crazy quilt of our affections and - your lack of them - I became more and more desirous of having you. Maybe it was first for the chase, at least that must have been a part of it; some of it was because to me then you were glamorous, you were my idea of what a girl ought to be. But still it was mostly a superficial thing - half real, and half imagination. When I heard that you had taken Bill's pin, I thought it was all over, forever. I started going with another girl, and tried to convince myself that I was forgetting you. Yet, I wanted to be sure, and so — the trip that spring day a couple of years ago, when I came up to see you along with George, who was trying all the way to tell me to turn around and go back to Columbus, I don't know what I was looking for, but if it was peace of mind, I didn't find it. I told George it was all over, and I lied to everyone else too. Then, I got gloriously drunk, and I have never been out with the girl I was dating since.

...period of making women... we're sure of one another... man and a girl can ever have... on solider footing and have more... most people who get married. But the idea of... four or five years more doesn't make me very happy. I just can't let you be away from me that long. I want my arms around you, and you as close to me as you can possibly get, I want to have your lips and eyes — and all of you, your mind and heart, and body for keeps, so that we can have the happiness we both know is ours. Maybe I'm crazy, but I think we have been crazy all along for not going ahead with our plans.

This has been a long letter dearest, maybe an unusual one. But this letter is as true a picture of my feelings as I can ever possibly give you. Maybe you won't want to take the chance, maybe my ideas are crazy, but I don't think so. Whenever I get to my permanent station I am due for a furlough. We could get married there, or we could get married in St. Louis...

...before, I had intended..., but for what I'm... to get to know!

...ting off because I was... through thinking anymore... want you to be my wife... not going to ask you... don't want that, going... if I'm in this country... matter where I go. I can get... now. I can get... and $128.00 a month... in the country would... off the past. If you... probably find if you... are they. - All down... getting at is, can you... regardless of anything... waters? All I've got is... is as great as it... can shout it, and... quite it, and whisper it... can't go on without... in a whole way, and a... re-adjustments afterwards... in every test a... dearest. Gladly, sure are... have more to go on than... But the idea of...

...Oh honey, please though... someplace as soon as you... can't guarantee our happiness... know that together we can... else but happy. I should... Monday for Jefferson Barracks... right away, I'll get it in time... something to think about in my... suit for now sweetheart, and... that you want to go... thing like what I'm suggesting... and I know it isn't... me, and we can be happy... most important, together.

Monday Night, April 19, 1943

Dearest Evelyn,

I got the letter that you wrote Thursday, today, and sweetheart ever since then I've been tingling all over, and my heart is still going like a sledge hammer, and my head is reeling. Oh darling, I want you so very much right with me in person right now, as you are now and always in my thoughts. I've told you for almost four years that I love you, and I've said it a million times to you and to myself. When I first started saying it, I didn't know quite what love was, but I know I felt differently about you than I ever had about anyone else. When I got a smile from you it did something to me, and a little teasing encouragement was all I needed to keep me working and trying to win you. The first time you decided not to see me again was more a blow to my pride than anything else for a while and then the idea dawned on me that I really missed you. When we had that first New Year's Eve together, that added to it all. I meant it even then when I gave you my pin, and persuaded you it was a joke, then through the whole crazy guilt of our affections and your lack of them I became more and more desirous of having you. Maybe it was just for the chase, at least that must have been a part of it; some of it was because to me then you were glamorous, you were my idea of what a girl ought to be. But still it was mostly a superficial thing—half real, and half imaginations. When I heard that you had taken Bills' pin, I thought it was all over, forever. I started going with another girl and tried to convince myself that I was forgetting you. Yet, I wanted to be sure, and so the trip that spring day a couple of years ago, when I came up to see you along with George, who was trying all the way to tell me to turn around and go back to Columbus. I don't know what I was looking for, but if it was peace of mind, I didn't find it. I told George it was all over, and I lied to everyone else too. Then, I got gloriously drunk, and I have never been out with the girl I was dating since.

Life all that spring was a series of dates and drunks, and damned foolishness. I don't know what made me ever write you again, or what made you answer. But I did know that when I was with you, I was happy again. Finally, through our rides, and swims, and walks, and dinners, and perfect nights in your porch swing, and parties, and nights before your fireplace, in each other's arms, and—everything else that happened to us. To the Christmas Holidays, and that New Years' Eve at my house. We built up a contentment and a knowledge of one another that grew into something a hell of a lot more than an ex-college boys' infatuation, and a college girls' leading a man on. It came to be us. It came to mean no pretense and few secrets; it came to be more than glamour. It came to be something built on a hard solid foundation. It came to be us Evelyn and Dick and real love, I wanted to marry you last summer, but I was afraid I would be drafted. I wanted to marry you before I left home, but I was afraid to ask you and have me be any place in the world but with you. When you came to Miami at Christmas time, I would have handcuffed you if need be had I not felt that by summer I would have had a commission and would have been well able to support you. I thought we should wait for that, and so did you. Well, it didn't happen. Perhaps, if I go back in the work I was in, I might eventually get a direct commission, perhaps I might get into C.L.C., where the sky is the limit as to how far I could go; perhaps I might do very well in the new Army Specialist Corps; perhaps, I may go to O.C.S. in Army Administration, or A.G.O., as they are recommending from here. But, there is another side to the picture too, that you may as well know now as later. Probably my address at Jefferson Barracks will have on it O.R.T.C., which means overseas replacement training center. The fact that I'm going there does not necessarily mean that I'll go over. But, I'll be placed in a pool, and wherever my talents call for, there will I go. If they need me at Lockbourne Air Base in Columbus, I'll go there. If they need me in North Africa that's where they'll send me. I'm not telling you that to alarm you, the chances are I'll be in this country someplace, but I can't count on it. Don't tell my mother that yet. I'll tell her when and if I go, and not before. I had intended to do the same with you, but for what I'm asking you now, you've got to know.

I kept putting everything off because I was always thinking. I'm through thinking anymore. All I know is that I want you to be my wife as soon as possible. I'm not going to ask you anything if I go over. I don't want that, going overseas married, but if I'm in this country, we can be together no matter where I go. I make $66.00 a month now. I can get a $20.00 ration allowance, and $28.00 a month for my wife. Most any camp in the country would let me live with you off the post. If you want to, you could probably find a job to keep you busy during the day. Oh damn it honey, what I'm getting at is, can you marry me this summer regardless of anything except a trip across the water? All I've got is my love for you, which is as great as it can ever possibly be. I can shout it, and carve it on trees, and write it, and whisper it in your ear. But I just can't go on without you indefinitely, through a whole war, and a period of making sensible re-adjustments afterwards. We're sure of one another dearest, by every test a man and a girl can ever have. Already, we are on solider footing and have more to go on than most people who get married. But the idea of four or five years more doesn't make me very happy. I first can't let you be away from me that long. I want my arms around you, and you as close to me as you can possibly get. I want to have your lips and eyes and all of you, your mind and heart, and body for keeps, so that we can have the happiness we both know is ours. Maybe I'm crazy, but I think we have been crazy all along for not going ahead with our plans.

This has been a long letter dearest, maybe an unusual one. But, this letter is as true a picture of my feelings as I can ever possibly give you. Maybe you won't want to take the chance, maybe my ideas are crazy, but I don't think so. Whenever I get to my permanent station I am dire for a furlough. We could get married then, or we could get married in St. Louis over Memorial Day. Oh honey, please though, please marry me someplace as soon as your school is over. I can't guarantee our happiness, but you and I know that together we can never be anything else but happy. I should leave about next Monday for Jefferson Barracks. If you answer this right away, I'll get it in time I think, to have something to think about in my trip north.

I'm going to quit for now sweetheart, and if you don't feel that you want to go through with anything like what I'm suggesting, I shan't blame you. I know it isn't sensible, but it <u>can</u> be done, and we <u>can</u> be happy and secure, and most important, <u>together</u>!

Dick

Wednesday
Afternoon.

Dearest Evelyn,

There are lots of other things I'd like to have called you besides Scarlet, but that really covers them all I guess. It's funny darling how I've been lately. But, I can't think of anything but you. Nothing else matters at all: You are in my thoughts all the day from the minute I wake until I sleep at night, and then I dream about you. When I'm loafing — which is most of the time lately — I conjure up pictures of you in my mind's eye, or get out your picture and look at it. Sometimes I can actually feel your presence right beside me, and I can hear your voice. Somehow, I know you're with me still, and oh sweetheart, I hate to open my eyes again to reality. I think if possible I love you more and more all the time. All I want is to be with you, I don't care where, just so long as you're around someplace. It's a terrible feeling in a way, and wonderful in another, but I know now what my German book meant when I used to read " du liest einer schöne gnadige fraulien, ich liebe dich, und ich wollte küsse du." Which all boils down to the same old story of blind love, whether it be in German or Hindustani or English. But, all of my telling you on paper that I love you is just so much stuff. If I had you here, I could whisper it to you, and shout it from the top of the mesa, and tell you with my eyes and arms, and lips, and every way there is.

In the letter I wrote you Monday, I was pretty unreasonable I suppose, and after I wrote it, I thought for a while before I mailed it. Not that I don't mean every word in it. Not that I don't want to marry you today or tomorrow, or any day you'll have me, if you will; but I've got no right to expect you to give up everything you have to come along madly on a wild chase to God only knows where with me. You've got everything back home to make you happy. You've got comforts and friends, and plenty to keep you occupied. If you marry me now, you'll lose about all of this. We probably wouldn't have the amount of money I outlined, but that really isn't very

these times. You probably would
... place that wouldn't be so hot,
... you would be associated with
... either. Maybe the job you
... all right, and maybe it would
... job as a waitress. After the
... we'd have to go back to
... in from scratch I hope.
... picture I can give you of
... to face if you marry me now.
... I'll go in this man's army
... very good start that is sure.
... promise you is that if
... to make you happy, and
... stand to do that, and
... the bad features of the thing,
... that much. — I know it is
... if you don't feel like taking
... I don't blame you at all,
... loving you just as much as ever.
... who messed up our really
... doing what they want here
... sweetheart, the choice is yours.
... you so very very much that
... with you, I'm really at the
... estly say I can't live without
... it's got to be up to
... me please Evelyn my darling,
... may happen? Do the good things
... outweigh the bad? All I
... that two months from now
... together for always and

... going to close for now. They
... tonight, and there is a
... How I wish you could be
... me! — But, I shall "walk
... military manner," and look at the
moon and think of you and long for you so very
hard, and miss you. Perhaps, if you are thinking
of me, it will be almost as if we're really
together.

All My Love for always and always,

Dick.

Wednesday Afternoon

Dearest Evelyn,

There are lots of other things I'd like to have called you besides dearest, but that really covers them all I guess. It's funny darling how I've been lately. But I can't think of anything but you. Nothing else matters at all: You are in my thoughts all the day from the minute I wake until I sleep at night, and then I dream about you. When I'm loafing—which is most of the time lately—I conjure up pictures of you in my minds eye, or get out your picture and look at it. Sometimes I can actually feel your presence right beside me, and I can hear your voice. Somehow, I know you're with me still, and oh sweetheart, I hate to open my eyes again to reality. I think if possible I love you more and more all the time. All I want is to be with you. I don't care where, just so long as you're around someplace. It's a terrible feeling in a way, and wonderful in another, but I know now what my German book meant when I used to read "deu bist einer schone gnadige fraulien, ich liebe dich, und ich wallte kusse tu." Which boils down to the same old story of blind love, whether it be in German or Hindustan, or English. But, all of my telling you on paper that I love you is just so much stuff. If I had you here, I could whisper it to you, and shout it from the top of the mesa, and tell you with my eyes and arms, and lips, and every way there is.

In the letter I wrote you Monday, I was pretty unreasonable I suppose, and after I wrote it, I thought for a while before I mailed it. Not that I don't mean every word in it. Not that I don't want to marry you today or tomorrow, or any day you'll have me, if you will; but I've got no right to expect you to give up everything you have to come along madly on a wild chase to God only knows where with me. You've got everything back home to make you happy. You've got comforts and friends, and plenty to keep you occupied. If you marry me now, you'll lose about all of this. We probably would have the amount of money I outlined, but that really isn't very much to go on in these times. You probably would have to live in a place that wouldn't be so hot, and most of the people you would be associated with would not be so hot either. Maybe the job you could get would be all right, and maybe it would be no more than a job as a waitress. After the War, if it ever does end, we'd have to go back to Grove City, and start in from scratch—broke.

That's the only picture I can give you of what you'll have to face if you marry me now. I don't know how far I'll go in this mans' army, but I'm not off to a very good start that's sure. The only thing I can promise you is that if loving you and wanting to make you happy, and being willing to work hard to do that, will compensate for some of the bad features of the thing, then you will have that much. I know it's going to be tough, and if you don't feel like taking that much of a chance, I don't blame you at all, and I'll go right on loving you just as much as ever. After all, it was me who messed up our really big chance by not being what they want here in an officer. So sweetheart, the choice is yours. I love you and love you so very very much that it hurts not to be with you. I'm really at the point where I can honestly say I can't live without you much longer, but—it's got to be up to you. Will you marry me please Evelyn my darling, in spite of all that may happen? Do the good things about our being together out weigh the bad? All I can do is hope, and pray that two months from now we'll be married and together for always and always.

Well honey, I'm going to close for now: They put us on guard duty tonight, and there is a full moon in Texas. How I wish you could be here to enjoy it with me! But, I shall "walk my post in a military manner," and look at the moon and think of you and long for you so very hard, and miss you. Perhaps, if you are thinking of me, it will be almost as if we're really together.

All My Love for Always and Always,

Dick

Wed. nite.

Darling,

I got your letters today telling me how you feel about my not making O.C.S., and also that you will marry me this June come hardship or come good times. Evelyn dearest, there is only one thing I can say and that is you are the most wonderful girl I've ever known or ever will know in this world or the next; and I love you with all my heart and soul and might. With each new and wonderful thing that you do or say, I only love you more, when I had already thought I loved you all there is. And sweetheart, I'm awfully in earnest when I tell you that I am humble in the presence of your love for me, I don't know why you love me, or how in the face of everything you keep on loving me, but I'm thankful for it sweetness, so thankful, and so happy, and so proud that everytime I think of you loving me a lump comes in my throat, and a strange pleasant prickly feeling spreads all over me. Yes darlingest, we do love each other more I think than any two people I know. We both feel exactly the same way, and did you notice? — We seem to feel the same way always at the same time! So that when I'm thinking of you very hard, I know somehow that you are with me, and are thinking about me too.

You say that you will marry me in June regardless of anything, regardless of security or anything else, and oh honey, I say the same thing over and over again. We've been too sensible too long. We will get married in June unless I go overseas, which I doubt that I'll do. And dearest, all I can say further is that I'll love you for always and always, and I'll try with everything I have to make you completely happy as long as we live. I want our marriage to be perfect in every way, and my darling I know it will be. We'd move any obstacles from our path together, and physically, mentally, and spiritually we'll be completely and inseparably united. — As to the practical side of our getting married, here's as much as I can tell you now honey:

I am due for a furlough right now, but I probably won't get one until after my permanent

won't be for a month or so yet If I am held at Jefferson Barracks ...th, I wish you would come ...t cross those bridges until later ...are nearly what the score is, so, ...to be married in June or ...home!

...m so happy tonight I could do ...right now. How else can I tell ...more than all the rest of everything ...offer? — Oh sweetheart, there ...this way that I can tell you in ...ust tried a million ways in which ...now, and make you realize it during ...going to have together.

...tonight my darling, I'll see you ...nigt, and all during my early ...t all during tomorrow; and

...so very much sweetheart, and I

...Dick.

POSTMARKED CAMP BARKELEY, TEXAS—APRIL 22, 1943

Wed. nite

Darling,

I got your letters today telling me how you feel about my not making O.C.S., and also that you will marry me this June come hardship or come good times. Evelyn dearest, there is only one thing I can say and that is you are the most wonderful girl I've ever known or ever will know in this world or the next; and I love you with all my heart and soul and might. With each new and wonderful thing that you do or say, I only love you more, when I had already thought I loved you more, when I had already thought I love you all there is. And sweetheart, I'm awfully in earnest when I tell you that I am humble in the presence of your love for me. I don't know why you love me, or how in the face of everything you keep on loving me, but I'm thankful for it, sweetness. So thankful, and so happy, and so proud that every time I think of you loving me a lump comes in my throat, and a strange prickly feeling spreads all over me. Yes darlingest, we do love each other more I think than any two people I know. We both feel exactly the same way, and did you notice? We seem to feel the same way always at the same time! So that when I'm thinking of you very hard, I know somehow that you are with me, and are thinking about me too.

You say that you will marry me in June regardless of anything, regardless of security or anything else, and oh honey, I say the same thing over and over again. We've been too sensible too long. We will get married in June unless I go overseas, which I doubt that I'll do. And dearest, all I can say further is that I'll love you for always and always, and I'll try with everything I have to make you completely happy as long as we live. I want our marriage to be perfect in every way, and my darling I know it will be. We'll move any obstacle from our path together, and physically, mentally, and spiritually we'll be completely and inseparably united. As to the practical side of our getting married, here's as much as I can tell you now honey.

I am due for a furlough right now, but I probably won't get one until after my permanent assignment which won't be for a month or so yet I don't imagine. If I am held at Jefferson Barracks longer than a month, I wish you would come there, but we can't cross those bridges until later when I know more nearly what the scare is. So, sit tight, and plan to be married in June or sooner, probably at home!

Oh honey, I'm so happy tonight I could do anything on earth right now. How else can I tell you I love you more than all the rest of everything the World has to offer? Oh sweetheart, there may not be any other way that I can tell you on paper, but there must be a million ways in which I can prove it to you, and make you realize it during the lifetime we're going to have together.

And now good night my darling, I'll see you while I dream tonight, and all during my early morning guard, and all during tomorrow; and forever.

I do love you so very much sweetheart, and I always will,

Dick

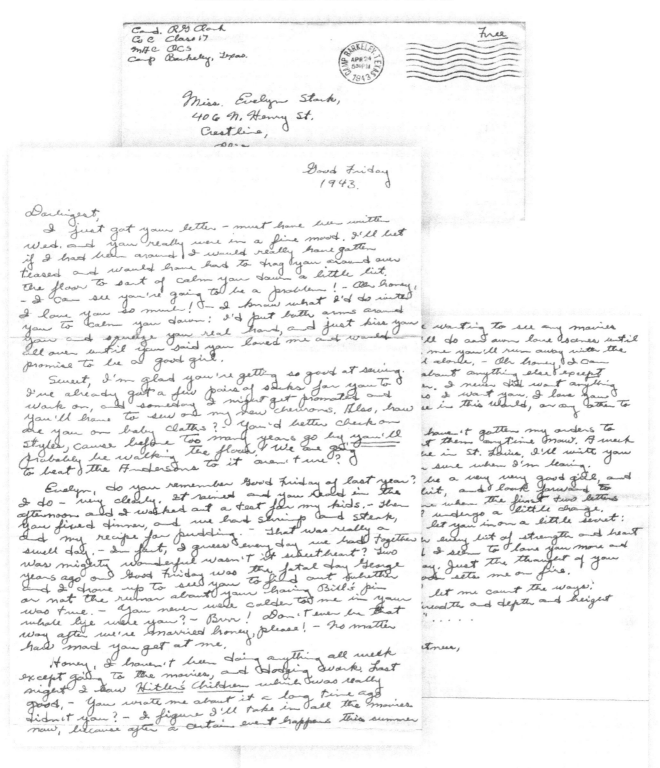

Cand. R.G. Clark
Co C Class 17
MAC OCS
Camp Barkeley, Texas.

CAMP BARKELEY, TEXAS
APR 24
5:30 PM
1943

Free

Miss. Evelyn Stark,
406 N. Henry St.
Crestline,

Good Friday
1943.

Darlingest,

I just got your letter - must have been written Wed. and you really were in a fine mood. I'll bet if I had been around I would really have gotten teased and would have had to drag you around over the floor to sort of calm you down a little bit. Oh honey, - I can see you're going to be a problem! - I love you so much! - I know what I'd do instead I'd put both arms around you to calm you down: I'd put both arms around you and squeeze you real hard, and just kiss you all over until you said you loved me and would promise to be a good girl.

Sweet, I'm glad you're getting so good at sewing. I've already got a few pairs of socks for you to work on, and someday I might get promoted and you'll have to sew on my new chevrons. Also, how are you on baby clothes? You'd better check on styles, cause before too many years go by you'll probably be walking the floor. We are going to beat the Andersons to it aren't we?

Evelyn, do you remember Good Friday of last year? I do - very clearly. It rained and you stood in the afternoon and I worked out a test for my kids. - Then you fixed dinner, and we had shrimp and steak, and my recipe for pudding. - That was really a swell day. - In fact, I guess every day we had together was mighty wonderful wasn't it sweetheart? Two years ago on Good Friday was the fatal day George and I drove up to see you to find out whether or not the rumor about your having Bill's pin was true. - You never were calder to me in your whole life were you? - Brrr! Don't ever be that way after we're married honey, please! - No matter how mad you get at me.

Honey, I haven't been doing anything all week except going to the movies, and dodging work. Last night I saw Hitler's Children which I was really good. - You wrote me about it a long time ago didn't you? - I figure I'll take in all the movies now, because after a certain event happens this summer

Good Friday 1943

Darlingest,

I just got your letter—must have been written Wed. and you really were in a fine mood. I'll bet if I had been around I would really have gotten teased and would have had to drag you around over the floor to sort of calm you down a little bit. I can see you're going to be a problem! Oh honey, I love you so much! I know what I'd do with you to calm you down: I'd put both arms around you and squeeze you real hard, and just kiss you all over until you said you loved me and would promise to be a good girl.

Sweet, I'm glad you're getting so good at sewing. I've already got a few pairs of socks for you to work on, and someday I might get promoted and you'll have to sew on my new chevrons. Also, how are you on baby clothes? You'd better check on styles, cause before too many years go by, you'll probably be walking the floor! We are going to beat the Andersons to it aren't we?

Evelyn, do you remember Good Friday of last year? I do—very clearly. It rained and you read in the afternoon and I worked on a test for my kids. Then you fixed dinner, and we had shrimp and steak, and my recipe for pudding. That was really a swell day. In fact, I guess every day we had together was mighty wonderful wasn't it sweetheart? Two years ago on Good Friday was the fatal day George and I drove up to see you to find out whether or not the rumor about your having Bill's pin was true. You never were colder to me in your whole life were you? Brrr! Don't ever be that way after we're married honey, please! No matter how mad you get at me.

Honey, I haven't been doing anything all week except going to the movies, and dodging work. Last night I saw Hitler's Children which was really good. You wrote me about it a long time ago didn't you? I figure I'll take in all the movies now, because after a certain event happens this summer I don't think I'll be wanting to see any movies for a long time. We'll do our own love scenes until you get so bored with me you'll run away with the girls and leave me all alone. Oh honey, I can hardly wait or think about anything else except you and I being together. I never did want anything so much in my life as I want you. I love you more than anything else in this world, or any other to come.

Sweetheart, I still haven't gotten my orders to leave yet, but I expect them anytime now. A week from today I should be in St. Louis. I'll write you as soon as I know for sure when I'm leaving. In the meantime, you be a very very good girl, and miss me just a wee bit, and look forward to the not too distant future when the first two letters in your last name will undergo a little change. If you'll do this, I'll let you in on a little secret: I love you dearest with every bit of strength and heart and mind I have, and I seem to love you more and more with each new day. Just the thought of you and I being together soon sets me on fire.

"How do I love thee? Let me count the ways. I love thee to the breadth and depth and height my soul can reach" . . .

Goodnight sweetness,

Dick

Easter
Sunday.

Hello sweetness,

Easter reminds me of last Easter with you, and that makes me sort of sad. I remember that day so very well darling. You had on your suit, while I had been anxiously awaiting, and your yellow blouse and hat. — Right sharp you looked in case I didn't tell you then. We went to church and heard Bob Tucker preach, and then to Hermie's, and then to the Dale with Bob and June. — Dinner at home with Mom and Bill, a walk, and then home. How I loved you that day, sweetheart! Maybe you're bored by my memories, but it does me so much good, because it brings you close to me again. — I can see you just as you were then honey.

There is no real news from here right now. I'm still awaiting orders to leave, and they surely ought to come tomorrow. As I've been telling you, all I do is dodge work, go to the movies, and think about you and I being together very soon now.

Honey, if I can just have you with me, I don't care where I go, or what I do. When you're around, I guess I lose all track of everything else except just having you with me.

...what causes it, I ...ld be that I love ...uppose?

...your grandmother? I ...she feels much better ...she's a good old gal. ...tion to our saying

...isn't really any news ...now, so I'm going to ...know for sure but I

...you're looking forward ...then forever just a tenth ...m. That will be the ...thing that could ever ...to anybody, as far as ...Everyday brings us one ...nearer honey, nearer to ... — I can't really tell ...when I think about ...e, but I can tell you ...ought of it gives me ...thrill.

...sweetheart, and keep ...will you? And oh ...it whatever you ...have all of my ...s and always dear.

Dick.

THE YOUNG MEN'S CHRISTIAN ASSOCIATIONS • THE NATIONAL CATHOLIC COMMUNITY SERVICE
THE SALVATION ARMY • THE YOUNG WOMEN'S CHRISTIAN ASSOCIATIONS
THE JEWISH WELFARE BOARD • THE NATIONAL TRAVELERS AID ASSOCIATION

306

Easter Sunday

Hello Sweetness,

Easter reminds me of last Easter with you, and that makes me sort of sad. I remember that day so very much darling: you had on your suit, which I had been anxiously awaiting, and your yellow blouse and hat. Right sharp you looked in case I didn't tell you then. We went to church and heard Bob Tucker preach, and then to Hennicks, and then to the Dale with Bob and June. Dinner at home with Mom and Bill, a walk, and then home. How I loved you that day, sweetheart! Maybe you're bored by my memories, but it does me so much good, because it brings you close to me again—I can see you just as you were then honey.

There is no real news from here right now. I'm still awaiting orders to leave, and they surely ought to come tomorrow. As I've been telling you all I do is dodge work, and go to the movies, and think about you and I being together very soon now.

Honey, if I can first have you with me, I don't care where I go, or what I do. When you're around, I guess I lose all track of everything else except just having you with me.

I don't know what causes it, I wonder if it could be that I love you. Do you suppose?

Evelyn, how is your grandmother? I surely hope that she feels much better than she did. She's a good old gal. Remember her reaction to our raising a large family?

Dearest, there isn't really any news from here right now, so I'm going to close until I know for sure when I leave.

I surely hope you're looking forward to being together forever just a tenth as much as I am. That will be the most wonderful thing that could ever possibly happen to anybody, as far as I'm concerned. Everyday brings us one day nearer one another honey, never to be parted again. I can't really tell you how I feel when I think about you marrying me, but I can tell you that just the thought if it gives me a tremendous thrill.

Be a good girl sweetheart, and keep on loving me—will you? And oh darling, do with it whatever you like, but you have all of my love for always and always dear.

Dick

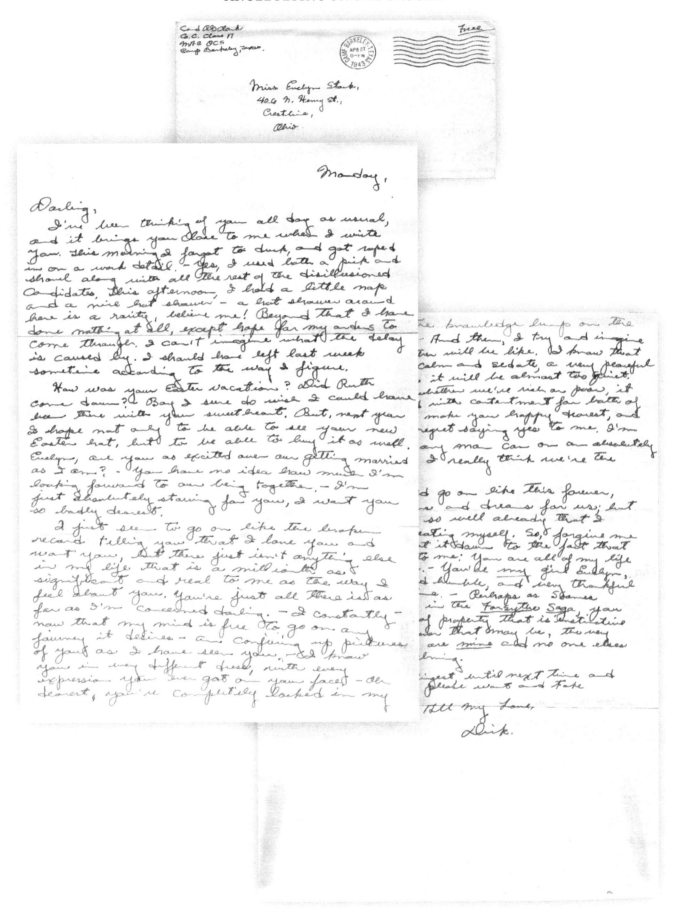

Monday,

Darling,

I've been thinking of you all day as usual, and it brings you close to me when I write you. This morning I forgot to duck, and got roped in on a work detail. — Yes, I used both a pick and shovel along with all the rest of the disillusioned candidates. This afternoon, I had a little nap and a nice hot shower — a hot shower around here is a rarity, believe me! Beyond that I have done nothing at all, except hope for my orders to come through. I can't imagine what the delay is caused by. I should have left last week sometime according to the way I figure.

How was your Easter vacation? Did Ruth come down? Boy I sure do wish I could have been there with you sweetheart. But, next year I hope not only to be able to see your new Easter hat, but to be able to buy it as well. Evelyn, are you as excited over our getting married as I am? — You have no idea how much I'm looking forward to our being together. — I'm just absolutely starving for you, I want you so badly dearest.

I just seem to go on like the broken record telling you that I love you and want you, but there just isn't anything else in my life that is a millionth as significant and real to me as the way I feel about you. You're just all there is as far as I'm concerned darling. — I constantly — now that my mind is free to go on any journey it desires — am conjuring up pictures of you as I have seen you. — I know you in every different dress, with every expression you ever got on your face — Oh dearest, you're completely locked in my

... knowledge lump on the ... And then, I try and imagine ... ... will be like. I know that ... calm and sedate, a very peaceful ... it will be almost too quiet. ... whether we're rich or poor, it ... with contentment for both of ... make you happy, dearest, and ... regret saying yes to me. I'm ... any man can on an absolutely ... I really think we're the ...

... go on like this forever, ... and dreams for us; but ... ... so well already that I ... ... eating myself. So, forgive me ... ... it down to the fact that ... ... to me: You are all of my life ... — You'll be my girl Evelyn, ... humble, and very thankful ... — Perhaps as Soames ... in the Forsythe Saga, you ... of property that is instinctive ... ... that may be, the very ... are mine and no one else's ... ... ing.

... est until next time and ... please wait and take

All my Love,

Dick.

Monday

Darling,

I've been thinking of you all day as usual, and it brings you close to me when I write you. This morning I forgot to duck, and got roped in on a work detail. Yes, I used both a pick and shovel along with all the rest of the disillusioned candidates. This afternoon, I had a little nap and a nice hot shower—a hot shower around here is a rarity, believe me! Beyond that I have done nothing at all, except hope for my orders to come through. I can't imagine what the delay is caused by. I should have left last week sometime according to the way I figure.

How was your Easter vacation? Did Ruth come down? Boy I sure do wish I could have been there with you sweetheart. But, next year I hope not only to be able to see your new Easter hat, but to be able to buy it as well. Evelyn, are you as excited over our getting married as I am? You have no idea how much I'm looking forward to our being together. I'm just absolutely starving for you, I want you so badly dearest.

I just seem to go on like the broken record telling you that I love you and want you, but there just isn't anything else in my life that is a millionth as significant and real to me as the way I feel about you. You're just all there is as far as I'm concerned darling. I constantly—now that my mind is free to go on any journey it desires—am conjuring up pictures of you as I have seen you. I know you in every different dress, with every expression you ever got on your face. Oh dearest, you're completely locked in my mind clear to the knowledge lump on the back of your head. And then, I try and imagine what our life together will be like. I know that most it will be calm and sedate, a very peaceful life indeed. Perhaps it will be almost too quiet. But, I know that whether we're rich or poor, it will be a life filled with contentment for both of us. I hope I can make you happy dearest, and I hope you'll never regret saying yes to me. I'm counting as much as any man can on an absolutely ideal marriage, and I really think we're the people to have that.

Dearest, I could go on like this forever, telling you my plans and dreams for us; but you know them all so well already that I know I'm only repeating myself. So, forgive me sweetheart, and put it down to the fact that you are life itself to me; you are all of my life goals rallied into one. You're _my_ girl Evelyn, and I'm proud and humble, and very thankful all at the same time. Perhaps as Soames Forsythe called it in the Forsythe Saga, you represent the idea of property that is instinctive in every man. However that may be, the very thought that you are mine and no one else's is almost overwhelming.

And now darlingest, until next time and forever and ever, please want and take

All My Love,

Dick

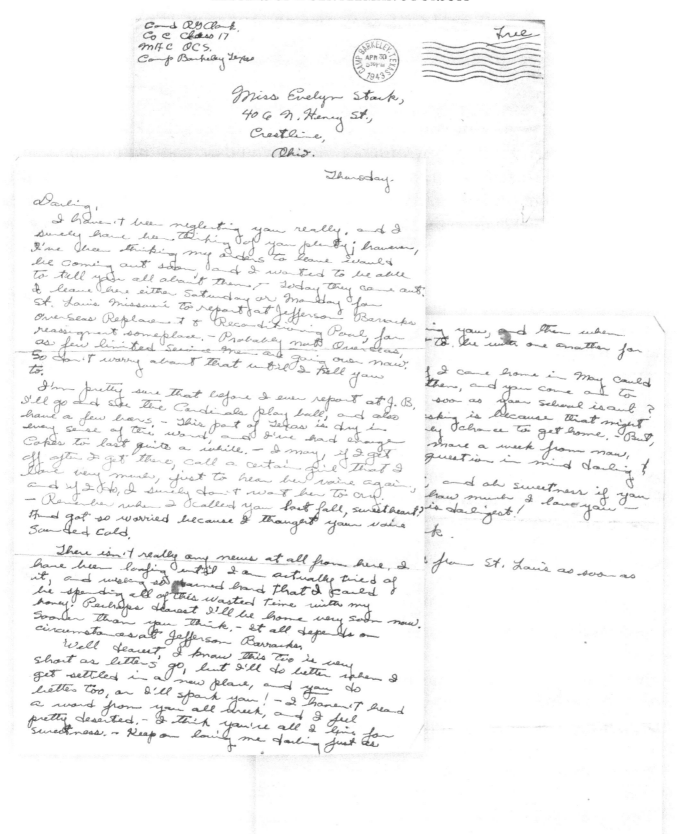

Comd R.G. Clark.
Co C Class 17
M.A.C. O.C.S.
Camp Barkeley Texas

CAMP BARKELEY TEXAS APR 30 1943

Free

Miss Evelyn Stark,
406 N. Henry St.,
Crestline,
Ohio.

Thursday.

Darling,

I haven't been neglecting you really, and I surely have been thinking of you plenty; however, I've been striking my orders to leave, I would be coming out soon, and I wanted to be able to tell you all about them. Today they came out. I leave here either Saturday or Monday for St. Louis Missouri to report at Jefferson Barracks Overseas Replacement & Reconditioning Pool, for reassignment someplace. — Probably not Overseas, as few limited Service men are going over now, So don't worry about that until I tell you to.

I'm pretty sure that before I even report at J.B. I'll go and see the Cardinals play ball, and also have a few beers. — This part of Texas is dry in every sense of the word, and I've had enough Cokes to last quite a while. — I may, if I get off after I get there, call a certain girl that I love very much, just to hear her voice again, and if I do, I surely don't want her to cry. — Remember when I called you last fall, sweetheart? I had got so worried because I thought your voice Sounded cold.

There isn't really any news at all from here, I have been loafing until I am actually tired of it, and wishing so darned hard that I could be spending all of this wasted time with my honey. Perhaps dearest I'll be home very soon now, Sooner than you think. — It all depends on circumstances at Jefferson Barracks.

Well dearest, I know this too is very short as letters go, but I'll do better when I get settled in a new place, and you do letters too, or I'll spank you! — I haven't heard a word from you all week, and I feel pretty deserted. — I think you're all I live for sweetness. — Keep on loving me darling just as

...ing you, and then when ...to be with one another for

...f I came home in May could ...them, and you come out to ...soon as your school is out? ...sking is because that might ...ly I chance to get home. — But, ...more a week from now, ...question in mind darling, ...and oh sweetness if you ...how much I love you — ...is darling!

...k.

...from St. Louis as soon as

POSTMARKED CAMP BARKELEY, TEXAS—APRIL 30, 1943

Thursday

Darling,

I haven't been neglecting you really, and I surely have been thinking of you plenty; however, I've been thinking my orders to leave would be coming out soon, and I wanted to be able to tell you all about them —Today they came out. I leave here either Saturday or Monday for St. Louis, Missouri to report at Jefferson Barracks Overseas Replacement & Reconditioning Pool, for reassignment someplace. Probably not Overseas, as few limited Service Men are going over now. So don't worry about that until I tell you to.

I'm pretty sure that before I ever report at J.B. I'll go and see the Cardinals play ball, and also have a few beers. This part of Texas is dry in every sense of the word, and I've had enough Cokes to last quite a while. I may, if I get off after I get there, call a certain girl that I love very much, just to hear her voice again, and if I do, I surely don't want her to cry. Remember when I called you last fall, sweetheart? And got so worried because I thought your voice sounded cold.

There isn't really any news at all from here. I have been loafing until I am actually tired of it, and wishing so darned hard that I could be spending all of this wasted time with my honey. Perhaps dearest I'll be home very soon now. Sooner than you think. It all depends on circumstance at Jefferson Barracks.

Well dearest, I know this too is very short as letters go, but I'll do better when I get settled in a new place, and you do better too, or I'll spank you! I haven't heard a word from you all week, and I feel pretty deserted. I think you're all I live for sweetness. Keep on loving me darling just as hard as I'm loving you, and then when we do finally get to be with one another for always—wow!

Incidentally, if I came home in May could we get married then, and you come on to my new station as soon as your school is out? The reason I'm asking is because that might possibly be my only chance to get home. But, we'll know much more a week from now, so just keep the question in mind darling!

Be good, dearest, and oh sweetness if you could ever guess how much I love you— just all there is darlingest!

Dick

P.S. I'll write from St. Louis as soon as possible honey.

(This is the last letter addressed as Miss Evelyn Stark)

Mr. and Mrs. Glenn J. Stark

announce the marriage

of their daughter

Evelyn Lucille

to

Mr. Richard Guy Clark

on Tuesday, the eighteenth of May

nineteen hundred and forty-three

Sunbury, Ohio

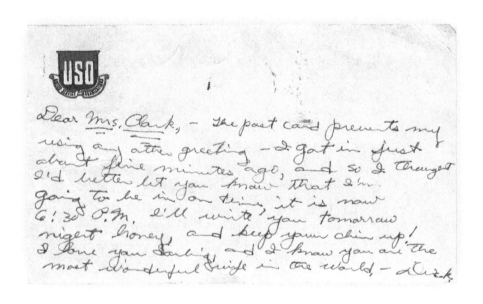

POSTMARKED ST. LOUIS, MISSOURI—MAY 20, 1943

Dear <u>Mrs. Clark</u>,

The post card prevents my using any other greeting. I got in just about five minutes ago, and so I thought I'd better let you know that I'm going to be in on time, it is now 6:30 P.M. I'll write you tomorrow night honey, and keep your chin up! I love you darling, and I know you are the most wonderful wife in the world.

- Dick

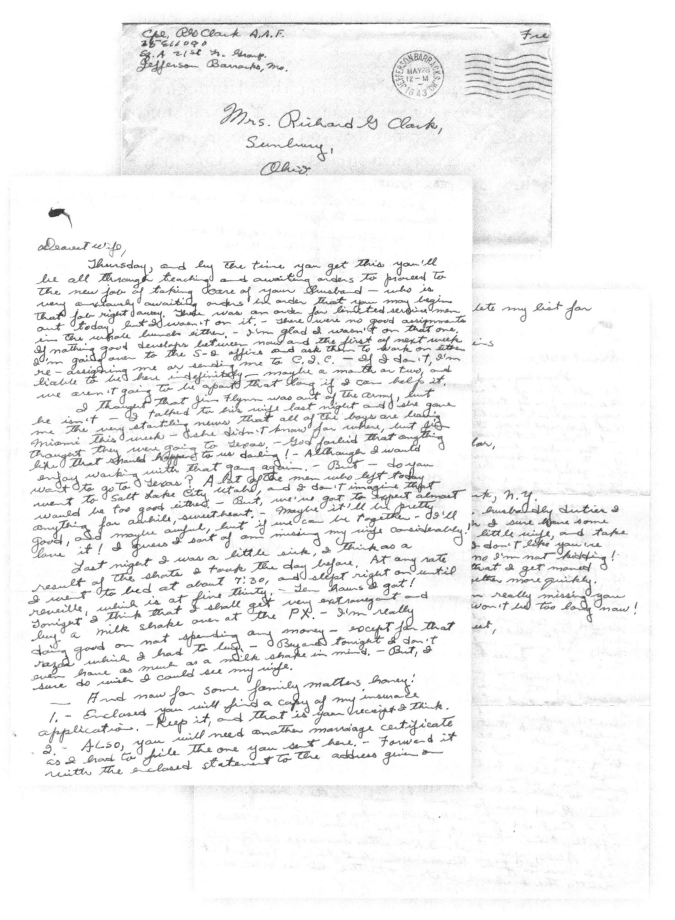

POSTMARKED JEFFERSON BARRACKS, MISSOURI—MAY 28, 1943

Dearest Wife,

Thursday, and by the time you get this you'll be all through teaching and awaiting orders to proceed to the new job of taking care of your husband—who is very anxiously awaiting orders in order that you may begin that job right away. There was an order for limited service men out today, but I wasn't on it. There were no good assignments in the whole bunch either. I'm glad I wasn't on that one. If nothing good develops between now and the first of next week I'm going over to the S-O office and ask them to work on either re-assigning me or sending me to C.I.C. If I don't, I'm liable to be here indefinitely—maybe a month or two, and we aren't going to be apart that long if I can help it.

I thought that Jim Flynn was out of the Army, but he isn't—I talked to his wife last night and she gave me the very startling news that all of the boys are leaving Miami this week—she didn't know for where, but Jim thought they were going to Texas—God forbid that anything like that should happen to us darling! Although I would enjoy working with that gang again. But—do you want to go to Texas? A lot of the men who left today went to Salt Lake City, Utah and I don't imagine that would be too good either. But, we've got to expect almost anything for awhile, sweetheart. Maybe it'll be pretty good, and maybe awful, but if we can be together—I'll love it! I guess I sort of am missing my wife considerably!

Last night I was a little sick, I think as a result of the shots I took the day before. At any rate I went to bed at about 7:30, and slept right on until reveille, which is at five thirty. Ten hours I got! Tonight I think that I shall get very extravagant and buy a milk shake over at the PX. I'm really doing good on not spending any money— except for that razor which I had to buy. Beyond tonight I don't even have as much as a milk shake in mind. But, I sure do wish I could see my wife.

And now for some family matter honey:
1. Enclosed you will find a copy of my insurance application. Keep it, and that is your receipt I think.

2. ALSO, you will need another marriage certificate as I had to file the one you sent here. Forward it with the enclosed statement to the address given on the sheet.

3. The addresses needed to complete my list for announcements are:
   a.   Ensign & Mrs. W.A. Hopkins
        1224 Ingraham N.W.
        Washington, D.C.

b. Lieut. Herb Emrich
    69th Fighter Sq.
    Bedford Airdrome,
    Bedford Mass

c. Ensign Richard P Taylor
    N.T.S. (1) 42065
    Fort Schuyler
    The Bronx, New York, N.Y.

I guess that is about all the husbandry duties I can perform right now. Although I sure have some others in mind! So, be a very good little wife, and take a little rest while you're home. I don't like you're having lost weight like you did—no I'm not kidding! So, rest up and relax, and hope that I get moved real soon so that we can be together more quickly.

I love you dearest wife, and I'm really missing you plenty these days. How I hope it won't be too long now!

All My Love, Dearest,

Dick

Tuesday
May 25 - '43

Dearest Wife,

I got a letter from you yesterday, and one again today, both of which certainly serve to bolster up my morale. I was really tickled about the GAF program. - I imagine the kids really did out do themselves in every way possible, and naturally they like you (and hate possible) - they don't to lose you - but honestly honey, they don't need you nearly as badly as I do. I sure am mighty proud of you though, because you are so well thought of by all of your studies. Also honey you are really a busy little wife taking care of my clothes, and the notes, and the announcements, not only busy, but awfully wonderful too, and awfully much loved by your husband,

Darling, I have been a little busy too; Last night I went over to make out your allotment and did so - enclosed you will find your receipt for same. - Keep it in a safe place until the money comes through, which should be between the first and tenth of July. - I guess we can't do any good for this month, but, the $50.00 will be there in another month. - Aren't you glad you married a man with so much money? Also, sweet, I took out an insurance policy for $5,000. with you as beneficiary, and mom as contingent beneficiary, and mom as contingent beneficiary, I already have a policy for her, and you have always been the second beneficiary on it. - Those papers will come through to you whenever the spirit moves the government to mail them. - So — now you are all fixed up dearest!

As far as my army life is concerned, I am learning all about the office work of a squadron, so that when + if I'm ever put to work in one after I'm assigned, I'll know what I'm doing. Also, they finally caught up with me on shots, and gave me three today. - My arms are both pretty sore, and I could do with a little very gentle physical therapy by my wife.

Tonight I'm going to bed early, and shave - in my new razor - which I had a heck of a time getting, and also which cost me a buck. - There's always something, darn it! I'm going to Louis one night this week and contact my old friend Jim Flynn - from my Miami days. - He got a discharge, he's a 44. Beyond that, life is just the same, day after day. - Wanting my wife with me, and wanting to be permanently assigned so that you can be with me - How I do long for that honey!

Sweetheart, I'm going to quit writing for now, but I will try and write a much longer one the next time.

I love you darling, and want you with me so much. - And, oh sweet, I'm so very glad that you are my wife that I fairly burst with pride in you. - You are truly the most wonderful wife in the whole world.

I guess I don't need to tell you that you have all my love, my least little bit, for always and always honey.

Dick.

P.S. - I'm glad you thought to go and see mom, I know that she appreciated it, and - well - keep it up dearest.

- Just think, we have been married a whole week now honey. - A whole week, not a year, but those times aren't very long - we have forever to love one another, don't we darling?

Tuesday, May 25- '43

Dearest Wife,

I got a letter from you yesterday, and one again today, both of which certainly serve to bolster up my morale. I was really tickled about the GAA program. I imagine the kids really did out do themselves in every way possible, and naturally they like you and hate to lose you—but honestly honey, they don't need you nearly as badly as I do. I sure am mightily proud of you though, because you are so well thought of by all of your students. Also honey, you are really a busy little wife taking care of my clothes, and the notes, and the announcements, not only busy, but awfully wonderful too, and awfully much loved by your husband.

Darling, I have been a little busy too: Last night I went over to make out your allotment, and did so—Enclosed you will find your receipt for same. Keep it in a safe place until the money comes through, which should be between the first and tenth of July. I guess we can't do any good for this month, but the $50.00 will be there in another month. Aren't you glad you married a man with so much money? Also, sweet, I took out an insurance policy for $5,000 with you as beneficiary, and Mom as contingent beneficiary. I already have a policy for her, and you have always been the second beneficiary on it. Those papers will come through to you whenever the spirit moves the government to mail them. So—now you are all fixed up dearest!

As far as my army life is concerned, I am learning all about the office work of a squadron, so that when & if I'm ever put to work in one after I'm assigned, I'll know what I'm doing. Also, they finally caught up with me on shots, and gave me three today. My arms are both pretty sore, and I could do with a little very gentle physical therapy by my wife.

Tonight I'm going to bed early, and shave—with my new razor—which I had a heck of a time getting, and also which cost me a buck. It's always something, darn it! I'm going to St. Louis one night this week and contact my good friend Jim Flynn— from my Miami days—Jim got a discharge, he's 44. Beyond that, life is just the same, day after day: Wanting my wife with me, and wanting to be permanently assigned so that you can be with me—How I do long for that honey!

Sweetheart, I'm going to quit writing for now, but I will try and write a much longer one the next time.

I love you darling, and want you with me so much. And, oh sweet, I'm so very glad that you are my wife that I fairly burst with pride in you. You are truly the most wonderful wife in the whole world.

I guess I don't need to tell you that you have all my love, every least little bit, for always and always honey.

Dick

P.S. I'm glad you thought to go and see mom, I know that she appreciated it, and—well—keep it up dearest.

P.S. Just think, we have been married a whole week now honey. A whole week, and soon a year, but those times aren't very long when we have forever to love one another, are they darling?

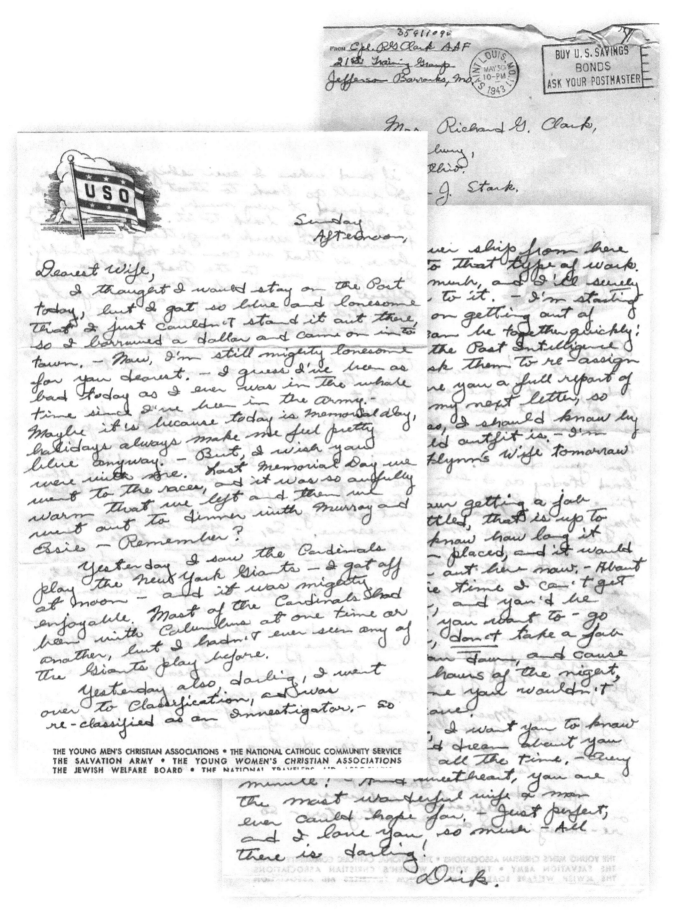

FROM Cpl. R.G. Clark AAF
21st Training Group
Jefferson Barracks, Mo.

35911090

ST. LOUIS, MO.
MAY 30
10-PM
1943

BUY U.S. SAVINGS
BONDS
ASK YOUR POSTMASTER

Mrs. Richard G. Clark,
[...]bury,
[...]hio.
[...]J. Stark.

USO

Sunday
Afternoon,

Dearest Wife,

I thought I would stay on the Post today, but I got so blue and lonesome that I just couldn't stand it out there, so I borrowed a dollar and came on into town. — Now, I'm still mighty lonesome for you dearest. — I guess I've been as bad today as I ever was in the whole time since I've been in the Army. — Maybe it is because today is Memorial day, holidays always make me feel pretty blue anyway. — But, I wish you were with me. Last Memorial Day we went to the races, and it was so awfully warm that we left and then we went out to dinner with Murray and Essie — Remember?

Yesterday I saw the Cardinals play the New York Giants — I got off at noon — and it was mighty enjoyable. Most of the Cardinals had been with Columbus at one time or another, but I hadn't ever seen any of the Giants play before.

Yesterday also, darling, I went over to Classification, and was re-classified as an Investigator. — So

THE YOUNG MEN'S CHRISTIAN ASSOCIATIONS • THE NATIONAL CATHOLIC COMMUNITY SERVICE
THE SALVATION ARMY • THE YOUNG WOMEN'S CHRISTIAN ASSOCIATIONS
THE JEWISH WELFARE BOARD • THE NATIONAL TRAVELERS AID ASSOCIATION

[...] ship from here [...] to that type of work. [...] much, and I'll surely [...] to it. — I'm starting [...] on getting out of [...] can be together quickly! [...] the Post Intelligence [...] ask them to re-assign [...] give you a full report of [...] my next letter, so [...] I should know by [...] old outfit is. — I'm [...] Flynn's Wife tomorrow

[...] getting a job [...] settled, that is up to [...] know how long it [...] placed, and it would [...] out here now. — About [...] the time I can't get [...] and you'd be [...] you want to — go [...] don't take a job [...] town, and cause [...] hours of the night, [...] you wouldn't [...]

[...] I want you to know [...] dream about you all the time. — Every minute! — sweetheart, you are the most wonderful wife a man ever could hope for. — Just perfect, and I love you so much — All there is darling!

Dick.

Sunday Afternoon

Dearest Wife,

I thought I would stay on the Post today, but I got so blue and lonesome that I just couldn't stand it out there, so I borrowed a dollar and came on into town. Now, I'm still mightily lonesome for you dearest. I guess I've been as bad today as I ever was in the whole time since I've been in the Army. Maybe it's because today is Memorial Day, holidays always make me feel pretty blue anyways. But, I wish you were with me. Last Memorial Day we went to the races, and it was so awfully warm that we left and then we went out to dinner with Murray and Essie—Remember?

Yesterday I saw the Cardinals play the New York Giants—I got off at noon—and it was mighty enjoyable. Most of the Cardinals had been with Columbus at one time or another but I hadn't ever seen any of the Giants play before.

Yesterday also darling, I went over to Classification, and was re-classified as an Investigator. So if and when I ever ship from here I will go back to that type of work. I enjoyed it very much, and I'll surely be glad to go back to it. I'm starting tomorrow to work on getting out of here, so that we can be together quickly! I'm going over to the Post Intelligence Office here, and ask them to re-assign me P.D.Q. I'll give you a full report of the proceedings in my next letter, so be waiting. Also, I should know by then where my old outfit is. I'm going to call Jim Flynn's' wife tomorrow night.

Honey, about your getting a job until I do get settled, that is up to you. I just can't know how long it will be before I'm placed, and it would be no good for you out there now. About three fourths of the time I can't get out at night here, and you'd be lonesome. So, if you want to—go ahead. However, don't take a job that might run you down, and cause you to work all hours of the night, and don't take one you wouldn't be allowed to leave.

Well dear wife, I want you to know that I love you and dream about you and plan for us all the time. Every minute! And sweetheart, you are the most wonderful wife a man ever could hope for. Just perfect, and I love you so much—All there is darling!

Dick

New York Giants vs St. Louis Cardinals May 29, 1943 Box Score

---

Baseball Almanac Box Scores
New York Giants 4, St. Louis Cardinals 5

Game played on Saturday, May 29, 1943 at Sportsman's Park III

New York Giants	ab	r	h	rbi
Bartell 3b	5	0	2	1
Jurges ss	4	1	1	0
Maynard cf	5	1	2	1
Ott rf	4	0	1	0
Lombardi c	5	1	1	1
Gordon lf	5	0	0	0
Witek 2b	4	1	1	0
Orengo 1b	5	0	2	0
Trinkle p	2	0	1	0
Barna ph	1	0	0	0
Coombs p	0	0	0	0
Wittig p	0	0	0	0
Totals	40	4	11	3

St. Louis Cardinals	ab	r	h	rbi
Klein 2b	5	2	2	1
Walker cf	5	0	1	0
Musial rf	3	0	1	0
O'Dea c	4	0	0	0
Adams pr	0	0	0	0
Sanders 1b	4	0	2	1
Garms 3b	4	1	2	0
Hopp lf	4	1	1	1
Marion ss	4	0	1	1
Krist p	3	1	0	0
Cooper p	1	0	1	0
Totals	37	5	11	4

```
New York    0  0  1    1  0  0    1  0  1  -  4  11  3
St. Louis   0  0  0    0  3  0    1  0  1  -  5  11  3
```

New York Giants	IP	H	R	ER	BB	SO
Trinkle	7.0	8	4	3	2	0
Coombs L(0-1)	1.1	2	1	1	0	0
Wittig	0.1	1	0	0	2	0
Totals	8.2	11	5	4	4	0

St. Louis Cardinals	IP	H	R	ER	BB	SO
Krist	7.1	10	3	3	3	3
Cooper W(4-3)	1.2	1	1	0	1	2
Totals	9.0	11	4	3	4	5

E–Lombardi (2), Witek (7), Orengo (4), Klein 2 (5), Musial (5). 2B–New York Orengo (1). 3B–New York Maynard (1), St. Louis Hopp (1). HR–New York Lombardi (2,7th inning off Krist 0 on), St. Louis Klein (4,7th inning off Trinkle 0 on). Team LOB–13. Team–10. SB–Garms (1). U–Al Barlick, Larry Goetz. T–2:21. A–2,585.

Game played on Saturday, May 29, 1943 at Sportsman's Park III

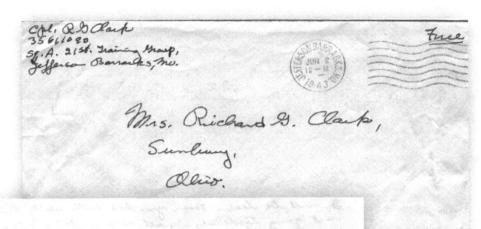

Tuesday.

Dearest Wife:

I got two lovely letters from you today darling, and I was really glad to get them. When I don't hear for a couple of days I sort of start to go slowly crazy, and I accuse the mail man of not getting all the mail out. — But everything is O.K. now! — I really laughed about you and the bird — I would surely have loved to have seen you. Did it dive bomb you, or let you have it from a high altitude? Honey, I don't know a thing about gardening, but I really am all for it. I think we can probably have the best garden in Grove City with you helping — it'll probably be me helping you though I suppose, — I didn't know how dumb I was about anything I guess. How I wish the day would soon come when we could start the garden, and the children etc.

Sweetheart, I don't know what to say about your coming to St. Louis, and planning to stay very long, with things as they are here now. Here's my set up — I can be out every night until two o'clock, but I must be in then. On Sundays, I can go out from 9:00 A.M. until 2:00 the following morning. It sounds good, but it isn't; because in the first place it takes about an hour to get into town, and an hour to have and also some nights — without warning — we are restricted altogether. I have looped in this paper here about apartments, but I hadn't checked on rooms as yet. Probably we can find a room pretty easily though. But, the devil of it is — a lot of the fellows I came in with are leaving today, and some more — who are on limited service are due to pull out before long. So far they have not put me on any order, but I am not going to be "frozen" here pending the investigation that is now underway on me — and you too darling. So — sit tight a week or so yet, and I'll try and find out what gives with my shipment — how soon etc. Then, if I find that ...

... ad better wait. But, if I'm ... reans let's plan on your ... ed of not having you ... be losing all of this time ... home that we would be ...

... now we've been married. ... no time together at all ... et together soon sweetheart. ... es of being in St. Louis ... is that I have nothing ... they want me here — then ... I'll be moved out.

... can think of that you ... rs. Frank Wright is ... ther, and a hell of a nice ... definitely need to visit ... is over, — what a lot ... the thought of them all ... make me very very ... war were over alright ...

... d letter from you today! ... did hit the jack pot ... but, I'm sorry I didn't ... was afraid I might need ... As to the new job — ... that out."

... to quit for now; probably ... so be a good wife, and ... anything else in the ... there is Evelyn sweet!

Your Husband,
Dick.

Tuesday

Dearest Wife,

I got two lovely letters from you today darling, and I was really glad to get them. When I don't hear for a couple of days I sort of start to go slowly crazy, and I accuse the mail man of not getting all the mail out. But everything is O.K. now. I really laughed about you and the bird. I would surely have loved to have seen you. Did it dive bomb you, or let you have it from a high altitude? Honey, I don't know a thing about gardening, but I really am all for it I think we can probably have the best garden in Grove City with you helping—it'll probably be me helping you though I suppose. I didn't know how dumb I was until I got in the Army. I don't know very much about anything I guess. How I wish the day would soon come when we could start the garden, and the children etc.

Sweetheart, I don't know what to say about your coming to St. Louis, and planning to stay very long, with things as they are here now. Here's my set up—I can be out every night until two o'clock, but I must be in then. On Sundays, I can go out from 9:00 A.M. until 2:00 the following morning. It sounds good, but it isn't, because in the first place it takes about an hour to get into town, and an hour to leave, and also some nights—without warning—we are restricted altogether. I have looked in the paper here about apartments, but I hadn't checked on rooms as yet. Probably we can find a room pretty easily though. But, the devil of it is—a lot of the fellows I came in with are leaving today, and some more—who are on Limited Service are due to pull out before long. So far they have not put me on any order, but I am not going to be "frozen" here pending the investigation that is now underway on me—and you too darling. So—sit tight a week or so yet, and I'll try and find out what gives with my shipment—how soon etc. Then, if I find that I will be leaving soon, you had better wait. But, if I'm not going to leave, by all means let's plan on you coming here. I'm awfully tired of not having you with me when we ought to be having all of this time together. I thought when I was home that we would be all settled by this time darling.

Honey, just three weeks now we've been married. And we've had practically no time together at all since. We've just got to get together soon sweetheart.

You asked about the chances of being in St. Louis permanently, and the answer is that I have nothing to do with that at all. If they want me here—then here I'll be, but otherwise—I'll be moved out.

The only other question I can think of that you wanted answered is that Mrs. Frank

Wright is Ann Wright (Dietsch's) mother, and a hell of a nice old gal she is too. We'll definitely need to visit her sometime when the war is over. What a lot of things we'll have to do! The thought of them all and of all our lives together make me very very happy, sweetheart. If only this war were over right now!

Darling, I just got a third letter from you today! It seems as though I really did hit the jack pot today, and am I glad! Sweet, I'm sorry I didn't send you more money, but I was afraid I might need it before the end of the month. As to the new job—we'll just have to "sweat that out."

Well dearest, I'm going to quit for now, probably I'll write again tomorrow, so be a good wife, and dearest—I love you more than anything else in the whole wide world. All there is Evelyn sweet!

Your Husband,

Dick

POSTMARKED JUNE 4, 1943—NO LETTER INSIDE

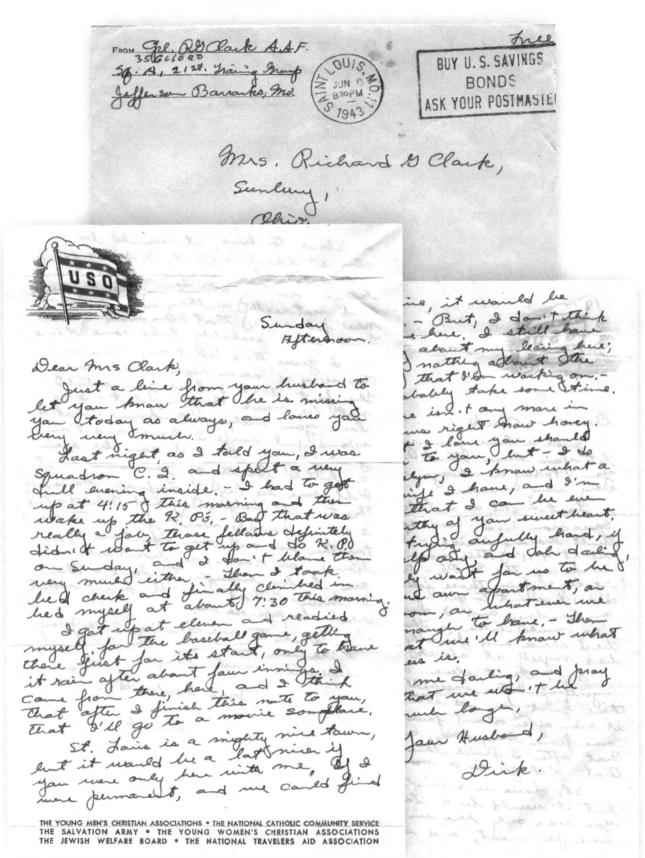

FROM Cpl. RG Clark A.A.F.
35611020
Sq. A, 21st Traing Group
Jefferson Barracks, Mo.

SAINT LOUIS. MO.
JUN 6
8:30 PM
1943

BUY U.S. SAVINGS
BONDS
ASK YOUR POSTMASTER

Free

Mrs. Richard G Clark,
Sunbury,
Ohio.

USO

Sunday
Afternoon.

Dear Mrs Clark,

Just a line from your husband to
let you know that he is missing
you today as always, and loves you
very very much.

Last night, as I told you, I was
Squadron C. Q. and spent a very
dull evening inside. — I had to get
up at 4:15 this morning and then
wake up the K. P's. — Boy that was
really a job, those fellows definitely
didn't want to get up and do K. P.
on Sunday, and I don't blame them
very much either. — Then I took
bed check and finally climbed in
bed myself at about 7:30 this morning.

I got up at eleven and readied
myself for the baseball game, getting
there just for its start, only to have
it rain after about four innings. I
came from there, here, and I think
that after I finish this note to you,
that I'll go to a movie someplace.

St. Louis is a mighty nice town,
but it would be a lot nicer if
you were only here with me. If I
were permanent, and we could find

THE YOUNG MEN'S CHRISTIAN ASSOCIATIONS • THE NATIONAL CATHOLIC COMMUNITY SERVICE
THE SALVATION ARMY • THE YOUNG WOMEN'S CHRISTIAN ASSOCIATIONS
THE JEWISH WELFARE BOARD • THE NATIONAL TRAVELERS AID ASSOCIATION

...ine, it would be
... — But, I don't think
... here. I still have
... about my leaving here;
... nothing about the
... that I'm working on. —
... probably take some time.
... isn't any more in
... me right now honey.
... I love you should
... to you, but — I do
...lyn, I know what a
... wife I have, and I'm
... that I can be ever
... worthy of your sweetheart.
... trying awfully hard, if
... help any, and oh darling,
... wait for us to be
... own apartment, or
...room, or whatever we
... enough to have, — Then
... that we'll know what
... ...ess is.

... me darling, and pray
... that we won't be
... much longer,

Your Husband,

Dick.

THE YOUNG MEN'S CHRISTIAN ASSOCIATIONS • THE NATIONAL CATHOLIC COMMUNITY SERVICE
THE SALVATION ARMY • THE YOUNG WOMEN'S CHRISTIAN ASSOCIATIONS
THE JEWISH WELFARE BOARD • THE NATIONAL TRAVELERS AID ASSOCIATION

Sunday Afternoon

Dear Mrs. Clark,

Just a line from your husband to let you know that he is missing you today as always, and loves you very very much.

Last night, as I told you, I was squadron C.L. and spent a very full evening inside. I had to get up at 4:15 this morning and then wake up the K.P.'s. Boy that was really a job, those fellows definitely didn't want to get up and do K.P. on Sunday, and I don't blame them very much either. Then I took bed check and finally climbed in bed myself at about 7:30 this morning.

I got up at eleven and readied myself for the baseball game, getting there first for its start, only to have it rain after about four innings. I came from there, here, and I think that after I finish this note to you, that I'll go to a movie someplace.

St. Louis is a mighty nice town, but it would be a lot nicer if you were only here with me. If I were permanent, and we could find a place to live, it would be almost ideal. But, I don't think we'll ever live here. I still have heard nothing about my leaving here; and naturally nothing about the new job angle that I'm working on. That will probably take some time.

I guess there isn't any more in the way of news right now honey. The fact that I love you should not be news to you, but—I do love you, Evelyn, I know what a wonderful wife I have, and I'm just praying that I can be even a little worthy of you sweetheart. I'll sure be trying awfully hard, if that will help any, and oh darling, I can hardly wait for us to be together in our own apartment, a home, or room, or whatever we are lucky enough to have. Then I know that we'll know what real happiness is.

Write to me darling, and pray with me that we won't be separated much longer.

Your Husband,

Dick

Philadelphia Phillies vs St. Louis Cardinals June 6, 1943 Box Score

----

Baseball Almanac Box Scores
Philadelphia Phillies 1, St. Louis Cardinals 1

Game played on Sunday, June 6, 1943 at Sportsman's Park III

Philadelphia Phillies	ab	r	h	rbi
Murtaugh 2b	2	1	1	0
Northey rf	3	0	1	0
Adams cf	2	0	0	0
Wasdell lf	2	0	0	0
Triplett lf	0	0	0	0
Dahlgren 1b	2	0	0	0
Stewart ss	1	0	0	0
May 3b	2	0	1	0
Livingston c	2	0	1	0
Johnson p	1	0	0	0
Totals	17	1	4	0

St. Louis Cardinals	ab	r	h	rbi
Klein 2b	3	0	0	0
Walker cf	3	0	1	0
Musial rf	2	0	0	0
Sanders 1b	1	1	0	0
O'Dea c	2	0	1	0
Garms lf	2	0	0	1
Brown 3b	2	0	0	0
Marion ss	2	0	1	0
Brecheen p	2	0	1	0
Totals	19	1	4	1

Philadelphia	1	0	0		0	0	–	1	4	1
St. Louis	0	1	0		0	0	–	1	4	1

Philadelphia Phillies	IP	H	R	ER	BB	SO
Johnson	5.0	4	1	1	1	0
Totals	5.0	4	1	1	1	0

St. Louis Cardinals	IP	H	R	ER	BB	SO
Brecheen	5.0	4	1	0	2	2
Totals	5.0	4	1	0	2	2

E–Wasdell (3), Walker (7). **SH**–Johnson (3). **Team LOB**–4. **Team**–4. U–Lou Jorda, Jocko Conlan, George Barr. T–1:21. A–10,943.

Game played on Sunday, June 6, 1943 at Sportsman's Park III

Cpl. R.G. Clark A.A.F.
35611090,
Sq. A. 21st Tring Grp
Jefferson Barracks, Mo.

Free
BUY U.S. SAVINGS
BONDS
ASK YOUR POSTMA

Mrs. Richard G. Clark,
Sunbury,
Ohio.

Dearest Wife,

It's a very hot - sticky afternoon here in St. Louis, and very dull too. I'm working - in theory - but actually there isn't a great deal to do except sit around and wish for you to be with me. - I'm having a heck of a time right now: In the first place, I can't seem to get any action towards being shipped, - I haven't been to the Post Intelligence office as yet, but I may go later on this afternoon. If they can't do anything to help me, I'm liable to be here for the duration - I doing nothing really constructive - but just more or less fooling around. I found out where everyone from Miami went, and that too made me feel bad. - They went to Amarilla Texas, which - from all I can gather - is the only place in the country that is worse than Abilene and Camp Barkeley. - I don't even know whether I'll ask to go back with them, That country would really be rougher for you I know. - What do you think?

The second thing to bother me - you'll laugh at this - I have been plagued with bed bugs for the last four days. They have just naturally chewed me up. I have big welts all over me which alternately hurt and itch, and I have been in misery. - They are getting big enough now to almost move the bed around, and all from eating me. - I have to eat more food than usual now to keep body and bugs together.

Third, I have lost a sheet - stolen almost out from under my nose, and a raincoat - likewise has disappeared, - Probably the whole thing will cost me about eight bucks or so out of my June pay - payable the first of July. - June first came and is now passing and I find that I don't get paid until about the tenth of the month. Right now I am at the "enough for one more pack of cigarets" stage, but I have a hot prospect for a loan all lined up, and so I should make out O.K. — But all of these various things add up to the fact that I figure God must be a little put out at your husband for something

whether it is or not, I do!

... were here at least just ... promise to have myself ... we are together, because ... ld add nothing whatever ... together.

... up all of your husband's ... - I surely do miss you ... e around nothing very bad ... even if it does I don't

... hear about your catching ... take care of yourself ... ... th. - So please rest, and get ... days dearest.

... ed me to death, - I would ... Paul, - After we're home ... have a lot of calls to ... - Oh darling, I do hope

... now, and write again soon. ...

... e to tell you how much ... and want you with me?

Dick.

P.S. — Two weeks today darling, you have been a bride!

331

Dearest Wife,

It's a very hot—sticky afternoon here in St. Louis, and very dull too. I'm working—in theory—but actually there isn't a great deal to do except sit around and wish for you to be with me. I'm having a heck of a time right now. In the first place, I can't seem to get any action towards being shipped. I haven't been to the Post Intelligence Office as yet, but I may go later on this afternoon. If they can't do anything to help me, I'm liable to be here for the duration—doing nothing really constructive—but just more or less fooling around. I found out where everyone from Miami went, and that too made me feel bad. They went to Amarillo, Texas, which—from all I can gather—is the only place in the country that is worse than Abilene and Camp Barkeley. I don't even know whether I'll ask to go back with them. That country would really be rough for you I know. What do you think?

The second thing to bother me—you'll laugh at this—I have been plagued with bed bugs for the last four days. They have just naturally chewed me up. I have big welts all over me which alternately hurt and itch, and I have been in misery. They are getting big enough now to almost move the bed around, and all from eating me. I have to eat more food than usual now to keep body and bugs together.

Third, I have lost a sheet—stolen almost out from under my nose, and a rain coat—like wise disappeared. Probably the whole thing will cost me about eight bucks and so out of my June pay—payable the first of July. June first came and is now passing and I find that I don't get paid until about the tenth of the month. Right now I am at the "enough for one more pack of cigarettes" stage, but I have a hot prospect for a loan all lined up, and so I should make out O.K. But all of these various things add up to the fact that I figure God must be a little put out at your husband for something or other. You could if you were here at least put something on my bites—I promise to have myself properly fumigated before we are together, because these damned bed bugs would add nothing whatever to our happy married life together.

So—that about sums up all of your husbands' misfortunes for the moment. I surely do miss you darling. Somehow when you're around nothing very bad can happen to me, and even if it does—I don't seem to mind very much.

I was mighty sorry to hear about you catching cold, darling. I do want you to take care of yourself and not get ill. You're far away the most precious thing I have on earth. So please rest, and get lots of sun, and be as always dearest.

Darling, the poem tickled me to death. I would like very much to meet Earl. After we're home safe & happy again, we'll have a lot of calls to make, and travelling to do.

Oh darling, I do hope it will be soon.

Well, I'll close for now, and write again soon. And you do the same.

Is it necessary for me to tell you how much I love you, and miss you and want you with me? Whether it is or not, I do!

Dick

P. S. Two weeks today darling, you have been a bride!

Cpl. R. G. Clark AAF
35411090
Sq. A - 21st. Training Group
Jefferson Barracks, Mo.

Free

Mrs. Richard G. Clark,
Sunbury,
Ohio.

Dearest Wife,

Thursday, and a rainy one at that. I had planned to go to the Baseball game tonight, so naturally it would rain. - I'm getting so that I kind of enjoy those games. Soldiers get in free, and I figure I might as well take advantage of all opportunities.

Still no real news about your husband, darling. Tuesday night I walked over and saw some new arrivals from Camp Barkely and got all the gossip. They said that the platoon I was in was going to graduate about fifteen men. Personally, there is no doubt in my mind but that I would not have been there for the ceremonies regardless. Yesterday was graduation down there, and I was a little blue for a few minutes. I did want a commission pretty badly. - Then, I had to take shots and consequently I became even bluer. - I positively can never catch any disease I feel sure. I don't know, but I guess yesterday was just a bad day. After the shots, I went back to work and had a very busy day. Then I was "C.Q." again last night, and right now I'm working on about three or four hours sleep. - Yeah honey, I'm out for sympathy from my wife I guess. Can't you give me just a little?

I got a letter from Bob yesterday. He's now back in Texas and I guess June isn't with him. He's kind of a dull instructor I guess. I wouldn't like that at all myself. He said that I should tell you that he'll collect a kiss from you as soon as he sees you again. - I guess he can have one, but no more.

shipping yet, but I may develop soon now. at opinion on - just you honey? What have decide to take a job, or a while? - Keep your h developments. - By the ipt on our allotment. - Save ime, you never know how p next.

e isn't any more news to ove you and miss you of you and at night I a before sleep will come. and you are always there. art of all my thoughts just belong Darling wife, should be.

lt in all of you that I ve you all there is.

nd,
Dick.

POSTMARKED JEFFERSON BARRACKS, MISSOURI—JUNE 9, 1943

Dearest Wife,

Thursday, and a rainy one at that. I had planned to go to the Baseball game tonight, so naturally it would rain. I'm getting so that I kind of enjoy those games. Soldiers get in free, and I figure I might as well take advantage of all the opportunities.

Still no real news about your husband, darling. Tuesday night I walked over and saw some new arrivals from Camp Barkeley and got all the gossip. They said that the platoon I was in was going to graduate about fifteen men. Personally, there is no doubt in my mind but that I would not have been there for the ceremonies regardless. Yesterday was graduation down there, and I was a little blue for a few minutes. I did want a commission pretty badly. Then, I had to take shots and consequently I became even bluer. I positively can never catch any disease I feel sure. I don't know, but I guess yesterday was just a bad day. After the shots, I went back to work and had a very busy day. Then I was "C.L." again last night, and right now I'm working on about three or four hours sleep. Yeah honey, I'm out for sympathy from my wife I guess. Can't you give me just a little?

I got a letter from Bob yesterday. He's now back in Texas and I guess June isn't with him. He's kind of a drill instructor I guess. I wouldn't like that at all myself. He said that I should tell you that he'll collect a kiss from you as soon as he sees you again. I guess he can have one, but no more.

Still no news about my shipping yet, but I do think that something may develop soon now. I have nothing to base that opinion on—just a hunch! What about you, honey? What have you been doing? Did you decide to take a job, or are you going to rest up for a while? Keep you husband informed on all such developments. By the way, I'm enclosing the receipt on our allotment. Save it, we may need it sometime, you never know how the Army will mess things up next.

Well dearest, I guess there isn't any more news to tell you, except that I love you and miss you a lot. All the time I think of you and at night I lay awake and think of you before sleep will come. With sleep comes dreaming, and you are always there. Awake or asleep you are a part of all my thoughts and dreams and plans. You just belong darling wife, and that is definitely as it should be.

There isn't a single fault in all of you that I know of, and—I just love you all there is.

Your Husband,

Dick

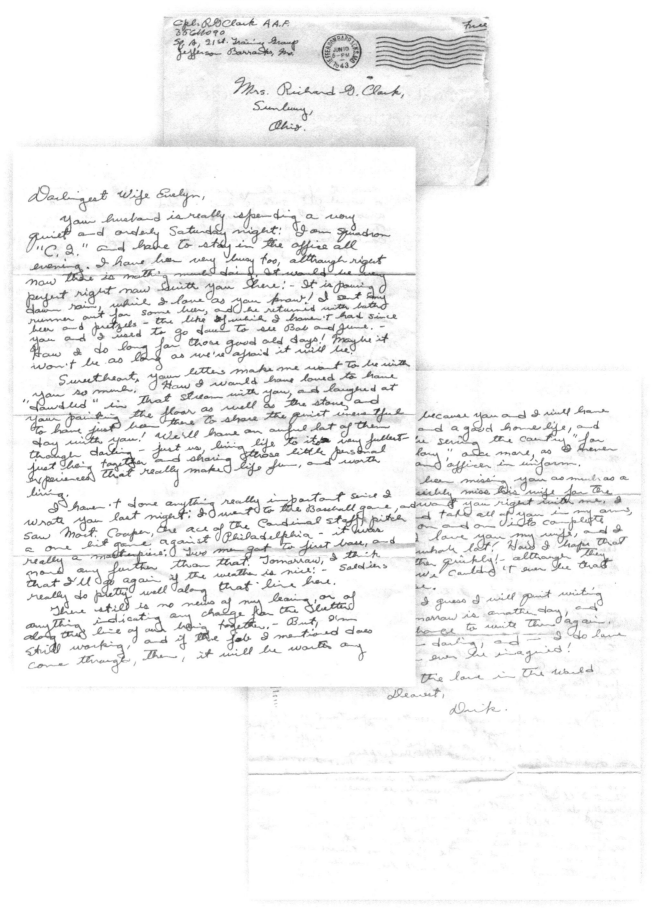

Darlingest Wife Evelyn,

Your husband is really spending a very quiet and orderly Saturday night: I am squadron "C. Q." and have to stay in the office all evening. I have been very busy too, although right now there is nothing much doing. It would be very perfect right now with you there! - It is pouring down rain, while I love as you know! I sent my runner out for some beer, and he returned with both beer and pretzels - the like of which I haven't had since you and I used to go down to see Bob and June. - How I do long for those good old days! Maybe it won't be as long as we're afraid it will be!

Sweetheart, your letters make me want to be with you so much. How I would have loved to have "paddled" in that stream with you, and laughed at your painting the floor as well as the stone, and to have just been there to share the quiet eventful day with you! We'll have an awful lot of them though darling - just us, living life to its very fullest, just being together and sharing those little personal experiences that really make life fun, and worth living.

I haven't done anything really important since I wrote you last night; I went to the Baseball game, saw Mort. Cooper, the ace of the Cardinal staff pitch a one hit game against Philadelphia - it was really a masterpiece! Two men got to first base, and none any further than that. Tomorrow, I think that I'll go again if the weather is nice! - Soldiers really do pretty well along that line here.

There still is no news of my leaving, or of anything indicating any change for the better along this line of our being together. - But, I'm still working, and if the job I mentioned does come through, then, it will be worth any

because you and I will have and a good home life, and be serving the country "for ... day" once more, as I ... an officer in uniform.

... been missing you as much as a ... ibly miss his wife for the ... want you right with me, I ... take all of you in my arms ... on and on ... to complete ... love you my wife, and I ... whole lot! How I hope that ... ther quickly! - although they ... we could it ever be that ...

I guess I will quit writing ... morrow is another day, and ... ace to write then again ... darling, and — I do love ... ever be imagined!

... the love in the world

Dearest,

Duck.

POSTMARKED JEFFERSON BARRACKS, MISSOURI—JUNE 10, 1943

Darlingest Wife Evelyn,

Your husband is really spending a very quiet and orderly Saturday night: I am squadron "C.I." and have to stay in the office all evening. I have been very busy too, although right now there is nothing much doing. It would be very perfect right now with you here: It is pouring down rain, which I love as you know! I sent my runner out for some beer, and he returned with both beer and pretzels—the like of which I haven't had since you and I used to go down to see Bob and June. How I do long for those good old days! Maybe it won't be as long as we're afraid it will be.

Sweetheart, your letters make me want to be with you so much. How I would have loved to have "dawdled" in that stream with you, and laughed at your painting the floor as well as the stove, and to have just been there to share the quiet uneventful day with you! We'll have an awful lot of them though darling—just us, living life to it's very fullest—just being together and sharing those little personal experiences that really make life fun, and worth living.

I haven't done anything really important since I wrote you last night: I went to the baseball game, and saw Mort. Cooper the ace of the Cardinal staff, pitch a one hit game against Philadelphia—it was really a masterpiece: Two men got to first base, and none any further than that. Tomorrow, I think that I'll go again if the weather is nice: Soldiers really do pretty well along that line here.

There still is no news of my leaving, or of anything indicating any change from the better along this line of our being together. But I'm still working, and if the job I mentioned does come through, then it will be worth any amount of waiting, because you and I will have a wonderful salary, and a good home life, and also I will truly be serving the country "for the honor and the glory," once more, as I never could have done as an officer in uniform.

Dearest, I have been missing you as much as a man could ever possibly miss his wife for the last week or so. I want you right with me. I want to touch you, and take all of you in my arms, and kiss you and on and on into complete blissful oblivion. I love you my wife, and I need you a whole whole lot! How I hope that they dispose of me rather quickly—although, they won't—naturally. We couldn't ever be that lucky I don't suppose.

Well dearest wife, I guess I will quit writing for tonight, but tomorrow is another day, and probably I'll get a chance to write then again. Good night my very own darling, and—I do love you more than can ever be imagined!

All the love in the World Dearest,

Dick

Pittsburgh Pirates vs St. Louis Cardinals June 9, 1943 Box Score

Baseball Almanac Box Scores
Pittsburgh Pirates 3, St. Louis Cardinals 4

Game played on Wednesday, June 9, 1943 at Sportsman's Park III

Pittsburgh Pirates	ab	r	h	rbi	St. Louis Cardinals	ab	r	h	rbi
Gustine 2b	4	0	0	0	Klein 2b	5	0	1	1
Russell lf	4	1	1	0	Walker cf	4	0	1	0
Elliott 3b	4	0	1	0	Musial rf	4	0	1	1
Barrett rf	4	0	0	0	Sanders 1b	4	0	0	0
Fletcher 1b	3	0	0	0	Cooper W. c	4	0	1	0
Lopez c	3	1	1	0	Garms lf	4	0	0	0
DiMaggio cf	4	1	2	1	Kurowski 3b	4	3	3	0
Geary ss	3	0	0	0	Marion ss	3	0	2	1
Sewell p	3	0	2	1	Cooper M. p	3	1	1	1
Totals	32	3	7	2	Totals	35	4	10	4

```
Pittsburgh   0  0  0    0  2  1    0  0  0  —   3   7   0
St. Louis    0  0  0    0  2  1    0  0  1  —   4  10   0
```

Pittsburgh Pirates	IP	H	R	ER	BB	SO
Sewell L(6-2)	8.2	10	4	4	1	1
Totals	8.2	10	4	4	1	1

St. Louis Cardinals	IP	H	R	ER	BB	SO
Cooper W(7-3)	9.0	7	3	3	2	5
Totals	9.0	7	3	3	2	5

E–None. DP–St. Louis 1. M. Cooper-Marion-Sanders. 2B–Pittsburgh DiMaggio (10); Sewell (1), St. Louis Walker (9); Kurowski (2); Marion (4); M. Cooper (2). 3B–St. Louis Kurowski (3). Team LOB–4. SH–M. Cooper (2). Team–7. U –Babe Pinelli, Al Barlick. T–1:48. A–2,365.

Game played on Wednesday, June 9, 1943 at Sportsman's Park III

Cpl. R.G. Clark A.A.F.
35611090
Sq. A. 2121 Tr. Group
Jefferson Barracks, Mo.

Mrs. Richard G. Clark,
Sunbury,
Ohio.

Dearest Wife Evelyn,

Saturday, and a terrifically warm one at that. It is so humid here that a person can just sit still and sweat. I know the finest place I can think of would be the backyard at the Stark house hold! Remember how cool it was last summer compared to the way it was in Columbus? We'll just simply have to live in a place where all is quiet and serene and cool, when this war is over. We'll garden, and raise children, and visit our neighbors and friends, and just be together – just us!

There is very little in the way of news – as usual. – Thursday as I told you I would, I went to the baseball game. Last night, I ate at the Service Club here on the post, and then visited some of my O.C.S. classmates for about three bottles of beer – then a shower and to bed. Today I'm working again, tonight I think that I'll go to St. Louis and take in a movie – just to get away from this place. Tomorrow two I'm going in to see the double header – still at the idea that the best in life is free. After that I am utterly at a loss for news, and the future is just as uncertain as it ever was. I'm still not on any shipment, I haven't heard a thing about the job I'm after, – nothing, – All I do is hope that something will happen, and wait, and grow more and more disgusted and blue and impatient to get definitely settled so that we can be together. – I thought I surely would be placed by now.

Honey, I know it's foolish, but if you want to come to St. Louis, come ahead, I want you with me, and I miss you so much. The only

... at I'll be shipped about
... here. – But, use your own
... weakened so much that I
... ming. – I want you honey!
... as my wife been up to
... hoping about all the
... everything that you do
...! I guess I just love my
... ibly can dearest. What did
... job at Kilgores? If the
... all, I wouldn't mind your
... come out here with me.
... OK with me darling, that

... e only with me right this
... and dream about you, and
... darling, the apple of my eye,
... whole world to me
... now sweet, and if you do
... ickly dearest.

Love a Husband can give,

Dick.

POSTMARKED JEFFERSON BARRACKS, MISSOURI—JUNE 15, 1943 (TUESDAY)

(Note this letter was written 6/12/43)

Dearest Wife Evelyn,

Saturday, and a terrifically warm one at that. It is so humid here that a person can just sit still and sweat. I know the first place I can think of would be the backyard at the Stark household! Remember how cool it was last summer compared to the way it was in Columbus? We'll just simply have to live in a place where all is quiet and serene and cool, when this War is over. We'll garden, and raise children, and visit our neighbors and friends, and just be together—just us!

There is very little in the way of news—as usual. Thursday as I told you I would, I went to the baseball game. Last night I ate at the Service Club here on the post, and then visited some of my O.C.S. classmates for about three bottles of beer—then a shower and to bed. Today I'm working again, tonight I think that I'll go to St. Louis and take in a movie—just to get away from this place. Tomorrow too I'm going in and see the double header—still at the idea that the best in life is free. After that I am utterly at a loss for news and the future is just as uncertain as it ever was. I'm still not on any shipment, I haven't heard a thing about the job I'm after,—nothing. All I do is hope that something will happen, and wait, and grow more and more disgusted and blue and impatient to get definitely settled so that we can be together. I thought I surely would be placed by now.

Honey, I know it's foolish, but if you want to come to St. Louis, come ahead. I want you with me, and I miss you so much. The only thing I'm afraid of is that I'll be shipped about the time you would get here. But, use your own judgement darling, I've weakened so much that I can't say no to your coming. I want you honey!

Sweetheart, what has my wife been up to lately? How I do enjoy hearing about all the mischief you get in, and everything that you do is just fine with me! I guess I just love my wife as much as I possibly can dearest. What did you do about getting a job at Kilgores? If the hours weren't so long, or off, I wouldn't mind you working there if you don't come out here with me. But, anything you do is OK with me darling, that is for sure!

Oh Evelyn if you were only with me right this minute! How I love you, and dream about you, and want you! You are my darling, the apple of my eye, just everything in the whole world to me sweetheart. Goodbye for now sweet, and if you do decide to come, come quickly dearest.

All the Love a Husband can give,

Dick

Pittsburgh Pirates vs St. Louis Cardinals June 10, 1943 Box Score

Baseball Almanac Box Scores
Pittsburgh Pirates 0, St. Louis Cardinals 5

Game played on Thursday, June 10, 1943 at Sportsman's Park III

Pittsburgh Pirates	ab	r	h	rbi
Gustine 2b	4	0	2	0
Russell lf	5	0	0	0
O'Brien rf	4	0	0	0
Elliott 3b	3	0	1	0
Fletcher 1b	3	0	0	0
Lopez c	3	0	1	0
DiMaggio cf	4	0	2	0
Geary ss	2	0	0	0
Gornicki p	1	0	0	0
Baker ph	1	0	0	0
Rescigno p	0	0	0	0
Shuman p	1	0	0	0
Colman ph	1	0	0	0
Totals	32	0	6	0

St. Louis Cardinals	ab	r	h	rbi
Klein 2b	4	0	1	1
Walker cf	4	0	1	0
Musial rf	4	0	0	0
Sanders 1b	4	0	0	0
O'Dea c	3	1	1	0
Garms lf	3	2	2	1
Kurowski 3b	2	0	0	0
Marion ss	3	2	2	1
Lanier p	2	0	1	2
Totals	29	5	8	5

```
Pittsburgh  0 0 0   0 0 0   0 0 0  -  0  6  2
St. Louis   0 2 0   3 0 0   0 0 x  -  5  8  1
```

Pittsburgh Pirates	IP	H	R	ER	BB	SO
Gornicki L(1-4)	3.0	4	2	2	0	1
Rescigno	0.1	3	3	3	0	0
Shuman	4.2	1	0	0	0	2
Totals	8.0	8	5	5	0	3

St. Louis Cardinals	IP	H	R	ER	BB	SO
Lanier W(3-3)	9.0	6	0	0	6	9
Totals	9.0	6	0	0	6	9

E–DiMaggio (5), Geary (6), Kurowski (4). **DP**–Pittsburgh 1. DiMaggio-Lopez, St. Louis 2. Marion-Sanders, Marion-Klein-Sanders. **2B**–St. Louis Klein (10); O'Dea (7); Marion (5). **Team LOB**–11. **SH**–Kurowski (3); Lanier (4). **Team**–2. **U**–Babe Pinelli, Ziggy Sears. **T**–2:03. **A**–13,356.

Game played on Thursday, June 10, 1943 at Sportsman's Park III

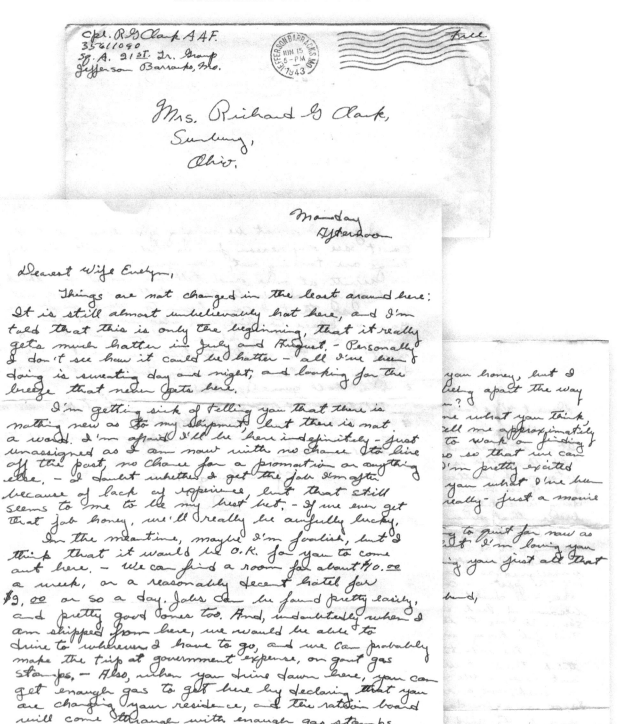

Cpl. R.G. Clark A.A.F.
35611090
Sq. A. 21ST. Tr. Group
Jefferson Barracks, Mo.

JEFFERSON BARRACKS MO
JUN 15
5 - PM
1943

Free

Mrs. Richard G Clark,
Sunbury,
Ohio.

Monday
Afternoon

Dearest Wife Evelyn,

Things are not changed in the least around here: It is still almost unbelievably hot here, and I'm told that this is only the beginning, that it really gets much hotter in July and August. — Personally I don't see how it could be hotter — all I've been doing is sweating day and night, and looking for the breeze that never gets here.

I'm getting sick of telling you that there is nothing new as to my shipment, but there is not a word. I'm afraid I'll be here indefinitely — just unassigned as I am now with no chance to live off the post, no chance for a promotion or anything else. — I doubt whether I get the job I'm after because of lack of experience, but that still seems to me to be my best bet. — If we ever get that job honey, we'll really be awfully lucky.

In the meantime, maybe I'm foolish, but I think that it would be O.K. for you to come out here. — We can find a room for about $10.00 a week, or a reasonably decent hotel for $9.00 or so a day. Jobs can be found pretty easily, and pretty good ones too. And, undoubtedly when I am shipped from here, we would be able to drive to wherever I have to go, and we can probably make the trip at government expense, on govt gas stamps. — Also, when you drive down here, you can get enough gas to get here by declaring that you are changing your residence, and the ration board will come through with enough gas stamps.

If you have a job by the time you get this letter, you'd probably better stay at home and keep at it, but otherwise — if you think it's a good idea let me know — and come ahead!

... you honey, but I ... being apart the way ... ? ... me what you think, ... tell me approximately ... to work on finding ... so that we can ... I'm pretty excited ... you what I've been ... really — just a movie ...

... to quit for now as ... If I'm loving you ... you just all that ...

... husband,

(Note this letter was written 6/14/43)

Monday Afternoon

Dearest Wife Evelyn,

Things are not changed in the least around here: It is still almost unbelieveably hot here, and I'm told that this is only the beginning, that it really gets much hotter in July and August. Personally I don't see how it could be hotter—all I've been doing is sweating day and night, and looking for the breeze that never gets here.

I'm getting sick of telling you that there is nothing new as to my shipment, but there is not a word. I'm afraid I'll be here indefinitely—just unassigned as I am now with no chance to live off the post, no chance for a promotion or anything else. I doubt whether I get the job I'm after because of lack of experience, but that still seems to me to be my best bet. If we even get that job honey, we'll really be awfully lucky.

In the meantime, maybe I'm foolish, but I think that it would be O.K. for you to come out here. We can find a room for about $10.00 a week, or a reasonably decent hotel for $2.00 or so a day. Jobs can be found pretty easily, and pretty good ones too. And, undoubtedly when I am shipped from here, we would be able to drive to wherever I have to go, and we can probably make the trip at government expense, on gov't gas stamps. Also, when you drive down here, you can get enough gas to get here by declaring that you are changing your residence, and the ration board will come through with enough gas stamps.

If you have a job by the time you get this letter, you'd probably better stay at home and keep at it, but other wise—if you think it's a good idea let me know—and come ahead!

I guess I must be missing you honey, but I can't see any reason for us being apart the way things are turning out, can you?

Write at once and tell me what you think, and if you decide to come, tell me approximately when so that I can begin to work on finding you a place to live, and also so that we can arrange a meeting place. I'm pretty excited right now, too excited to tell you what I've been doing since Saturday—nothing really—just a movie and a ball game yesterday.

Well sweetheart, I'm going to quit for now as I must get back to work; but I'm loving you and missing you, and wanting you just all that a husband can.

Your Loving Husband,

Dick

Pittsburgh Pirates vs St. Louis Cardinals June 13, 1943 Box Score

Baseball Almanac Box Scores
Pittsburgh Pirates 10, St. Louis Cardinals 3

Game played on Sunday, June 13, 1943 at Sportsman's Park III

Pittsburgh Pirates	ab	r	h	rbi
Gustine 2b	6	1	3	3
O'Brien rf	6	1	3	2
Russell lf	4	1	2	1
Elliott 3b	3	2	1	0
Fletcher 1b	5	2	2	0
Baker c	2	0	1	1
Lopez c	3	0	1	1
DiMaggio cf	3	2	2	1
Barrett cf	0	0	0	0
Geary ss	5	0	0	0
Hebert p	4	1	1	1
Totals	41	10	16	10

St. Louis Cardinals	ab	r	h	rbi
Klein 2b	3	1	1	0
Brown ss	2	0	1	0
Walker cf	5	1	2	1
Musial rf	5	1	2	0
Demaree lf	4	0	2	2
Cooper c	4	0	0	0
Kurowski 3b	3	0	0	0
Garms 3b	1	0	0	0
Sanders 1b	2	0	0	0
Hopp 1b	0	0	0	0
Marion ss	3	0	2	0
Fallon 2b	1	0	0	0
Brecheen p	0	0	0	0
Gumbert p	0	0	0	0
Dickson p	3	0	1	0
Litwhiler ph	1	0	0	0
Totals	37	3	11	3

```
Pittsburgh  7 0 0   0 1 2   0 0 0  -  10  16  1
St. Louis   2 0 0   0 0 0   0 1 0  -   3  11  1
```

Pittsburgh Pirates	IP	H	R	ER	BB	SO
Hebert W(4-3)	9.0	11	3	3	2	1
Totals	9.0	11	3	3	2	1

St. Louis Cardinals	IP	H	R	ER	BB	SO
Brecheen L(2-2)	0.0	3	5	5	2	0
Gumbert	0.2	2	2	2	2	0
Dickson	8.1	11	3	3	5	3
Totals	9.0	16	10	10	9	3

E–Elliott (8), Fallon (1). DP–Pittsburgh 1. Fletcher-Geary-Fletcher, St. Louis 2. Klein-Sanders, W. Cooper-Marion-Kurowski. 2B–Pittsburgh Gustine (4); O'Brien (4), St. Louis Musial (12); Demaree (1); Dickson (1). 3B–St. Louis Brown (2); Walker (3). Team LOB–13. Team–9. SB–Russell (3). U–Ziggy Sears, Babe Pinelli, Al Barlick.

Game played on Sunday, June 13, 1943 at Sportsman's Park III

Pittsburgh Pirates vs St. Louis Cardinals June 13, 1943 Box Score

Baseball Almanac Box Scores
Pittsburgh Pirates 4, St. Louis Cardinals 4

Game played on Sunday, June 13, 1943 at Sportsman's Park III

Pittsburgh Pirates	ab	r	h	rbi		St. Louis Cardinals	ab	r	h	rbi
Gustine 2b	7	1	4	0		Klein 2b	6	0	3	0
Russell lf	3	1	0	0		Walker cf	6	1	2	1
Colman rf	2	0	0	0		Garms lf	6	1	2	0
O'Brien ph	1	0	0	0		Musial rf	5	1	1	0
Barrett rf	0	0	0	0		O'Dea c	4	0	1	1
Elliott 3b	6	1	1	2		Litwhiler pr	0	0	0	0
Fletcher 1b	3	1	1	2		Cooper c	1	0	1	0
Lopez c	6	0	2	0		Hopp 1b	6	0	2	2
DiMaggio cf	6	0	0	0		Kurowski 3b	6	0	2	0
Geary ss	6	0	0	0		Marion ss	5	0	1	0
Klinger p	5	0	1	0		Krist p	3	1	1	0
Totals	45	4	9	4		Lanier p	0	0	0	0
						Totals	48	4	16	4

```
Pittsburgh   1 0 1   0 0 0   2 0 0   0 0 0  -  4   9  1
St. Louis    0 0 3   0 0 1   0 0 0   0 0 0  -  4  16  0
```

Pittsburgh Pirates	IP	H	R	ER	BB	SO
Klinger	12.0	16	4	4	4	5
Totals	12.0	16	4	4	4	5

St. Louis Cardinals	IP	H	R	ER	BB	SO
Krist	7.1	8	4	4	7	4
Lanier	4.2	1	0	0	2	5
Totals	12.0	9	4	4	9	9

E–Geary (7). DP–Pittsburgh 1. Fletcher-Geary. 2B–Pittsburgh Gustine (5), St. Louis Walker (10); Garms (3); Musial (13); W. Cooper (5); Hopp (2). HR–Pittsburgh Fletcher (3,7th inning off Krist 1 on). HBP–Fletcher (4). **Team LOB**–15. SH–Klein (5); Walker (12); Lanier 2 (6). **Team**–16. U–Babe Pinelli, Al Barlick, Ziggy Sears. T–3:16. A–16,255.

Game played on Sunday, June 13, 1943 at Sportsman's Park III

Tuesday,

Dearest Wife,

Just a little note darling on account of I have been thinking of you all day, and all last night, Almost without interruption. Dearest, the way you wrote yesterday, you must have thought I wouldn't want you to go to W. Va. Darling, I want you to be happy, and you do need a rest and a little fun. I hope you're having a swell time down there right now. — I'll bet that when you and Ruth are together you really do get a lot of talking done.

Honey, last night Will Osborne put on a show for us here on the post, and how I did wish for you then. The moon is getting fuller every night, and his music was good, and just enough romantic to make me long terrifically for my wife. — All evening I was seing you as you were the night we got married — you looked awfully swell that night darling, and I was and am mighty proud of my wife. Four weeks today darling we've been married, and how I wish we had been together all of the time. — But we will be from now on if you're willing.

I still think it will be O.K. for you to come out now if you think so too, and I sure want you to do so, It may be that if you come my orders will come through real quick, and if they do we can then travel together to our next post. Would you like that?

Well dearest, it's back to work for me now, so have a good time sweetheart, and write me and miss me, and plan to come to St. Louis real soon, I love you darling wife all the love there is in the world
Dick,

Tuesday

Dearest Wife,

Just a little note darling on account I have been thinking of you all day, and all last night, almost without interruption. Dearest, the way you wrote yesterday, you must have thought I wouldn't want you to go to W.Va. Darling, I want you to be happy, and you do need a rest and a little fun. I hope you're having a swell time down there right now. I'll bet that when you and Ruth are together you really do get a lot of talking done.

Honey, last night Will Osborne put on a show for us here on the post, and how I did wish for you then: The moon is getting fuller every night, and his music was good, and just enough romantic to make me long terrifically for my wife. All evening I was seeing you as you were the night we got married—you looked awfully swell that night darling, and I was and am mighty proud of my wife. Four weeks today darling we've been married, and how I wish we had been together all of the time. But we will be from now on, if you're willing.

I still think it will be O.K. for you to come out now if you think so too, and I sure want you to do so. It may be that if you come my orders will come through real quick, and if they do we can then travel together to our next post. Would you like that?

Well dearest, it's back to work for me now. So have a good time sweetheart, and write me and miss me, and plan to come to St. Louis real soon. I love you darling wife all the love there is in the world,

Dick

Wed. Afternoon.

Hi Sun Burn!

Life goes on darling. One day drags through to a close to be followed by another - similar - one. Days pile up somehow into weeks and time goes by. It's dull and boring here now, and very hot and sticky. I guess that all of my ambition has now departed, and I am stagnate - just watching the world go by, and hoping that soon something good will happen. — It's a terrible feeling.

Dearest, I surely hope you are enjoying yourself a lot this week, and that you aren't nearly as sun burned as you sounded. I can just see those red shoulders, and I hope I have a nice sun kissed wife when she gets back. I know that you won't get this until you are back, but I hope you're just swimming and relaxing, and enjoying life to its fullest. I surely do wish I was with you there on a vacation or something. — Did you get the recipe for fixing the ham up Southern style? — Also, I don't know what to think about me being at the foot of the bed. — I can think of a much better spot than that for me.

Sweetness, what have you decided about coming on to St. Louis? I'm anxiously awaiting a reply on that one. I do miss you dear, and I want you with me if possible, and I think it's possible if you do. — So, write and tell me what you think, and - here's hoping it won't be too long now until we're together. Be a good girl and love me dearest, as I do you - all a husband possibly can.

Dick.

351

Wed. Afternoon

Hi Sun Burn!

Life goes on darling. One day drags through to a close to be followed by another—similar—one. Days pile up somehow into weeks and time goes by. Its dull and boring here now, and very hot and sticky. I guess that all of my ambition has now departed, and I am stagnate—just watching the world go by, and hoping that soon something good will happen. It's a terrible feeling.

Dearest, I surely hope you are enjoying yourself a lot this week, and that you aren't nearly as sun burned as you sounded. I can just see those red shoulders, and I hope I have a nice sun kissed wife when she gets back. I know that you won't get this until you are back, but I hope you're just swimming and relaxing, and enjoying life to its fullest. I surely do wish I was with you there on a vacation or something. Did you get the recipe for fixing the ham up Southern style? Also, I don't know what to think about me being at the foot of the bed. I can think of a much better spot than that for me.

Sweetness, what have you decided about coming on to St. Louis? I'm anxiously awaiting a reply on that one. I do miss you dearest, and I want you with me if possible, and I think it's possible if you do. So, write and tell me what you think, and—here's hoping it won't be too long now until we're together. Be a good girl and love me dearest, as I do you—all a husband possibly can.

Dick

Cpl R G Clark AAF
3561090
Sq. A, 21st. Tr. Group.
Jefferson Barracks, Mo.

Free

Mrs. Richard G Clark,
Sunbury,
Ohio.

Hi-Darling,

Friday – fish day – and all of the fish will be G.I. Time still flies and nothing much happens around here to even tell you about. Yesterday I worked all day on about three hours sleep – I went to the ballgame Wed. night and didn't get in until about two. – Then yesterday I also had another shot to take and it hurt. Last night I ate at the cafeteria in the P.X. Then read for a while – _Time_, and went out and looked at the moon. It was very beautiful and full and Summery, a perfect night to have had my wife with me. – How I would have enjoyed that! As it was I got lonesome and indulged in some wishful thinking. – Wishing that we were together, no matter where, but preferably in our own _home_, on our own front porch; or else out in the woods, or along a lake or ocean. – We have a lot of living left to do darling. – A whole lifetime full. How I hate the army and this war for keeping us apart, and keeping us from beginning on all the things that we need to do together.

Tomorrow – Saturday – I am C.Q. again, and so I'll have lots of time for thinking about us. That's about all I get done anymore. Just dreaming day and night about my wonderful wife. And you are wonderful, darling! Do you know that? You'll never know quite how grand I think you are, and how I miss you and how awfully much I love you. I'm so proud of you sweetheart, and I know that no one else has a wife as nice as mine. – No one! You're just perfect and all there is in the world for me dearest.

forward to hearing when
, and I'll really hunt for
, or maybe it would be
up in a hotel and let you
the day time. – I think it
uld give you something to do.
what goes on!

you Wednesday letter, and
of the state senator! – You
men on I'll fly over on my
al you away. – I'm glad
this down there dear, and I
with you.

that I'm in love with my
this! Do you suppose?

our Husband

Dick.

POSTMARKED JEFFERSON BARRACKS, MISSOURI—JUNE 18, 1943

Hi Darling,

Friday—fish day—and all of the fish will be G.I. Time, still flies and nothing much happens around here to even tell you about. Yesterday I worked all day on about three hours sleep—I went to the ball game Wed. night and didn't get in until about two. Then yesterday I also had another shot to take and it hurt. Last night I ate at the cafeteria in the P.X. then read for awhile and went out and looked at the moon. It was very beautiful and full and summery, a perfect night to have had my wife with me. How I would have enjoyed that! As it was I got lonesome and indulged in some wishful thinking—Wishing that we were together, no matter where, but preferably in our own home, on our own front porch; or else out in the woods, or along a lake or ocean. We have a lot of living left to do darling. A whole lifetime full. How I hate the army, and this war for keeping us apart, and keeping us from beginning on all the things that we need to do together.

Tomorrow—Saturday—I am C. I. again, and so I'll have lots of time for thinking about us. That's about all I get done anymore—just dreaming day and night about my wonderful wife. And you are wonderful, darling! Do you know that? You'll never know quite how grand I think you are, and how I miss you and how awfully much I love you. I'm so proud of you sweetheart, and I know that no one else has a wife as nice as mine. No one! You're just perfect and all there is in the world for me dearest.

Honey, I'm looking forward to hearing when you're coming to St. Louis, and I'll really hunt for a spot for you to stay, or maybe it would be better to put you up in a hotel and let you find a place during the day time. I think it would, because it would give you something to do. Anyway, let me know what goes on!

Sweet, I just got your Wednesday letter, and I'm mighty jealous of the state senator! You stay away from those men or I'll fly over on my magic carpet and steal you away. I'm glad you're having a good time down there dear, and I really wish I were there with you.

I guess it's just that I'm in love with my wife through—all of this! Do you suppose?

Your Husband,

Dick

Cincinnati Reds vs St. Louis Cardinals June 16, 1943 Box Score

- -

Baseball Almanac Box Scores
Cincinnati Reds 4, St. Louis Cardinals 1

Game played on Wednesday, June 16, 1943 at Sportsman's Park III

Cincinnati Reds	ab	r	h	rbi		St. Louis Cardinals	ab	r	h	rbi
Frey 2b	5	0	0	0		Klein 2b	4	0	0	0
Clay rf	4	0	0	0		Walker cf	5	0	0	0
Walker cf	5	0	2	0		Demaree lf	4	1	1	0
McCormick 1b	5	1	1	0		Musial rf	5	0	0	0
Mesner 3b	4	0	1	0		Cooper c	5	0	1	0
Tipton lf	3	2	0	0		Kurowski 3b	4	0	2	1
Miller ss	4	1	1	2		Marion ss	5	0	1	0
Mueller c	4	0	1	1		Sanders 1b	2	0	0	0
Vander Meer p	4	0	2	1		Litwhiler ph	0	0	0	0
Totals	38	4	8	4		Hopp 1b	1	0	0	0
						Brown ph	1	0	0	0
						Pollet p	4	0	0	0
						Totals	40	1	5	1

```
Cincinnati  0 0 0   0 1 0   0 0 0   0 3  -  4  8  2
St. Louis   0 0 0   1 0 0   0 0 0   0 0  -  1  5  4
```

Cincinnati Reds	IP	H	R	ER	BB	SO
Vander Meer W(6-5)	11.0	5	1	0	4	9
Totals	11.0	5	1	0	4	9

St. Louis Cardinals	IP	H	R	ER	BB	SO
Pollet L(5-2)	11.0	8	4	3	5	6
Totals	11.0	8	4	3	5	6

E–Clay (1), Vander Meer (3), Klein (7), Marion 2 (5), Hopp (2). DP–St. Louis 2. Kurowski-Klein-Sanders, Musial-Kurowski. PB–W. Cooper (5). 2B–Cincinnati Miller (11); Mueller (5), St. Louis W. Cooper (6); Kurowski (3). 3B–St. Louis Marion (1). SH–Frey (3); Tipton (3); Vander Meer (2). Team LOB–9. Team–10. U–George Magerkurth, Tom Dunn, Bill Stewart. T–3:05. A–14,229.

Game played on Wednesday, June 16, 1943 at Sportsman's Park III

Cpl. RG Clark AAF
35611090
Sq. A 21st Trg Group
Jefferson Barracks, Mo.

SAINT LOUIS MO.
JUN 10
9 PM
1943

BUY U.S. SAVINGS
BONDS
ASK YOUR POSTMASTER

Mrs. Richard G. Clark,
Sunbury,

Saturday Afternoon

Darlingest wife Evelyn,

Surprise, I thought th at in case you want to frame this letter that
I had better write it on a typewriter, so here goes. I have a little
bit of news that might be of some interest to you, and you might even
like it. The fact is that you had better now come to St louis after all:
You see, it really wouldn't be very practical just now, because
I'M SHIPPING OUT TO WRIGHT FIELD, DAYTON OHIO PROBABLY THIS COMING WEEK.
It's almost unbelievable, and it is entirely luck: I had nothing to do with
it myself, except to cheer when the news came out today. I don't know for
sure what I'll be doing, but I imagine that it will be in the same line
of work that I have been engaged in since I've been in the army. I'm
going to the Material Command, which is supply headquarters for the
Air Corps. - I'll write you all the details when I get more information,
and I'll let you know the day I ship. I don't know that yet, but I imagine
that next week I'll be close enough that I could see my wife over Sat.
and Sunday. Oh my Lord iisn't it wonderful? More than I ever dreamed of.
If it is a permanetn assignment, and I think that it is, you can get a
job in Dayton, or in the vicinity teaching, and we can be together, almost
as we wish it. Or if you don't want to each, I imagine tha there are
plenty of jobs to be had for the asking around that town. I'm just keeping
my fingers crossed for fear something will happen to mess us up. But it
looks as though everything will be all right with the world after all.
If we get set up the way I hope that we will, and hear tha we can, I will
forget all about my chances for the job I have applied for. So start cheering,
and begin to make plans accordingly.

There is really no other news right now, but that should be enough to
keep you thinking for a while. I enjoyed reading the letter from Betty
Trego, and it made me a little sad too. I surely do agree that it will be nice
when we can get back to normal, and live like God meant us to. By the
way, Mom informed me that a package from Tom and Toots had come to her,
and she wondered what to do with it. I told her to keep it that you would
be down, so you had better go down this week sometime. I guess that that
is about all in this letter, - They just took over the typewriter
So I'll continue in pen. - Be a good girl dearest, and
be ready to come to Dayton when you get invitations
from me. - And keep on loving me honey. - It
will only be a little while now at most until
we are together. All my love goes to my wife, and
there is an awfully, tremendous amount of it
Darling.

Your Husband,
Dick.

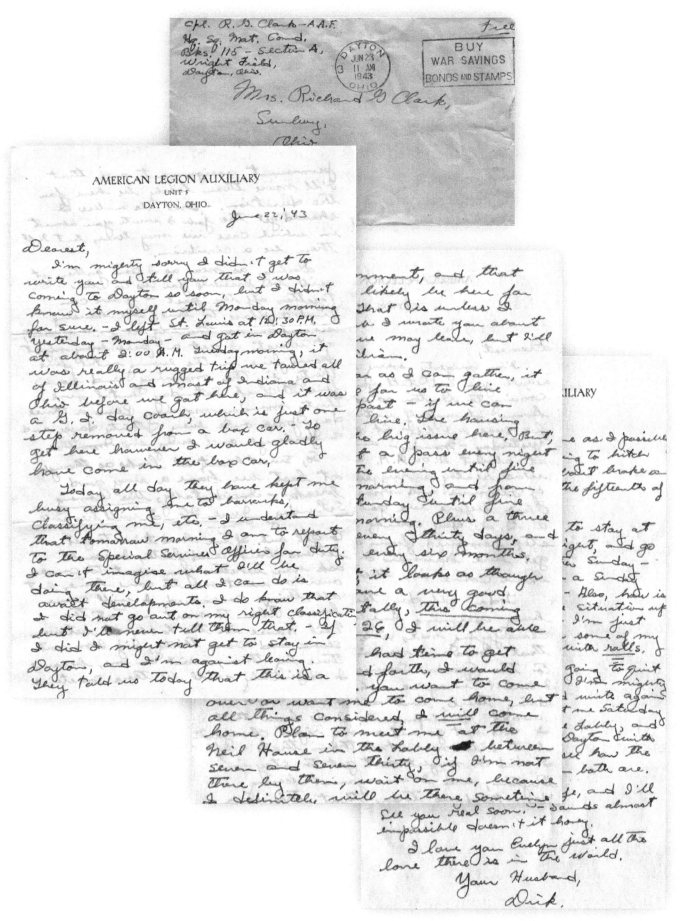

AMERICAN LEGION AUXILIARY
UNIT 5
DAYTON, OHIO.

June 22, '43

Dearest,

I'm mighty sorry I didn't get to write you and tell you that I was coming to Dayton so soon, but I didn't know it myself until Monday morning for sure. - I left St. Louis at 12:30 P.M. yesterday - Monday - and got in Dayton at about 2:00 A.M. Sunday morning, it was really a rugged trip we toured all of Illinois and most of Indiana and Ohio before we got here, and it was a G. I. day coach, which is just one step removed from a box car. - To get here however I would gladly have come in the box car,

Today all day they have kept me busy assigning me to barracks, classifying me, etc. - I understand that tomorrow morning I am to report to the Special Services Officer for duty. I can't imagine what I'll be doing there, but all I can do is await developments. I do know that I did not go out on my right classification but I'll never tell them that. - If I did I might not get to stay in Dayton, and I'm against leaving. They told us today that this is a

...ment, and that ...likely be here for ...That is unless I ...I write you about ...we may leave, but I'll ...them.

...as I can gather, it ...for us to live ...past - if we can ...line. The housing ...big issue here. But, ...of a pass every night ...evening until five ...morning and from ...Sunday until five ...morning. Plus a three ...every thirty days, and ...every six months.

...it looks as though ...are a very good ...Sally, this coming ...26, I will be able ...had time to get ...forth, I would ...you want to come ...me to come home, but all things considered, I will come home. Plan to meet me at the Neil House in the lobby between seven and seven thirty, if I'm not there by then, wait on me, because I definitely will be there sometime. See you real soon. - Sounds almost impossible doesn't it honey.

I love you Evelyn just all the love there is in the world.

Your Husband,
Dick.

...ILIARY

...as possible ...to hitch ...broke a ...fifteenth of ...to stay at ...night, and go ...Sunday - ...a Sunday ...Also, how is ...situation up ...I'm just ...some of my ...with ralls. I ...going to quit ...I'm mighty ...write again ...me Saturday ...lately, and ...Dayton write ...how the ...bath are. ...fe, and I'll

June 22, '43

Dearest,

I'm mighty sorry I didn't get to write you and tell you that I was coming to Dayton so soon, but I didn't know it myself until Monday morning for sure. I left St. Louis at 12:30 P.M. yesterday—Monday—and got in Dayton about 2:00A.M. Tuesday morning, it was really a rugged trip we toured all of Illinois and most of Indiana and Ohio before we got here, and it was a G.I. day coach, which is just one step removed from a box car. To get here however I would gladly have come in the box car.

Today all day they have kept me busy assigning me to barracks, classifying me, etc. I understand that tomorrow morning I am to report to the Special Services Officer for duty. I can't imagine what I'll be doing there, but all I can do is await developments. I do know that I did not go out on my right classification, but I'll never tell them that. If I did I might not get to stay in Dayton, and I'm against leaving. They told us today that this is a permanent assignment, and that I'll more than likely be here for the duration. That is unless I should get the job I wrote you about in which case we may leave, but I'll then be a civilian.

Darling, as near as I can gather, it will be possible for us to live together off the post—if we can find a place to live. The housing situation is the big issue here. But, at worst, I get a pass every night from five in the evening until five thirty in the morning, and from five o'clock Saturday until five thirty Monday morning. Plus a three day pass once every thirty days, and a furlough once every six months.

So, sweetheart, it looks as though at last we have a very good break! Incidentally, this coming Saturday, June 26, I will be able to get out. If we had time to get letters back and forth, I would ask you whether you want to come over or want me to come home, but all things considered, I will come home. Plan to meet me at the Neil House in the Lobby between seven and seven thirty, if I'm not there by then, wait on me, because I definitely will be there sometime as near to that time as I possibly can make it. I'm going to hitch hike over, I'm just about broke and I won't get paid until the fifteenth of July.

If it's O.K., let's plan to stay at your house Saturday night, and go down and see my mother Sunday—maybe we can work in a Sunday evening dinner on her. Also, how is the fried chicken and pie situation up on the Stark manor? I'm just hinting dearest wife for some of my own wifes' cooking—with <u>rolls</u>.

Well sweetness, I'm going to quit for now and go to bed. I'm mighty tired, but I'll try and write again this week. If not, meet me Saturday evening in the Neil House Lobby, and plan to come back to Dayton with me dearest. You can see how the job and room situation both are.

Goodnight darling wife, and I'll see you real soon. Sounds almost impossible doesn't it honey?

I love you Evelyn just all the love there is in this world.

Your Husband,

Dick

1946

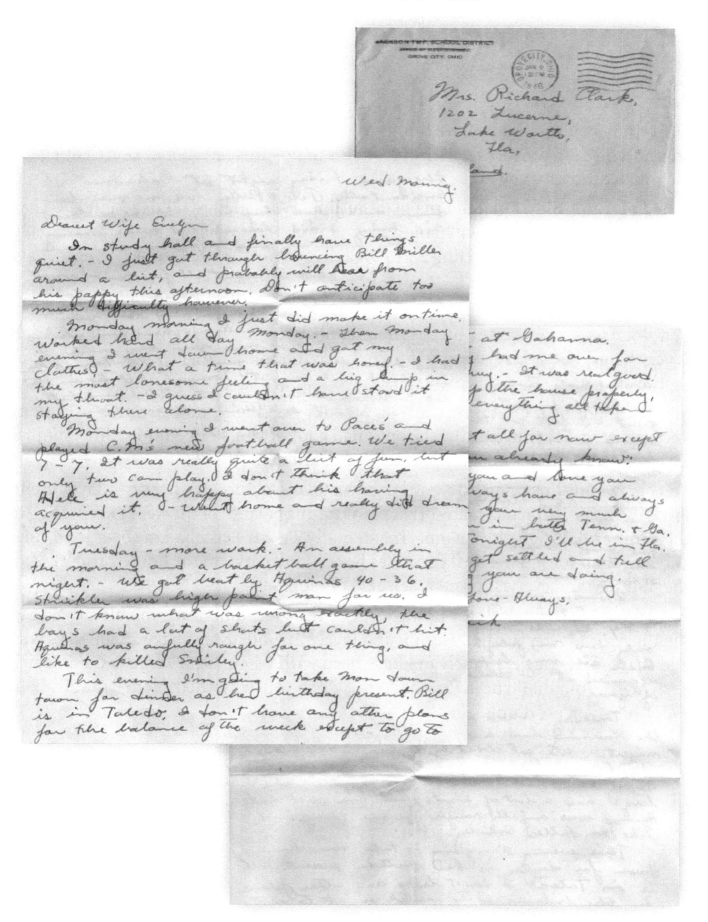

Wed. morning.

Dearest Wife Evelyn

In study hall and finally have things quiet. - I just got through bouncing Bill Miller around a bit, and probably will hear from his pappy this afternoon. Don't anticipate too much difficulty however.

Monday morning I just did make it on time. Worked hard all day Monday. - Then Monday evening I went down home and got my clothes. - What a time that was honey. - I had the most lonesome feeling and a big lump in my throat. - I guess I couldn't have stood it staying there alone.

Monday evening I went over to Pace's and played C.M's new football game. We tied 7 - 7. It was really quite a bit of fun, but only two can play. I don't think that Hele is very happy about his having acquired it. - went home and really did dream of you.

Tuesday - more work. - An assembly in the morning and a basket ball game that night. - We got beat by Aquinas 40 - 36. Strinkle was high point man for us. I don't know what was wrong exactly, the boys had a lot of shots but couldn't hit. Aquinas was awfully rough for one thing, and like to killed Smiley.

This evening I'm going to take Mom down town for dinner as her birthday present. Bill is in Toledo, I don't have any other plans for the balance of the week except to go to

[right panel, partial]
at Gahanna.
had me over for
... It was real good.
the house properly,
everything all taken
all for now except
already know:
you and love you
always have and always
you very much
in both Tenn. & Ga.
tonight I'll be in Fla.
get settled and tell
you are doing.
Love - Always,

Mrs. Richard Clark,
1202 Lucerne,
Lake Worth,
Fla.

Wednesday Morning

Dearest Wife Evelyn,

In study hall and finally have things quiet. I just got through bouncing Bill Miller around a bit, and probably will hear from his pappy this afternoon. Don't anticipate too much difficulty however.

Monday morning I just did make it on time. Worked hard all day Monday. Then Monday evening I went down home and got my clothes. What a time that was honey. I had the most lonesome feeling and a big lump in my throat. I guess I couldn't have stood it staying there alone.

Monday evening I went over to Paces' and played C.M.'s new football game. We tied 7–7. It was really quite a bit of fun, but only two can play. I don't think that Adele is very happy about his having acquired it. Went home and really did dream of you.

Tuesday—more work. An assembly in the morning and a basketball game that night. We got beat by Aquinas 40–36. Strikler was high point man for us. I don't know what was wrong exactly, the boys had a lot of shots but couldn't hit. Aquinas was awfully rough for one thing, and liked to kill Smiley.

This evening I'm going to take Mom down town for dinner as her birthday present. Bill is in Toledo. I don't have any other plans for the balance of the week except to go to the game Friday night at Gahanna. Incidentally, Pete & Betty had me over for dinner and had chop suey. It was real good. Yes honey I did close up the house properly. Got the plumber and everything all taken care of Monday.

I guess that's about all for now except to tell you something you already know: That is, that I love you and love you and love you, and always have and always will; and that I miss you very much and have been with you in both Tenn. & Ga. in spirit each night. Tonight I'll be in Fla. too. Write when you get settled and tell me all about everything you are doing.

All My Love—Always,

Dick

JACKSON TOWNSHIP BOARD OF EDUCATION
OFFICE OF THE CLERK
GROVE CITY, OHIO

Mrs. Richard Clark,
1202 Lucerne,
Lake Worth,
Fla.

To E. J. Freeland.

Wednesday,

Dearest Evelyn,

Study Hall again, and they are pretty quiet right now. Boy have I been lucky since I wrote you Sunday night; Monday I graded papers almost all day, and until eleven o'clock Monday night. Tuesday I got my grades on the grade sheets, and averaged everything up for the semester in addition to teaching all of my classes. Last night we played Ashville a basketball game, and lost for the third straight time. I don't know what has happened to them, but they look like a different team. I think what they really need is you watching them. – I know I would do a lot better with that sort of inspiration.

Tonight I have to chaperon that damned Sophomore skating party, so if I wire you from a hospital bed you'll know what happened. Tomorrow night I have no plans, but I suppose something will turn up that I won't want to do. Friday we play Circleville down there, and unless the boys snap out of it, will get beat again.

Additional news of interest only to my wife is that I love her and miss her more and more every day. I even have a tough time going to sleep because I'm thinking about you and that gets me to wishing we were both home in our own little bed, and that we could be cuddled up – even with your cold feet on my stomach darling.

Incidentally, my financial status is solvent, and I'm sure will continue to be: I've got about $32.00 left, and even after I pay Wall for the lockers should wind up O.K. Plus that, I got back a check from that insurance company for $28.60, because they

application, on account ... ... and am going to ... ... out P.D.Q. I ... ... my meeting with the ... the Masons, so it looks ... ... approved – I'll be taken in ... back.

... king back, have you seen ... get, and when are you ... marking off the days on ... ... miss your sweetheart, ... now on we'll take all ... ... awful to be that ... ... and I'm afraid ... ... up with me.

... dearest, and tell me ... ... ruby, and if your Ho– ... ... da, and if your Ho– ... ... re, because I need to ... ... I miss you and I want ... ... y more and more

my Love,

Dick.

Wednesday

Dearest Evelyn,

Study Hall again, and they are pretty quiet right now. Boy have I been busy since I wrote you Sunday night: Monday I graded papers almost all day, and until eleven o'clock Monday night. Tuesday I got my grades on the grade sheets, and averaged everything up for the semester in addition to teaching all of my classes. Last night we played Ashville, a basketball game, and lost for the third straight time. I don't know what has happened to them, but they look like a different team. I think what they really need is you watching them. I know I would do a lot better with that sort of inspiration. Tonight I have to chaperon that damned sophomore skating party, so if I wire you from a hospital bed you'll know what happened. Tomorrow night I have no plans, but I suppose something will turn up that I won't want to do. Friday we play Circleville down there, and unless the boys snap out of it, will get beat again.

Additional news of interest only to my wife is that I love her and miss her more and more every day. I even have a tough time going to sleep because I'm thinking about you and that gets me to wishing we were both home in our own little bed, and that we could be cuddled up—even with your cold feet on my stomach darling.

Incidentally, my financial status is solvent, and I'm sure will continue to be: I've got about $32.00 left, and even after I pay Wade for the locker, should wind up O.K. Plus that, I got back a check from that insurance company for $28.60, because they turned down my policy application, on account of C.D.D. I have the papers and am going to take that government policy out P.D.Q. Tonight after school, I have my meeting with the investigating committee for the Masons, so it looks as though—if I am approved—I'll be taken in about the time you get back.

Speaking of you getting back, have you seen about bus transportation yet, and when are you coming? I want to start marking off the days on the calendar. I guess I just miss you sweetheart, and I know that from now on we'll take all of our trips together. It's awful to be that much in love, but I am, and I'm afraid you'll first have to put up with me.

Write to me often dearest, and tell me what you're doing, and why it took you so long to get to Florida, and if you do—tell me that you love me, because I need to be told all the time. I miss you and want you and love you honey more and more every day.

All My Love,

Dick

GROVE CITY Lodge No. **689**

Free and Accepted Masons of Ohio

Grove City, Ohio, *Jan 29d* 19*46*

Mr. *Richard Fey Clark*.

Dear Sir:

You have been elected by unanimous ballot to receive the Mysteries of Freemasonry. In your petition soliciting this honor you stated you had a favorable opinion of our Institution—a statement which we have accepted; but a few words concerning the Fraternity may help you to better understand its design.

Freemasonry is an organized society of men symbolically applying the principles of operative Masonry and architecture to the science and art of character building. Our purpose is to make men, to build character, to bind men together in bonds of brotherly love and friendship.

You should approach Masonry clean in body, in heart and in a receptive mind with an eagerness to learn the significance of the Institution—for only in this state can your preparation be worthy of what you are about to receive. Be assured there is nothing of a light or trifling character in the degrees. Any intimation you may have had to the contrary is false. There is a profound meaning in every step of your progress.

The symbolism of Freemasonry deals only with the intellectual moral and spiritual values of life. If you were biased by improper solicitation of friends: influenced by mercenary motives: if you cannot cheerfully conform to the ancient established usages and customs of the Fraternity or be prepared to give to it your steady and undivided loyalty, it is better then you remain outside its ranks. You may say we are insisting upon this in advance of your full knowledge of the Institution; but we were likewise assuming much in your behalf when we accepted your petition thus admitting our obligations to you in advance of actual fraternal association. We have no doubt that the principles of the Order will command your loyal, active and sincere cooperation in furthering the interest of Freemasonry in general and this Lodge in particular.

Please present yourself for the conferring of the Entered Apprentice

Degree at *7·30* P. M., *Feb. 4th*, 19*46* at the Hall of *GROVE CITY* Lodge No. *689*, F. & A. M., located at *Grove City*, Ohio.

Sincerely

J. M. Campbell, Secretary

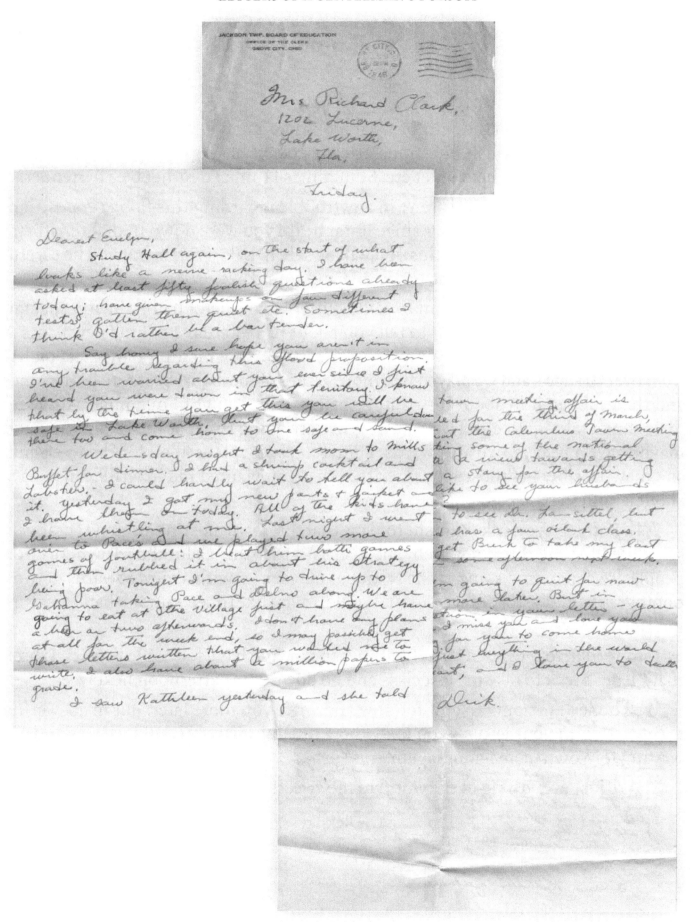

JACKSON TWP. BOARD OF EDUCATION
OFFICE OF THE CLERK
GROVE CITY, OHIO

Mrs. Richard Clark,
1206 Lucerne,
Lake Worth,
Fla.

Friday.

Dearest Evelyn,

Study Hall again, on the start of what looks like a nerve-racking day. I have been asked at least fifty foolish questions already today; have given makeups on four different tests, gotten them quiet etc. Sometimes I think I'd rather be a bartender.

Say honey I sure hope you aren't in any trouble regarding this flood proposition. I've been worried about you ever since I just heard you were down in that territory. I know that by the time you get this you will be safe in Lake Worth, but you be careful down there too and come home to me safe and sound.

Wednesday night I took mom to Mills Buffet for dinner. I had a shrimp cocktail and Lobster. — I could hardly wait to tell you about it. Yesterday I got my new pants & jacket and I have them on today. All of the girls have been whistling at me. Last night I went over to Pace's and we played two more games of football. I beat him both games and then rubbed it in about his strategy being poor. Tonight I'm going to drive up to Gahanna taking Pace and Delno along. We are going to eat at the Village first and maybe have a beer or two afterwards. I don't have any plans at all for the week end, so I may possibly get those letters written that you wanted me to write. I also have about a million papers to grade.

I saw Kathleen yesterday and she told

town meeting affair is ...ed for the ...ins of March, ...at the Columbus Town Meeting ...king some of the national ...a view towards getting ...a story for the affair. ...like to see your husbands ...?

...to see Dr. Lansittel, but ...d has a four o'clock class. ...get Breih to take my last ...some afternoon next week.

...m going to quit for now ...more later. But in ...tion in your letter — you ...d miss you and love you ...for you to come home ...just anything in the world ...ant, and I love you to death.

Dick.

Friday

Dearest Evelyn,

Study Hall again, on the start of what looks like a nerve-racking day. I have been asked at least fifty foolish questions already today; have given makeups on four different tests, gotten them quiet etc. Sometimes I think I'd rather be a bartender.

Say honey I sure hope you aren't in any trouble regarding this flood proposition. I've been worried about you ever since I first heard you were down in that territory. I know that by the time you get this you will be safe in Lake Worth, but you be careful down there too and come home to me safe and sound.

Wednesday night I took mom to Mills Buffet for dinner. I had a shrimp cocktail and lobster. I could hardly wait to tell you about it. Yesterday I got my new pants & jacket and I have them on today. All of the kids have been whistling at me. Last night I went over to Pace's and we played two more games of football; I beat him both games and then rubbed it in about his strategy being poor. Tonight I'm going to drive up to Gahanna taking Pace and Delno along. We are going to eat at the Village first and maybe have a beer or two afterwards. I don't have any plans at all for the week end, so I may possibly get those letters written that you wanted me to write. I also have about a million papers to grade.

I saw Kathleen yesterday and she told me that this town meeting affair is tentatively scheduled for the third of March, she also said that this Columbus Town Meeting people are contacting some of the National magazines with a view towards getting photographs and a story for the affair. Wouldn't you like to see your husbands picture in Life?

I stopped in to see Dr. Lansitel but he wasn't in, and has a four o'clock class. I think that I'll get Breck to take my last class and go down some afternoon next week.

Well honey I'm going to quit for now and write you more later. But in answering the question in your letter—you know how much I miss you and love you and am waiting for you to come home again.

You're just everything in the world to me sweetheart, and I love you to death.

Dick

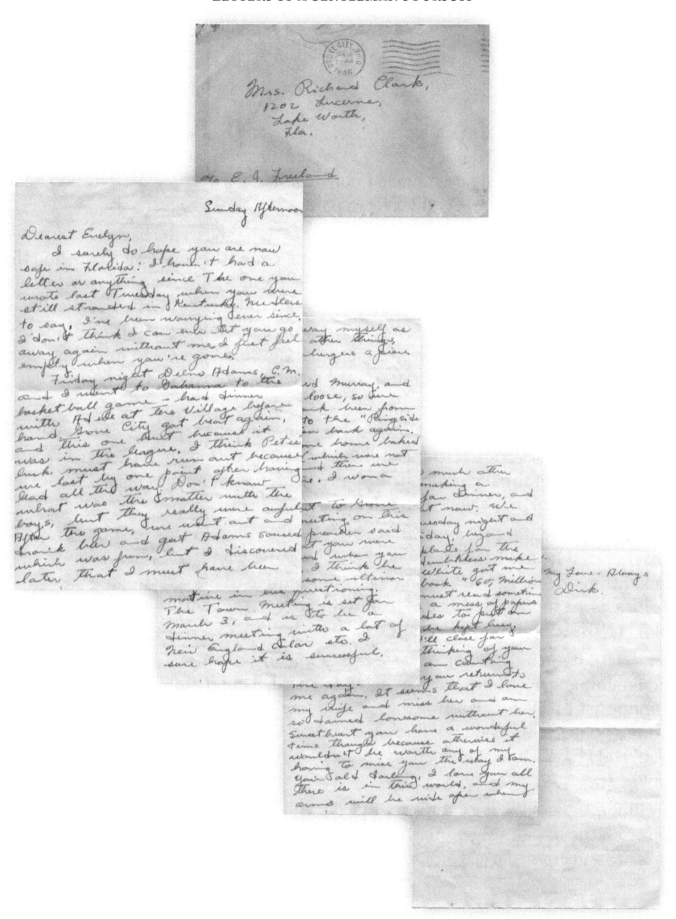

Mrs. Richard Clark,
1202 Lucerne,
Lake Worth,
Fla.

c/o E. I. Freeland

Sunday Afternoon

Dearest Evelyn,

I surely do hope you are now safe in Florida! I haven't had a letter or anything since The one you wrote last Tuesday when you were still stranded in Kentucky. Needless to say, I've been worrying ever since. I don't think I can ever let you go away again without me, I just feel empty when you're gone.

Friday night Delno Adams, C.M. and I went to Gahanna to the basketball game — had dinner with Adele at the Village before hand. Grove City got beat again, and this one hurt because it was in the league. I think Pete's luck must have run out because we lost by one point after having lead all the way. Don't know what was the matter with the boys, but they really were awful. After the game, we went out and drank beer and got Adams soused which was fun, but I discovered later, that I must have been ... the questioning. The Town meeting is set for March 3, and is to be a dinner meeting with a lot of New England color etc. I sure hope it is successful.

... me again. It seems that I love my wife and miss her and am so darned lonesome without her. Sweetheart you have a wonderful time though because otherwise it wouldn't be worth any of my having to miss you the way I am. Your gal & darling, I love you all there is in this world, and my arms will be wide open when ...

All my Love - Always
Dick.

POSTMARKED GROVE CITY, OHIO—JANUARY 14, 1946

Sunday Afternoon

Dearest Evelyn,

I surely do hope you are now safe in Florida: I haven't had a letter or anything since the one you wrote last Tuesday when you were still stranded in Kentucky. Needless to say, I've been worrying ever since. I don't think I can ever let you go away again without me. I just feel empty when you're gone.

Friday night Delno Adams, C.M. and I went to Gahanna to the basketball game—had dinner with Adele at the Village beforehand. Grove City got beat again, and this one hurt because it was in the league. I think Pete's luck must have run out because we lost by one point after having lead all the way. Don't know what was the matter with the boys, but they really were awful. After the game, we went out and drank beer and got Adams soused which was fun, but I discovered later that I must have been a little that way myself as was C.M. Among other things, we ate <u>four</u> hamburgers a piece <u>with</u> onion.

Saturday I called Murray and Essie turned him loose, so we shot pool and drank beer from Frombes and Hi to the "Ringside" at Broad, and then back again. Essie fixed us some home baked ham sandwiches (which were not as good as yours) and then we played gin rummie. I won a dollar.

Today I drove out to Grove City to another meeting on this lecture series. The preacher said he has heard that you were away and wondered when you would be back. I think he may have had some ulterior motive in his questioning. The Town Meeting is set for March 3, and is to be a dinner meeting with a lot of New England color etc. I sure hope it is successful.

I don't know much other news. Mom is making a butterscotch pie for dinner, and I'm hungry right now. We play Ashville Tuesday night and Circleville on Friday, beyond that I have no plans for the week, but will doubtless make some. Kathleen White got me Henry Wallaces' book "60 Million Jobs," which I must read sometime soon, and I have a mess of papers to grade, and grades to post on the cards, so I'll be kept busy.

Honey, I guess I'll close for now, but I'm thinking of you every minute and am counting the days until you return, to me again. It seems that I love my wife and miss her and am so darned lonesome without her. Sweetheart you have a wonderful time though because otherwise it wouldn't be worth any of my having to miss you the way I am. You're all darling, I love you all there is in this world, and my arms will be wide open when you come back.

All My Love—Always,

Dick

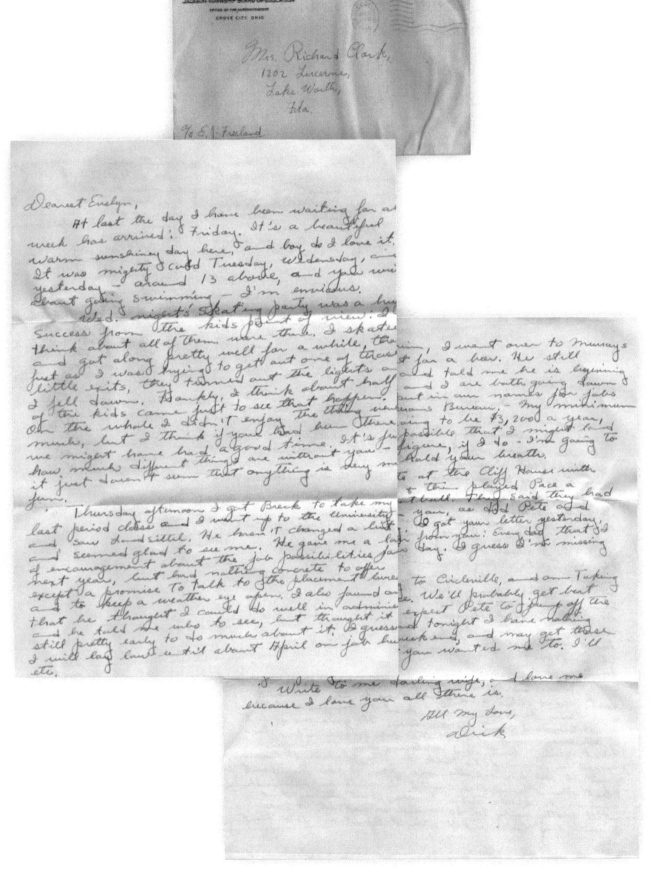

POSTMARKED GROVE CITY, OHIO—JANUARY 18, 1946

Dearest Evelyn,

At last the day I have been waiting for all week has arrived! Friday. It's a beautiful warm sunshiney day here, and boy do I love it. It was mighty cold Tuesday, Wednesday, and yesterday—around 13 above, and you write about going swimming —I'm envious.

Wed. Nights' skating party was a huge success from the kids point of view: I think about all of them were there. I skated, and got along pretty well for a while, then just as I was trying to get out one of those little exits, they turned out the lights and I fell down. Frankly, I think about half of the kids came just to see that happen. On the whole I didn't enjoy the thing very much, but I think if you had been there we might have had a good time. It's funny how much different things are without you—it just doesn't seem that anything is very much fun.

Thursday afternoon I got Breck to take my last period class and I went up to the University and saw Lansitel. He hasn't changed a bit and seemed glad to see me. He gave me a lot of encouragement about the job possibilities for next year, but had nothing concrete to offer except a promise to talk to the placement bureau and to keep a weather eye open. I also found out that he thought I could do well in administration and he told me who to see, but thought it still pretty early to do much about it. I guess I will lay low until about April on job hunting etc.

After seeing him, I went over to Murrays and we went out of for a beer. He still doesn't have a job and told me he is beginning to worry a little. He and I are both going down Sat. morning and put in our names for jobs with this new Veterans Bureau. My minimum salary accepted is going to be $3,200 a year, and I think it's possible that I might land something at that figure, if I do—I'm going to take it, but don't hold your breath.

Last night I ate at the Cliff House with Mom and the Paces & then played Pace a couple of games of football. They said they had gotten a card from you, as did Pete and Betty this morning. I got your letter yesterday, and was I glad to hear from you: Every day that I hear is a red letter day. I guess I'm missing my honey.

Tonight I'm going to Circleville, and am taking C.M. along with me. We'll probably get beat again, and, if so, I expect Pete to jump off the nearest bridge. Beyond tonight I have nothing lined up for the week end, and may get those letters written that you wanted me to. I'll try anyway.

Write to me darling wife, and love me because I love you all there is,

All My Love,

Dick

JACKSON TWP. BOARD OF EDUCATION
OFFICE OF THE CLERK
GROVE CITY, OHIO

Mrs. Richard Clark,
1202 Lucerne,
Lake Worth,
Fla,

To E. J. Freeland

Dearest Evelyn,

Blue Monday for sure honey. I got up this morning to find considerable snow on the ground, and still more snow falling. I slipped and slid all the way out to school, and it took me just under an hour to get here. I really envy you your trip darling, but mostly I just wish I was with you.

Well, we got beat again Friday night at Circleville 40-35. I don't know what the trouble is, but I think it's largely just a question of the ability to put the ball in the basket. C. M. went with me, and after the game we had a few and got home around 12:30. Saturday morning Murray and I went down to the Veterans Administration to see about the job possibilities. Got application blanks out, and am filling them out, and getting Mom busy lining up the necessary drag. I'm putting $3,200 as my minimum salary to be accepted, and if I can get this one guy (Herb Lape) to go to bat for me, I'm going to ask for $3,600. — I don't know why I've gotten the urge all of a sudden to get out of Grove City High School, but I'm sure trying. I think it's mostly your being gone that's doing it, I just ain't happy or content without you. What do you think about me trying for a job like that honey? Do you think it's smart or not? I know that actually there is time enough for us to worry about taking such a job when it's offered, but I'd kind of like your opinion. It would be a job somewhere in Ohio, under permanent civil

Mom and Bill and I
I had Filet of Sole etc.)
at George and June
June had a real good meal.
George had gotten better the
Bronze Star while overseas.
George I would still hit
with a club the way she

downstairs and talk to
awhile, and then over to talk
out this job proposition.
day Groveport and if we're
hitting, that had better

getting your letters and
morale builders, especially
sent telling me you want
me Sunday. If you want
the reservations, you can fly
one almost fifty dollars
is Friday. If you get in
stranded call me at
come and get you, I'm any
about getting the house opened
so that everything will be
get home, Have a good time
know that I'll love you
ys,

Dick

Dearest Evelyn,

Blue Monday for sure honey. I got up this morning to find considerable snow on the ground, and still more snow falling. I slipped and slid all the way out to school, and it took me just under an hour to get here. I really envy you your trip darling, but mostly I just wish I was with you.

Well, we got heat again Friday night at Circleville 40-35. I don't know what the trouble is, but I think it's largely just a question of the ability to put the ball in the basket. C.M. went with me, and after the game we had a few and got home around 12:30. Saturday morning Murray and I went down to the Veterans Administration to see about the job possibilities. Got application blanks and am filling them out, and getting Mom busy lining up the necessary drag. I'm putting $3,200 as my minimum salary to be accepted, and if I can get this one guy (Herb Lape) to go to bat for me, I'm going to ask for $3,600. I don't know why I've gotten the urge all of a sudden to get out of Grove City High School, but I'm sure trying. I think it's mostly your being gone that's doing it, I just ain't happy or content without you. What do you think about me trying for a job like that honey? Do you think it's smart or not? I know that actually there is time enough for us to worry about taking such a job when it's offered, but I'd kind of like your opinion. It would be a job somewhere in Ohio, under permanent Civil Service (Federal.)

Saturday night, Mom and Bill and I ate at Marzettis (I had Filet of Sole etc.) Yesterday I was over at George and June Wolfes' for dinner. June had a real good meal. Found out that George had gotten both the Air Medal and the Bronze Star while overseas. Incidentally, if I were George I would still hit her over the head with a club the way she orders him around.

Tonight I'm going downstairs and talk to Anne and Ted for a while, and then over to talk to Byron Harth about this job proposition. Tomorrow night we play Groveport and if we're ever going to start hitting, that had better be the time.

Honey, I've been getting your letters and they have been great morale builders, especially the last one you sent telling me you would be starting for home Sunday. If you want to, and can get the reservation, you can fly home: We still have almost fifty dollars here, and pay day is Friday. If you get in Cincinnati and are stranded call me at school and I will come and get you. In any event, I think I'll start getting the house opened up next Monday so that everything will be ready when you get home. Have a good time dearest wife, and you know that I'll love you all there is always,

Dick

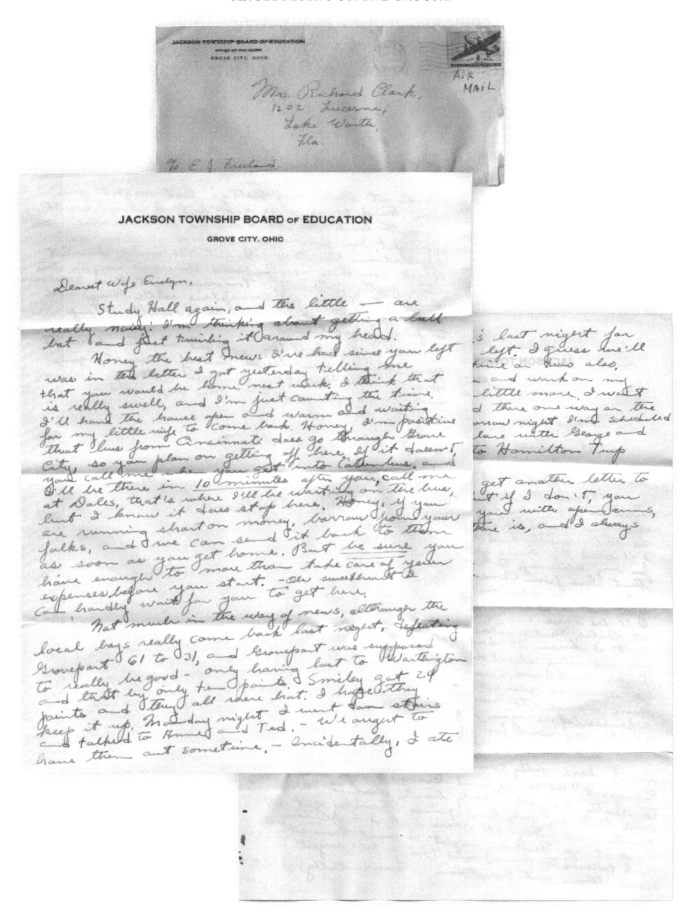

Mrs. Richard Clark,
1202 Lucerne,
Lake Worth,
Fla.

% E.J. Freeland.

JACKSON TOWNSHIP BOARD of EDUCATION

GROVE CITY, OHIO

Dearest Wife Evelyn,

Study Hall again, and the little — are really noisy! I'm thinking about getting a ball bat and just twirling it around my head.

Honey the best news I've had since you left was in the letter I got yesterday telling me that you would be home next week. I think that is really swell, and I'm just counting the time. I'll have the house open and warm and waiting for my little wife to come back. Honey, I'm positive that bus from Cincinnati does go through Grove City, so you plan on getting off here, if it doesn't, you call me when you get into Columbus, and I'll be there in 10 minutes after your call me at Dales, that's where I'll be waiting on the bus, but I know it does stop here. Honey, if you are running short on money, borrow from your folks, and we can send it back to them as soon as you get home. But be sure you have enough to more than take care of your expenses before you start. — Oh sweetheart I can hardly wait for you to get here.

Not much in the way of news, although the local boys really came back last night, defeating Groveport 61 to 31, and Groveport was supposed to really be good — only having lost to Worthington and that by only ten points. Smiley got 24 points and they all were hot. I hope they keep it up. Monday night I went down stairs and talked to Annie and Ted. — We ought to have them out sometime. — Incidentally, I ate

[...] last night for [...] left. I guess we'll [...] time in here also, [...] and work on my [...] little more. I was [...] there one way or the [...] morrow night I'm scheduled [...] lane with George and [...] to Hamilton Twp

[...] get another letter to [...] but if I don't, you [...] you with open arms, [...] one is, and I always

POSTMARKED GROVE CITY, OHIO—JANUARY 23, 1946

Dearest Wife Evelyn,

Study Hall again, and the little ---- are really noisy: I'm thinking about getting a ball bat and just twirling it around my head.

Honey the best news I've had since you left was in the letter I got yesterday telling me that you would be home next week. I think that is really swell, and I'm just counting the time. I'll have the house open and warm and waiting for my little wife to come back. Honey, I'm positive that bus from Cincinnati does go through Grove City, so you plan on getting off here. If it doesn't you call me when you get into Columbus, and I'll be there in <u>10 minutes</u> after you, call me at Dales, that's where I'll be waiting on the bus, but I know it does stop here. Honey, if you are running short on money, borrow from your folks, and we can send it back to them as soon as you get home. But <u>be sure</u> you have enough to more than take care of your expenses before you start. Oh sweetheart I can hardly wait for you to get here.

Not much in the way of news, although the local boys really came back last night, defeating Groveport 61 to 31, and Groveport was supposed to really be good—only having lost to Worthington and that by only ten points. Smiley got 24 points and they all were hot. I hope they keep it up, Monday night I went down stairs and talked to Anne and Ted. We ought to have them out sometime. Incidentally, I ate over at Pete and Betty's last night for the third time since you left. I guess we'll have to look after them a time or two also. Tonight I'm going to stay in and work on my application for this job a little more. I want to get something accomplished there one way or the other pretty quickly. Tomorrow night I'm scheduled to go out to dinner some place with George and June, and Friday we got to Hamilton Turp to play basketball.

Honey, I'll try and get another letter to you before you leave, but if I don't, you know I'm waiting for you with open arms, and loving you just all there is, and I always will.

Dick

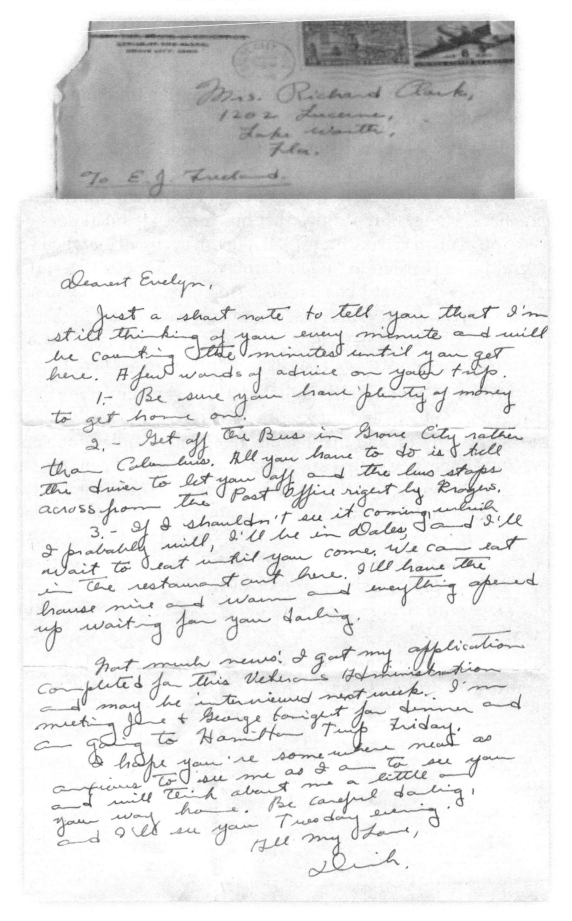

Dearest Evelyn,

Just a short note to tell you that I'm still thinking of you every minute and will be counting the minutes until you get here. A few words of advice on your trip.

1.- Be sure you have plenty of money to get home on.

2.- Get off the Bus in Grove City rather than Columbus. All you have to do is tell the driver to let you off and the bus stops across from the Post Office right by Krogers.

3.- If I shouldn't see it coming, which I probably will, I'll be in Dales, and I'll wait to eat until you come. We can eat in the restaurant out here. I'll have the house nice and warm and everything opened up waiting for you darling.

Not much news. I got my application completed for this Veterans Administration and may be interviewed next week. I'm meeting Jane & George tonight for dinner and am going to Hamilton Twp Friday.

I hope you're somewhere near as anxious to see me as I am to see you and will think about me a little on your way home. Be careful darling, and I'll see you Tuesday evening.

All my Love,
Dick.

POSTMARKED GROVE CITY, OHIO—JANUARY 24, 1946

Dearest Evelyn,

Just a note to tell you that I'm still thinking of you every minute and will be counting the minutes until you get here. A few words of advice on your trip.

1. Be sure you have plenty of money to get home on.

2. Get off the bus in Grove City rather than Columbus. All you have to do is tell the driver to let you off and the bus stops across from the Post Office right by Krogers.

3. If I shouldn't see it coming, which I probably will, I'll be in Dales, and I'll wait to eat until you come. We can eat in the restaurant out here. I'll have the house nice and warm and everything opened up waiting for you darling.

Not much news: I got my application completed for this Veterans Administration and may be interviewed next week. I'm meeting June & George tonight for dinner and am going to Hamilton Turp Friday.

I hope you're somewhere near as anxious to see me as I am to see you and will think about me a little on your way home. Be careful darling, and I'll see you Tuesday evening.

Dick

Afterword

From Richard G. Clarks' autobiography, <u>Torts and Dry Martinis</u>:

"On a hot July afternoon in 1939, I was playing a pinball machine in Hennicks with three or four others when I looked up and saw a tall, blue-eyed, ash-blonde come up the steps into the restaurant. Lightning must have struck me. I did not know who she was, but I knew I had to find out. I immediately got out of the pinball game and grabbed one of the waiters who was a friend of mine, and told him to find out who that girl was. I guess I just stared at her. In a day or so, the waiter told me that her name was Evelyn Stark, that she went to Ohio Wesleyan, and was attending Ohio State for the summer school only. I arranged to get acquainted and managed to get a date with her a couple of weeks later. I thought she was wonderful then and I still do. Unfortunately, so did several other guys, and while I chased hell out of her from then on, and dated her whenever she would go out with me, I made little progress for a long time. If I got nothing else out of college, I met Evelyn. She was then, and has always been since, the most important person in my life. I do not know what my life might have been like had I not met her, but I do know it has been great with her, and I would not have been as happy. I know that there is not supposed to be such a thing as love at first sight, but I was the exception to the rule. Fortunately, or unfortunately the same thing did not happen to her. For a long time she was not very receptive to me. One of the many times when she was trying to get rid of me, she wrote a letter to me and said, "Honey, I love the life you lead, but I couldn't stand it all the time." I guess she still has problems, but she has learned to sort of roll with the punches over the years."

• July 1939 Dick (20) sees Evelyn (20) at Hennicks

• July 21, 1939 First Date to the Valley Dale to see Artie Shaw

• December 20, 1939 First Saved letter

• Officially Going Steady 1942

• Summer 1942 Dick Pinned Evelyn

• Fall 1942 reported on 11/11/42 for Service (on Armistice Day)

• Fort Benjamin, Indiana 1st Stop in Military as Private (11/11–11/18/1942)

• Miami, Florida 2nd Stop in Military (11/18/42–3/7/1943)

• Camp Barkeley, Abilene, Texas 3rd Stop in Military as Candidate (3/8/1943–4/30/1943)

• May 18, 1943 Married Sunbury, Ohio

• Jefferson Barracks, St. Louis, Missouri 4th Stop in Military as Corporal (5/1943–6/1943)

• Wright Field, Dayton, Ohio 5th & Final Stop in Military as Corporal (6/1943–9/1945)

It has been a privilege to share my grandparents romance with the world. There are gaps in the letters, specifically January 14, 1940–July 21, 1940; February 10, 1941–February 10, 1942. I venture to guess that Grandma was "dating" others, and things just weren't great for Grandpa during that time, as you get that sense through the letters, and the excerpt from his autobiography. I know my grandmother would NOT have saved any letter that were "untoward." She was always a positive person, always shining light wherever she went. Once Grandma moved to Dayton, it is logical the letters stopped. It picked back up when Grandma accompanied her parents to Lake Worth, Florida, for January 1946.

I found it interesting that my grandfather took German in school, let alone quoted in a April 22, 1943 letter, "deu bist einer schone gnadige fraulien, ich liebe dich, und ich wallte kusse tu," which translates as "You are a lovely, merciful woman, I love you, and I kiss you."

Notice that Barkley was changed to Barkeley in the postmark on 4/12/43. I wonder if this was some type of military joke some private in the post office did unbeknownst to others.

The recipes I have included are ones that were "passed down" to me or from where I know my grandmother would have retrieved the recipe. The yellow rolls were always a family treasure!

Grove City, an idealic small town in southwest Ohio in the 20th century holds a very special place in my heart. In 1946, the Clarks started out in a house on the corner of Conner and Lincoln, almost overlooking the cemetery. Here is how Grandpa described the home: "The little house we rented in Grove City was near the edge of town, almost directly across the road from the cemetery. It was a small, four-room cottage. Naturally it was painted white. It had a full basement and a coal furnace, which I had to hand fire. There was no thermostat. One attempted to control the heat by opening and closing a draft."

Married for forty-four years, my grandparents rest next to each other in the Grove City Cemetery (Section 433F, Row 2, Number 6) along with my mother, Marcia Jo. My grandma told me that they picked their cemetery location, as it would be overseen from where they first began in their little cottage together. I can just imagine the talks they had in their 20s foreseeing what would happen when they reached their retirement years.

Final words from Torts and Dry Martinis: "We were young. I had a good job, we lived in a little white cottage and life was good. I do not remember any of the rainy days—only the sunshine."

May you always remember the sunshine days.

Postmark Locations of Love Letters

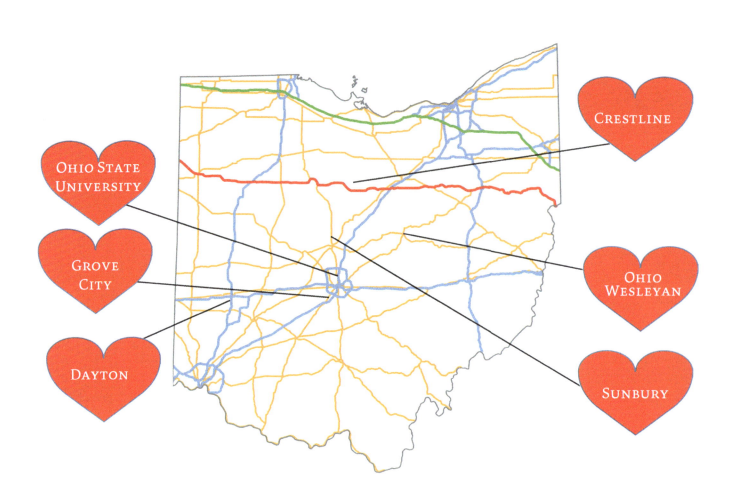

Recipes

FRIED CHICKEN

From: *Better Homes and Gardens Cookbook*

Serves: 4

Instructions

Combine flour and seasonings in paper or plastic bag; add 2 or 3 pieces of chicken at a time and shake.

Place on a rack to let coating dry. Heat fat (⅓ inch deep in skillet) till it will sizzle a drop of water.

Brown meaty pieces first; then slip others in. Don't crowd—you may need two skillets.

Brown one side; turn with tongs so not to pierce.

When lightly browned, 15 to 20 minutes, reduce heat; cover tightly. (If cover isn't tight, add 1 tbsp water.)

Cook until tender, 30 to 40 minutes.

Uncover last 10 minutes to crisp.

Cast iron skillet recommended.

Ingredients

¾ cups all-purpose flour

1 tbsp salt

1 tbsp paprika

¼ tsp pepper

1 2½–3 pound, ready-to-cook chicken, cut up

Fat for frying

CHERRY PUDDING *(OR ANY FRUIT)*

From: *Evelyn Clark, Grove City, OH*

Ingredients

½ cup sugar

2 tbsp shortening (Crisco)

1 cup flour

1 tsp baking powder

Dash salt

½ cup milk

1½ cups pitted cherries (sour)

1½ cups (or less) sugar

Instructions

Cream together shortening & sugar.

Sift flour & baking powder & salt together.

Add the creamed mixture to flour mixture.

Add milk, stir.

Mix and put on bottom of lightly greased casserole.

Mix 1½ cups of pitted cherries (sour) & 1½ cups of sugar or less.

Put cherry mixture on top of dough.

Sprinkle ½ cup HOT water on top.

Bake at 350°F for 30–45 min. until brown.

Serve with milk to pour over if desired.

DATE NUT PUDDING

From: *"Great" Grandma Ruth Clark*

Serves: 12

Instructions

To boiling water, add soda.

Pour over chopped dates. Let stand until ready to use.

Sift flour.

Cream butter & sugar.

Add eggs & vanilla.

Add dates & hot water.

Then add flour.

Flour nuts and add to batter.

Use pan larger than 7" x 11". Bake at 250°F for 1 hour or longer.

Serve with whipped whipping cream, no sugar added.

Ingredients

½ cup butter

2 cups sugar

2 well-beaten eggs

2 cups flour

2 tsp baking soda

2 cups boiling water

2 cups chopped dates

1 cup chopped nuts *(walnuts or pecans)*

1 tsp vanilla

Butterscotch Pie

From: *Better Homes & Gardens*

Instructions

In a saucepan, combine sugar, flour, and salt; gradually stir in milk. Cook and stir over medium heat till mixture boils and thickens.

Cook 2 minutes longer. Remove from heat. Stir small amount of hot mixture into yolks; return to hot mixture; cook 2 minutes, stirring constantly. Remove from heat. Add butter and vanilla; cool to room temperature. *(To prevent a crust forming, put clear plastic wrap or waxed paper directly on top, touching surface of the hot pudding, clear to sides of bowl.)* Pour into baked pastry shell.

Meringue:

Beat 3 egg whites with ¼ teaspoon cream of tartar and ½ tsp vanilla till soft peaks form. Gradually add 6 tbsp of sugar, beating till stiff peaks form and all sugar is dissolved. Spread atop pie, sealing pastry. Bake in moderate over (350°F) about 12 to 15 minutes, or till meringue is golden. Cool.

Ingredients

¾ cup brown sugar

⅓ cup all-purpose flour *or* 3 tbsp cornstarch

¼ tsp salt

2 cups milk

3 egg yolks, slightly beaten

2 tbsp butter

1 tsp vanilla

1 9-inch baked pastry shell

Pecan Pie

From: *"Great" Grandma Ruth Clark*

Serves: 12

Instructions

Beat and bake at 325°F for 45-50 minutes until top is firm (*less is gooier & more is crisper*).

1 9-inch pie crust (*use Better Homes & Garden Recipe and make with Crisco shortening*).

Ingredients

3 eggs, slightly beaten

Then add:

1 cup Karo corn syrup, light

1 cup pecans, broken

½ cup white Sugar

1 tsp vanilla (*fresh; should not taste like alcohol*)

YELLOW ROLLS

From: *Evelyn Clark (07/06/73)*
via Mrs. Jones on unmarked notecard

Ingredients

2 eggs, beaten

¼ cup sugar

½ cup warm milk

½ cup melted fat (*e.g. Crisco*)

1 package cake yeast

2 cups flour, or more

Instructions

Work yeast in sugar (1 tsp) until a liquid.

Mix eggs and sugar and milk together.

Add shortening.

Last, add flour.

Place in greased bowl. Cover, leave in warm place for 2 hours (Evelyn used to put it in her front window in her bedroom on Park Place, as it had a small seating area.).

Place on floured board.

Knead and make into rolls.

Roll into a circle, cut in triangles, roll from long side to point.

Place, point up on baking sheet. Cover with linen towel.

Let rise, again, 1–2 hours.

Bake 375°F for 12 minutes.

Serve hot with butter!

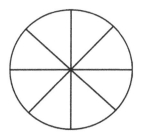

CHOCOLATE CHIP COOKIES

From: *Original Toll House Chocolate Chip Cookies* (c. 1938)
Serves: 5 dozen cookies

Instructions

Preheat oven to 375°F

Combine flour, baking soda, and salt in small bowl.

Beat butter, granulated sugar, brown sugar, and vanilla extract in large mixing bowl until creamy.

Add eggs—one at a time—beating well after each addition.

Gradually beat in flour mixture.

Stir in morsels and nuts.

Drop by rounded tablespoon onto ungreased cookie sheet.

Bake for 9 to 11 minutes or until golden brown.

Cool on baking sheets for 2 minutes, remove to wire racks to cool completely.

Ingredients

2¼ cups all-purpose flour

1 tsp baking soda

1 tsp salt

1 cup or 2 sticks butter

¾ cup granulated sugar

¾ cup brown sugar

1 tsp vanilla

2 large eggs

2 cups chocolate morsels

1 cup chopped nuts (*optional*)

MARSHMALLOW CREAM FUDGE

From: *Evelyn Clark*

Instructions

Stir marshmallow cream, evaporated milk, butter, sugar, and salt in a saucepan. Bring to a full boil stirring constantly. Stir and boil 5 min over medium heat.

Remove from heat.

Stir in chocolate, vanilla, and nuts until chocolate is melted.

Pour into greased pan (8 x 8 x 2in.).

Chill until firm.

Ingredients

1 jar marshmallow cream (7.5 oz)

1 6 oz. can (¾ cup) evaporated milk

¼ cup butter

1½ cup white sugar

¼ tsp salt

1 12 oz. package semisweet chocolate bars

1 tsp vanilla

½ cup chopped nuts

Photos

Richard G. Clark | 1944 Army

Richard G. Clark & Jerome Stark | 1944 Army

House on Conner Street, Grove City OH

Across from the Grove City Cemetery, it overlooks where Dick & Evelyn now reside. Grandma told me they picked this cemetery spot because of just that reason. Peeking out the front door is Evelyn holding her daughter, Marcia Jo.

Wedding & Shower Cards

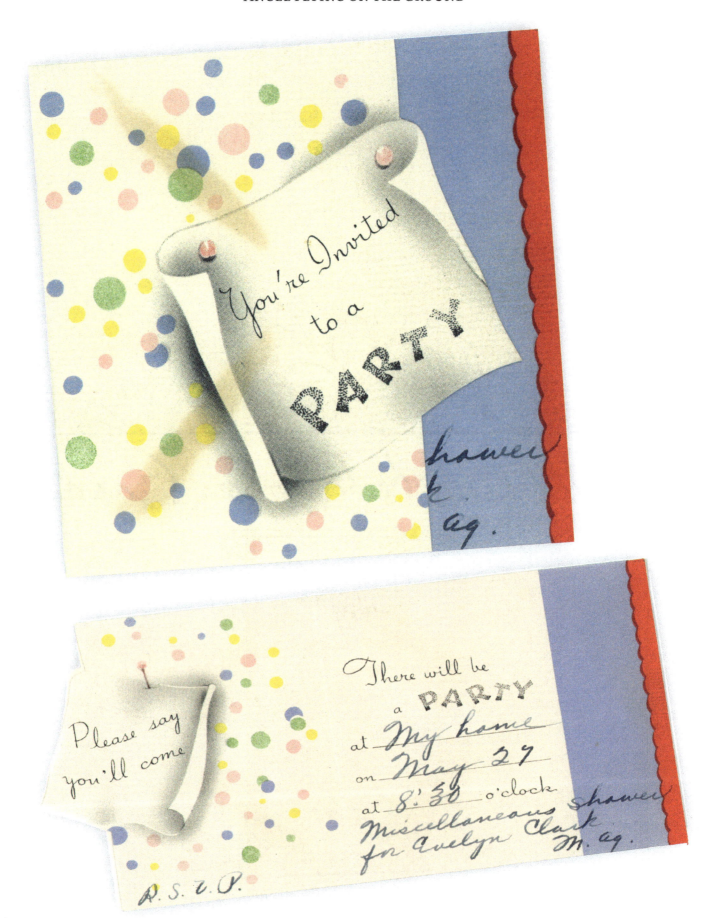

A SHOWER GIFT
for You

It's SHOWERING today
Without a single cloud in view.
For it's SHOWERING
A heap of sunny wishes right on you!
Mother.

For the
BRIDE

Volumes of best wishes!
May your married life
Be the daily record
Of a happy Wife!
Dot

A Bridal Gift

May life be filled
with joy for you –
A special joy that grows
Still deeper and
more wonderful
As each year
comes and goes

Alice & Buz

Congratulations and Best Wishes

This brings congratulations
And a little wedding toast:

"May days ahead
bring everything
You want the very most."

Mary Alice

Hearty
congratulations!
In sincere friendliness
Comes a wish that
life may bring you
Continued happiness

BEST WISHES
on Your
Wedding Day

As you start out together,
　　Now that you're Man and Wife,
Here's wishing Love's Sweet Melody
　Will bless you all thru Life;

May every dream and plan you've made
　　Be realized for you,
　And may the years ahead be bright
　　With joy and gladness, too.

Edna Mae Marshall

Marion, Marilyn,
Burnell, Betty, Janet,
Margaret, Donna, Jeanne +
Naomi.
We hope that you
will be very happy
+ have a big family.

From part of the
Fourth. Grade.

TO THE BRIDE and GROOM

CONGRATULATIONS
and
may married life
exceed your fondest
expectations.

THE HAPPY NEWLYWEDS

GOOD WISHES
to the charming bride,
To the groom,
CONGRATULATIONS~
May married life
be wonderful
And exceed all expectations.

Pauline Hetrick
Mary E. Craig
Mary Alice Foster
Freada Miller
Helen H. Millar
Arthur T Enoch
Cleo J H Donaldson
Merle Hutson
Cora B. Cover
Elizabeth O'Leary
Maurice Davis

Dorothy Barton
Miriam Burns
Alice Solinger
Ednah Smith
Rocky Crocker
Minerva Morton
Leonard L. Hill
Karl E. Hackman
Mary Ag. Keller
Zona Morkel

Russell B. & Elfrieda
K. Smith
Inez M. Hunter
Aglea a Perry
Sam Brown
Emma L. Wintere
Miriam Reynolds
E. F. Hetrick
Jake Minich

Made in the USA
Coppell, TX
03 June 2022

78319736R00227